Tim Paisley and Friends

There are some things which
cannot be learned quickly, and
time, which is all we have, must
be paid heavily for their
acquiring. They are the very
simplest things and because it
takes a man's life to know them
the little new that each man gets
from life is very costly and the
only heritage he has to leave.

Ernest Hemingway

Published by Angling Books Ltd.

First published in 2002 by
Angling Books Ltd.,
272, London Road,
Sheffield S2 4NA.

Reprinted June 2003

British Library Cataloguing-in-Publication Data
A catalogue reference for this book is available from
the British Library

ISBN 1-871700-70-1

Illustrations by Frank Warwick
Additional drawings by Dave Ramsay
Photographs by the author and as acknowledged
elsewhere

Typeset by the author

Designed by the author and
Carp Fishing News Ltd,
Newport,
East Yorkshire HU15 2QG.

Layout and Production by
Carp Fishing News Ltd.
and Sandholme Publishing

Print management by John Mason Design and Print
Aylesbury HP21 9DZ.

Printed and bound by Butler & Tanner Ltd., Caxton
Road, Frome, Somerset BA11 1NF.

Dedications

There are many people I would love to dedicate this book to. If you aren't included in the special little group that follows – well you almost were!

To the late Alan Smith, Maurice Ingham and Tag Barnes, who were admired, and appreciated, and are sadly missed.

To Micky Sly and John Lilley, for long-term friendship beyond the call of duty.

To my neglected, but much-loved, offspring Tim Jnr. and Suzy.

To Pip and Jemima, the future of Carpworld and Crafty Carper.

And to the remarkable, beloved Mary, who brings economic order from carp fishing addiction and artistic chaos.

Bibliography

Books by Tim Paisley

Carp Fishing, 1988
Carp Season, 1988
Big Carp (Tim Paisley & Friends), 1990
Carp Amid the Storm, 1992
From the Bivvy, 1994
To Catch a Carp (Tim Paisley & Friends), 1997
A Century of Carp Fishing, with Kevin Clifford and Chris Ball, 2000

Books compiled and contributed to by Tim

For the Love of Carp, 1989
Carp in Focus, 1990
Carp Baits, with Bill Cottam, 1991

Books contributed to by Tim

Tim Paisley has also contributed to a number of carp and angling books, including *Carp: the Quest for the Queen* by John Bailey and Martyn Page; *Carp Now and Then*, by Rod Hutchinson; *Fox Pool* by Rob Maylin; *Ritchie on Carp* by Ritchie MacDonald; *Carpworld Yearbook* published by Angling Publications; *Carp Hunters*, published by the Carp Society; *Master Fisherman; Carp* by Kevin Clifford; *Lessons From the Fish*, published by Second Chance; *Carp Tales* by Paul Selman; and *Carp Tales Two* by Paul Selman.

Books by the Contributors to *Carp!*

Redmire Pool, Kevin Clifford and Len Arbery, 1984
A History of Carp Fishing, Kevin Clifford, 1992
Master Fisherman; Carp, Kevin Clifford, 1994
The King Carp Waters, Chris Ball, 1993
Floater Fishing by Chris Ball & Brian Skoyles, 1991
Practical Carp Fishing, Julian Cundiff, 1993
Successful Carp Fishing, Julian Cundiff, 1995
The Beekay Guide to Carp Rigs, Julian Cundiff and Kevin Maddocks, 1996
The Beekay Guide to Starting Carping, Julian Cundiff, 1995
Strategic Carp Fishing, Rob Hughes and Simon Crow, 1997
Discover Carp Fishing by Simon Crow and Rob Hughes, 2002
A La Decouverte de la Carpe, Simon Crow et Rob Hughes, 1998
In Pursuit of the Largest, Terry Hearn, 1998

Acknowledgements

Steve Briggs, for sharing in the indelible events of the year 2000 and inadvertently inspiring much of the material that follows.

In no particular order, Chris Ball, Kevin Clifford, Frank Warwick, Simon Crow, Steve Briggs, Erwin Vos, Alijn Danau, Julian Cundiff, Terry Hearn, Kevin Knight, John van Eck and Simon Horton for their invaluable written contributions.

Frank Warwick for inspiration, his chapters, and his illustrations.

Everyone who helped with the photographic work and illustrative material, including the contributors, the B.C.S.G., Mick Perry and Mainline Baits, Carp Fishing News Ltd., Bill Cottam and Nutrabaits, Rod Hutchinson, Lee Jackson, Rob Hughes, Dave Lane, Keith Jenkins, Ian Chillcott, Dave Ramsay, Kath Hutchinson, and Kevin Maddocks.

All my generous carp fishing sponsors, especially Alan Young, Alistair Bond of Rod Hutchinson Rods, Rod Hutchinson, Kevin Nash, Steve Morgan & Kevin Knight of Mainline Baits, Bill Cottam, Richard Skidmore & Lee Walton of Nutrabaits, Bryan Jarrett of Hinders, Jim Rawcliffe of Tails Up, Dave Chilton of Kryston, Ray Dale-Smith of Carp 'R' Us, Cliff Fox & Max Cottis at Fox International, and Danny Fairbrass & the talented team at Korda.

Kev Clifford for his technical expertise and input, and the rest of the Carp Fishing News and Sandholme Publishing team – namely Dave Jessop for pulling it all together, Jon Hurst for his invaluable contribution during the final stages, Dave Ramsay for his design and layout input, and Rob Wooler and Alan Hutchinson for their layout work – for their various contributions at the production stage.

John Mason for placing and supervising the printing.

Preface

By the time this volume appears I will have lived with it for well over a year! When you plan a book of this nature you have no real grasp of the amount of effort required, however many books you have been involved in before. You start out with a vague concept of the basis for the book, and the beginnings are usually very low key. Five years on from *To Catch a Carp* I was becoming increasingly aware that there were areas of carp fishing that weren't covered by that book, or any other book on carp fishing for that matter, and the sketchy outline of the basis of *Carp!* was born.

The book developed from there, and in so doing extended to include material that is as much about carp as it is about carp fishing. In particular the chapters by Kevin Clifford and Simon Horton are worthy of a place in a reference book on carp. Their material on the carp, and the chapters on overseas carp fishing, extend the scope of *Carp!* well beyond the terms of reference of any carp book that has gone before.

The size and scope of this book reflect the number of areas of carp fishing that deserve detailed coverage. You would think that a book of 160,000+ words could claim to be a fairly comprehensive volume, but I can make no such claim. There are areas covered in *To Catch a Carp* that aren't covered here. In the pages that follow there is no specific material on stalking or floater fishing: the bait and rig chapters could be far more detailed; carp fishing photography, carp care, and casting are three subjects which require specialised coverage, but aren't included here. The pursuit of carp now represents such a huge, growing kaleidoscope of subjects that it is becoming increasingly difficult to cover them comprehensively in a single volume. I stress at the end of *The Winds of Change* chapter that any book on carp has to be read in the context of the latest developments covered in monthly and weekly carp publications – particularly material on baits and rigs – and I will emphasise that again here.

Writing and compiling *Carp!*, and co-ordinating the efforts of the contributors has been a fifteen-month labour of love. When I started out I had in mind a big book of around 120,000 words. The final word-count is 160,000 plus. Quickly said, but there is a great deal of experience, knowledge, enthusiasm, commitment and dedication demonstrated by the contributors in arriving at a book of this size! I simply cannot thank them enough for their massive contribution to *Carp!*.

Then next year, and the year after, there will be new methods to be looked at, new sets of questions to be answered, and new avenues to be explored. That is the nature of carp and carp fishing, and explains why there are so many magazines and books about our beloved species. If I have one regret about the book it is that is doesn't attempt to explain why carp mean so much to us. Many moons ago I interviewed the unimaginative Kev Clifford for Carp Fisher, and asked him "Why carp fishing?" His reply keeps coming back to me. "I suppose because they have captured my imagination." As they have mine, and many thousands of others all over the world. So this is for all the hopeless cases out there whose imaginations have been captured by carp!

Tim Paisley, August 2002

Contents

Chapters by the author unless otherwise stated

Happiness is... The author with a Raduta common of 73lb 13oz, the biggest carp caught in the world in 2001. Picture by Andy Chambers.

The Winds of Change

The winds of change gently blowing. With Rob Hughes and Simon Crow after their victory at Fishabil in the World Carp Cup of 1996.

The space and beauty of Lac de Madine in eastern France made a big impression on me, and helped change my attitude to fishing abroad.

My biggest fish from Madine was this big-framed mirror of 39lb 12oz. An October 1999 blank at the venue had me rethinking my whole approach to fishing distant waters on a restricted timescale.

My most recent technical book on carp fishing, *To Catch a Carp*, was published by Crowood Press in the autumn of 1997, which means it was written and compiled up to and during the winter of 96/97. The book has stood the test of time. My comments in Acknowledgements and Preface in that book could well have formed the introduction to this book. The book was written on the basis that carp fishing is many different things to many people, and books and magazines have to recognise that fact.

When I compiled *To Catch a Carp* I felt it would be my last technical carp book. I'm not getting any younger, and I didn't feel there would be enough changes looming, or enough new personal experiences to live through, to make the material for another technical book necessary, or even possible. How naive! In fact from a personal angle the final third of the 90s marked the end of one carp fishing era, and the start of a new one. The main thrust of my carp fishing since 1970 had been on home waters, and I had no great wish to change direction. But in retrospect the wind of change had started to blow in 1996, when I watched my friends Rob Hughes and Simon Crow win the World Carp Cup at Fishabil. Even then the change was slow developing, but when I went to the 2,500 acre Lac de Madine in eastern France for the World Carp Classic in September 1998 the wind became a bit of a gale!

Lac de Madine had a big impact on me. I was bowled over by the beauty and space of eastern France, and by the exciting new dimension of fishing a water where there might not be a carp within a mile of you. The potential size of the fish was an inspiration, too. My previous attitude that France was a land where you went for holiday carp fishing changed overnight. Pleasure fishing is pleasure fishing in any language. But just as there is a big fish circuit in this country, there is one in Europe, too, and their idea of a big fish is one over 25 kilos! Forty pounds-plus is still a tough home waters objective; a more comfortable European achievement. In Europe 25 kilos is big fish reality. Wow! My personal best for home and abroad coincidentally stood at 38lb 8oz at the time, from the Mangrove and Fishabil.

I made a couple of trips to Madine and had a few fish to 39lb 12oz. Fishing that big, sprawling, lovely venue opened my eyes to big water fishing, and caused a complete rethink in my approach to spending a limited amount of time fishing distant waters.

I went to Domaine de Boux in central France in late October 1999 and had a memorable session there in the company of Frank Warwick and Simon Horton. On Thursday 28th October 1999 I caught my first forty-plus, a huge mirror of 59lb 2oz. The following day I caught the same fish again at 58lb 14oz! Then, in the early hours of the day we were leaving, the Saturday, I had my first actual forty at 43½lb. It was one of the nicest sessions I've ever fished, made even more memorable by the stunning, colourful late autumn

9

Late October 1999, and a memorable session at Domaine de Boux in the company of friends and brilliant carp anglers Frank Warwick and Simon Horton. Sadly Si's labrador, Wild Thing, is no longer with us.

My first overseas monster – the Domaine de Boux mirror of 59lb 2oz being returned.

Steve Briggs and I are in the middle of that crowd of spectators on our way to winning the World Carp Cup 2000 at Fishabil.

One of the 37 carp that helped Steve and I set new world records for 48-hour and 72-hour carp matches on the way to winning at Fishabil with a weight of just under 500lb.

conditions, the company of two brilliant carp anglers, and a succession of fish beyond my previous experience.

Enter Steve Briggs. I first encountered Steve on Darenth Tip Lake in the mid-80s. In the late 90s I became friendly with him through his growing friendship with Rob Hughes and Simon Crow. I wanted a partner for the World Carp Cup 2000 at Fishabil, and felt Steve could be the right man. Everyone's idea of a nice guy; easy company, laid-back, and a successful, talented angler on circuit waters both in England and all over Europe. Steve came along for the ride, and we won the event by some margin, setting new world record weights (since beaten by Andy Murray and Mitch Smith) for 48-hour and 72-hour carp matches in the process.

"How come you've never fished Cassien?" asked Steve during the match. Yeh, how come? He offered to take me there at the back end of the year and show me the ropes. He duly did so, for a two-week late November/early December session during which we both landed big fish, Steve with fish of 42½ and 51½lb, and my haul including fish of 43½lb, 44lb 2oz, 44lb 4oz and the famous Half Moon Scale at 63lb. It was an incredible session on a venue which is stunning in any language – in terms of history, scenery and contents. Steve has been fishing Cassien on a regular basis since the mid-80s so when it came to the choice of author for a Cassien chapter for this book he was the natural choice.

"How come you've not fished Lake Raduta?" asked Steve during the Cassien session. Oh no, here we go again! The quick answer was that Raduta was at the end of an aeroplane flight, and planes are equal first with dentists on my list of cowardly aversions. In addition I was only just starting to spread my wings in terms of overseas fishing and didn't know if I was mentally ready for a water with the reputation of Raduta. But if I wanted a 50lb-plus common, or a chance of an increase in my new personal best of 63lb, Raduta was where I would have to go. So I booked for a two-week session starting on 21st April 2001, travelling to Romania more in hope than expectation. But I got lucky again... During the session I had fish of 44lb 12oz, 46lb and 46lb 4oz, plus what turned out to be the biggest carp caught in the World in 2001, a 1st of May common of 73lb 13oz. The stuff that dreams are made of? I'd never even dreamed of catching a fish of that size!

The huge fish came from an area of bank known as the Shepherd's Cottage stretch – more specifically from a spot familiar to the Brits as Briggsy's Swim – an area anglers tend to avoid because of the amount of small(er) carp activity you get while you are fishing it! I mention the name of the area to top off the impact Steve has had on my fishing since the turn of the century. We won the World Carp Cup together in June 2000. He took me to Cassien in November 2000. Steve it was who suggested I go to Raduta in April 2001.

For me fishing the big overseas venues was like learning to carp-fish all over again. It was new, exciting and addictive. For the present trekking off to

"Why haven't you been to Cassien?" asked Steve, so we went in November 2000. Late in the session we had simultaneous captures of a mirror of 51½lb (top) and 63lb. We were quite a double-act that year! The 63 is the famous Half Moon Scale, one of the most coveted fish in France.

Fishing "Steve's Swim" on the Shepherd's Cottage stretch at Lake Raduta in Romania.

At Raduta I got lucky again and caught the biggest carp in the world in 2001! The big common of 73lb 13oz going back, 1ˢᵗ May 2001. Sadly this was the last capture of the great fish. It died almost exactly a year later.

Romania or France has become part of my way of life. Flying still scares the living daylights out of me, but pursuing the huge monsters in distant waters is like any other goal in life; if you want it enough you have to overcome the barriers. In the case of fishing overseas the mental and logistical barriers can be just as daunting as the angling difficulties.

Realistically I am just one of thousands of carp anglers who now travel abroad for at least some of their carp fishing. In addition to which there is a growing multitude of overseas carp anglers, many of them very talented, and successful, and setting new standards in terms of the size of the target carp and the numbers of big fish caught.

We tend to think of carp fishing in terms of what it represents to us on a personal basis at any given moment. As an editor of two carp magazines I can't afford to be too influenced by what carp fishing means to me at any given time: I have to recognise that it is many different things to different people. Hooking your first eight-pounder gives the same feeling of excitement and disbelief as catching a fish in excess of seventy pounds. At the time they are equally memorable. Size and a sense of achievement lie – like beauty – in the eyes of the beholder. The buzzer sounding is the same thrill in any language. But our perception of size undoubtedly changes. As you go through your carp fishing life the big-deal fish become harder to catch – but that is a personal thing. For many of us the compulsion to get out there and fish stays the same. I'll never forget the capture of the six-pound mirror that changed my life, and I've seen that same wonder and excitement reflected many times since in the faces of others when a carp, a double, a twenty, a thirty, or something bigger, gives someone I'm fishing with that special buzz.

What I didn't realise when I compiled *To Catch a Carp* was how quickly overseas fishing would grow, and how suddenly I would be captured by the phenomenon. It is a part of the carp-fishing scene, although still not a part that everyone can aspire to. But unarguably it is part of carp fishing now, and it will become a bigger and bigger part with the passage of time. Travel to France on a Friday night Channel crossing now and you get an early clue about the numbers that are already treating Europe as an extension of the Home Counties! Travel to Cassien in November and you will find more Brits wintering there than on any English carp water! I will not live to see just how big an impact carp fishing will have on a global scale: many of the younger readers of this book will live through an even greater expansion in overseas fishing than has taken place during the last decade.

As in previous books I've called on a number of friends to contribute chapters covering areas which require their personal expertise to do justice to the subject. But I have another reason for asking other writers to contribute to my books. To me carp people are as big a part of carp fishing as the carp are. Asking them to write is an acknowledgement of their expertise and experience. My overseas contributors are as well known in their own countries as the biggest of our home stars are here. I have met these guys on

Erwin Vos, author of the chapter on the carp of the Netherlands.

European star Alijn Danau, editor of the Belgian VBK Magazine and author of two highly acclaimed books on carp fishing.

Fisheries and carp fishing expert Simon Horton with a 53lb mirror from Lac de Madine, a remarkable capture. Si's comments about Potamogeton aroused my curiosity.

Carp in their environment.

my travels, feel fortunate to be able to number them in my growing circle of friends, and appreciate the trouble they have taken to compile their chapters about the carp scene in their own countries. In the end I drew the line at chapters about Holland, Belgium and the big-fish waters of France – the closest overseas countries to England. Special thanks to friends Alijn Danau and Erwin Vos for taking time off from their hectic schedules to write their contributions. European star Alijn posted his as he set off for Cassien, and Erwin had to take a break from his for a week's carp fishing in Italy!

There was a case for including material on carp fishing in Germany, Austria, Italy, Spain, Portugal, USA and Canada. Material by European household names Christian Finkelde from Germany and Roberto Ripamonti from Italy was on the list for possible inclusion, but there had to be deletions from the original shopping list. Apart from Lake Raduta all the waters covered in *Carp!* are a modest journey by car and car ferry from home. If I live long enough to compile another technical book then it won't be possible to ignore the claims for inclusion from emerging carp scenes in a growing number of countries.

I see this book as a follow-up to *To Catch a Carp*, not simply in terms of the global impact of carp fishing, but because of its coverage of some of the areas of carp lore that haven't been given adequate coverage in previous books.

For instance travelling to a variety of venues has made me more curious about the various types of weed you find in carp waters. How attractive are the different weeds to carp, and how significant are they in terms of the presence of natural food? A chance comment by Simon Horton strengthened my curiosity about weed-types. I was intrigued by the Madine carp's clear attraction to the potamogeton beds, and remarked on it. "Bloodworm lives around potamogeton beds," commented Si. I'd never been a great lover of pot beds, but my enthusiasm for them has grown since that moment! Si got the unenviable job of writing about carp and weed, and his chapter gradually grew and extended to cover the whole cycle of carp, their feeding and their environment. Fascinating, ground-breaking and revealing material.

I get asked questions about the life cycle of the carp, and don't know where to point people to find suitable material. I consider some of my friends to be experts on the subject, including Simon Crow, Si Horton and Kev Clifford. Writing a chapter about the carp itself is a job for a pro – and as I'd already talked the two Simons into writing chapters on other subjects, my friend Kev Clifford was entrusted with the difficult job of compressing material which could fill a number of volumes on carp into a single chapter. Prolific author Kev doesn't write as much as he used to so I think researching and compiling his chapter came as something of a culture shock to him! But he went to his usual painstaking lengths and the end result is an academic, pioneering piece of writing which will be extended for inclusion in the next edition of Kevin's very special book *A History of Carp Fishing*. I'm proud that

Kevin Clifford, one-time high-profile carper, now successful specimen hunter, publisher and author. Kev's chapter on the carp includes some new information on the background of the species.

Archivist and long-time carper Chris Ball: his painstaking chapter about – and list of – the big fish caught in this country makes remarkable reading.

My friend Simon Crow, global carping guru whose chapters on the big fish waters of France and the monster carp of the world are essential reading for any would-be overseas big-fish carper.

this book is the setting for the initial results of some of Kev's research.

I think carp anglers love lists of carp captures. I remember in the 70s poring in wonder over the list at the back of the *First British Carp Study Group* book, published in 1973. I've got it in front of me now: *"A List of Carp Over 30lb."* There are 56 captures in that list, including just seven over 40lb. It would take a large book to publish a list of thirty-pound captures now; a small one to update the captures of forty-pound-plus fish. So I've asked big fish list compiler and carp fishing archivist Chris Ball to write me a chapter on –

A LIST OF CARP OVER 30lb

44-00	R. Walker	Redmire	1952	Bal Crust
43-13½	C. Yates	Redmire	1972	Caddis
42-00	R. Clay	Billing	1966	Honey Paste
40-08	E. Price	Redmire	1959	Bal Crust
40-03	J. Hilton	Redmire	1972	Slug
40-00½	R. Groombridge	Boxmoor	1966	Fltg Crust
40-00	J. McLoud	Redmire	1972	Maggot
38-08	R. Bowskill	Redmire	1966	Lobworm
38-01	T. Mintram	Redmire	1970	Maggot
37-08	F. Staples	Bures Lake	1969	Maggot
36-10	J. Hilton	Redmire	1972	Maggot
36-04	B. Quinlan	Redmire	1970	Maggot
36-04	B. Walkden	Redmire	1972	Maggot
35-00	J. Hilton	Redmire	1967	Paste
34-08	J. Ward	Robinson Crusoe	1959	Fltg Crust
34-08	W. Beta	Cut	1965	Cheese
34-00	P. Chillingsworth	Billing	1970	Cheese
33-12	P. Harvey	Cut	1964	Potato
33-12	P. Hemmingway	Cut	1965	Potato
33-11	D. Moulds	York	1965	Fltg Crust
33-08	J. Brough	Send	1966	Potato
33-02	B. Reynolds	Billing	1964	Paste
33-00	R. Bowskill	Redmire	1967	Maggot
32-08	J. Hilton	Redmire	1971	Maggot
32-00	P. Dukes	Boxmoor	1969	
32-00	K. Rowley	Ashlea	1970	Fltg Flake
32-00	P. Shatford	Billing	1964	Bal Crust
31-12	P. Stacey	Waveney	1971	Potato
31-10	J. Duffett	Layer	1971	Lob
31-08	B. Chapman	Ashlea	1971	Maggot
31-08	R. Jones	Eggetts	1972	Maggot
31-08	B. Richards	Redmire	1956	
31-06	J. Hilton	Redmire	1971	Maggot
31-04	R. Walker	Redmire	1954	Flake
31-04	B. Richards	Redmire	1951	
31-00	P. Frost	Tidden Foot	1960	
31-00	P. Baddley	Redmire	1970	
30-12	P. Stacey	Waveney	1971	Potato
30-12	K. Murray	Cuttle Mill	1971	Cheese
30-12	K. Cayer	Farnborough	1972	Bread Paste
30-08	R. Measure	Hunton	1964	
30-08	J. McLoud	Redmire	1971	Lob
30-08	M. Harris	Kent	1971	
30-08	D. Wesley	Cut	1968	Paste
30-08	A. Campion	Thames	1972	Fltg Crust
30-06	E. Proctor	Johnsons	1972	Flake
30-06	B. Quinlan	Redmire	1972	Maggot
30-04	K. Ewington	Redmire	1971	Maggot

95

The list from the First British Carp Study Group book, which held my attention and fuelled my dreams in the seventies.

and compile a list documenting – the fifty-pound-plus captures that have been reported in this country. Big-fish lists are historical documents. Statistics do not make judgements. I've no doubt the list in the First BCSG book excited a certain amount of comment at the time over the inclusion of the big Cuttle Mill fish, which were just as controversial in the seventies as Darenth fish – and possibly those from a number of other home waters – are now. There are fish in the list in this book that some readers may not approve of, or wish to fish for. But they were caught in this country and weighed over 50lb, which are the only criteria applied to their inclusion here. They are history, and to distort history is a corruption of reality.

My friend Simon Crow is already acknowledged as a global carp-fishing expert. He receives details of big carp captures from all over the World, and writes regular big carp columns for *Carpworld*, *Carp-Talk* and a number of overseas carp magazines. His inclusion as the author of the global Big Carp chapter needs no comment. The fact that he has also written the chapter on big carp waters in France is less easily explained. Fact is my first choice of author for the French chapter wanted far too much money. My second choice was far too busy. As was my third... Time was starting to run out, and what

Dutch carper John Van Eck, secretive and successful. The chapter on the Orient is based mainly on the experiences and pictures of John and his friends.

The great Terry Hearn needs no introduction. His chapter tells us the secrets of locating carp waters – and the carp in them.

Frank Warwick, talented artist and angler in action at Birch Grove.

Crowy doesn't know first-hand about French waters he is in a position to find out. So if anyone raises their eyebrows about the choice of Simon to write about France, I can assure them that my request raised Crowy's eyebrows, too. I think he was also too busy, but he's just a guy who can't say no!

I should add that John van Eck's enlightening and exciting chapter on the daunting Orient owes a great deal to Crowy's friendship with John, and his patience in steadily extracting the material from the highly secretive, highly successful Dutch carper! Thanks to John for his input and superb pictures.

Terry Hearn and Frank Warwick have two of the greatest minds in carp fishing. Their perception, their understanding of carp, and the depth of their carp fishing knowledge are second to none. I taped some brilliant material with Terry for *Carpworld*, and he agreed to rewrite a couple of the features so they could have a more permanent record in here. Dazzling stuff.

Frank's chapter on the Method actually came in as an article, and instantly got hijacked and updated for inclusion here! Then I wanted a chapter on single high-attract hookbait fishing, spent ten seconds thinking about attempting it myself, before asking Frank to do it. At the time of writing the carp world is full of brightly coloured, high-attract hookbaits. As far as I'm concerned Frank is the original thinker behind the concept (going back twenty years or so), and his tactical and technical thoughts on the subject are laid out here for us all to benefit from. As Frank is also the artist responsible for making sense of the author's weird scribblings – referred to by we lesser mortals as "rough drawings" (dog rough!) – his contribution to the book has been considerable and invaluable. Frank is a rig expert and great thinker and entrusting the drawings to him gives an author great confidence.

Kev Knight's chapter on what I refer to as Mainline's new age baits first appeared in a bait series I wrote for *Carp-Talk*. Kev and Steve Morgan have been a great help to me with bait over the last decade or so. My thanks to both of them and to Kev for updating the original material, which reflects Mainline's research, thinking and successes on the food-source type of bait my carp fishing is invariably based on. New concepts of bait development and design are becoming increasingly difficult to pioneer, but Mainline have managed to find a new and significant avenue with their successive dedicated baits.

Finally, my friend and co-conspirator in the compilation of *Carpworld* and *Crafty Carper*, Julian Cundiff. Material on local, short-session carping is in great demand. Overseas fishing is still a minority pursuit. As is fishing circuit waters for big carp. I find Julian's attitude to carp fishing totally refreshing. He is happy catching fish from 5lb to 35lb. He has a rabbit to look after so doesn't travel far for his carp fishing, or indulge in long sessions! He does what the majority of carpers want to do. He escapes to a local lake as often as possible – often for overnighters between working days – and gets the indicators moving as frequently as possible. Never mind the weight, give me a buzz! Jules tells us how he does it – and how you can do it – in his

Kev Knight, partner in Mainline Baits and one of the pioneers of dedicated new-age carp baits.

Julian Cundiff, another household name, here explaining how to do what he does best – catch lots of carp in very little fishing time.

enlightening chapter, and I'm sure many of you will take inspiration from both his attitude and his approach.

A huge thank-you to all my very talented, high-profile friends who have contributed so much to the content and balance of this book. There is a lifetime of experience, accumulated knowledge and understanding in writing a chapter for a book, and I appreciate the dedication and effort that has gone into the compilation of all the guest chapters included here.

What was there left for me to cover?! Quite a lot! I've written over half the book. The reason for the inclusion of most of my chapters is obvious, although one or two may need a word of explanation. In the 80s I spent some years studying water, pH and the basis of the scientific reaction between carp and their food sources. We receive an increasing amount of material, and a significant number of questions, on this heavy area of biochemistry and biophysics, so I've given it some coverage here as a reference point. Boats, feature finders, equipment for abroad are subjects that haven't received specialised coverage in previous books. Big-water fishing is growing in popularity with the spread of carp fishing to the huge inland seas of Europe and beyond. So I guess I would describe some sections of this volume as an update of *To Catch a Carp*, extended to focus on areas not previously covered, and to reflect the excitement and growth of the overseas carp scene.

Much of the material in the pages that follow is valid for any carp water, home or overseas. Those who don't fish abroad, or only go on holiday to fish overstocked puddles, look on overseas fishing as easy. Some overseas waters are. Just as there are some easy overstocked puddles in this country. But would you like our home carp fishing to be judged on the basis of overstocked puddles, or on the basis of the daunting Wraysbury One, Yateley Car Park Lake or Conningbrook (home of the carp record at the time of writing this)? There are some very tough waters in foreign lands, many of them complicated by

Big-water, long-session fishing. A bivvy, a boat, four rods and 2,500 acres of the daunting Lake Raduta.

More dreams coming true in the autumn of 2001 in the shape of these stunning mirrors of 55lb 4oz from Raduta and 57lb from Cassien.

Conningbrook, home of the record fish at the time of writing. Would you like our carp fishing in this country to be judged on the basis of overstocked puddles, or hard waters such as this one?

Dreams can come true. With Briggsy after winning the World Carp Cup 2000.

the fact that they cover hundreds, or even thousands, of acres!

One of the problems with writing technical or practical books is that they are out of date by the time they appear! The book has to be in production for two months before it goes to the printers and binders. The printer wants it for at least six weeks. In the meantime there is a summer of carp fishing passing by. For instance *Carp!* will be published shortly after the 2002 Carp World Cup at Lake Raduta, in which Steve Briggs and I, plus a number of other English pairings, are competing. There will be no mention of that event in here, whatever the outcome. Similarly there will be recent captures which don't appear on the home and overseas big fish lists, simply because they occurred too late for inclusion. Most importantly new rigs, new methods and new baits will be evolving – and significant new waters will be making their impact – throughout the book's incubation period.

This book is designed to give you a basis for your thinking, and to encourage understanding. Carp monthlies and weeklies are available to keep you up to date with all the latest developments, and changes in direction. The greatest wish any author can have is that his material entertains the reader, and promotes understanding. *Carp!* is simply a starting point: a foundation on which to base your own thinking, and carp fishing approach. Use it as such, rather than as a manual outlining methods and ideas to be slavishly copied. The more you understand about carp and carp fishing the greater your chances become of successfully harnessing methods and changes and incorporating them into your own ideas and concepts. To be really successful on the basis of your own thinking you need to write and constantly rewrite your own carp fishing manual in your head on the basis of the reactions of the carp you are fishing for and the methods and developments available to you.

There is an old adage which says that we start off wanting to catch a carp. Then we want to catch lots of carp. Then we want to catch a big carp. Then, when we've achieved our own version of those goals, we finish up fishing to our own terms of reference, be it for beautiful carp, big carp, record carp, lots of carp, surface-caught carp, river carp, or any old carp. Whatever your current objectives (and they may well change with the passage of time) I hope that in the pages that follow my friends and I help you enjoy your carp fishing and achieve your objectives.

But do open your mind and dream a little. If nothing else the last six years since I wrote and compiled *To Catch a Carp* have taught me that even dreams you don't dare to dream can come true! Writers are the pedlars of dreams, and if ever there was a pursuit built on dreams it is carp fishing. As a carp angler, an editor of two magazines, and a writer of books, I am very lucky. My life is built around trying to make dreams come true – my own and those of the readers. Hopefully in the pages that follow my friends and I can both inspire dreams, and help make them come true.

Background of a Species

Kevin Clifford

The ancestor of our modern carp almost certainly evolved some two million years ago around the area of the Caspian Sea. Then, between two million years ago and 11,000 years ago glaciers advanced and receded four times across the northern quarter of the planet resulting in the carp's distribution shrinking dramatically. With the ending of the last ice age our modern carp, *Cyprinus carpio carpio*, again spread naturally from the Caspian Sea area into the Black and Aral Sea basins, west along the Danube and into eastern mainland Asia.

Its further distribution, outside this region, was brought about by man's intervention. The main source of the earliest human transfers may well have been around the upper Danube where the Quadi Celts had their Divinium fort and the Romans their town of Carnuntum. This was the major crossing point of the river with the much-used Amber Road. One proposition is that the Romans transferred wild carp from the Danube to their western provinces as well as back to Italy. However, as a source of food in its homeland carp were held in little regard. Having ready access to coastal waters, the Romans often exploited species where fresh and saltwater mixed, such as the mullet – and the various varieties of eel were probably their most cultivated fish (Higginbotham, 1997).

The generally held view has been that after the fall of the Roman Empire carp distribution and breeding was continued by religious communities, then in the 12th-13th century it was further spread in a westerly direction through Europe by Franco-Burgundanian secular development. However, Richard Hoffmann, comparing archaeological finds with early written records, is critical of Eugene Balon's Roman/monastic approach, suggesting a mainly secular distribution and domestication.

By whatever means carp were probably first introduced into Britain in the late-14th or early-15th century (Hickling, 1971; Clifford, 1992; Currie, 1991), but as in Italy, for much the same reasons, they never achieved any major significance in fish culture.

---

460 BC Chinese scholar Fan Li publishes oldest known fish culture (probably carp) document.

2-11th Cent. Carp spread west and north from its natural habitat of Piedmont zone of Danube River – at some juncture with human assistance into new watersheds (e.g. River Rhine). When this actually took place is a matter of some conjecture between Professor Eugene Balon and Dr Richard Hoffman.

11-12th Cent. Active construction of fishponds and domestication of carp begins.

12-15th Cent. Culture of carp becomes common on secular estates throughout Europe in heyday of European pond building.

1547 Janus Dubravius writes first authoritative book on carp culture.

Past propositions (Hickling, 1962 et al) that the carp, *Cyprinus carpio*, originated in, and spread to Europe from, China is extremely unlikely. The detailed work of Balon(1969) and others has demonstrated that the carp evolved independently in China, resulting in a subspecies, *Cyprinus carpio haematopterus*; and whilst there is some evidence of domesticated common carp going from Europe to Asia, introductions in the reverse direction have not been claimed until recently. These two subspecies can be identified most easily by their gill rakers and vertebrae – the Far Eastern type having somewhat fewer of both.

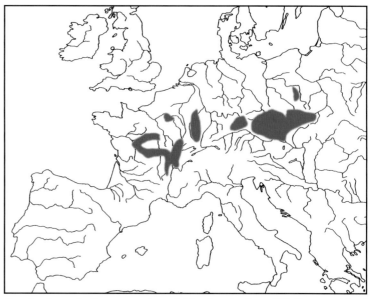

Map showing major European regions of fish culture in about 1500 (from Dr. Richard Hoffman – copyright TFH Publications Inc.).

Whilst there is evidence that the Chinese have been involved in carp domestication for at least 2,500 years (in 460BC Fan Li, a Chinese scholar, published a short document relating to carp culture), the domestication of the carp in Europe took place much more recently. By the 1500s a number of written studies on pond carp culture appear (Dubravius, 1547; Strumienski, 1573). However, probably the earliest European references made to breeding carp in ponds were by the Count of Champagne in 1258 and Albertus Magnus in the 1260s. Whilst there is documentation of pond building (for the rearing of fish as against a simple holding enclosure) taking place in Europe in the 11th century, the main thrust began to take place later, in the 12th and 13th century.

Sadly, the true ancestor of our modern-day domesticated carp (*Cyprinus carpio carpio*), the wild carp, is almost extinct – only nowadays existing in small pockets in central Europe and Asia. In the Czech Republic it occurs sporadically in the lower part of the River Dyje (Thaya) at its confluence with the River Morava and parts of the lower Morava river itself (a tributary of the Danube) – (Lusková et al., 2000).

The modern domesticated carp does not 'revert' back to the wild carp if left to its own devices. Over many generations such feral carp may end up appearing identical, for all practical purposes, to their distant ancestors, but the feral common carp will always be genetically different to its true 'wild' ancestor.

A River Danube wild carp. Photograph courtesy of Dr. Radu Suciu, Danube Delta Research Institute, Tulcea, Romania.

The carp is a highly adaptable fish that can survive in a wide variety of environments and in a range of pH from 5 to 9. Its low oxygen requirements (3-4ppm), robust nature and fast growth have resulted in its utilisation as a food source becoming very important worldwide. In 1996 some 1.99 million tons (FAO) were farmed globally, with roughly some 30 tons estimated as being produced annually in the UK. By way of contrast the Czech Republic produces yearly some 16,000 tons and the Ukraine 44,000 tons.

The variant of the wild carp that anglers come across today, in the ponds, lakes and rivers of Europe, is the domesticated farmed carp – in the past often referred to in the UK as the king carp – and its feral descendants. The term is associated with carp that have enhanced growth and often irregular scale patterns. No one knows exactly when the first deliberate selective breeding for improved growth and body shape took place, but it has occurred for hundreds of years in central Europe. There is little, if any, room for further improvement in enhanced growth of carp through simple mass selection (Schäperclaus, 1958; Moav & Wolfarth, 1973) although some gains have been made by cross-breeding established lines and the inducement of sterility, but future major advances in this area will seemingly come through genetic engineering. (This type of research is being carried out by Dr Rex Dunham at Auburn University, Alabama, USA, and the State Key Laboratory of Freshwater Ecology and Biotechnology, Chinese Academy of Sciences, Luojishan, China, and outdoor tests of transgenic common carp have already taken place in the United States and China – Hallerman and Kapuscinski, 1990).

Fish culture improvements have, however, been made in more recent times via selective breeding for other characteristics such as fecundity, survival ability of fry, disease resistance, muscle and fat content, cold tolerance, body shape, etc. Despite the generally held view to the contrary, the deepest-bodied carp do not necessarily have the highest growth potential (Hollebecq and Haffray, 1999).

The Russian Ropsha carp strain – the result of long-term selection between the domesticated Galician strain and Amur wild carp for cold weather resistance.

The scaling of domesticated carp occurs in four basic forms – the common (often termed 'scaled' by the scientific community), the mirror (scattered), the linear (or line) and the leather (nude). The occurrence of these basic scale types is governed by two pairs of autosomal genes, located in different pairs of chromosomes. The ability to produce these variously scaled carp originally came about through naturally occurring mutations which were then bred together. Interestingly, the mirror carp shows a great variability in the number and arrangement of its scales – from 'fully-scaled' mirrors to those with just a line along the back and a few near the tail. This diversity is caused by at least ten modifier genes that influence the variation in scale covering.

These genes also have a profound effect upon the development of the carp and its viability. In simple terms they have an adverse effect upon numerous physical characteristics of the carp as the scale covering is reduced. The leather carp is affected to the greatest extent, less so the linear, with the mirror the least affected. Table 1 gives a comparison of the deleterious effects of the 'scale' genes in carp.

A number of genetic abnormalities have also been observed in domesticated carp – one of the most common of these being the absence of ventral fins. Two known examples of this were seen in fish caught at Redmire Pool, and in one American lake over 40% of the carp exhibited this trait (Thompson and Adams, 1936). Other examples include an additional preanal fin, dolphin-like head and distortion of the vertebrae.

Because of their intensive farming background domesticated carp are particularly susceptible to a great variety of diseases, more so than many other species of fish and, because of their widespread commercial movements (recreational introductions, fish farm activities and koi aquaculture) these diseases are readily transferred. Common parasites, such as argulus (fish louse) and piscicola (leeches) generally do not cause too much damage to a robust adult carp if their infestation is light or temporary, however, if heavy they can be severely debilitating, even leading to death. Other parasites such as tapeworms (an example is Bothriocephalus) usually cause severe damage even in light infestations. Bacteria and fungi can also infect carp, but these are mainly a problem only when the fish is stressed, in poor condition or

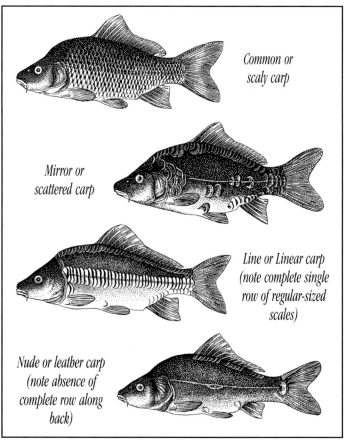

Common or scaly carp

Mirror or scattered carp

Line or Linear carp (note complete single row of regular-sized scales)

Nude or leather carp (note absence of complete row along back)

The four principal types of scale cover in carp (from Kirpichnikov, 1981).

Parameter	Common	Mirror	Linear	Leather
Weight of 2 year old fish	100	94-96	86-91	83-84
Mean number of gill rakers (var. of means)	24.6-25.1	24.3-24.8	19.4-21.6	18.5-20.5
Mean number of pharyngeal teeth	9.22	9.58	7.63	7.44
Ability for fin regeneration	100	76	39	19
Erythrocyte count	1.93	1.99	1.76	1.69
Haemoglobin	9.02	8.87	8.18	8.28
Critical lethal temperature °C	37.6	37.5	36.8	36.6
Survival time under oxygen defect (min)	210	210	132	132

Table 1. Some physical effects of the scale covering of carp – Results from Probst (1953), Steffens (1966), Kirpichnikov (1945), Chan (1969).

damaged, or primarily infected with another type of disease. The virus is the other category of disease that infects carp and has been the cause of extensive economic losses in European and Far Eastern fish farms and recreational fisheries. Identification of viral agents is often difficult and many instances of carp disease occur throughout the world where a virus is suspected but cannot be isolated. Since the early 1970s there have been a number of regular outbreaks in the UK of what has become known as Spring Viremia of Carp (SVC). These are often associated with a recent stocking of carp and the disease manifests itself in the spring period during rising water temperatures. There is some evidence that below 10°C carp are unable to produce certain antibodies which severely reduces their immune capability, allowing SVC (and perhaps other diseases) to prevail. In water temperatures above 15°C fish losses due to SVC appear to cease and the disease often fails to reappear in surviving stocks. However, the viral cause of SVC has not been proven conclusively, and there is some evidence to suggest that the agent may in fact be a disease with a combined bacterial and viral make-up. Clearly, there is some way to go before this particular disease is fully understood.

There are also a number of emerging carp diseases that are giving serious cause for concern. These include several dangerous viruses, similar to SVC but genetically distinct, which have been isolated in recent years; and in 1998 and 1999 a herpes-type virus caused massive mortalities along Israel's coastal plain – losses amounted to 400 metric tons of common carp and £2.5 million worth of koi carp intended for export.

Carp diseases show little regard for national borders and can spread in a multitude of ways – both with and without human intervention. Those intending to stock their fisheries with carp should proceed with great caution, take advice from reputable, independent sources (that preferably do not have a connection with the supply of fish), and use fish dealers/farmers who have a well-established reputation for handling carp that do not suffer mortalities. However, there are no guarantees!

Carp culture has promoted a variety of carp forms, these finding demand in food production, recreational angling and ornamental koi commerce. All of these outlets have relied upon certain factors for their success – the propagation of naturally occurring mutations and selective breeding (and latterly genetic manipulation).

Colouration in carp is affected by the presence or absence, or the proportions of each, of three pigmentation cells. The first, which contains melanin, is responsible for dark colouration. The second carry reddish-yellow pigments, and the third type of cells carry guanine crystals and produce iridescence. The

Red or orange carp are not an uncommon mutation and occur through the inheritance of a single recessive gene. The author holds a 14lb example from the UK.

absence of the first and second-type cells produce white colouration and other combinations can produce yellow, orange, red, blue, grey or black fish – even transparency is possible. Mutant forms are also found that include gold colourations. Whilst a carp's colour is genetically determined, it can be altered to a degree by the clarity of the water and the fish's age.

During domestication a number of races, then local strains, were developed in parts of Europe and Asia as a result of breeding objectives under different environmental and geographical conditions. There appears to be considerable confusion and misinformation amongst a number of British angling writers as to the identification of these breeds, with most of the identification being based on hearsay.

In central Europe carp farming often flourished in particular areas – the famous Trebon area of South Bohemia once supported over 620

Carp farming in the famous Trebon area of South Bohemia prior to the 2nd World War. Both mirror and common carp were cultivated.

fish farming family businesses, and in the heyday of pond building (the 15th-16th century) the country had some 444,800 acres under water. At one time there was hardly a single community in the regions of Bohemia and Moravia that didn't have its own carp-rearing pond. Today the Trebon region has only seven carp producers left, but some of these surviving establishments are very large – the Rybnikarstvi Trebon and Rybnikarstvi Hluboká jointly-owned farms have bred carp for over 600 years and nowadays manage some 16,368 acres of ponds.

Another famous area of historic carp farming were the Milicz Ponds, close to Beslau in the Silesia region of Poland. Around 100 ponds covering an area of 19,000 acres were created in the 12th/13th century by Cistersian monks.

In the domestication of carp the term 'race' or 'land-race' is therefore generally used to describe a cultivated carp population in a geographically limited area, whereas the term 'strain' is usually used to describe individuals of a smaller population within this race. However, the use of these terms – race, strain, form, variety, breed – has tended to become homogenised, even amongst the scientific community.

By the 19th century the cultivation of carp in Europe had resulted in a handful of distinct races of carp – the main ones being the Galician, Franconian, Lausitian and Aischgründer from Germany and the Bohemian from the region that later became Czechoslovakia (at the time part of the Austrian-Hungarian Empire). Then, during the early part of the 20th century these geographically distinct races began to become intermingled, with each other and with other derivatives, resulting in various local strains. Subsequently, carp from much further afield were also mixed with these

Abb. 8.
Galizier Karpfen.
1500 g schwer, Körperverhältnis 1 : 2,45. ⅓ natürliche Größe.

Abb. 6.
Aischgründer Karpfen.
1500 g schwer, Körperverhältnis 1 : 2. ⅓ natürliche Größe.

Top: The Galician or Galizier carp race. Lower: The high-backed Aischgründer race. Photographs from Hofmann (1927).

European races and strains (for example in 1939 wild carp from the River Amur were first crossed with the Galician race by the Russian professor, Valentin Kirpichnikov).

These breeds were distinct in varying degrees from the aforementioned races – and a few of the well-known ones are the Hluboká carp from Czechoslovakia, the Dinkelsbühler from Germany, the Dinnyés strain from central Hungary, the Göd carp from Northern Hungary, the Sumony and Palonya strains from Southern Hungary, the Našice carp from Yugoslavia, the Fresinet and Dumbrava-Sibin strains from Romania and the Poljana race from Eastern Serbia. Further afield and genetically older there is the Big Belly race, raised for hundreds of years in China (and taxonomically classed a subspecies), plus the Yamato carp from Japan. In addition there were a great many local European strains selectively developed in the early part of the 19th century. In the former Czechoslovakia alone, research by the State Fisheries in 1954 identified within the country 17 common scaled strains, 11 mirror scaled strains and 9 leather (nude) strains – although many of them disappeared in the 1950/60s. A few of these were the Valtický mirror, the Pohorelický grey mirror, Chlumský common carp and the Mšecký leather carp.

These breeds were either produced selectively for specific reasons or demonstrated biological traits based on geographical or local environmental factors. For example the Ropsha carp was deliberately developed to thrive in an extremely cold environment, whilst the Krasnodar strain (work began in 1963) was produced to be resistant to endemic disease in Southern Russia. On the other hand the Ukrainian frame (mirror) carp has a rapid growth rate in warm climates, but performs badly in cooler environments and has poor disease resistance. The Czech Hluboká was the result of long-term selection in the first three decades of the 20th century. It was high-backed and considered one of the best-performing strains till the 1950s. This strain disappeared in the 1970s.

Whilst one of the main aims of the European domestication of carp has been improved growth (but not the only one), the Chinese Big Belly has evolved (rather than being developed) to make the best of overstocked, intensely-manured ponds shared with several other species. They demonstrate rapid growth at the larval stage but retarded growth thereafter. However, they are admirably suited to their particular environment and, amongst other traits, show high resistance to oxygen deficiency.

After the 1st World War the German Agricultural Union (D.L.G.) attempted to establish certain standards and classifications for breeding their four main races of carp – the Aischgründer, Galician, Franconian and Lausitzer. The Aischgründer and Galician were 'high-backed' – that is their length to height ratio was low (1.7 to 2.6) whilst the Franconian and Lausitzer were 'wide-backed' with a higher index of 2.6 to 3. However these 'criteria' appear to have been somewhat artificial, unrealistic and unachievable, and never found favour with the fish farmers.

With the increasing ease of transportation that modern industrialisation brought about, almost all of these ancient races were dissipated and lost. For example the Aischgründer carp had been a local geographical form that had been reared in a 120,000-acre area of Bavaria by small peasant farms for hundreds of years with little change. At the time it was the shortest, most high-backed carp of all the known domesticated carp. It was valued and admired because of its exceptional length to height ratio, even though it had poor viability and an inferior growth rate to other carp races of that period (Hofmann, I. – 1927). Wunder (1949) subsequently stated that its exceptional 'hump-back' and high length to height ratio was not due to good development of dorsal musculature but to malformation and ossification of its vertebral column. This was probably caused by excessive inbreeding.

The 2nd World War had a profound effect upon almost all the breeds of carp in Europe, such as the aforementioned Aischgründer and Galician races. Many farms and their original stocks were destroyed and their workers lost or displaced. In the devastated Germany the remnants of their once long-established and famous races were subsequently unified into a single breed.

Similarly, throughout Europe in the years that followed the 2nd World War the fragments of these once 'pure' races and strains were bred together to produce new strains or so-called 'hybrids' (intraspecific hybridisation can counteract inbreeding depression and can result in heterosis – an increase in growth or improvement in other functions over that of the parents). This was carried out with the deliberate intent of achieving better growth performance and/or other improvements.

In the wild, natural populations of different breeds of carp readily intermingled and formed 'mongrel' offspring added to at intervals with disparate additional introductions.

SZARVAS P. 34

The Starvas P34 hybrid – partially developed to provide Hungarian anglers with a vigorous, hard-fighting, longer-shaped common carp.

Examples of some of these more recently developed 'hybrid' strains are the Dor-70 from Israel (work began in 1958) and the Szarvas line from Hungary (work started in 1977), the best being the 215, P31 and P34 (the latter being developed partially for recreational angling requirements as perceived in Hungary – S. Gorda, pers. communication). As was the case with the P34, some other breeds have also been deliberately developed for angling partly incorporating the 'wild' genotype. This was the case with the semi-governmental OVB (Netherlands Organisation for the Improvement of Inland Fisheries), who produced a strain that comprised 25% 'wild' carp which has been released into many Dutch fisheries. However, the inclusion of the 'wild' genotype in the simple OVB cross resulted in a diminution of growth rate whereas the more recent and elaborate Hungarian P34 cross produces a carp with excellent growth rate.

The Milevsky mirror carp – one of many Czech strains.

However, two characteristics sought by many western European carp anglers in recent years (and certainly in the UK since 1950), namely ultimate size and longevity, have never deliberately been considered in carp culture. Understandably so, since both these traits by their very nature would demand many decades to measure the results of such a breeding programme and, for economic reasons, could hardly be contemplated.

Today there are numerous strains and 'hybrid crosses' throughout Europe and Asia held at carp-breeding establishments. In the

Czech Republic 11 important strains of carp are maintained at the live gene bank of the Research Institute of Fish Culture and Hydrobiology, University of South Bohemia, Vodnany. A similar project exists in Hungary where 19 different strains of carp have been identified, broodstock of which are maintained at the Fish Culture Research Institute in Szarvas in an attempt to preserve the gene pool (they also hold 15 foreign strains). A further collection is kept in Poland, at the Institute of Ichthyobiology and Aquaculture of the Polish Academy of Sciences, in Golysz. In Russia, at the Research Institute of Pond Fisheries, Moscow Province, a cryopreserved carp sperm bank has been established for similar reasons.

There are four well-known Russian strains – firstly, the previously mentioned Ropsha carp, developed in the province of St. Petersburg from the Galician race, and the Amur wild carp. There is also the Para strain, the Middle Russian strain (initiated in 1960 at the Yakota Experimental Fish Farm, Moscow) and the Krasnodar strain. There are also a number of other Russian crosses such as the Yazhelbitsy (work began in 1959), Srednerusskiy, Belorussian and Sarboyanskiy strains – plus the Ramchatiy and Cheshuichaty strains from the Ukraine (work began in 1954) which were later used (in 1960) in an attempt to produce SVC-resistant breeds. There is also the Plovdiv strain from Bulgaria – and further afield in Indonesia there are the Puten and Majalaya strains; in Vietnam the Baccan, Hotay and South Haivan strains, and in China the Jian. There are many more throughout Europe and Asia.

In the UK domesticated carp have been commercially imported for more than 100 years from a great many continental sources including Holland, Belgium, France, Italy, Germany and Croatia, but we have no history of carp breeding or selection similar to that which has taken place throughout central and eastern Europe.

The earliest introductions of 'substantially' domesticated carp (king carp) into the UK appear to have taken place sometime around 1800, and by the 1850s there had been several releases of what were then known as "Spiegel Karpe" or "Spiegelkarpfen" (the latter being the correct German term and means mirror or looking-glass carp) – records suggest that the majority, if not all, of these early stockings appear to have derived from Germany. By the turn of the century carp were being imported on a regular basis and fish dealers were advertising their availability in the press at that time.

From around 1880 to 1907 considerable numbers of king carp were supplied by Thomas Ford's Manor Fishery of Lincolnshire. The origins of these carp are unknown at present, though the presumption must be that they came from Europe. Then, a few years after the 1914-1918 War, Donald Leney of the Surrey Trout Farm began importing carp from Holland. During the period 1925 to 1955 the majority of the carp imported into the UK were via Don Leney, and almost all of these (with a few exceptions) came from the same source in Holland. These were being bred at a Dutch fish farm (Nederlandsche Heidemaatschappi) – and mainly based on the statements of Don Leney these have been dutifully accepted as deriving from brood stock of the widespread Galician race. However, the author has obtained a contemporary chapter (of a book) written by the manager of Nederlandsche Heidemaatschappi, A.J.L. Looijen (Donald Leney's contact), which details the beginnings of the company from 1899. It clearly states that the brood stock obtained for the fledgling company came from Lausitz, that eastern portion of the kingdom of Saxony and the adjacent portion of Prussia watered by the upper River Spree (north of Dresden). At this time Lausitz was a noted area of carp

A delivery of fish being made by the Surrey Trout Farm who were responsible for most of the carp stocking in the UK between 1925 and 1945.

farming and had evolved its own equally famous race of carp (as mentioned earlier – the Lausitzer race – which was distinct from the Galician race). However, the Lausitzer carp were known to be fully scaled. Adding more confusion was an article written in *Coarse Fisherman* (October 1986) by famous 1950s carp angler Pat Russell. During a holiday in Holland he had spoken to a Mr J. Dogger, who had worked at Nederlandsche Heidemaatschappi during its early years, and Mr Dogger claimed that the farm had actually crossed two famous races of carp to obtain its offspring – the Galician and the Aischgründer. The author will be elaborating on this in a new edition of his book *A History of Carp Fishing*, but suffice to say that the latest evidence confirms that Leney's Dutch imports were very probably of the Galician race.

Since the early 1970s some very limited commercial carp breeding has taken place in the UK by independent fish farms (Humberside Fisheries in 1975, Newhay Fisheries/Warburtons Ltd (1976), Severn-Trent Water Authority at Calverton in 1976) and other groups although, to the best of the author's knowledge, these were little more than an exercise in carp production with virtually no work going into selection development, with the origins of the brood stock being unclear. In the case of Newhay/Warburtons Ltd those used may well have been of the Dinkelsbühler race which had been imported from Germany by Newhay for some years prior to the date of their breeding work.

More recent attempts have been made to create, or recreate, quality British stock (Castle Carp, Sparsholt College and others). This is a feasible objective although for it to succeed and produce meaningful breeds of 'British' carp it has to be a long-term project, and is a far more complex and costly operation than might initially be imagined by the general carp angler. The author has some doubts that the necessary work to produce a significant new genotype, if that were to be a desired objective, could be funded only from the existing limited sale of carp for stocking purposes.

Simon Scott of Sparsholt College feeding small carp. Several existing strains and crosses are being studied – Redmire's Galicians, Sutton-on-Hone fish and Priory Fisheries' carp.

Mature carp (in the wild in central Europe the males are at least 2-3 years old and females 3-4 years old) usually spawn between the end of May and mid-July in the UK when the combination of water temperature and day length is optimal. The final arbiter is water temperature and a figure of 18-20°C is usually given by most authorities as necessary for spawning. Swee and McCrimmon (1966), during extended observations of carp in Ontario, found that the lowest temperature carp would spawn was 17°C and this figure was also mentioned by Balon (1995). However, Crivelli (1980) reported an even lower temperature of 15-16°C during his work on the Camargue, in Southern France, and Osipova (1979) reported wild specimens spawning at 15°C in the Kubyshev Reservoir.

Notwithstanding the differences given in past studies, it would seem that carp will adapt in time to spawning at lower temperatures at the extremes of their natural distribution range, even within the lifetime of a single fish. When the necessary environmental conditions are reached, chemosensory interaction and visual stimuli takes place between male and female carp, and spawning begins – usually over weed, fibrous tree roots, flooded grass, etc. – invariably in shallow water.

If the air temperature is settled and similar throughout the UK then spawning can take place within a few days all over the country. For example in 1975 carp first spawned at South Cave in Yorkshire on the 8th June, at Redmire Pool in Herefordshire on the 10th June, at Moston in Cheshire on the 10th June and at Brandesburton in East Yorkshire on the 12th June. However, in 1977 the carp spawned at South Cave on 1st June but not until July 15th at Brandesburton. The following year, in 1978, the carp spawned at Brandesburton on June 2nd, but did not spawn at all at South Cave.

The spawning procedure is often accompanied by a great deal of physical activity, usually with one or two females being attended by several male carp. At times the males push into the females and as the carp swim along they 'thrash' the water as the eggs are shed. Sometimes the spawning can be over in a few hours of extreme intense activity – in other years it can take place spasmodically over several days, or even weeks, with long periods of resting. In 1976 the carp at South Cave spawned first on the 7th and 8th June. On the 9th June odd fish were still occasionally spawning. Then on the 23rd June some further spawning again took place.

There have been a number of reliable reports in the UK of second spawnings during particular years – but it is apparently unknown if this is by fish who also took part in the earlier spawning. From his observations Crivella (1980) thought that some individual carp in the Camargue may spawn a second time, in October and November.

Observations have shown that some individual carp fail to spawn and do not take part in the annual spawning procedure. For example during a period of some ten years a large carp in a pond at Newport, East Yorkshire, was never seen to show the slightest interest in the spawning activity of the 20 or so other carp that the pond contained. Sterility can occur for various reasons in fish, and a not inconsiderable number of female carp in the UK are assumed to be 'spawn bound'. Not all mature eggs are shed by the female carp, and if some remain in the ovaries these are normally absorbed. However, if proportionally large numbers of eggs are not shed for any reason (e.g. failure of the necessary environmental requirements) then the ovaries are unable to reabsorb them. The carp then becomes 'spawn bound' and future passage of eggs may become impossible. This problem has been well documented – Bieniarz & Epler (1976); and English (1952) who found a large number of carp in such a condition in Clear Lake, Iowa. Whilst unusual in carp there have also been examples of gonad abnormalities, including hermaphroditism. In the examples of hermaphrodite carp found in studies, both ovaries and testes were present and self-fertilisation was possible.

Date	Spawning time	Density of spawners	Water temp °C
18 May	Early afternoon	X	22
23 May	All afternoon	XXX	21-25
24 May	Morning	XXXXX	19-25
25 May	Midday	XXX	15-17
26 May	Late morning	XX	15-19
31 May	Late morning	X	15-19
2 June	All morning	X	15-21
13 June	All morning	XXXX	19-26
14 June	All morning	XXX	20-26
15 June	All day	XXXXX	18-21
18 June	Late morning	X	19-22
19 June	Late morning	XXXX	19-24
20 June	Late morning	XXXXX	21-24
21 June	Late morning	XXXX	21-24
26 June	Late morning	XXX	17-20

1964 spawning activity in shallow area of St. Lawrence, Canada (from Swee & McCrimmon, 1966). Density of spawners: X= very few; XX=up to 50; XXX=50 to 100; XXXX=100 to 1000; XXXXX=over 1000. Unlike small ponds/lakes where the majority of the carp population usually participates in simultaneous spawning, in large watersheds spawning is progressive as shoals of carp gather at slightly different times.

At spawning time the gonad weight of the mature European female carp can represent between 10-30% of total body weight, and of the male much less at around 7-10%. The eggs are small, about 1mm in diameter which swell to about 1.6mm after contact with water. They are slightly opaque, soft and sticky and, after being shed, become attached to aquatic vegetation. The eggs harden within 15-30 minutes. A single female carp, weighing 20lb, can release in the region of two million eggs. Swee and McCrimmon (1966) examined carp from the St. Lawrence river and found 36,000

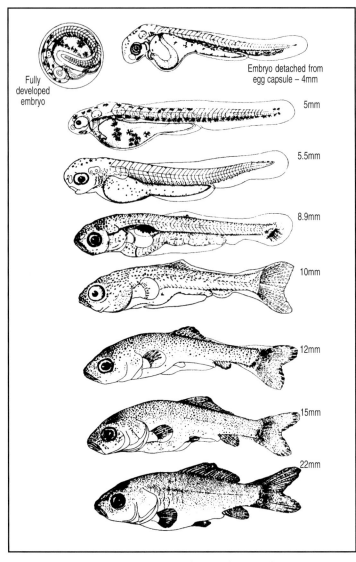

Early development stages of carp – (modified from Lippson and Moran, 1974).

Fully developed embryo

Embryo detached from egg capsule – 4mm

5mm

5.5mm

8.9mm

10mm

12mm

15mm

22mm

eggs in a four-year-old carp and 2,208,000 eggs in a 16-year-old female weighing 22.3lb.

Clearly, there is a very high natural mortality of eggs and young fry.

Depending on temperature, the eggs hatch in about three to ten days (four days at a constant 23°C). From observations Swee and McCrimmon (1966) found that a decrease in water temperature to 11°C or below was lethal to the eggs.

The fry after hatching are some 4-5mm in length and grow rapidly, feeding on zooplankton. The author's studies concluded that at this stage their feeding response is activated visually by movement, immobile items of food rarely being investigated; and in confined, artificial rearing experiments he noted some cannibalistic tendencies amongst a small number of domesticated carp fry. This resulted in extremely fast growth and these particular individuals had to be segregated. Alikunhi (1958) also found newly hatched carp fry would only feed on zooplankton, but conversely Swee & McCrimmon (1966) found both zooplankton and phytoplankton in the digestive tracts of Canadian carp fry.

At 8mm the yolk sac will have disappeared; at 16-18mm scale formation begins and is completed by the time the young carp are 22-25mm in length.

By the end of October, some 20 weeks after birth, the carp have the potential to be between two and seven inches in length (50-180mm), depending on available food and water temperature. By this stage their choice of food has become more varied and will include a wide spectrum of invertebrate life including chironomids, caddis and other hexapods, small molluscs, ostracods, crustaceans, algae and various plant material.

Over the next few years the carp's feeding behaviour will change – the importance of locating food by sight will become less dominant and eventually it will achieve a great deal of its natural intake of food by 'grazing'. The availability of natural food items will usually dictate what adult carp eat – in some waters their diet may be high in plant material (55% – Rehder, 1959) whilst at other sites much lower (11% – Sigler, 1958). However, carp are no different to many other species of fish and animals, being opportunistic feeders when situations arise, by taking advantage of readily available food items – even though these may not form part of their usual diet. The author has observed carp consuming large quantities of tadpoles at South Cave, and Sigler (1958) found some 30% of consumed items consisted of small fish in a considerable proportion of carp he examined in one particular lake. Sigler also relates another occurrence of young carp (25-50mm long) being eaten by large (10-20lb) carp.

Carp can often be observed to feed in a random manner – being apparently unconcerned about what is being ingested; at other times they can be highly selective in their diet. Stein, Kitchell and Kezevinc (1974) demonstrated a high degree of selectivity by carp in their choice of mollusc species, feeding to a large extent (over 80%) upon one thin shell variety even though its occurrence represented only about 15% of the total mollusc availability in Skadar Lake.

Adult carp therefore locate their food by sight, olfaction (smell) and taste. An item of food may be recognised from previous experience, in which case memory and learning must play a part – a subject we shall deal with later in this chapter. If the item of food is unrecognised then a conscious decision to take or reject it is made via olfaction and taste signals. In this case instinctive behaviour is the underlying model. Olfaction is by far the most acute sense of the two, requiring only a few molecules of a soluble substance in the carp's nasal chamber to evoke a response.

Food item	% water	% crude protein	% pure protein	% fat	% Carbo-hydrate
Daphnia pulex	90.67	5.42	1.47	0.61	4.07
Daphnia magna	91.60	3.53	2.98	0.62	2.63
Chironomus gregarius	87.18	8.21	6.21	1.4	2.42
Cloeon dipterum	77.32	13.05		5.96	1.87
Tubifex	87.15	8.06	4.23	2.00	1.88
Planorbis planorbis	73.00	10.58	7.10	0.65	8.72
Anabolia	77.099	11.13	8.61	0.95	5.06

Some food items of (mostly young) carp and their composition (from Halver, 1972).

Awareness of a food item is usually initiated by olfaction – water movement carrying recognisable scents to the fish. A number of scientific studies have taken place that have tried to isolate chemicals that elicit feeding responses, and these often appear to be species-specific. It may be, however, that naturally occurring chemical feeding triggers are mixtures of several compounds, rather than a single one. Nevertheless, some basic amino acids do appear to bring about feeding stimulation in several species of fish – amongst these probably Betaine has shown the widest appeal. Its use in carp fishing baits has existed for more than a decade, although it is only in recent years that it has found widespead application. A further commercial development that is related is in the use of Finnstim, a product developed for the aquaculture feed industry by Danish food ingredient producers, Danisco, and now being used extensively in carp fishing baits. Finnstim is comprised mainly of Betaine, with some other amino acids. Further amino acids that may be associated with feeding stimulation are Glycine, Alanine, Proline and Cysteine. However, some studies have demonstrated that certain amino acids individually can act as repellents, yet when combined together can attract and initiate feeding responses. Other substances that have also been shown to elicit feeding reactions are some nucleotides and quaternary amines.

The detection of food, whether it is performed visually or by smell, is almost certainly not the arbiter that decides whether the food item should be finally ingested or rejected. This is ultimately made by gustatory (taste) signals received via specialised cells situated mainly in the mouth, but also found on the lips, barbels and gill cavities.

Carp bait manufacturers seemingly have three meaningful methods of developing bait. The first is to use 'field-testers' to try out new formulations, who may also be encouraged to alter or adjust the ingredients. The collective information from the testers is then fed back to the bait manufacturer. The second method used is observation of captive carp in tanks/aquaria and their reaction to bait ingredients and formulations. This method has certainly been used by Mainline Baits of Essex in the development of some of their baits. The third alternative is when agencies outside the carp fishing domain, usually from the food or aquaculture industry, offer their commercial developments. This was the case with the Trigga bait from Nutrabaits.

The natural food of carp is high in protein – some 50% dry weight (Mann 1961; Schaperclaus 1962-63) – being derived from crustaceans, worms, insect larvae, molluscs, etc. However, the protein requirement of carp, as a proportion of their intake, is lower at some 32% (Billard, 1999). Fat, carbohydrate, vitamins and minerals are also obtained from these sources, as well as vegetable matter, which are all utilised. Efficiency of food conversion varies, dependent on a number of factors. Intensive carp farming using dry pellet feed in recirculating water ponds has reported conversion ratios of 3.5kg feed per kilogram of carp. Some generalised tests using natural foods suggest that a 40:1 conversion ratio is achieved when carp feed on molluscs and 24:1 when feeding on crustaceans.

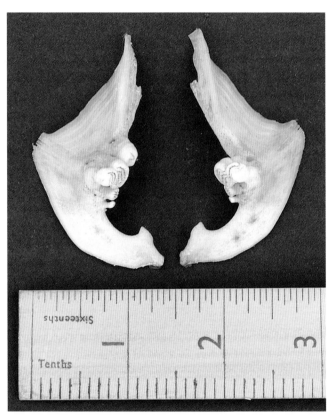

Pharyngeal teeth from a 31lb carp.

Carp possess two sets of pharyngeal teeth that are able to crush and grind ingested food items, and as this species does not possess a true stomach, food is digested whilst passing through the intestine. As food is pushed along the intestine by muscles in the gut wall it is broken down by enzymes. When large amounts of food are ingested digestion is usually at a faster rate than when small amounts of food are eaten; but when food availability is considerable gut contents can be expelled without complete digestion. There can, therefore, be considerable variation in food passage time, dependent on digestibility and availability of the food, temperature, pH (which is particularly applicable to artificial foods) and neural mechanisms – but several hours would normally be expected during summer temperatures in the UK.

Digestion is the process by which ingested materials are reduced to molecules of small enough size to allow passage through the gut wall into the bloodstream. This generally means that proteins are hydrolysed to amino acids, digestible carbohydrates to simple sugars, and lipids to fatty acids and glycerol. Materials not absorbed are by definition indigestible and are eventually expelled. Digestibility of most natural proteins and lipids is around 80% to 90%, whereas plant material, containing mostly cellulose, is hardly utilised at all.

The products of digestion are then absorbed into the body of the carp where oxidation processes occur, producing energy. In the first place energy is used for maintenance before being made available for growth. If food becomes scarce, protein and fat may be broken down from the carp's body to provide the energy needed for maintenance. When this happens the fish loses weight.

Growth in carp is highly variable and is mainly dependent on food availability and type, temperature and the degree of selective breeding of an individual. A weight of 20lb after ten years is not unusual in a natural environment in the UK, although much faster growth rates have been achieved – especially in warmer European countries. It was reported that at the famous Hluboká farm ponds in Bohemia some of the best growth rates in central Europe were achieved – 24lb (11kg) in four years, and 37lb (17kg) in five years (František Volf in *Fishing with a Camera*, 1954).

Christoph Meske first demonstrated in Germany (in 1966), with his Ahrensburg closed-cycle warm water system, that it is technically possible to achieve considerably enhanced growth rates – up to 4½lb in less than 12 months held at a constant 23°C. Similar experiments were performed by Severn-Trent Water Authority (Keith Easton) at Calverton, UK, in 1978, using polytunnels to warm outdoor ponds. This resulted in carp weighing 2lb after two years, and 6lb after three years. Vilis Michaels burnt waste chipboard from a local factory to warm pond water at his Newhay Fisheries carp farm in Yorkshire (UK) in the early-1980s, and recently Simon Scott of Sparsholt College (UK) has used warm water to obtain carp weighing up to 10lb in 18 months.

However, the actual commercial viability of achieving enhanced growth on a large scale through artificially warmed water remains doubtful, and whether or not the enhanced growth gain, produced in such a manner, will be retained in subsequent years after the carp's release into a natural environment is questionable.

Textbooks on carp culture usually state that carp growth is minimal (or even ceases – Halver 1972) below 15°C, and that 20°C is required for reasonable growth. However, this view is probably derived from the farming of young carp and there is some evidence that as carp grow older they are able to adapt to feeding in colder temperatures. László Horváth, with Tamás and Seagrave, in their book, *Carp and Pond Fish Culture*, state that fish grow fast when the water temperature remains steadily above 12-14°C. The present author agrees with this opinion.

Interestingly, laboratory studies suggest that one-year-old carp, when given a choice, preferred a temperature of around 32°C (Pitt, Garside & Hepburn, 1956) and that optimal growth for carp occurs at a temperature of 30-32°C (Teskeredziae, 1991). However, Reynolds and Casterlin (1977), in their study, found that carp preferred a slightly lower temperature of 29°C. This variation may be due to genetic differences in the strain of carp or the age of the fish used in the experiments. In young carp the upper lethal temperature was determined to be 43-44°C by Lirski and Opuszynski (1988).

In an amazing experiment with goldfish *(Carassius auratus)*, Rozin and Mayer (1961) found that after a training period, the fish could press a lever which allowed them to adjust the water temperature. They then maintained it between 33.5°C and 36°C.

Carp do feed in low temperatures as anglers regularly demonstrate.

It has been noted that the growth rate of carp is adversely affected in brackish water – Soller (1965), Wang (1977) and Privolnev (1977) demonstrated that the rate of growth in carp decreases with an increase in salinity. However, carp can tolerate high levels of salinity – as high as 12% for ten weeks (total length of the study) or four weeks at 17% (Al-Hamed, M.I., 1971). Carp are known to sometimes naturally inhabit, or move through, saline water (Fernandez-Delgado, C., 1990), (Barraclough, W.E.; Robinson, D.G., 1971), (Kuliyev and Agayarova, 1984), (Crivelli, A.J. 1980).

Another aspect of the carp's adaptability is their high tolerance of turbidity. The lethal level is in the region of 165,000ppm (Wallen, 1951) which is considerably higher than the amount which restricts light penetration.

As water temperature falls feeding decreases. In one study about 25% of the carp were still responding to food at

4°C whilst at 3°C feeding ceased altogether (Krajuchin, 1955). In another study (Rajbanshi, 1966) it was concluded that feeding ceased at 5°C. These experiments tally very closely with similar ones carried out by the author in 1976 with one-year-old carp.

However, many scientific tests are carried out using small fish and may not always apply identically to larger specimens. For example, small fish have a higher metabolic rate than large fish and therefore need to eat relatively more to support this. Schäperclaus (1933) estimated the energy requirement of a 12gm carp as 24.48kcal/kg of weight necessary for 24 hours versus a requirement of only 7.97kcal/kg of weight in the same period for carp weighing 600gm. On the other hand there is strong evidence to suggest that older carp over a number of years can acclimatise to feeding in lower temperatures. Metabolism increases with temperature – a rise of 10°C will double the carp's biological activity (oxygen requirement and general metabolism will be twice as high at 30°C compared to 20°C).

Naturally occurring hybrids of the carp (*Cyprinus carpio*) with other species have been observed – the main two being crosses with the goldfish (*Carassius auratus*) and the crucian carp (*Carassius carassius*). However, a great many artificial hybrids have also been produced around the world, with species such as silver carp (*Hypophthalmichthys molitrix*), big head carp (*Aristichthys nobilis*), grass carp (*Ctenophayngodon idella*), tench

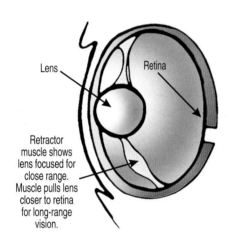

Lens

Retina

Retractor muscle shows lens focused for close range. Muscle pulls lens closer to retina for long-range vision.

(*Tinca tinca*), rosy barb (*Barbus conchonius*) and tilapia (*Oreochromis hornorum*), but few at present appear to offer any real advantages in terms of fish culture.

How important a part sight plays in the well-being of a carp is open to question and probably depends greatly on the age of the fish. Very young carp certainly depend on sight to locate food and avoid predation, but as they grow older this dependency seems to diminish. Certainly with larger carp blindness does not appear to inhibit their ability to thrive.

The general make-up of a carp's eye is not dissimilar to that of a human, although there are some differences (e.g. the carp's eye focuses its more spherical lens by moving it back or forth with a tiny muscle; in our case focusing is achieved by changing the shape of the lens). As with humans, carp have both cones and rods cells contained in the retina. The rods are very sensitive to light, even very small amounts of light, but can only discern in shades of grey. The different type of cones, however, are not as sensitive to light but are responsible for colour vision. Humans have three types of cones and these respond to red, green and blue light. Carp, and some other fish, have a fourth type of cone which is sensitive to ultraviolet light, giving them a range beyond that of man. Of course, colour recognition is complex and fish probably do not perceive colour in exactly the same way as humans.

However, the cells in the carp's eye do not alone decide what colours are seen. The colour of an object is simply the quantity of light reflected from its surface. The deeper the object is in the water, the more the shades of red, yellow and green disappear. Only a few metres underwater much of the red/yellow spectrum disappears; eventually only the blue spectrum

Colour	10 feet	20 feet	30 feet
Red	6.5%	0.4%	0.025%
Orange	50%	25%	12%
Yellow	73%	53%	40%
Green	88%	78%	69%

Table showing how the penetration of light is affected at various depths for different colours (figures given for very clear water). So, yellow shows up much better than red.

32

remains. The clarity of water also has a big impact on how far light penetrates and the distance a fish can see. Even in the very clearest lakes almost all the light is filtered out by the time 8 metres (26ft) is reached. Turbidity in most fisheries, caused by plankton and suspended silt particles, reduces the carp's visibility, at best, to some 3-4 metres (10-13ft).

Carp are amongst a small group that has the most acute hearing sensitivity and auditory bandwidth of all fish species. This ability is due to the existence of Weberian ossicles, a chain of bones connecting the inner ears to the swim bladder. In the past the general opinion was that the range of notes audible to fish is less than that which is audible to humans, and that the ability to discriminate different notes and the intensity or direction is also poorer. However, more recent studies suggest that carp have quite remarkable hearing abilities and the following statement is made by Ava Chase from the Rowland Institute for Science in his paper 'Music Discriminations by Carp (Cyprinus carpio)' published in *Animal Learning & Behaviour 2001, 29 (4):* "Prior to this series of experiments, the prevailing opinion appeared to be scepticism as to whether koi could discriminate one piece of music from another under any circumstances. Now it appears that these animals can discriminate polyphonic music, discriminate melodic patterns, and even classify music by artistic genre. As far as I know, these experiments presented the most complex auditory stimuli to which fish have ever been shown capable of making sophisticated discriminative responses."

These revelations explained observations made by the author some 25 years ago at Redmire Pool, where carp were seen on a number of occasions whilst feeding on the shallows, to 'take flight' at the sound of a human voice. It would appear that some of the Redmire carp had learned to associate danger with the human voice.

Scientists age fish by looking at certain of their bony parts, usually their scales or opecular bones, and reading their 'growth rings'. Until fairly recently most biologists believed that, unlike birds and mammals, fish continued to grow throughout their lives (Maitland, 1977; Lagler, Bardach, Miller, 1962) so that these growth rings also represented their age. However, carp in captivity and in the wild can live for very much longer than the growing period of their scales or opecular bones would suggest, and the author was mainly responsible for bringing this to widespread notice with

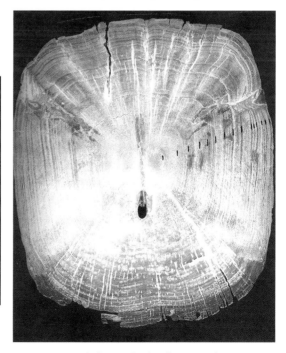

Source	Original scale reading 1952	Reading on scale after demise 1971
Percy Austin 1952	15 years+	
Jim Gregory (BCSG) 1972		13-14 years. Some signs that edges of scales have eroded
George Sharman 1978		15 years
Dr Bruno Broughton Dr Keith Easton (Severn/Trent WA)	14-15 years+	12 years or more depending where scales are read. 14/15 yrs could be found at one point

Scale readings carried out on scales of Walker's 44lb carp when it was caught in 1952 and transferred to London Zoo, and scales removed in 1971 when it died. The latter scales provide no indication of the 19 years it lived in the Zoo.

A scale from Richard Walker's record carp with the year checks marked.

documentary evidence (Clifford 1976, 1984). We now know that carp can regularly live in the wild for more than 40 years, and in extreme cases to around 70 years (the carp known as Raspberry at Redmire Pool was amongst several shown to be over 60 years old). During their long lives individual carp can be caught by anglers dozens of times from intensively fished waters.

Several well-respected angling authors have in the past claimed the carp's memory is very poor, on one occasion referring to an experiment with goldfish that purported to suggest that the memory of those species lasts just a few seconds (probably *A Method to Study Short-term Memory (STM) in the Goldfish* by Ralph S. Ryback which actually considered the effects of alcohol on the STM of the goldfish because of its known effects on human memory!).

Of course memory is a very complex subject and scientists often refer to the process of retention in humans falling into three categories: immediate or working memory, short-term memory and long-term memory – which may operate by different processes within the brain. Comparatively few scientific studies have been carried out with fish, but the widespread opinion corroborates most experienced anglers' views that fish do possess good long-term memory. The Dutch scientist Beukema carried out some useful studies on carp in 1970 and found that carp learnt very quickly to avoid capture once they had been hooked. These caught fish were left unfished for during the winter and spring. The following summer tests were carried out on the catchability of these previously hooked carp, comparing them with previously unfished for carp, all being held in the same ponds. The results demonstrated that the unfished for carp were 3-4 times more vulnerable to angling than carp with a one-year-old capture experience. (Similar work carried out by Ron Linfield, 1980, at Grey Mist Mere in Cheshire, produced different results, with the carp demonstrating higher rates of recapture. Linfield suggested that this may well be linked to the greater total fish density and relatively intense competition for food in Grey Mist Mere.)

Dr Keith Jones (PF Fishing Research Director) demonstrated that large-mouth bass, after several fruitless attacks on an artificial minnow, gave up. Two weeks later a similar artificial minnow, similar in shape but distinguishable from the first, was presented to the same group of bass. The bass showed little interest, although a second group of 'naïve' bass readily attacked it. The original group of bass retained this memory until the completion of the experiment – some

Redmire's famous resident – 'Raspberry'. First caught in 1961 at 23lb (top) and 38 years later weighing 26¼lb in 1999. The fish was almost certainly from the original stocking (1934) making it 67 years old.

three months after the initial test. In his summary Dr Jones stated: "I, personally, have little doubt the fish will probably bear the memory of their experience for the rest of their lives." In a 1985 comparative study by Coble, Farabee and Anderson (University of Wisconsin) on the memory of 14 different fish species, common carp were found to have excellent learning ability and retained their learned behaviour for months.

It has been suggested that the carp's brain is so small that there is little room in it available for memory. But the size of the brain is not necessarily a test of memory capability. The Clarke's Nutcracker, a type of American crow, only has a small brain but may possess the animal world's best memory. It collects some 30,000 pine seeds over a three-week period, then carefully buries them over an area of 200 square miles. During the following eight months it succeeds in recovering over 90% of them. I think it would be acknowledged that such a feat would be beyond the capability of human memory.

Similarly, there are those who dismiss the possibility of carp having intelligence – in that they cannot think or reason like humans. Intelligence is an extremely complex subject yet laymen often describe it in terms of human attributes. We consider humans to have the most intelligence and tend to compare the abilities of other animals in this respect with our own. Yet there is no basis in the assumption that all intelligence is 'human-like' intelligence. Evolution has caused different species to develop different information-processing systems to respond to stimuli that exist in their cognisance. Various human concepts have been used to try to define intelligence – abstract thought, reasoning, self-awareness. Are these a natural consequence of neurological evolution that sets us apart from some other species? Or should we be looking for a definition of intelligence that explains how animals interrelate with their environment rather than how closely they mimic human behaviour? The author's own view is that carp do possess some rudimentary intelligence and are capable of behaviour that can be construed as 'logical'. A dog sees a rabbit through the window – it doesn't smash through the glass in its attempt to catch it, it runs to the door. No one has trained it to do that, it's worked it out for itself. On a university campus in Japan carrion crows wait for the traffic lights to turn to red. As soon as they do the birds hop in front of the cars and drop walnuts brought from nearby trees. After the lights have changed to green and the cars have driven over the walnuts, the crows return for their meal. If the tyres miss the walnuts the crows move them to different spots. No one 'conditioned' the crows to do this, they worked it out themselves. Alex is an African Grey parrot that has been studied by Dr Irene Pepperberg for 20 years. Alex has a large vocabulary, can count, can identify and name 40 different objects and understands the concepts of 'same', 'different', 'absence', 'quantity' and 'size'. There is good evidence to suggest that Alex may one day be able to read. Is it therefore so foolish to totally dismiss the possibility that even a fragment of rudimentary intelligence could be present in carp?

Acknowledgement: The author would particularly like to thank Martin Flajšhans of the Department of Fish Genetics and Breeding, Research Institute of Fish Culture and Hydrobiology, University of South Bohemia, for his considerable patience in dealing with my queries, his kindness in checking the draft chapter for factual errors and providing the photographs used on pages 2, 3, 7 and the lower one on page 8.

Literature cited:

Al-Hamed, M.I. (1971). Salinity tolerance of common carp. *Bul.l Iraq Nat. Hist. Mus. (Univ. Baghdad)., Vol 5, No 1, pp 1-7.*

Balon, E.K. (1969) Studies on the wild carp. New opinions concerning the origins of the carp. *Práce Laboratória Rybárstva (2): 99-120.*

Balon, E.K. (1974). Domestication of the carp. *Misc. Publ. R. Ont. Mus. pp 1-38.*

Balon, E.K. (1995). Origin and domestication of the wild carp: from Roman gourmets to the swimming flowers. *Aquaculture 129;3-48.*

Barraclough, W.E.; Robinson, D.G. (1971). Anomalous occurrence of carp in the marine environment. *J. Fish Res Board Can., Vol 28, No 9, pp 1345-1347.*

Beukema, J.J. (1970). Angling experiments with carp: Decreasing catchability through one-trial learning. *Netherlands Journal of Zoology 20 (1): 81-92.*

Bieniarz, K, Epler, P. (1976). Preliminary results of the in vivo studies on ovarian resorption in carp. *J. Fish Biol. (1976) 8, 449-451.*

Billard, R. (1999). Carp, Biology and Culture. *Praxis, Chichester.*

Chan, M. T. (1969). Viability of some physiological traits in common carp of different genotype. *Genetika, Selekcija I Hybridizacija Ryb (Moscow). Nauka Publ. (edited by B.I. Cherfas) pp117-123.*

Clifford, K. (1976). Age concern. *Coarse Fisherman. May 1976, pp14-15.*

Clifford, K. (1992). A History of Carp Fishing. *Sandholme Publishing Ltd.*

Clifford, K; Arbery, L. (1976). Redmire Pool. *Beekay Publishers, Middlesex.*

Crivelli, A.J. (1981). The biology of the common carp in the Camargue, southern France. *J. Fish Biol. 18, 271-290.*

Currie, C. K. (1991). The early history of the carp and its economic significance in England. *Agricultural History Review, Vol. 39, Part 2.*

Dubravius, J. (1547). About the Fish Ponds and the Fish Living Therein.

English, T.S. (1952). Growth studies of the carp in Clear Lake, Iowa.

Iowa St. Coll. J. Sci. 24, 527-540.

Fernandez-Delgado, C. (1990). Life history patterns of the common carp in the estuary of the Guadalquivir River in south-west Spain. *Hydrobiologia; 206(1):19-28.*

Halver, J.E. (1972). Fish Nutrition. *Academic Press (New York).*

Hickling, C.F. (1962). Fish Culture. *Faber & Faber (London).*

Hickling, C.F. (1971). Prior More's fishponds. *Medieval Archaeology, XV, 1971.*

Higginbotham, J. (1997). Piscinae. Artificial Fishponds in Roman Italy. *University of North Carolina Press.*

Hoffman, R.C. (1994). Remains and verbal evidence of carp in medieval Europe. *Musee Royal de l'Afrique Centrale. No 274.*

Hofmann, I., Die Aischgründer Karpfenrasse. *Z. Fisch., 25(3): 291-365.*

Hollebecq, M.G.; Haffray, P (1999). Carp, Biology and Culture. (Ed. R. Billard). *Praxis, Chichester.*

Kirpichnikov, V.S. (1945). The effects of rearing conditions on viability, growth rate and morphology of the carp with different genotypes. *Doklady (Reports) Akademii Nauk SSSR (Moscow) 47: pp521-524.*

Kirpichnikov, V.S. (1981). Genetic Bases of Fish Selection. *Springer Verlag (Berlin).*

Krajuchin (1955). Quoted by W. Schäperclaus (1961) p 408.

Kuliyev, Z.M.; A.E. Agarayova. (1984). Ecological-morphometrical characteristics of wild carp of the central and southern Caspian. *Journal of Ichthyology 24(3):9-17.*

Linfield, R.S.J. (1980). Catchability and stock density of common carp in a lake fishery. *Fish. Mgmt. 11, No 1.*

Lippson, A.J.; Moran, R.L. (1974). Manual for identification of early development stages of fishes on the Potomac River estuary. *Martin Marietta Corporation prepared for Maryland Power Plant Siting Program, PPSP-MP-13, Annapolis, Maryland. 282p.*

Lirski, A.; Opuszynski, K. (1988). Upper lethal temperatures for carp and the phytophagous fishes in the first period of life. *Roczniki Nauk Rolniczych, Seria H: Rybactwo RNRRB9, Vol. 101, No. 4, pp 31-49.*

Maitland, P.S. (1977). Freshwater fishes of Britain and Europe. *Hamlyn, London.*

Mann, H. (1961). In Fish as Food. Vol 1, 77-102. *Academic Press (New York).*

Meske C. (1966). der Fischwirt 12, 303-316.

Moav, R., Wohlfarth, G.W. (1973). Carp Breeding in Israel. *John Wiley & Sons (New York).*

Osipova, V.B. (1979). A contribution to the ecology of the carp in the Chermshan arm of Kuybyshev Reservoir. *Journal of Ichthyology 19(5):151-154.*

Privolnev, T.I. (1977). Effect of environmental salinity on water metabolism in freshwater fish. In **Karzinkin G.S.** Metabolism and biochemistry of fishes. *Indian National Scientific Documentation Centre 371-378.*

Probst, E. (1953). Die Beschuppung des Karpfens. *Münchner Beitrage für Fluss- und Abwasserbiologie 1: pp150-227.*

Rajbanshi, K.G. (1966). *Der Fischwirt. (4) 99-102.*

Rehder, D.D. (1959). Some aspects of the life history of the carp in the Des Moines River, Boone County, Iowa. *Iowa State Jounals of Science. (34) No 1 pp 11-26.*

Reynolds, W.W.; Casterlin, M.E. (1977). Temperature preferences of four fish species in an electronic thermoregulatory shuttlebox. *The Progressive Fish Culturist*, Vol. 39, No. 3, pp 123-125.

Rozin, P. N., Mayer, J. (1961). Thermal reinforcement and thermoregulatory behaviour in the goldfish, carassius auratus. *Science 134: 942-943.*

Schäperclaus, W. (1933). Lehrbuch der Teichwirtschaft. *Parley, Berlin.*

Schäperclaus, W. (1962-63). *Z. Fisch. Hilfswiss. 14 (3/4), 265-300.*

Sigler, W.F. (1958). The ecology and use of carp in Utah. *Utah State University. Bulletin 405*

Soller, M. (1965). Carp growth in brackish water. *Bamidegeh 17, 16-23.*

Steffens, W. (1966). Die Beziehungen zwischen der Beschuppung und dem Wachstum sowie einigen meristschen Merkmalen beim Karpfen. *Biologisches Zentralblatt 85: pp273-287.*

Stein, R.A., Kitchell, J.F. (1975). Selective predation by carp on benthic molluscs in Skadar Lake, Yugoslavia. *J. Fish Biol. 391-399.*

Swee, U. B.; McCrimmon, H.R. (1966). Reproductive Biology of the carp in Lake St. Lawrence, Ontario. *Trans. Am. Fish. Soc. (95), pp372-380.*

Taylor, J.; Mahon, R. (1977). Hybridization of Cyprinus carpio and Carassius auratus, the first two exotic species in the lower Laurentian Great Lakes. *Environmental Biology of Fishes 1(2):205-208.*

Thomson, D.H., Adams L.A. (1936). A rare wild carp lacking pelvic fins. *Copeia No 1: 210.*

Wallen, I. E., (1951). The direct effect of turbidity on fishes. *Oklahoma Agricultural and Mechanical University Biological Bulletin 48(2):1-27.*

Wang, J., H. Lui, H. Po, and L. Fan. (1997). Influence of salinity on food consumption, growth and energy conversion efficiency of common carp fingerlings. *Aquaculture 148:115-124.*

Carp and Their Environment

Simon Horton M.Sc.

It is actually quite amazing what goes on beneath the other side of the mirror: the internal workings of our local pond are nothing short of a science fiction film! To put things into perspective humans are able to live and breathe air that has the same daily oxygen content. Fish have to deal with daily oxygen fluctuations of the order of 100%; like if we woke up every morning on the summit of Everest, had lunch at sea level, then dinner in an oxygen tent. I think it would take us some considerable time to get used to this pattern, but we would adapt, and tune our own feeding patterns accordingly.

Fish, and especially carp, are well adapted to their environment. They have biological and physical systems that enable them to thrive in an element that is not stable, and is affected by multiple external factors. However, their adaptation relies on a sensible use of time and space. The golden rule is very simple; it is only worth feeding on something if the energy taken from that element is superior to the energy spent looking for it and digesting it. That is simple bioenergetics. If we had to walk 100 miles every day for a small meal then it would not add up. We would lose weight and ultimately die. There is a first lesson to be learnt from bioenergetics, and that is that our baits may be competing with more significant items that are deeply engrained in the feeding pattern of the fish. That said, natural feeding patterns are tuned to the seasonal variation in abundance of the different items. A carp will switch specifically onto bloodworms (chironomids) only when the bloodworm beds are most abundant, even though some bloodworms are present all year round. It is just that carp optimise the use of the available resources. The different food items present in the carp's diet all have seasonal changes in abundance. The carp are instinctively aware of these fluctuations and switch diet accordingly. Why spend hours mouthing the benthic silt for bloodworm when there is a massive mid-water hatch of daphnia

Carp in their environment…

… And in their natural environment. This big carp is wandering over a sparse bed of Canadian pondweed.

(cladocerans), and equally why spend hours looking for daphnia when hundreds of vulnerable crayfish are just sitting on the bottom whilst moulting? Understanding what the natural daily and seasonal diet of the carp is will at least help you position your bait in an area where the carp are likely to be feeding on a selected item. I suppose you could call this bio plumbing! Equally, a little understanding of the habitat of the food items will help you associate water features such as weed, plateaux and silt patches with certain forms of natural food resources.

Looking a step ahead, the largest carp are often fish (genetics aside) that are more efficient than the others at locating and using

Weed can be a carp heaven.

the natural resources present. Knowing the resources used may only bring you closer to them… However, as good as our watercraft and water knowledge may be, they do not account for the full explanation of carp behaviour, simply because our dear carp may have very individualistic habits or "feeding traits" and may abandon all their principles out of curiosity. The following explanations of the functioning of some of the carp's environment may help explain success or failure on some sessions, but do not provide a foolproof guide to catching carp. As long as the carp keeps some mystery I think our sport has some bright days ahead. From a personal point of view I don't feel so much of a donkey if I can blame my miserable blank on the abundance of tadpoles rather than my inadequate angling! Whatever the situation, those who think they know it all are usually those the furthest away from the truth; absolute knowledge shuts the door on progressive day-to-day learning.

Macrophytes and Oxygen Fluctuations

The familiar lily pads. A covering like this can lead to a low stock density with the odd lump among them.

Macrophytes and hydrophytes – commonly termed as weed – have a major effect on the oxygen, carbon and nitrogen cycle of a water body. Their constitution and maintenance through the use of photosynthesis contribute to the establishment of a natural physico-chemical balance that is critical to other more elaborate life forms. Broadly speaking their effects are:

• To mobilise in their tissue carbon, nitrogen, phosphorous and pollutants (changing free inorganic and organic compounds into organic matter again)
• To contribute to the breakdown of complex organic matter

- To produce oxygen in the daytime through photosynthesis
- To excrete carbon dioxide at night through respiration and thus to influence pH
- To provide habitat for the fixation of algae and thus food for protozoa, crustacea, insects and fish
- To provide decaying vegetable matter for the detritivorous zoobenthos
- To diminish bankside erosion through wave breakdown and root system sediment fixation
- To make anglers moan because it can complicate presentation and fish retrieval!

As you can see that is quite an agenda for a bit of green stuff! We will not look into all these aspects but focus on those having a direct implication on our daily fishing.

Firstly, diurnal photosynthesis of submerged macrophytes produces plenty of oxygen to the point of obtaining 100% water oxygen saturation, or even supersaturation. However, the same plants consume oxygen by respiration at night and produce carbon dioxide. On weedy waters where the plants cover 50% or more of the lake surface this implies that diurnal oxygen levels will be high, but nocturnal oxygen levels will be very low. That is exaggerated if water temperature is high as the amount of oxygen that water may hold is dependent on temperature. Water saturated 100% in oxygen at 20°C contains much less oxygen than water saturated 100% in oxygen at 10°C.

Bait versus naturals? No, let's try bait and naturals.

Fish require oxygen for their maintenance breathing, and even more so for the breakdown and assimilation of the organic compounds they have eaten. The amount of oxygen present in the water therefore regulates the actual quantity of food a fish can eat before reaching satiation. Equally the more organically rich the food item is the less the fish can eat before reaching satiation.

Nocturnal oxygen levels are particularly low (anaerobic conditions) in the lower part of the water column (hypolimnion) because that is the furthest away from the surface interface with air and oxygen – which is the only area where oxygen can diffuse into water at night. Fish and invertebrates can feel this and therefore migrate to the aerobic surface waters (epilimnion) during periods where oxygen is scarce. Even some chironomids (bloodworm) will migrate out of the benthic silt into the water column to satisfy their oxygen requirement. Well if you know that, it is easy to understand that at such times these food items will be more readily available to the carp: they will take advantage of the fact that the benthic invertebrates are out of their cover and more vulnerable for predation.

During late night and early morning it is not unusual for the surface of the silt to become red with bloodworm that have crawled out of the benthic substrate in the search for the rare oxygen. However, as oxygen is a limiting factor in feeding carp cannot take full advantage of this situation so the inherent feeding strategy is to have regular short feeding spells. They eat little but often so as not to overload their oxygen demand. It is possible for them to visit the

Natural food extracted from a small clump of weed.

39

hypolimnion for a couple of quick mouthfuls, but they cannot sustain feeding over long periods in anaerobic conditions. Fish that have just fed on the oxygen-depleted benthos are likely to emerge on the surface regularly so as to flush their gill lamellae and gill rakers of silt and debris. Crashing at the surface with open operculas helps to rapidly eliminate any fine and abrasive debris that may have accumulated during feeding. This is just **one** reason why fish crash at the surface, but the tuned carp angler's ear will distinguish between the sound of a carp clearing its gills and the sound of just a rolling fish. A similar phenomenon occurs in waters where carp

Varied habitat conditions lead to biodiversity.

feed specifically on crayfish. The sound of carp emerging resembles a human "burp", and this is due to the fish trying to eliminate crayfish shell debris out of the gill lamellae. The carp pokes its head out of the water with open operculas and mouth, and whilst dropping back down the air expelled out of the oesophagus and buccal cavity creates a rather extraordinary sound.

Anyway, back to weed! So, firstly, on weedy waters during the night carp are likely to be close to the surface in the margins or on bars where food and oxygen are abundant. Secondly, if you are fishing the hypolimnion where oxygen is rarer you are more likely to catch them quickly if you use a little quantity of readily digestible bait. A big bed of bait means that the carp has to make several visits to get through it. The fish will sit next to or above the food, have a quick feed, stop for digestion and then feed again. It has absolutely no choice as there is not enough oxygen to support a continued and intense feeding effort. The presence of food in the intestines mobilises a lot of oxygen-vectoring blood cells. During digestion it is very difficult for a fish to do anything else if the supply of oxygen is restricted. Hyperventilation through the gills is possible, but relatively inefficient and energetically demanding.

Wind can create extra surface aeration; therefore, a windy night will offer slightly less restrictive oxygen conditions and contribute to the concentration of vertically migrated organisms in the windward marginal fringe. It is worth bearing in mind that it takes more than a breeze to de-stratify a lake so really the water oxygen abundance is likely to be restricted to the first 3-4 feet of the water column.

Oxygen is not the only restrictive factor in a weedy water. During daytime photosynthesis carbon dioxide is taken up by the plants in massive proportions and then equally rejected at night. The amount of dissolved CO_2 is really determinant for the water pH. During daytime it is not uncommon for the pH to rise from 7 (neutral) to over 8.5. In fish terms that is a difference of over 15,000 times change in concentration of hydrogen ions. In human terms the equivalent is to have a morning soak in a mild solution of acid and to have an evening bath in some quicklime. Carp are built for these changes and their osmotic regulation enables them to maintain a constant internal salt and ion concentration. However, the osmotic regulation does entail the use of more energy, and causes some discomfort, and inhibits feeding during the rapid changes in pH that occur at dawn and dusk.

The hydrogen content of water has massive consequences on the efficiency of our boiled baits. A low pH bait will be leaching out flavours and goodies big style during the day as the hydrogen ions tend to be sucked out, whereas it will act like a sponge with low diffusion during the night. A high pH bait will do the opposite. I am sure that some of you will have noticed how some boilies suck in obnoxious silt and smell terrible once retrieved, whereas other baits remain unchanged even when presented in acidic black silt. As anglers are not expected to walk round lakes with pH and oxygen meters, obtaining some insight into the type of pH is a matter of trying out different baits and inspecting them on return. One tip is to check the weed for signs of calcium deposits. If the surface of the weed is covered in a fine and uneven layer of calcium carbonate deposit that is brittle and rough under the finger (similar to the tartar in the kettle) you know that the lake has a high pH.

It is all very well understanding that weed is good for carp but it is not a great help in carp location if you have just acres of the various species of weed in front of you. There are in fact several species of macrophytes that stand head and shoulders above the rest in terms of benefits to the fish. Carp like to spend hours basking under water lilies and occasionally sucking away at a few snails and amoebas, but in fact lilies (nuphar & nymphea) do not provide ideal conditions for biodiversity. Waters encroached with lilies (over 60% of surface) are rather unproductive and support a weak biomass of fish. The floating leaves leave little room for algae phytoplankton photosynthesis below the lily "canopy"; few algae means little food for zooplankton and little zooplankton means little food for our dear fish fry… So fry survival is low and, hey presto, that means that those who survive have little

Carp bubbling next to a bed of potamogeton in an English pool. The weed is a bloodworm haven and natural target for carp.

The French version of potamogeton has bigger leaves than the English type – and carp seem to love it!

intraspecific competition (competition within the same species) and therefore we have the foundations of a fishery that has the potential for a few lumps in it! So next time you have broken your PB in this undisclosed estate lake covered in lilies thank the weed for its not-so-modest contribution.

Weed species with underwater foliage offer a greater surface for the proliferation of phyto- & zooplankton. Furthermore their underwater respiration and photosynthesis bear more impact on the water's physico-chemical properties. The foliage surface is even more consequent if the leaves are fine and fragmented, such as with milfoil (myriophyllum), ranunculus and chara. These also provide an ideal source of food for the detritivore crustaceans that thrive on decaying plant matter during the regeneration and fall. I am sure you have spotted marginal clusters of asellus and gammarus (small freshwater shrimps) that feed on fallen leaves and decaying aquatic weed. The margins and windward plateaux are often alive with these guys, especially after a couple of days of strong wind congregating all sorts of debris.

Canadian pondweed (Elodea canadensis) is now fairly common throughout Europe. Its capacity to encroach on certain waters has contributed to the elimination of other aquatic plants in some lakes. Its high oxygen-producing and demanding process through photosynthesis and respiration does create some unfriendly conditions for other forms of invertebrate life. So Canadian pondweed offers a useful feature to cast next to as carp may use its edge as a route, but a nocturnal bait presented smack bang in the middle of the stuff is a bait placed in an environment that is temporarily devoid of oxygen.

Apart from bait positioning it is worth bearing this in mind if you intend to sack a fish overnight. Sacking fish in weed is extremely dangerous, as suffocation is a definite possibility.

The potamogeton species of weed, with their floating-leaved and submerged variants, offer a far better support and lifestyle for biodiversity to settle in, on or around. Their root system is often the site of big bloodworm beds and much sought-after tubifex worms. The plant's diffuse foliage and vascular system allows water flow-through that prevents complete nocturnal anaerobic conditions. Being non-invasive other beneficial macrophytes such as milfoil and hornwort can also proliferate around beds of potamogeton. Water snails such as limnea can create important colonies on these three plant species, and it is not rare to observe a density of over one hundred snails per square metre. Aquatic snails can represent up to 90% of a carp's diet during their period of hyperabundance (usually between end of June to mid August). As such this plant community provides a variety of suitable invertebrate and fish microhabitats. Inevitably this plant community creates ideal holding areas for carp where they do not have to move far to forage for different food sources. Feeding at close quarters implies savings on the energy budget, which means better growth for the fish. Weed species such as milfoil and to a lesser extent hornwort also provide ideal spawning media for carp to shed their eggs onto.

Emergent littoral macrophytes such as reedmace, bulrushes, iris, typha and juncus also make an important contribution to the habitat of the carp. Their presence is located on a major ecotone where the plants have simultaneous contact between water, air and soil. These plants are prime natural filters that are efficient at absorbing and fixating all sorts of pollutants. Their absorption of nitrogen and carbon slows down eutrophication – which is the enrichment of a water body in organic matter. As such this natural filter helps to prevent harmful blue/green and red algae blooms. They also act as effective silt traps and natural wind barriers that prevent bankside erosion. The interstices between the plants provide ideal fish fry refuge against predators. Many insects also climb their stems and aerial foliage for their final emergence and metamorphosis. Carp use the stem interstices for lying up in during periods of inactivity and may find food at close hand on the rough and slightly elevated ledge that is created on the edge of a bank of reeds.

The marginal fringe offers more than meets the eye.

Well-Planned Coincidences

There are numerous phenomena to be noticed whilst enjoying a session on the bank: occurrences are plentiful, and amongst those one in particular has always got me thinking. Why on earth do carp decide to feed at the exact same moment all around the lake? How many times have you been rudely awoken by a buzzer only to notice that head torches are also switched on in other distant swims? On the big waters fish that may be miles apart have "chosen" to start feeding within seconds of each other. It takes one hell of a stimulus for this to happen. It is virtually impossible to fully understand and master this invisible feeding trigger, but being aware of the favourable times, and to some extent anticipating them, can improve your chances of capture dramatically. As discussed in the previous section all water quality parameters are cyclical; it is therefore very logical that the fish should adopt cyclical feeding patterns.

Helping in the organisation of numerous carp matches across France has enabled me to record some significant data on feeding frequencies. These data corroborate the presence of marked feeding peaks, and what is even more interesting is that these peaks also show signs of being quite size-specific. There are periods in a 24-hour cycle where you are

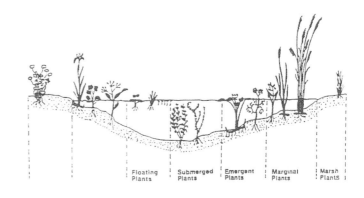

Floating Plants | Submerged Plants | Emergent Plants | Marginal Plants | Marsh Plants

more likely to catch bigger fish! I would love to say that these peaks are in the same time window for every lake, but this is not the case. The feeding hours are very site-specific but appear to be separated by common periods of inactivity that depend mostly on seasonality. However, the fact that smaller fish have different peaks of activity to bigger fish strongly suggests a different feeding pattern. The energy maintenance requirements of adult mature carp are different to young growers; hence it is perfectly logical for them to make a different use of time and space in the quest for the food sources that suit their ongoing energy requirements. Furthermore, differences in body mass have vast implications on the energy budget; for instance all small animals breathe faster and have a fast heart rate compared to larger animals. That is because the smaller the body mass, the greater it is subject to the surrounding environmental conditions. A mouse breathes faster than an elephant… Faster metabolism in young carp implies a greater demand for readily available energy, and if the individuals are "small" then they need to feed on the food source more regularly as their body cannot proportionally stock enough energy reserves.

Now here is an interesting one: true common carp have a faster metabolism than mirror and leather carp. Have you never noticed that commons tend to behave differently to the mirrors and that the commons tend to come out in

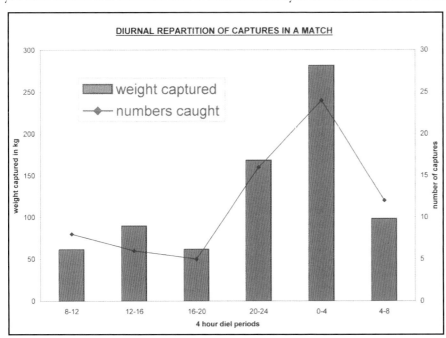

"flurries"? Similarly you may have noticed that certain baits work better than others with common carp. Frightening stuff really, but the source of this differential behaviour is bioenergetics. Common carp tend to have more red blood cells than their more sparsely scaled fellows. That is because their metabolism is faster. Having more blood cells opens the door for a faster digestion rate, and, more importantly, to the faster digestion of more organically rich complex food items. With this in mind it is no surprise that commons may thrive on bivalves and crustaceans. Similarly it explains the regular capture of common carp on livebait. True commons are known to have a more "pelagic" lifestyle; they move a lot more and are prepared to travel further in their daily feeding. They are defined as having a larger "home range". Thinking about it this difference in build and behaviour is usually perceptible during a fight after hooking. Commons are a lot more "wiry", nervous and their powerful surges last longer.

By trying to understand how the carp live and behave I firmly believe that we can position ourselves closer to the right spots, offer them an adapted bait and be ready at the right time. I consider the life of a carp to be very similar to a game of chess, each element of the carp's life and environment being represented as a pawn. In the carp's life these pawns

Please make the next one as pretty as this.

are moved around and the fish reacts accordingly, but instinctively. Similarly to the wonderful board game my interest is to understand the positive and negative interactions between each pawn (biotic and abiotic interactions). The possibilities are plentiful but they all have a meaning. Fish react to stimuli; these are created by the interactions of the natural physical and chemical elements present in their environment (abiotic factors) and by the interactions of all the other living entities (biotic factors). In the latter we can consider predation, and inter and intraspecific competition for food (competition with bream, roach or competition with other carp).

We have discussed oxygen variations in relation to photosynthetic activity. It is now time to look at temperature as a major variable. Fish are poikilothermic creatures (body temperature equals surrounding temperature), which implies that the fish has no direct body temperature regulation and that internal processes such as digestion are dependent on seasonality. A low temperature reduces metabolic activity and the carp's ability to digest complex organic compounds. A standard daily winter ration is around 0.3% to 0.7% body weight (70 grams per day for a 10kg fish). Whereas during summer temperatures this ration is likely to be between 4% and 6% body weight (600 grams per day for a 10kg fish).

Ever felt that your baits were in the wrong place?

These figures are precious as the winter biorhythm has different limiting factors to the summer biorhythm.

The first paradox that explains the lack of constant feeding during the summer is the temperature and oxygen relationship. The hotter the water the less it can physically hold oxygen at 100% saturation. Add plant respiration to this and you understand that the main summer restrictive factor is oxygen. In the winter, low water temperatures and the lack of photosynthesis mean that oxygen is plentiful (10 times more than in summer) and that diurnal variations are pretty much absent. However, metabolic slowdown due to lower temperatures means that the fish cannot make full use of this oxygen abundance.

Characteristics of winter biorhythms are:
- Lesser abundance of natural food resources
- Longer digestion time
- Lesser fish activity, so a lower quantitative food demand
- The fish have a maintenance energy regime
- Stable water quality parameters

Temperature is the limiting factor but the carp can satisfy its requirements with little food, feeding periods are short and well spaced in time. Fish tend to avoid moving away from food sources. Exceptions to this exist. In lakes where intraspecific competition is strong two scenarios are found. The fish overwinter and tend to avoid activity because food is scarce, which leads to stunted populations, or the fish maintain an intense quest for food. The latter scenario is typical of lakes receiving strong and prolonged angling pressure. The continuous input of artificial baits alters the energy balance of the fish. Food in the winter is no longer a limiting factor: stimulated by the daily presence of food and being accustomed to competing for food the fish maintain a regular daily activity. The fish uses more energy but it also gains more energy, and the equilibrium is changed. However, this increase in winter activity bears no impact on the carp's capacity to digest food quickly, as the efficiency of gut enzymes is temperature-controlled. From an angler's perspective the only way to prevent long waits between takes is to use a digestible bait in a normal quantity, or to use very little of a complex bait. The choice of strategy is yours.

Characteristics of summer biorhythms:
- Hyperabundance of natural food
- Rapid digestion time
- Increased fish activity and movement
- Important energy demand for growth, storage and gametogenesis
- Important diurnal variations in water quality parameters

The carp is devoid of a marked stomach and digestion relies on the food passage through the long intestine. The nature of the food determines how much oxygen is required for its digestion, and to some extent the time it takes for the food to pass. In a natural lake without artificial bait, a fish will adapt its feeding frequency to the nature of the food it has available within the tolerance of the surrounding oxygen levels. A fish feeding on bloodworm will have more regular feeding spells than a fish feeding on crustaceans because the bloodworms are more digestible so they put less oxygen stress on the fish. But as they are also less nutritive the quantitative requirement is greater. We can therefore understand the "preoccupation" state the fish reaches. It needs to filter through a

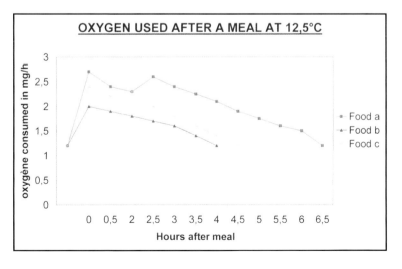

45

lot of silt and needs plenty of bloodworm before it reaches satiation whereas just a few "meaty" items suffice to reach satiation.

At this point it is worth summarising feeding. Two systems control the rate of consumption: 1) systemic demand, which is for the energy and nutrients generated by the metabolic rate: 2) the speed at which the fish can digest the food.

These two interact to generate a motivational state of hunger and generate appetite. "Hunger is the propensity to feed when given the opportunity, whilst appetite is the quantity of food consumed before the fish ceases to feed voluntarily." (R.J. Wootton. 1990.)

It's nice when the hard work and brainstorming pay off.

The Pathway to Big Carp

There are no two ways about it, the capture of a large specimen always gets the grapevine going. Tales of hairy moments and photos of proud captors are spread around the carp world. But why are some fish bigger than others? And can some elements give you an indication as to the growth potential of a venue or a specific fish?

Generations of fish farmers and scientists have worked hard on the question of optimum growth of carp in intensive and extensive production systems. Research has focused on two main areas: 1) the strain, which has the genetic phenotype expressing growth, and 2) diets, where they have looked at diets giving the fastest growth at the least cost.

Applied aquaculture research has given us a few explanations of the differential growth rates of carp, but the research has mainly focused on the production of 2-5kg fish for the table. So in fact we have relatively little scientific data on the mean terminal growth potential of the different strains. The fish farmer knows his growth rate but has little requirement for the knowledge on how many years the fish can grow, what the terminal weight may be and what the life expectancy is likely to be. Hence we look towards the natural environment for data on different strains in different biotopes.

Fortunately amongst the good habits carp anglers have we record weights and take photos, these two elements

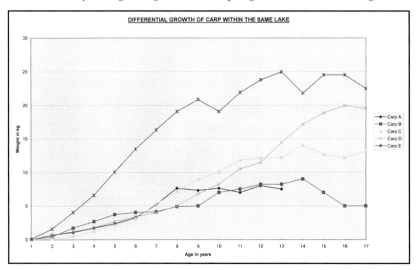

being necessary for the identification and monitoring of exceptional specimens. Terminal weight and the speed at which a fish may reach it are dependent on the variables defined later, but first we need to define what growth is. If the rate of food consumption is adequate, a fish can synthesize new tissue as well as meet the energy costs of maintenance. The tissues may be kept within the body as net growth under the form of storage products (fat), or muscle tissue, or alternatively allocated to the production of gametes (eggs) until their release. Growth and reproduction are complementary processes but the process of natural selection leads to patterns of growth that tend to maximise the lifetime production of offspring.

In other words a carp's system will always allocate whatever resources it has available to the production of viable eggs rather than make provision for weight increases! The reproductive strategy is the most intimate link between the fish and its environment. The well-being of the species is more important than that of the individual. Furthermore, individual growth is obtained when sufficient resources are present and when the fish has optimal foraging. However, in a favourable environment reproductive success with plenty of recruitment (offspring survival) implies that the carp is likely to end up in a situation of strong intraspecific competition that depletes the resources… So ideally the perfect big carp environment is a lake where individual growth is good because of a suitable thermal regime (6 months over 20°C), where there is enough food to satisfy gametogenesis and individual growth, but where recruitment is weak due to unfavourable biotic and abiotic conditions in the early stages of

"Growth and reproduction are complementary processes, but the process of natural selection leads to patterns of growth that tend to maximise the lifetime production of offspring." Carp spawning, seen from close quarters.

life. It is no coincidence that both St. Cassien and Sarulesti (Raduta) hold large carp, although they are not genetically related. Both lakes benefit from an optimal thermal regime for growth and have a low fry survival rate due to the abundant presence of piscivorous predators. Mother nature runs a good business: when reproductive success is low only the strongest, fastest-growing fry survive, hence fine young specimens are selected from their youngest age. In environments where recruitment is high, the overall biomass production of carp is high but this is distributed amongst more individuals, hence a lower average weight or, taking it to the extreme, a stunted population.

So a high biodiversity warm water lake with carp present at no more than 100kg per hectare and plenty of predators is likely to produce, or contain, big carp. Similarly subalpine or submountainous lakes in general are likely to generate big carp because springtime biotic conditions are poor for the fry (little phyto- and zooplankton) but excellent for growers, because the macrobenthos is plentiful. In theory providing a suitable environment for carp to become large is fairly straightforward; however, producing super specimens is a different game with more variables coming into play. The following summarises the main elements affecting the growth of a likely super specimen:

Stock assessment, a vital part of fishery management.

First-class parameters
- The genetic strain (morphology and weight of parents, predisposition for growth, selection…)
- Environment of growth (biotope assembly, productivity and stability)

Second-class parameters
- Biotic interactions (competition, human and natural predation, reproduction, disease)
- Abiotic interactions (water quality content and stability, temperature) create the foundations for a specific **population dynamic**
- Sex of fish (females more fragile but have a greater weight amplitude)

Third-class parameters
- Population accidents
- Luck and individual resilience

Similarly to humans the carp have in their inherited genes a coding that guides them towards a certain morphology (and scale phenotype). Broadly speaking the morphology is defined by the expression of a certain body frame that has typical ratios for height/length/weight and also ratios for appendages and specific body angles. These morphometric data allow us to differentiate accurately the various strains in a mixed population. Even the naked eye can distinguish the main differences. It is straightforward to spot a French Champagne region fish, a torpedo common or a Dink. Where the morphometrics become interesting is when you can identify the potential big lads amongst the others even at an early ontogenic stage. Having measured the frame ratios of the exceptional fish of the same strain it is possible to compare these to smaller, younger fish so as to analyse their morphological similarity. By only keeping the fish that have the desirable ratios it is possible to save on years of grading and lost food (resources) in order to end up with a population that is composed of individuals that have a greater terminal weight potential.

One line of thought that I would like to look into more is chemoreception. It would be interesting to know if a super specimen is a fish that has a greater ability to detect a food source that is more profitable for itself. There is no doubt that carp can clearly distinguish between simple and complex molecules, and that those stimulate feeding, but I do not know if extra big carp have a greater threshold of stimulus before feeding. Logically big carp are fish that have an inherent wise management of their energy budget and also they **should** be fish that are compelled to feed more than the others. However, given the capture statistics on many private and public waters I suspect that some of these fish don't feed a great deal more than their smaller counterparts. Does this mean they are far more selective in their diet and opt for items of higher nutritional value?

When it is up to genetics our wildest dreams can be answered.

I hope that some of the information I've covered gives you an insight into what actually goes on within and around your favourite fish. This chapter is in no way exhaustive, the elements included being only a mere fragment of the complexity of a carp's life. There are still many lines of thought to be pushed further and I sincerely hope that in the foreseeable future some serious scientific work will be undertaken in the ecology of carp.

Finding Waters, Finding Fish

Terry is recognised far beyond these shores as one of the finest carp anglers ever. His results have been exceptional. He has charisma. He is one of the nicest guys you could hope to meet. We all want to hear or read what he has to say. But unfortunately Terry doesn't enjoy writing. His output has been limited to articles in Big Carp **magazine, a regular column for** Angling Times, **a couple of series of taped interviews in** Carpworld, **and his acclaimed book** In Pursuit of the Largest. **I wanted to include some of Terry's words of wisdom in this book, and he agreed to update a couple of features from the** Carpworld Terry Hearn Tapes, **based on conversations that took place at his home in Surrey. I feel the material used here deserves a more permanent record than gathering dust in back issues of a magazine.**

Let's talk a bit about the general approach to fishing big fish waters. Presumably you're just like everyone else when it comes to finding suitable venues. No one picks up the phone and says, "Look, there's a forty-five-pounder in our water, will you come and fish for it?" You have to sort out these target fish and target waters for yourself. What is your starting point?

Terry Hearn

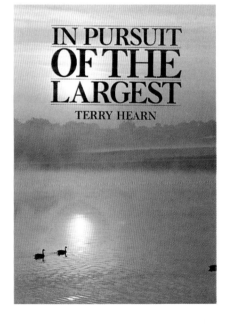

This is a question I'm often asked. "How do you get into all these waters?" Fact is that a good 95% of them anyone can get into. I think a lot of it is down to joining them early rather than leaving it too late. Once waters become well known for their big fish then quite often the membership does close, otherwise they would become too busy. What I've always done over the years is to keep a close eye on the weeklies, *Carp-Talk* and *Angling Times*, and look out for the possible growth of individual big fish, and of course the known big fish themselves. You can keep track of them as they are coming out at bigger weights, and growing.

As an example of planning for the future this past year has been the most expensive ever for me in that I've spent over £700 on tickets. Half of these I knew I wasn't going to fish this season, or possibly even next! But I knew that

Reluctant writer Terry selecting the pictures for another exciting piece of material.

49

if I didn't buy these tickets this year then my chances of getting into the waters concerned in a year or two would be very slim. I've just had to buy the tickets now to get in there for the future. So a lot of it is about keeping your eye on the papers, keeping a check on which waters are producing what fish, and then getting tickets for the waters you want to fish, or may want to fish in the future. I'm talking about big fish waters here, but of course the same applies to any kind of water. If it's the one you want to be in then you have to keep an eye on it for when it is open for membership.

When you say "looking into it" you don't always see the true name of the water in the weeklies, so then you've got to decode the name that's being published to find out which water it really is.

Don't overlook the possibility that your local specialist or tackle shop may be able to point you in the direction of a suitable water.

Well with most venues the grapevine knows the location of almost all the big fish so the true identity of the water isn't normally a problem. When you are in a situation where you don't know you have to start out somewhere, so ask!

Don't overlook the obvious, like asking at your local tackle shop about where fish are being caught from. Where you've got anglers like Lee Jackson and Roy Wheeler from the Tackle Box, Brian Jarrett, Mike Winstone and John Claridge in Hinders and Shaun Harrison in Walkers of Trowell what they don't know about waters in their areas isn't worth knowing! There will be other high-profile anglers in other specialist shops, and even the little corner tackle shop will probably know the whereabouts of the best carp waters in the area. Tackle shops can be a real help in directing you to any type of venue, from the heavily stocked day ticket water to the big fish syndicate venues.

Start asking for information but be a bit subtle about it. Sometimes you've got to be a part of the carp scene to find information that isn't readily available. To be involved in the grapevine you've got to become accepted as part of the scene. You hear about the captures of the target fish straight away, as soon as they happen. You're waiting for it to appear in the paper, but you already know it's been caught. There's an element of paying your dues here. There is a big carp scene and you have to earn acceptance into that scene through your efforts, your captures and your reputation, and you gradually become part of the grapevine. The big carp scene is a surprisingly extensive one, but to become part of it you have to earn the respect of other carp anglers before you become privy

I keep a record of all waters and fish that interest me in a special plastic folder!

Carp monthlies and Carp-Talk *are super sources of information when you are looking for waters to fish.*

Sometimes you just know that it's going to happen. The Brook mirror at 50lb+.

to information that isn't publicly available, or freely published. The starting point here is joining a water and start fishing it. Just being there and trying is part of paying your dues, and it puts you into contact with other big carp hunters. Once they start talking to you then you become part of the grapevine. It can be tough when you are on the outside looking in, but once you're in you feel a lot more comfortable about it!

Fair comment! Let's talk about a route you go down frequently. You see a picture of a big fish from a water you don't have a ticket for. How do you go about tracking down the fish and making a move to get to fish the water where it lives?

Well normally my starting point is to find out exactly which water we are talking about, then I'd try to find someone who is a member, then get the exact address or phone number off them. Then you ring up and find out exactly what the situation is about membership. Sometimes you have to go on a waiting list, but if you are quick enough off the mark then you may well get a ticket straightaway. To be honest very rarely do I have any problems getting into waters. Normally you know if it's a closed shop so you don't even bother trying.

But subject to a waiting list nearly all the big fish waters that you fish are open to anyone?

Yes, definitely. All of the waters, in fact. RMC Angling with all their big fish venues is a terrific starting point – they control Wraysbury, Yateley, Horton and a number of others. Wm. Boyers have big fish waters. Then there's Richmond Park and so on, and a number of lesser-known club waters. Some of the big-fish venues are actually day ticket waters that anyone can go and fish. All of them are open to anyone provided there are places available. On the other hand there are some waters I know I can never get in, yet friends in the area can ring up and join. There are some famous big fish waters with a geographical radius limit for membership: you have to live within a certain distance of the water to gain membership. Some waters don't like publicity, and as a high-profile angler it can be harder for me to get into some of these than it can for other anglers. There are some big carp appearing regularly in the weeklies that I know I'll never fish for because of publicity bans and radius restrictions.

Another well-documented fish, but one that isn't easy to catch. An elusive long golden common from the Brook weighing in at 39lb 12oz.

51

Right: Prelude to a record. Everyone knows where this fish lives, but not everyone wants to take on the daunting Wraysbury Number One. Mallins at 40lb 12oz.

Once you've found a water you can gain membership of you just send off your application and keep your fingers crossed?

Exactly. I've been on one or two waiting lists for years. For example at the time of writing I've been on the Dinton Pastures list for the past six years! I've also been on the list for another cracking water in the area where Martin Clarke had his amazing trio of forties in 2001. There are several other waters that I've got my name down for and have been trying to get into for quite some time, so readers have to understand that getting into a water can take a long time for anyone. It's part of carp fishing. I can't emphasise enough that getting into waters early is the thing to aim for. Once they are really well known and all the big carp hunters want to catch those target fish then it can take years to join the club or the syndicate.

On a lot of the waters you fish you are targeting one fish. I know from reading your material and hearing you talk that you set a great deal of store by doing your homework on that fish as a starting point to fishing for it.

That's right. Absolutely. I'll always go back over as many past captures of the target fish as I can trace. I'll go back through the weeklies to check on the circumstances of previous captures to see if I can find any

Two days later I landed Wraysbury's Mary at 55lb 13oz, a capture which set a new carp record.

information regarding the successful swim, or bait, or tactic. It all helps build up a picture of the fish and its habits and the possible timing of the captures. The timing can be the most important aspect of all with some of these big fish. They just seem to come out three or four times a year, and almost always at around the same time of year in each instance. Other fish seem to go on a feeding spree and can get caught a couple of times within a short space of time then not get caught again until the same time the following year. I keep a plastic folder of cuttings containing information about waters and captures, and this file is the starting point for many of my big fish campaigns.

Fill us in on the background to one or two of your big fish campaigns. For instance presumably the late lamented Bazil would be a very well-documented fish?

Yeh. Just through fishing on the Yateley complex you got to hear about all of the Bazil captures through people who had been there at the time. You learnt an awful lot at Yateley. Everyone was friendly. Everyone was talking to each other, so in addition to Bazil you learnt a great deal about the other lakes on the complex at the same time. Like the Car Park Lake. You learnt where Heather was caught from. Sometimes you'd be on the complex when one of the big fish was caught, so you were learning all sorts. What rigs they were caught on, what baits, the producing swims and hot spots.

Watching and waiting.

But to be honest in most cases, when it's a brand new venue to you, you don't really learn a lot until you get there and start mingling with the other anglers, chatting. You all learn off each other on those sorts of waters.

The north end of Yateley Car Park lake as seen from the tree tops. Everything becomes so clear.

Looking back over your experiences I've got the impression that you've had to work a lot harder to learn about some waters than others, Toll Pits and Sutton in particular.

Yeh, definitely. Whenever I've been lucky enough to get a quick result with a big fish it's been on the lower-stocked waters, or certainly the waters that haven't got so many big fish. I think fish like that are easier to target. If you get a bite it's likely to be from the big fish! But on waters with a number of big fish and mixed stocks in them you're fishing to get bites. That's the main problem. On those waters it's very difficult to target individual fish. You just have to work through the fish that are willing to come your way and hope that the big one turns up. It certainly takes longer.

A great deal of carp fishing is down to hard work and determination. Some readers perhaps feel there is a magic formula. How much of your success do you feel is as a result of hard work and persistence, and how much is down to some sort of instinct, being tuned into the waters you fish?

I think an awful lot of it is down to being tuned into the water and the fish. With me it only seems to happen every now and then, when you know for certain you are about to catch a big fish. On occasions you really do get a strong feeling about it. This only happens when you are on your own. When you are with other people it's as though this fine-tuning and sixth sense is all blocked out, but when you are on your own your perception of the circumstances that you need to aspire to for a capture becomes so much clearer.

This heightened perception, or anticipation, comes across very clearly prior to one or two of the captures in your book In Pursuit of the Largest. *I recall that you had trouble sleeping the night before you caught the big Brook fish, and the same was true of some of your other captures, even when you'd been after that fish for quite some time.*

Above Left: For the best views you need to go higher – but be careful!
Top right: Pads – they can be good but I'd prefer a big bed of Canadian pond weed any day.
Above right: A very carpy spot on the Mere, one of the big mirror's favourite haunts. My first summer there the water was incredibly clear. The strip of bright green silkweed between the bar and the weed columns is in 8-9 feet of water.

On the shallows... The crystal clear waters of Linear's Manor made spotting the fish a fairly simple task.

Yes, with the Brook fish, and others, I got that feeling that I just knew I was going to catch a big fish. It happened last year with Black Spot. It was the second night of the session. I'd caught the 26-pounder the night before and I just knew the following night was the night for the big one. That was one of those nights when I just couldn't sleep, forever looking at the isotopes, waiting for it to roar off. I think it's an instinct that you've narrowed it down to the point that the fish has got to feed in that spot, and that the whole build-up says it has to happen that night, or the following morning. The Sussex capture of Black Spot from Plankton was a perfect example. At around 20 acres it's not a small lake, but through climbing trees and having a good look round the shallow areas I could rule out so much of the lake that in my mind the big 'un was right there, where I was fishing. That was the only area it could possibly be in. It was snaggy. It had cover. So I think that in your mind you finish up convincing yourself that you are about to catch the fish to the extent that you are just shaking with anticipation and excitement. You know it's just got to happen.

A lot of our readers would love to catch a thirty-pounder. They'll be fishing a club water with lots of doubles and some twenties in it, and a thirty-pounder that comes out two or three times each year – and that's their dream fish. It can be difficult to single out a big fish from a population of other fish. Have you got any advice as to the best way of going about this?

This ghostly shape beneath the overhanging bushes is the Yateley Car Park lake's 'Arfur'. Watching the Car Park Lake's low stock of carp at such close quarters taught me a great deal about their feeding habits.

A nice spot as seen from a boat; not too open, not too blatant. Notice the old rusty scaffold pole lying across it. This type of clear spot is fairly common and you'll regularly see a sunken branch, or perhaps an old brick or something similar, in the centre of a clear patch. Carp love to use such objects to rub their flanks against – which is often how a clear spot starts off.

When it comes to those more heavily stocked waters that have got lots of doubles, a fair few twenties, then one thirty, you can be up against it for singling out the big fish – unless you can see it and possibly stalk it. There are a great many waters like this. I imagine Orchid, where you fished, is such a venue where targeting a big fish can be really tricky. All you can do is keep fishing it and catch as many fish as possible, and hope that the one you are after is going to come along.

There are a couple of areas you can help yourself with. Swim selection is definitely the best basis for location when you are trying to single out a big fish on waters of this type. Some big fish are very territorial. I did a couple of spring campaigns on Linear Fisheries' Manor Farm in Oxford. There were two possible 40lb+ fish in there at the time, a fish called Pop-Eye, and another one called Cut-Tail. After two successive springs fishing the water I ended up with nine different thirties, but I didn't catch either of the big target fish. I caught pretty much everything else bar those two! The way I fished Manor was to follow the wind, move around all the time. But whenever the two big fish came out it tended to be from the same swims – although it wasn't until I'd finished the two campaigns that I was able to piece the capture pattern together. In hindsight I think that's where I went wrong. I should have fished the two swims that tended to produce those two big fish.

You may be able to give yourself an edge with bait, too. The big fish in a water may be falling to a certain bait. If they are it may pay to get on it. If you want a big fish be sure you are using a proven big fish bait. I changed when I moved on

55

to fishing exclusively for big fish. Because a bait catches carp it doesn't mean to say it's going to appeal to the big carp. I guess this is an area covered elsewhere in the book, but from a personal point of view I can't emphasise enough the importance of the right type of bait if you are after a big fish.

Do you set much store by the history of target fish captures in terms of when they get caught, or do you just go anyway?

Apart from when it feels dead in the middle of winter when I sometimes go and fish for other species, I tend to fish for big carp all the time. Some of the time you know you are just waiting, but while you are waiting you are building up the picture which will lead to the eventual capture. Some carp take longer to catch than others, not just because of the timing but because you have to break down their defences and

The main Snake Pit snags. When I fished there during the early spring there wasn't much weed present and consequently the fish used to virtually live amongst this twisted mass of underwater trees.

get inside their heads more gradually. You know some times of the year are better for big carp than others. April and May are especially good, as autumn can be, but there's a chance at any time of the year. If you try to narrow down the chance to a known brief period then you may miss out on chances that present themselves at other times. I'm aware of when big fish are likely to get caught, but I don't limit my fishing to those times. Readers with limited time may want to give some extra thought to timing. Most carpers take a week off at the start of the season, or in the summer. If they only have one full week's fishing each year on top of their shorter sessions, that time off might be better taken in the late spring or autumn.

OK. We've found a suitable venue, and even given some thought to how you go about finding the fish. Obviously the whole spectrum of the location of carp is one of your greatest strengths. Do you want to talk a bit about the trouble you will go to to find carp?

I don't really see locating carp as going to any trouble because I'm enjoying myself. I'm walking around, exploring the lake, climbing trees... If there's access to a boat, even better. But the thing is I'm learning all the time. If the water's clear you can see likely spots. Even if you can't actually find the carp you can quite often find where they've been, which shows you you're getting on the right track. It also helps to be able to rule out areas. You don't actually have to find the carp: sometimes you can rule out so much of the lake that the only area where you can't see the bottom, or you can't get to because it's snaggy, then that's where they must be.

Fishing on the end of a big wind isn't always productive. On Sonning I found that once the cold winds were blowing it was best to head for the more sheltered areas.

OK, let's take a water where you can go out in a boat. What are you looking for when you go out in a boat?

Using a boat to explore a target venue is all-important. Even if boats aren't permitted for fishing you may be able to get

56

permission to go out in one during the close season – on waters where there is one. With a boat you can learn in a day what it may take you two seasons to piece together from the bank. Tell-tale signs I look for from a boat are clear areas, particularly if there's weed everywhere else around the area. If there's no fish in a lake then weed will cover most of the bottom, but when you get fish in a lake, and birds on it, that's when you get clear areas, and those are the spots I'm looking for. A water doesn't have to be clear for you to be able to define the clear spots. Areas that look disturbed – more coloured than the rest of the lake or surrounding areas – need to be investigated. If you can imagine an area in a field full of long grass, if someone goes in there and has a picnic, then afterwards it's blatantly obvious that someone's

been there. It's all flattened down and disturbed. It's exactly the same when you're out in a boat; you're looking down at an underwater field if you like, consisting of weed and other features, and you can see an area where all the weed fronds are all twisted, and turned round the wrong way. You can see it's been disturbed, and fed on, and it's often quite easy to identify these spots.

A lot of your fishing has been on gravel pits, which a lot of our readers will fish. You're out in a boat on a gravel pit. What are you looking for in terms of the most appealing features to you on a gravel pit?

Where you see them isn't necessarily where you can catch them. These 'oldy worldy' commons living in a large pit not too far from the Mere could often be seen sunning themselves amongst weed over deep water at one end of the lake...
...but it wasn't until a good wind took them to the other end and onto the shallows that they became catchable (below).

A cracking common of 33lb 5oz, my best from the 100 acre Oxford pit. Here feedback from the tench anglers put us on the track.

On a wide expanse of open water I'd be looking for any of the bars, or other features, that come up from the bottom. Probably the first areas I check out are the corners, particularly the corner where the southerly winds blow into. I've often found the corner where the north-easterly wind blows into to be productive. As a rule on a lot of the waters I fish the south-facing bank is definitely the best bank to fish. That bank receives the sun summer and winter and the best areas are often on the south-facing side of the lake. So I'd start by checking out all the corners, then figure out the points of the compass and identify and explore the south-facing bank.

What about bars? Are they just routes that the carp favour, or is there something about them that is a feeding attraction to the carp? And if so which part of the bars should we be concentrating on?

I think there's an element of both aspects, but I feel that the route side of it is the most important aspect. For example if you watch grebes diving on a lake they will very often tell you the exact route where the bars run. Well it's more than "often" really, because all the time, particularly in winter when the weed's died down and there are only the permanent features out there, the grebes are working the bars and they'll tell you exactly where they run. The grebes are following the routes of the smaller fish species and more often than not the carp are following exactly the same routes.

Concealment is almost as important as location. Making myself invisible in an exposed spot on the Toll pits.

Your mention of grebes brings up an interesting point about birds. Have you found any relation between the movement of carp and other waterbirds, for instance coots and tufties?

Certainly over at Horseshoe, where all the coots seem to be ganged up, then the carp seem to be there, too – or vice versa, perhaps. Horseshoe's very heavily stocked so when there's heavy feeding going on there might be bits of weed and other debris coming up from the bottom. Watching through the binoculars you can see the coots constantly feeding off the surface. Maybe they're feeding on bits of food that the carp are digging up from the bottom.

I've just experienced a similar sort of thing in France where the coots were moving up and down the lake, and when the coots were in front of me the carp were, too. What about tufties?

Coots seem to get on all right with the carp but tufties don't seem to be too happy about them. Often when I've got a lot of bait out and I know the carp are coming in on the bait, then you'll see the tufties holding back from the area. If one is brave enough to go down then up he comes pretty sharpish.

So there's no redeeming features with tufties at all then?

No, definitely not!

Let's get back to bars. You say a bar may be like a well-defined route. If you find a bar that appeals to you as a feature how do you place your bait there?

In hot weather, during high pressure, I'd look for the highest point on the bar. The fish are going to be high in the water and I'd be aiming to get my bait as close as possible to the fish. But for the most part, like during the night-time and at other possible feeding times – and during the cooler part of the year – I'll fish on the back of the bars, simply because it's easier to identify really. You're casting over the back of the bar and pulling back to it. You cast out, feel it coming back smooth when you're pulling the lead along the bottom, wait for the tap-tap, up with the marker float, and that's the spot at the back of the bar. I've always found these to be good areas. It's probably just the same as pulling the lead down the near side of the bar but the precise bottom of the bar is easier to identify with a lead or a marker float. The fish are likely to hug the bars when they are on the move.

Do you look on snags as an obvious location feature?

Yeh, next to weed snags have got to be one of the first places to look – particularly on the pressured venues. Normally I find that if a lake's heavily weeded then the snags don't come into the equation as much, but when you get a lake that's not got much weed at all then it seems they'll always use the snags.

Going back to weed, do you find there are weeds that carp relate to and others that they aren't as enthusiastic about, or is weed simply weed?

I've never noticed any great difference. I think they like any weed that reaches the surface and gives them cover. If it doesn't reach the surface they may not like it as much. Thinking about it I think I'd prefer a heavy bed of Canadian to a set of pads. I think they prefer to be in a denser weedbed than a sparser one. Silkweed I love. I like the fluffy, candy-floss type stuff. You can fish straight into this stuff without it affecting the rig People get scared of it because when you reel the rig in it's all in a ball and it looks hideous, but if you drop it all back in the edge it seems to sort itself out and the rig is still fishing efficiently, it all fluffs back out again. I've never had a problem with silkweed.

Success in the shape of the Toll Pits mirror known as Lesters at 40lb 2oz.

I know you've used pop-ups a lot but if you were fishing over silkweed would you favour them, or would you actually go down into the weed?

I've done both. On the Car Park Lake, I remember looking down at the end of one of the bars from a tree and you could see this great ball of silkweed, a very pale, lime-green colour. It was a very big ball and came up about three feet off the bottom. I kept seeing tench and some of the smaller stockie carp disappearing into this green ball of silkweed and I just cast a stringer into it, with a straight bottom bait presentation. I caught two tench off that spot. No carp, but I felt that if I could catch the tench there then I was in with a chance of catching carp that way, too. One thing you have to watch if you're fishing a stiff-linked pop-up rig in silkweed is that the weed can clog up the hinged loop and stop the rig from working properly. That's why I was experimenting with bottom baits in that particular situation. I think a bottom bait in a PVA bag is probably the best presentation when you're casting into silkweed.

Always look for the chance of a fish off the top. I've always got floating baits with me.

You're out in a boat – or you're casting around – on a gravel pit and you find patches of silt. How do you look on these features? Areas to be avoided, or possible feeding spots?

Silt pockets are areas that are normally feeding spots but I've found it can be difficult to get takes from them. If I find patches of silt where I'm seeing carp, or seeing them bubbling there, then I'll try to find a firm area adjacent to it to present my bait on. As long as it's not raised too high above the bottom I'd rather fish a firm area than fish the silt itself. The base of the bar I was talking about earlier is typical of this situation. There might be silt at the very bottom of the bar, but I prefer to fish just onto the harder bottom of the bar itself. Fish that are feeding in very silty spots have got their head in the bottom and there's a chance they won't even find the bait.

I know you've fished silty waters. How have you selected the spots to fish on this type of venue? How do you go about deciding where to position your hookbaits?

The silty venues I've fished have had very few features. There was just the silt and that was it! One particular water I remember was Silvermere in Cobham – that was very silty. On there we noticed that when you threw your freebies in the edge they'd actually disappear into the silt, because the silt was so fine, like a thick milk shake almost. What I finished up using successfully on there was peanuts, which actually lay on top of the silt, which helped keep the bait available to the carp. All the carp that were getting caught there were being caught on single hookbaits popped-up off the bottom, and all the freebies were buried in the silt. So you needed quite a blatant presentation to get a take there.

Because I've fished silty waters I get a lot of questions about silt. People seem to be very nervous of it. I think the water you are talking about is fairly exceptional, but it is a feeding medium for them, isn't it, silt? Carp aren't afraid of it.

This welcome Toll Pits mirror of 24lb 3oz came off the top during a long, difficult period when the fish weren't feeding strongly on bottom baits.

If there's nothing else available then they've got to be feeding in it, yes. This particular lake didn't have anywhere else. All the lake bed was soft silt.

Earlier in the conversation you mentioned observation. How much store do you set by the carp actually showing you where to position your baits?

Most of my fishing is based around letting the carp show me where to put the baits. Whether they're rolling, or jumping, or bubbling, or if I can see them from climbing trees or going out in the boat, whatever, I'll do my best to let the carp tell me the spot. Other than that a lot of it's guesswork.

Fair comment. We're talking mostly about smaller waters here, waters you can observe, and explore fairly thoroughly. I know from reading your Angling Times *column, your book and your other material that on the bigger waters you set a great deal of store by wind direction.*

Wind direction has always been a starting point when I turn up at a lake. Especially in the early part of the year before the weed has come up, and in the warmer months, for a good percentage of the time I find the fish on the end of the wind. They do follow the wind. Really the only time that I find there is an exception to this is when a water is very heavily weeded, when they are going to be in the weed irrespective of wind or other possible influences. Weed can stop them dead in their tracks. If there's a massive weedbed halfway down the lake then they won't bother going any further.

Returning the Big Black Mirror to the Mere, one of my happier carp fishing moments – and it shows. Oddly enough I almost slipped up on the location aspect here. I nodded off, and the wind changed. If I'd been awake I'd probably have moved with it!

Going on a bit, when you're going onto a big new water how much is past capture history part of your starting point, or is wind your usual early guide? How do you start on a big new water, like the 100-acre Oxfordshire water you've spent some time on?

In the case of the big Oxfordshire pit it was a combination of a number of factors. There were a couple of tench anglers who'd fished there for a number of years, and they'd hooked a few carp – lost a few and landed a few. So we had a good starting point there. The tench anglers were mainly float fishing and had caught carp from the margins, and it happened that they'd caught them on the end of the prevailing wind as well. This history all helped, and we did have quite a lot to go on when we first started fishing there.

How often are you right on location with your first choice of swim?

Well, I get it wrong quite a lot! But I won't sit there knowing I've got it wrong. If I've done a night and in the morning it feels wrong, or I know it's wrong from seeing fish elsewhere, then I'm on the move. I don't just look for fish prior to setting up. There are often long periods of the day when you know the carp aren't going to feed, and when I'm at the water I'll spend at least some of this time each day looking for fish

When you're talking about wind direction, I guess this can change your choice of swim fairly quickly. In general terms you're talking about the prevailing wind, but I recall when we relived your capture of the big Mere fish you commented that those fish would have moved on the change of wind – and that by the time you woke up Laney had moved with them!

Yeh! Definitely. The Mere fish always follow the wind, and that was a south-west wind as well. Good wind. I finished up catching the big fish in that case, and I bet the rest of the fish had already moved past me on the wind. Sometimes the bigger ones do act a bit differently to the rest, and can hang back. A lot of the big fish are loners and may act and think differently. A good example of this was the story Dave Mallin told about fishing the Priory for the Pet. The Priory is a really big pit, and Clive Tillotson and Dave had moved onto a really strong southerly wind. They were sitting on the north bank, rubbing their hands, with everything looking right, when the Pet was caught from the margins of the southerly bank at 40lb+. It came out from the calm water at the back of the wind, and they just couldn't believe it! So the wind direction can be a guide, but it doesn't guarantee success, and it doesn't always take account of the big loners.

We can't really leave the subject of location without touching on the extra dimension aspect that is associated with your name. You are consultant for a range of carp products launched by Drennan under the initials ESP, which I think stands for Extra Sensory Perception. Can I ask you if this is an allusion to a highly developed understanding of carp through advanced watercraft, or if you are at times visited by some sort of divine inspiration that says "fish there" for no apparent reason?

No divine inspiration, Tim! I think the name ESP was perhaps a bit tongue in cheek, based on what people were saying about my results rather than how I was achieving them! We all have to rely on guesswork or instinct at times. I guess ESP is one of those "when all else fails" senses. It comes through strongest on waters you know well. When there are no fish coming out, and no movement to be seen, you have to make an inspired guess (or what you hope is an inspired guess!) as to where the fish are likely to be, and where they might pick up a bait. When the fishing's slow the carp aren't following the usual guidelines we've discussed here. Like we've just talked about the Pet coming out from the wrong bank, and the big Mere mirror being slower to move on the wind than the other fish in the water. When you're fishing really well, and are in tune with the carp, you develop a level of understanding that lets you make apparently unorthodox decisions. When you're fishing for one target fish you perhaps start to develop an understanding of that fish's movements and thinking. Looking back I've been more in tune with some waters and some target fish than others. I think ESP is a sort of instinctive understanding, which is part watercraft and part experience. I tend to rely on it when I get a very strong feeling to do something, or when all else fails! Catching carp isn't easy, and at times we all need all the help we can get in carp fishing.

Terrific stuff. Thanks for all that, and good luck.

Local Waters – Limited Time

Julian Cundiff

Two months of hard work pays off. A 27.00 on my first trip to the lake 'with tackle'.

Although the lure of big carp is a tremendous pull for many anglers, in reality the majority of anglers who fish for carp may never be in a position to go down that avenue, due to real life, imposed or self-imposed! Family commitments, work commitments, social and financial commitments and so on mean that many of us have more chance of a week in Tenerife with the wife and kids than a week at Cassien after Lucy or Half Moon Scale, or a session on Yateley Car Park Lake after one of its prizes. Read the chapters in this book carefully and you will see that the self-discipline required to catch such fish (be they here or abroad) is tremendous, and the majority of anglers who fish for carp simply don't have that mindset. You've got to really want to catch Benson, or Arfur, or Lucy so much that failure is not acceptable. Is that really you? Well perhaps not at the moment anyway! You can't plan life to the nth degree, and even if you can't imagine such a scenario now it may well happen in the future. But for the moment let's examine the position many of us find ourselves in.

The brief Tim gave me for this chapter was to write of local waters and limited time, which I guess sums up what many of us have to live with. So what pedigree do I have to write about such a subject? Well my life has always been a whirlwind of conflicting demands, and having to juggle my love of carp fishing with my other varied interests – such as girls, weight training, boxing, Formula One, WWF, motocross etc. – has never been easy. Add that to a five-day week, nine-to-five job, a brilliant family situation, additional duties with *Carpworld* and *Crafty Carper*, plus conferences, slide shows, exhibitions and such like and it would be very easy for me to find carp fishing an unwanted distraction. However I need to fish on a regular basis; if I didn't I would go what I think is known as 'stir crazy'. All work and no play does not a happy Jules make. For that reason, ever

You can't do too much work in advance. It's mid-February and I'm spending a cold evening looking for fish.

since 1986 when I really started to take my carp fishing seriously, I have concentrated on local waters on a limited timescale. Two or three overnighters per week, every week, between March and early December – I love it! And if I can do it, you can as well.

It's easy to believe (usually quite wrongly) that you don't have time to carp fish regularly and effectively: the reality is that if I sat down with you for a couple of hours we could come up with a game plan which, if you stuck to it, could change your carp fishing for ever, provided you have the mindset to do it. I'd love to sit down with you in person but unfortunately that isn't possible so you are going to have to make do with a chapter trying to convince you, instead. Start reading this with an open mind. Have no preconceived ideas and you'll realise that you too can get the best from your local waters in limited time.

Right, enough of the preamble, let's get down to business. Whatever time of year you are reading this, if you are not satisfied with your results sit back and take stock. Obviously if you are on a roll you would be silly to do that – I certainly wouldn't – but I would guess that many of you feel there is still work to be done, and that perhaps your results could be improved upon. If that's the case then put the tackle in the garage, forget about getting it out for a while and start to focus on making your future carp fishing time more productive.

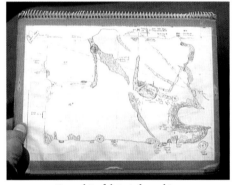

Every bit of data is logged in.

Whenever I hit a brick wall in my carp fishing I take a step back to take two steps forwards, and time and time again doing this has repaid me generously. When things are not working out as they should one night at home thinking about it isn't going to solve things, is it? Better to take a week or two off from the fishing (don't worry, the world won't stop), think about every aspect of your approach, and put as much right as you can. With me on that point? Good, let's start thinking.

Firstly, how much time do you realistically have available to you? Most of us have work and social commitments and a family to care for and support. Life is a balancing act and you have to decide how important carp fishing is to you, and how much time you are willing to put into it. Do you want it enough? If you do you will find a way; find an hour, find a night or two; find the time. Remember the title of the chapter; local waters, limited time. Make that time a little less limited and you are well on the way to success.

Once you have decided how much time you will have at your disposal don't simply see it as a short-term thing; look at it as long term, as a way of life. Don't force yourself into a corner by giving yourself a limited timescale to achieve things. Look at the big picture. Obviously there will be certain weeks or months when you can put more or less time in due to illness, holidays, weather and so on, but view this local water approach as a way of life, not just a passing phase. Even during difficult domestic circumstances, or during my 'down' periods, I have always looked at the big picture and forced

The strain is showing. A fourth over-nighter in a row. Trying hard!

myself on, rather than lying down, giving up, or taking long periods 'out'.

A good description of the way-of-life concept is 'campaign angling'. I'm prepared to do it for as long as it takes to succeed, and if that means twelve months or more, then so be it. By limiting yourself to the 'nice' months from May to September you will definitely be limiting your potential for success. Rome wasn't built in a day and to have consistent success on your waters in limited time you must not limit the big picture. The varying seasons will obviously have an effect on

On short sessions sleep will cost you dearly.

your efforts but avoid thinking too far ahead. Simply view it as one long road and one you will travel come rain or shine. Later in the chapter I will cover how to get the best from your fishing all year round, but if your mindset is the same in November as it is in May you will be well on course.

Next step is your choice of venue. Quite simply the more often you can visit or fish your water the more successful you should be. You will be aware of the time you have available, and you need to make the most of that time. Perhaps you are going to fish an overnighter, or two, each week? Maybe one day midweek? Maybe just the odd evening session, or Sundays? Whatever your time schedule is you can only make it work if you pick the right venue. So how do you go about doing that?

Well first you have to decide what size of carp you want to catch, and what you are prepared to put up with to catch that size of carp. Say you want to catch lots of twenties each year, but the only place to do it is a horrible, overpriced and badly run day ticket water. You need to weigh up the situation. For me it's not just a question of what I'm fishing for, but the venue I'm fishing, too. I have to enjoy it! It's all right saying you can put up with anything, but can you? One of my favourite venues is Three Lakes at Selby, Yorkshire, which I've fished on and off for years. In 1999 it went day

Get a rod to it now.

ticket after years as a syndicate venue, and with its day-ticket status came an increase in pressure, and all that goes with it. Last year I wanted to catch a big carp and I knew that Three Lakes was my best venue for that in the time I had available. However, I had to accept that it would be busy, that I would struggle to get in a going swim, and that all I could do was grit my teeth and work hard when I was at the venue. A need to balance the size of the fish with personal surroundings was made and I was rewarded with a personal best within three months. Game over! So be realistic in your objectives.

Do you want to catch singles, doubles,

twenties, thirties, or bigger!? Perhaps you want to catch a personal best? Which local venue has the best stock of the size of fish you are targeting which will beat your personal best? Make a list. The ones which have the most fish in them of the size you want should theoretically be your best choice. However, once you've drawn up the list remember what I said earlier about the surroundings and situation you are prepared to fish in. It's an unfortunate state of play today that you have to consider how waters are run, facilities, security and so on. Some waters which produce big fish I wouldn't touch for love nor money due to the nature of some of the people who fish such waters, and the poor way in which they are run.

Don't just think size-wise, consider the big picture. Shortlist at the ready, and in my opinion you now have to narrow it down to one water only for each campaign. Which venue can you afford to fish? I don't just simply mean its fishery fees but also the travel implications. Most of you will travel to your chosen venue by car, so not only do you need to consider how much it costs to fish the day-ticket, club or syndicate water, but how much it costs you in fuel, too. Some of you may well be lucky and live very close to the ideal water, but all venues involve some travelling. On a one-off

The rods are out but I think the carp will move in an hour or two so I'm barrowed up and ready to move.

basis this isn't necessarily a factor, but this is a campaign you are putting together so the long-term costs have to be assessed.

In addition every minute in the car compared to time on the bank has to be taken into consideration. The more time you put in on the road equates to less time at the venue. A water on the way to work (or back) is ideal as you can incorporate it into your work schedule. What is the road to the venue like? Rush-hour traffic? Best route? Quickest route? Cheapest route? All these aspects have to be considered to make the most of limited time on local venues.

Having weighed up all the pros and cons you need to start to get down to the nitty-gritty of planning a campaign which will bring results in both the short and long term. The name of the game here is research, and whether you've fished the venue or not before, knowledge is power and ignorance certainly isn't bliss! Firstly you need to visit the venue as often as you can to get a feel for the place and to start drawing up plans for your fishing. If your venue is well known or has been written about, get the articles together and keep them in a folder. Magazines such as *Carp-Talk*, *Carpworld*, *Crafty Carper* etc. publish thousands of words about venues, so start researching your chosen one. There are fact sheets available from Angling Publications, day-ticket reviews in most carp and angling weeklies and monthlies, and in-session features in some of the carp monthlies. All this material can give you valuable venue information.

How about using the internet if you have access to it? Whilst it does have its detractors the net is a brilliant medium for research. You can join in forums, post questions and enquire online. Make it work to your advantage. Visit your local tackle shops to see if they can help. Many shops have photo display boards with local catches on them. The best specialist shops have at least one carp fishing assistant who will be familiar with local venues. Don't make a nuisance of yourself, but get what information you can while you are doing your shopping.

The Carp Society has regional organisers all around the country so join the Society and go to the local meetings for possible help about venues from the RO or other members. Whatever advice you get from these sources take it with an open mind, write it down and add it to the folder of information you've already got. If that sounds over the top why do you think anglers like Terry Hearn, Jim Gibbinson, Tim Paisley and company are so successful? Because on top of anything else they may have going for them they put the spadework in. From overhead shots of Orchid and capture files (Tim), to old *Angling Times* clippings (Terry), nothing is too much trouble for the top carp anglers, and it shouldn't be for you, either.

It may be that you already know your chosen water well, but even if that's the case you still need to prepare that file. Map of the water, big fish captures, baits which have worked, times of the year when the big fish get caught, and so on. Complacency can be your greatest enemy, especially if you feel you really know the water. How often have we all been surprised by some newcomer turning up and catching the biggest fish from our favourite venue using tactics that couldn't possibly work there!

For the purposes of this chapter let's presume you don't know the water well and instead have to start from scratch. You've assessed the venue as being your best choice on limited time, so let's get some reconnaissance visits in. If I didn't know the water at all I would spend at least one – preferably two – week(s) visiting the water, especially in the summer months. Too many anglers make the mistake of turning up and doing their spadework with the fishing tackle in tow.

Recast in the middle of the night was rewarded with this 33.04.

Big mistake! You will be desperate to get your rods cast out and almost certainly won't be in a position to look, look, and look again as you really should.

Your early visits should be used to draw a map of the venue marking on it any visual features, obvious sight lines and significant bankside features. Ascertain where North, South, East and West are so you can equate your plan of the water to weather forecasts and wind directions. Ensure you visit the water at different times of the day, including dawn, dusk and noon. Carp may show at any time and it's important to pick up on any visual indications. Some waters are better morning waters than evening waters, and it may be that the carp favour certain areas of the lake at certain times of the day.

The visits may teach you something about angler pressure, and hopefully give you the chance to schedule your sessions to periods of favourable angler pressure. Ensure that you visit the water midweek as well as at weekends. Maybe Sundays are quiet? Sunday afternoons and evenings can be the quietest time of the week on some venues. Midweek could be quiet? This early spadework will save you some heartache. If other anglers are present see how they can help you – intentionally or unintentionally! Some anglers can be very helpful and very honest and will tell you all about features, hot spots, going baits and so

Keep feeding it in but watch for changes in the carp's feeding patterns.

on. Others will be a little more reticent to pass this knowledge on, so don't make a nuisance of yourself.

Even if anglers are not forthcoming you can pick up some ideas, using some subtlety of course! Where are their lines pointing? Are they using much bait? Large baits or small baits? Long-range casting or short-range? Buckets of particles or seeds next to the swim? Wet nets? Are some swims favoured more than others? Which swims do the most successful anglers favour? Don't stand around making a nuisance of yourself, use some common sense. Putting the binoculars on anglers is guaranteed to get you noticed for the wrong reasons from the start. And once you start to visit the water regularly and become part of the scene anglers who weren't willing to pass on information to start with will become more forthcoming, particularly as you build some knowledge of your own that you can exchange with them.

Wherever the knowledge and information comes from write it all down and build up that dossier.

Well that's a lot of the hard work done already. We are almost ready to go fishing! Now you need to look carefully at bait and bait application. Really this area will depend on the water and your personal whims so it would be wrong of me to say you must get on the Grange, Big Fish Mix, Formula One or whatever. As a starting point have a look at the bait chapters in this book: if you have any doubts about bait read and reread them. Because I have total confidence in the Nutrabaits range I would definitely choose something from their stable, so my choice would almost certainly be Trigga, Big Fish Mix or Biollix. If you have total confidence in a certain bait company's products then don't let me influence your thinking. Stick with your chosen bait, be it Mainline's Activ-8, Nashbait's Formula One or Monster Pursuit, or Essential Products' Shellfish B5.

It may be that one particular bait is dominating your water. On limited time you would be silly not to get on it. I have known waters to be totally dominated by a bait and if I hadn't had my allegiance to Nutrabaits I'd have gone straight onto the going bait. Why make it difficult for yourself? Let the others bait up for you and you can reap the rewards during the limited time you can put in. As you start to use the bait you will be contributing to its success by your own bait application. **But** don't put all your eggs in one basket and stock up with tons of one size of bait; use a

Limited time does not mean limited results, as I proved here.

degree of caution and imagination, please. I may well have a freezer full of Big Fish Mix but I'll certainly have lots of variations on the bait theme as back-up on short sessions and limited visits.

No matter which local water you decide to target I'd have a good stock of the following – subject to any bait restrictions on the venue, of course. Hemp and tiger nuts, either raw or ready prepared by Dynamite Baits. Alternative high-attract hookbaits (bottom baits and pop-ups) from Heathrow Bait Services, and Dynamite Baits' Frank Warwick range. Trout pellets and betaine pellets in a variety of sizes from Hinders, The Bait Company and Haiths. Chum mixers and an alternative floater, and sweetcorn. That will do for starters. On limited-time visits the carp won't always be feeding strongly and you may need to try to buy a bite at times. Quick breakdown pellets and other tiny groundbaits are ideal for focusing the carp's attention on your main bait or hookbait. Sometimes you will need to fish single hookbaits at long range, maybe spod at distance or PVA bag to a feature. On other occasions it may be floaters or stalking under the rod tip.

To be versatile you need to be able to ring the changes without carrying the kitchen sink around with you. Whatever tackle you own will almost certainly suffice but ensure that your mobility isn't hampered and your options aren't limited by too much gear! If you are on very limited time it may be that you only need to carry one rod which can be used for stalking, floater fishing, or PVA bagging. For short morning or evening sessions this approach is brilliant and providing you can find your carp it can even be possible to outfish anglers who have more time at their disposal. A rod, reel, landing net, weigh sling, mat and all the incidentals in a small rucksack or holdall are all you need. Many carp anglers admit that stalking or floater fishing are the weakest areas in their armoury. Work at being successful in these skills and you may find yourself with a head start over many other anglers on your chosen venue.

Ball pellets and boilies are a wonderful combination when they are fine-tuned correctly.

Let's presume that most of you have a little longer than very short sessions available to you and will wish to adopt more conventional, semi-static tactics to catch your carp. Most of my own carp fishing is done on an overnight basis, twelve hours maximum, which is quite limited really, but long enough to mean that I need to be fully tooled up. Three rods, a spod rod and marker float rod, two landing nets, Viper bivvy and so on. These are my 'essentials' starting point. Out of interest I have drawn up a list of the major items of tackle I carry with me. These can all be placed on my barrow and taken to any swim with the minimum of effort, then packed up and moved to another swim in a very short period of time should the need arise.

The following are all carried in a large Nash Quiver which houses all the made-up rods in separate rod sleeves:

3 x 12' x 3½lb TC. rods with Big Pit Reels	1 spod rod and reel
1 marker rod and reel	1 floater/stalking rod & reel
1 Nash Viper bivvy	6 single banksticks
1 rod pod	2 landing nets
1 throwing stick	baiting spoon & landing net

The following items fit in a large Fox bedchair bag:

1 bedchair	1 seat	Buzzer heads
1 groundsheet	Bivvy pegs	Visual indicators in cases

The following items fit in a large Nash Stacksack Carryall:

Sleeping bag and pillow	Rig boxes, wallets and cases
Marker floats and spods	Camera case
Scales and weigh sling	Spare spools of line

The following bait items fit in a large white bait bucket:

Ready prepared particles	Pellets and groundbait
Lots of tubs of hookbaits	Method bait and catapults

The carp are on the move, and so am I – with all the items in the table on board

All those items will fit on the barrow, which is a lot easier than carrying them by hand. Whilst there is a lot to be said for really cutting your tackle down when you have limited time, I would prefer to be in a position where I am able to take advantage of any opportunities which arise **and** fish comfortably, so that I want to return on a regular basis. A fully laden barrow is not much harder to move around than a half laden one so I don't cut corners when it comes to being equipped to catch carp from my local waters on limited time.

69

Right, it looks like everything is ready; your tackle and baits are up to scratch, so let's go carp fishing for real!

You have made a plan of the time you have available and your preliminary visits have given you some good clues as to where the carp will be. Things are looking good! Tackle in the car. Don't forget any vital items, or the bait, and away we go. I must admit that because I have limited time in which to catch carp, once I am in the car I am totally focused and dedicated to catching carp. The mobile phone is switched off. The radio is kept off, and even though I am concentrating on my driving my mind is a computer of carp information. Which way will the wind be blowing? What has the weather been like and how may conditions affect the carp? What tactics, rigs and baits are likely to be most successful? What did I learn from my last trip? Mind in gear all the time – thinking, thinking, thinking!

Although my mind will constantly be mulling over the prospects and alternatives I avoid making any decisions

In amongst 'em. Only feet from some very large carp, and on tenterhooks.

until I get to the lake. You have limited time to get it right and need to find the carp, not hope that they find you. Whilst there is nothing wrong with having some preliminary ideas you mustn't become stereotyped with your thoughts and planning. Once you decide on swim and tactics in advance you are in trouble. There will be times when you are on a roll and will find carp locked up in certain areas of the lake on a succession of visits, but even then you need to be aware that no two days are alike, and that you may have to make slight adjustments to your tactics each session.

The water is here. Let's go fishing – soon!

If the car park is secure there is no problem with leaving your tackle in the car but if not you need to leave it with an angler you can trust, or you will have to wheel it round with you in the barrow – commonly known as doing it the hard way! Nothing could be worse for your campaign than losing all your tackle early on because you left it in the car and some thief broke in and stole it. But let's presume the car park is secure so you can leave your tackle in the car for a while. Now what? Whether it is raining or sunny, whether you are in a hurry or not, it is always best to look round the water at least once before you decide on a swim. On very large waters it may well be impossible to do a full lap before you fish but you must manage your time effectively. Your research will have given you some pointers as to where the carp may be but nothing beats the 'here and now' approach.

You have to weigh up how much time you have available with how much looking you should do. For that reason you need to create as much time as possible for your fishing. If you only have the chance to fish one day per week then make that day as long as possible. At Three Lakes when I could only do a day and a night each week I would get to the lake very early in the morning. In the summer months it would not be unusual for me to be at the lake well before 3.00 a.m. so I could walk the water for an hour before I decided on a swim. At Norfolk's Catch 22, which involved a three to four-hour drive (not exactly local water fishing, admittedly!), I would leave home at 2.00 a.m. in the winter so I could get to the venue well before dawn to look for rolling fish. Even on overnighters I will be creative to leave work early to buy myself extra time. Lots of half-day holidays; working on Saturdays so I can leave early once or twice a week. Maybe using flexitime or shift work to your best advantage. Don't be negative. Be positive and creative, even in terms of the time available to you for your fishing.

Providing you have a reasonable amount of time to spend looking, and you are in any doubt, I would always be prepared to spend more time looking than fishing. You may well be lucky and find the carp straightaway, or it may take some time to come up with a sound choice of swim. Don't be in a hurry to set up. That will not automatically catch you carp quickly; in fact it may have quite the opposite effect. Look and look properly. Do not simply walk round the water for the sake of it; do it purposefully. Nooks and crannies; near in and far out; all areas warrant your full attention.

I've no wish to turn this into a chapter on location so use your common sense, and the advice elsewhere in this book, and make your swim choice sensibly. The best advice I can give you is to pick a swim which offers you the best chance during the time you have available to you. Think about that advice carefully... What does it really mean? It means you need to pick swims which give you maximum potential for the limited time you can put in on that session. Maybe you can only fish the night. In that case you need to select a swim where the carp are known to feed at night. Maybe you can only do evenings. Where are the carp in the evening, and will they take a bait in that area?

When it comes to short session fishing known feeding times can be both heaven and hell. If you can identify periods of time when the carp feed strongly and you can fish those times it's heaven, but if they occur when you can't fish – it's hell! There will definitely be times of year when the carp lock themselves into certain time zones when they are most likely to "make a mistake", and all around the lake buzzers will sound within that time span. For the long-session angler this isn't a problem, but for you and me on our short sessions it can create a love or hate situation. Time and time again I've had to pack up at 7.00 a.m. to get ready to go to work knowing full well that the next feeding time was 8.00-9.00 a.m. – aaahhh!

To take advantage of known feeding times you need to be creative and do all you can to be there at the time. In my case I would have to fish weekends rather than my normal over-nighters to be there for breakfast time feeding spells. At Catch 22 the strongest feeding period was 8 – 10 a.m. so even though it was well over a three hour drive to the venue I was always fishing by 6.00 a.m.: that's right, a 2.00 a.m. start to the session to take advantage of the known feeding times! At the Tilery late afternoon was the time you just had to be there so Sundays always meant sitting tight until the evening – which did not please my dad, who ran me to the water and back in those days. Identify the strongest feeding times and be creative with your time to do all you can to make sure you are there at the times which are most likely to produce.

Three hours looking, twenty minutes fishing, and I'm in.

Sometimes you have to avoid carp you can see to put yourself in a better position for the rest of the session. Time and again I have set up on carp only to find that those carp weren't feeding, and when they did decide to feed it was not in that swim! Carp will have preferred places to feed during the day and night, and it is up to you to find those places. You have limited time, so try to make the most of it. Even when you have decided on a certain swim your carp brain

Carp were showing in open water, so I waited with a lightweight marker ready to mark the spot.

should not be turned off. You may well have made your initial decision but is it still valid? Has someone else moved to give you a better choice?

One of the keys to limited time is to be impatient rather than too patient. Once my rods are cast out I will not be in a hurry to get my shelter set up, unless of course it is raining, or dark. It is far easier to pack up three rods and reels than it is a bivvy and bedchair. Dave Lane is the master of such restless swim-change tactics and we all know how successful he has been!

Tactics-wise no method should be dismissed, so from stalking to floaters, natural baits to single hookers, you need to have an open mind and an impatient brain. Nothing should be too much trouble, and with three rods at your disposal there is no excuse for not trying variations on a theme at any stage of the session. From casting to rolling fish, to working a swim, to alternating hookbaits and tactics you really have to work hard during your limited time to get the best from it.

Because you will hopefully be fishing fairly regularly you need to log your data and results in a diary so you can refer back to it. Maybe a carp shows in a certain spot on a number of occasions. Maybe certain swims produce regularly in certain wind conditions. Even if you aren't in those swims at the time you can log down your observations of the fishing of others, and learn from them. You cannot hope to remember everything that happens so always have that pen and paper to hand. Although you should not accept blanks lightly, they will happen, so look at the big picture as well as the short-term one. You may well have blanked today, but what information and lessons can you draw from the blank? Occasionally information gleaned may seem of little significance at the time, but on many occasions you will have learnt something, something from which you can benefit on future occasions. At the very least you will have given the carp some bait for free – which may help lower their defences on your next session. At worst you will have learnt that you will have to try harder to get it right next time out!

When fishing a water on a limited-time basis a lot of your success will depend on how strong your mindset is. Have you really got what it takes to do it week in, week out, month in, month out? There will be good times when it seems to flow nicely, but there will also be times when nothing seems to work. Keep faith and don't be distracted from your campaign. Even if you cannot fish as regularly as you would like, keep in touch with the water by visiting it regularly and finding out what is or isn't happening. Let the successes and failures of others aid your long-term prospects.

Whatever happens don't limit yourself to a set period in which to get it right. Instead be prepared to keep at it all year round. It may well be late in the year when your success comes, but if you've already fallen by the wayside then that success will not happen. Local waters on limited time can bring tremendous results providing you have the strength of character, self-belief and determination to do it, and keep doing it. I know that if I can do it so can you. Go and prove me right.

One of 22 carp in a day in winter means I got it right!

Heavy Chemistry

"Mystery is all involved..."

I wrote some material on the subjects of pH, water, carp and attractors in the early 80s. "Heavy!" was the consensus. It is. Now I see an increasing number of letters and articles touching on the subject of pH, and its significance in terms of water, flavours, and attraction generally. So I'll revisit the subject here and place a very basic outline of the science of pH, water and carp's chemoreception on record as a reference point. 90% of what follows is scientific fact. I have added some conjecture in an effort to explain an undefined phenomenon – nutritional recognition.

Attractors. But how do they attract? How do we smell food? Through air. Water is a liquid gas... It's not bait that's complicated. The science of life is.

When I first became involved with carp baits there were a number of aspects of them that fascinated me. To start with I simply didn't believe Fred Wilton's idea that a carp could somehow instinctively assess the nutritional value of a bait – or be conditioned to eat a bait because of its nutritional value is probably a better way of putting it. Fred was right of course, but he was so far ahead of his time that his thinking took some catching up with!

Then, on top of Fred's revolutionary concept, came the revelation that carp were attracted by a range of substances. Amino acids caused a bit of a furore in the 70s. Scientific papers detailing experiments with fish to assess the feeding stimulation provoked by certain amino acids were in great demand. Work on the subject came out of the Lowestoft Institute, and from a group of overseas professors, headed by the great Japanese researcher Toshiaka J. Hara, living in Canada.

The Black Majic bait of the 70s was designed on the basis of the Lowestoft Institute work. Rod Hutchinson wrote about amino acids in his first book, *Rod Hutchinson's Carp Book*. I was already experimenting with nutritional baits, and trying to read up on this revolutionary concept in visits to the reference library when I read Rod's chapter on aminos. Stunning, ground-breaking stuff it was, too. But it presented me with a major problem.

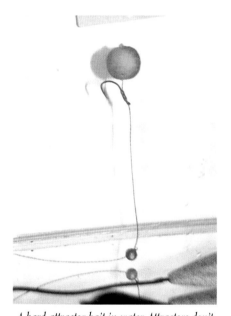

A hard attractor bait in water. Attractors don't necessarily dissolve; what they do is interact with the carp's senses through the medium of water. I think of "attraction" as an electrical current from a small battery gradually running down.

Briefly, there are two groups of amino acids – which as chemicals are solids, usually in crystalline or powder form – hydrophilic (water-loving), which dissolve, and hydrophobic (water-hating), which don't. We learnt that carp were stimulated in the medium of water by some aminos, so on the basis of our vague concept of underwater attraction you would presume the most stimulatory to be the hydrophilic (dissolving) type. Not so. The most stimulatory turned out to be among the non-dissolving hydrophobic group. How could that be? How could something that didn't dissolve attract? And was there a connection between amino acids – the component parts of proteins – stimulating carp, and carp having an instinct for evaluating the nutritional quality of a protein-containing bait?

Now you would think that a reference library would contain books dealing with areas like that. You would be wrong! Fred Wilton wasn't only

73

ahead of the carp world, he was ahead of the entire world with his theory. Nowadays I would shrug at the lack of relevant material and get on with something else. In those days I was absolutely fascinated by the concept of attraction – what I now know to be chemoreception – and looked for an alternative exploratory route to go down. For instance, was it even scientifically possible for a solid to attract in an underwater environment? The only starting point was to study water, and there was plenty of authoritative scientific material on that mysterious environment.

Here is a starting point for water, the introductory paragraph to the chapter on water in Lehninger's Biochemistry:

"Water not only makes up 70 to 90 percent of the weight of most forms of life, it also represents the continuous phase of living organisms. Because it is familiar and ubiquitous, water is often regarded as a bland, inert liquid, a mere space filler in living organisms. Actually, however, it is a highly reactive substance with unusual properties that distinguish it from most other common liquids. We now recognise that water and its ionisation products, hydronium and hydroxide ions, are important determinants of the characteristic structure and biological properties of proteins and nucleic acids, as well as membranes, ribosomes, and many other cell components."

That's a start. Water isn't simple. If you think what follows is heavy, you should see the weight of the material I had to plough through to come up with this simplified explanation of chemical (biochemical to be strictly accurate) reactions in an underwater environment! I'll outline the basics of the phenomenon, then try to explain it in more detail for those who are as fascinated by "attraction" as I am.

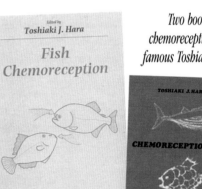
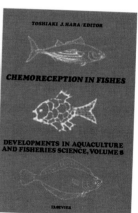

Two books on chemoreception by the famous Toshiaka J. Hara.

Solids and non aqueous liquids can attract underwater. Water is a liquid gas. H_2O. H = Hydrogen. O = Oxygen. Water is a molecular structure with a ratio of two Hydrogen ions to one Oxygen ion. It is referred to as H_2O, but the construction is a fluid one and the Hydrogen ions are highly mobile, passing from one molecule to the next. So water is actually stated as $H_3O + OH- = H_2O$.

Attraction between carp and their food sources is a molecular reaction! The stimulatory message is passed through what is known as Hydrogen bonding, or ionisation, via the Hydrogen ions. When an amino acid, or an ester, is introduced into water it ionises and interacts with the carp's receptors. This is actually a description of how we smell things in the medium of air. As with carp our receptors recognise the source of the smell. For instance we can differentiate between food smells and flower smells without seeing what we are smelling. Even food smells which we don't exactly recognise we can identify as food.

Underwater smell is known as chemoreception, more precisely olfaction. Chemical taste is known as gustation. Carp smell what is an apparent food source, and take it into their mouth. They then taste it to check to see if it is food. They have receptors all over their bodies, but I think (conjecture) that their nutritional awareness is via their receptors to an enzyme linkage.

Carp have been identifying their food sources by smell for millions of years. Naturally occurring chemicals are their food signals. In experiments certain individual amino acids evoked strong feeding responses. Certain groups of aminos when coupled with betaine are said to be synergistic and evoke a much stronger feeding response, suggesting (to me) that these combinations mirror the carp's identifying scents for natural foods. In turn the best attractors mirror the natural food scents, too. The closer we get to the exact food message carp have been reacting to over millions of years with our baits or attractors the more effective the source of attraction is likely to prove.

A quote, from chapter nine of Fish Chemoreception by Toshiaka J. Hara. The chapter is on Gustation.

"Receptor molecules (most probably glycoproteins) that detect and preferentially pass biologically important information have evolved and have been positioned in the membranes of the receptor cells. These receptor molecules, upon being activated by their specific stimulus or stimuli, initiate a series of molecular events that can result in behavioural responses, such as food search and ingestion."

Precise identification of a food source via the receptors is known as a lock and key effect. The molecular message has to be the right shape to provide the key to unlock the receptors.

Carp have no stomach. Their food is digested in the intestinal tract. It is in the intestines for a far shorter period of time than food is in our stomach/intestine systems. The more digestible and nutritional the food is the more benefit the carp will derive from eating it. I can find no scientific explanation of nutritional recognition. I will conjecture that because carp have no stomach hunger must represent a nutritional need. Their system needs food, and their receptors help them find it. They will eat until they are nutritionally fulfilled, i.e. until their nutritional requirement is appeased.

There is some conjecture and rationalisation of a currently unexplained area – nutritional recognition – in that last passage. For the rest the smell and taste relationships between carp and their food sources has been heavily researched and is well documented. I'm not even sure the Japanese professors are aware of Fred Wilton's theory yet, which shows just how advanced Fred was in his late 60s' thinking.

Frank Warwick, a very successful angler and acknowledged attractor bait guru. Frank sets great store by the concept that different pHs of flavour work better in different waters. Frank has a range of hookbaits available through Dynamite Baits.

What's pH got to do with it?

pH stands for **p**ositive **H**ydrogen and is a logarithmic statement of the positive Hydrogen content of a substance. In the context of carp fishing its significance is usually in relation to the pH of water and attractors introduced into it.

pH is stated as a logarithmic scale, with a pH of 7 being neutral. Neutral pH means there are an equal number of H_3O (hydronium) and OH- (hydroxyl) ions present in a volume of water at 25°C. Logarithmic scale means that a one-unit increase or decrease in pH levels actually represents a tenfold change. Small changes in pH are significant. In carp waters pH can vary at different levels in the water, and will be affected by changes in temperature, through the effect of sunlight, because of the presence of weed, and as a result of the influence by rainfall. The pH of rainfall can vary from area to area. There was a great deal of controversy about acid rain some years ago. Acid means of low pH.

Fish are influenced by changes in pH. In America it is recognised that certain species favour certain pH levels, which can be a real aid to location, particularly in big, deep waters. Carp will have a favoured pH level, although this will almost certainly vary from water to water, and depend on the normal pH of the carp's home.

A water with a mean pH of less than 7.0 is said to be acidic. Carp have a remarkable tolerance range for changes in pH, being able to survive in acidic conditions as low as pH 5, and alkaline conditions as high as pH 10. Water with a pH in excess of 7.0 is said to be alkaline, or basic. Most quality carp waters have an alkaline pH. Within reason the higher the pH the greater the natural life in a water tends to be. I seem to recall that in its prime Redmire was measured as having a pH of 8.4. Recent tests indicate that Birch Grove has a winter pH of 7.2, which is similar to the pH of tap water.

Attractors stimulate carp's senses. The chemistry of attraction from amino acids, betaine and flavours and most other known attractors is via ionisation. A chemical reaction. It is enough to know that without fully understanding it. What it does help to understand is that stimulation is not in the form of the attractor "leaching out" into the water, but rather more like the current of a battery passing from one point (the attractor) to another point (the carp's receptors). A rock-hard bait can attract without dissolving.

Batteries run down. In the same way I suspect that sources of attraction gradually lose their power, too. Some

A range of successful baits and flavours. They don't have to smell "good" to us to be of great significance to the carp. In fact some of the most successful attractors smell pretty revolting! What we are trying to do is mirror the "here is food" message carp have been responding to for centuries.

baits have better overnight pulling power than others. The source of the attraction continues to be effective over a longer period than in baits which don't have the same attractor life. By the same token some baits simply represent too strong a source of attraction when they are introduced, and may be at their most effective some hours after immersion. The chemical formula of the bait is changing from the moment it is immersed.

You may see references to "regulating the pH of the bait". I don't think that is possible. Most foods have a pH of around 7, which is neutral. Foodstuffs are buffered against change, which means that when you mix low pH attractors with neutral pH ingredients in pH terms the two remain independent of each other. You don't change the pH of the bait, you simply introduce different levels of pH to the bait and into the water. Only certain items in the bait will ionise, and thereby attract.

I've undoubtedly oversimplified a very complex area here and have deliberately focused on concepts rather than trying to deal with specifics. It's all right people saying "keep it simple" but the relationship between carp and their food sources is not a simple area! It embraces aquaculture, biochemistry, biophysics, nutrition and fish physiology. The important concept to understand is that hard baits can attract. That idea can give you confidence and belief. From thereon the rest is taken care of by the bait companies, for whom I have the greatest respect, and in whom I have the greatest confidence. There was a time when I needed to know "Why?" and " How?" Now I simply need to know with what, and please will you send me a freezer full of it?!

Another quote to finish with – from Bob Dylan:

"Mystery is all involved, it can't be understood or solved."

The pH scale		
[H+], M	pH	[OH-], M
1.0	0	10^{-14}
0.1	1	10^{-13}
0.01	2	10^{-12}
0.001	3	10^{-11}
0.0001	4	10^{-10}
0.00001	5	10^{-9}
10^{-6}	6	10^{-8}
10^{-7}	7	10^{-7}
10^{-8}	8	10^{-6}
10^{-9}	9	10^{-5}
10^{-10}	10	10^{-4}
10^{-11}	11	0.001
10^{-12}	12	0.01
10^{-13}	13	0.1
10^{-14}	14	1.0

Sources
Fish Chemoreception, 1992. edited by Toshiaka J. Hara.
Chemoreception in Fishes, 1984. edited by Toshiaka J. Hara.
Biochemistry by Albert L. Lehninger. 1975.
The Carp by Simon Crow, Carp Fisher 35.

Bait Talk – Bait Choice by Design

Basic Instincts

I guess it's true to say that very rarely do any of us go fishing without taking at least some boilies with us, even if it's just a jar of attractor baits to fish as singles, or in conjunction with a groundbait situation.

Boilies. What a multitude of concepts, buoyancies, textures, shapes, colours, sizes, ingredients and attractors that single word embraces. The word boilies will conjure up so many different pictures in the minds of readers that we are going to have to go through the thinking behind the various categories of bait and examine what role each design, or type, is likely to be able to fulfil. Long term or short term? Is there really a difference? Frozen or preserved? Does it make any difference? Ready-made or specially made? 50/50 Mix, Birdfood, Fishmeal, Predigested, Enzyme active, Four Seasons, Protein HNV? If there was a collective word for baits I would have to go with "a confusion of baits". The scene is a confused one; there are too many choices; there are too many brilliant baits.

Don't worry, I'm confused, too. I have a couple of freezers containing four of the best baits known to man or beast. My confusion is simple. Which is the best one to use for a week in France? Which is the best one to pull me a big fish in a few days' fishing? Which of the four is likely to appeal most to a 50lb common I'm dreaming about catching? Which is going to get me the best results during my winter fishing on two or three different home venues? The same bait? If I thought so the answer would be simple. Activ-8, Grange Red, Trigga, Protavit-Liver. At least my freezer choice is limited to four. I don't have to worry about those hundreds of brilliant baits out there that don't reside in my freezer!

But I do...

Straight to it. You choose or design your boilie on the basis of the type of fishing you will be doing. Let's start with two categories, Attractor Baits and Food Baits. To many anglers the flavour is the bait. To others the ingredients are the bait. For many of us the overall package – the balance of the attractors to the food ingredients – is the bait.

Flavours attract both carp and carp anglers. Opening bottles and sniffing is the equivalent of studying rigs – the stuff that dreams are built on. "Get your nose round that!" Here is a concept that is readily understandable and embraced with some enthusiasm. We are attracted by flavours, therefore we can relate to carp being attracted to them. Many of the packaged baits are identified by their flavours, so the flavour becomes the bait. The flavour is like a woman's scent,

Part of the bait section of the Carp Cabin, Sheffield. Why so many different bottles, tubs, bags and packets?

Boilies! What a multitude of categories and attitudes that single word embraces!

an attractor. It is a direct appeal to the carp's senses, an effort to convince the carp that what it has before it is highly desirable. As with human relationships, will the bait still be as desirable when the carp gets to know it better?

At the bottom end of the bait scale the flavour gives a promise of food that is not fulfilled by the food content of the bait. The success of the bait relies entirely on the fish being convinced by the smell of the bait. The simplest baits are based on ingredients like ground rice, semolina and soya flour. For a bait-maker to supply his customers with ready-made baits at a competitive price something has to give, and what gives is the cost of the ingredients – and therefore the food value – of the bait.

I'm not bracketing all ready-mades together here. All will be based on successful flavours and attractor combinations. Some have a better food content than others. From the mid-80s until the late 90s "ready-mades" meant shelf-life preserved baits of indeterminate age. The situation is now confused by the reappearance of frozen ready-mades. Reappearance? Yes! The initial Richworth ready-mades were frozen: Richworth supplied shops with freezers to store them. Preserved "shelf-life" boilies followed some time later. By definition a "frozen ready-made" is a different bait to a preserved ready-made. Preserved baits are much more convenient than frozen ones, but are they as good? I think not, a personal opinion shared by many, but not a proven fact!

Where preservatives are used in shelf-life boilies different preservation methods and ingredients may be in use. And in some situations ready-mades can be extremely successful. Short-session fishing; fishing for naive carp; winter fishing; unpressured or overstocked waters; heavily pressured well-stocked waters where the carp's senses gradually become flavour-saturated; heavily baited waters where the carp are accustomed to quality baits (and

Are you more interested in what's in the bottles, or what's in the container?

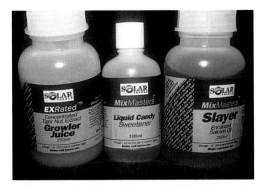

Flavours or foods? Does it matter? Well yes. You can't overload a food, but you can a flavour.

for a time treat all baits as being food sources). All these types of venues may respond to cheap and cheerful baits which appeal to the carp's basic feeding instincts.

If you are going to make your own cheap and cheerful flavour-based attractor bait check out the most successful ready-made flavour combinations and take one of those as your starting point. Then boost the food quality of the bait by adding liquid foods like Minamino, Liquid Liver, Liquid Yeast, Corn Steep Liquor or one or two of the other stunning liquid food/attractors that are now available to your recipe.

Effective carp catchers, but for how long will they be effective?

Why aren't all baits cheap and cheerful flavour-based attractor baits? Well such baits appeal to the carp's most basic feeding instinct. "That smells good, I'll eat it." Over a period of time a carp's system will evaluate the food value of the bait and its effectiveness may start to diminish for a number of reasons, the two most obvious being as follows.

1) Attractor baits tend to be overloaded with attractors, which may have an adverse effect on the carp's senses. We soon know if we eat something that doesn't agree with us. The same thing can happen with carp. I keep coming back to the curry simile on this aspect of bait. All curries smell pretty good to me, but I can only eat the mildest, and my staple diet is nutritional, ungarnished food.

2) Baits are in competition with other food sources, both baits and naturals. Over a period of time carp's systems assess the food quality of their diet and tend to select the most nutritious. Sooner or later a selective feeding instinct gradually takes over from the most basic instant-appeal instinct. If that wasn't the case we would all still be using balls of semolina and soya laced with a couple of flavours, a few glug-glugs of sweetener and Minamino (in its many guises!).

The starting point for most carp anglers is a cheap and cheerful bait. Why wouldn't it be? I get the impression that a high percentage of overseas anglers still think that the flavour is more important than the content of the bait. This is possibly a by-product of fishing big, unpressured inland seas, but to me the different attitude to bait explains why the British keep winning the prestigious international matches. And it is also my experience that overseas carp always respond to quality baits, which is not to say that in many waters they won't still respond to cheap and cheerful versions. Travelling the distances I do for overseas fishing I equip myself with a mix of ready-mades and quality baits.

Nutrabaits started here! The pantry in the mid-80s. A few blind alleys and a few real winners.

In a book which may have some international appeal I should add that the attitude to the quality of the bait appears to vary from country to country. My own experiences suggest, for instance, that Belgian and German carp anglers are more food-content conscious than most of my friends in France!

Ready-mades will take you so far. Most people reach a point in their carp fishing when they wish to move on. So where to from cheap and cheerful attractor baits? What are the alternatives?

Your next step will depend on cost, seasonality, and the type of fishing you are doing. To me a compromise between attractor baits and food baits is the ideal next step. If I were simply a warm weather carper I would definitely lean towards flavoured fishmeals. Check out the listings of the bait-rolling companies in magazine advertising and you will see how popular this type of bait is.

Then there are the successful baits that fall into a rather vague category that only the manufacturers can define. I refer to these as new-age baits. The bait company tells you the recipe and doesn't leave you scope to mess up a perfectly good base mix by over-flavouring it! Mainline successfully broke the mould of categorised carp baits when they came up with their Grange with CSL package. They followed this with Activ-8, Assassinate-PT10 and NRG. Nutrabaits' Trigga, Richworth's Multi-Plex and Bio-Plex and Rod Hutchinson's Addicted are among the growing range of new-age baits which are proving successful. These baits are designed to make a direct appeal to the carp's feeding instincts, as opposed to their basic instincts. There is a new vista opening up which seems to spell out the fact that carp baits are going to move in a slightly different direction to the old flavour attractor routine.

But we're getting ahead of ourselves. We're on from ready-mades. Where to from there? Birdfoods, Fishmeals, All Season Mixes, Protein/HNV mixes. Get the bait books. Study the bait videos. Form a bait team. Out of the confusion must come conviction. "That is the route I need to go down." The bait as a source of instant appeal. The bait as a source of confidence for your fishing. The bait as a food source.

And it's when you think of bait as a food source that you start to understand that your boilie has to offer more than smell and taste appeal. By and large ready-mades are the sweeties of the food industry. If we want to be healthy we have to find a more substantial diet of fish and chips, or meat and veg. Carp are no different.

Bait Lore

Most of the bait thoughts I have in my head have been originated by, contributed to, or influenced by the pioneering and ongoing efforts of others. Fred Wilton's nutritional bait concept. Rod Hutchinson's pioneering work on attractors, birdfood baits and tiny sources of preoccupation. Steve Morgan's and Kevin Knight's thinking on new-age baits. Andy Little's throwaway "food source" comment. Premier Baits' resurrection and extension of the fishmeal bait concept in the late 80s. The work Bill

Bill Cottam of Nutrabaits. Knowledgeable, no bullshit bait man, and a very successful carp angler.

Cottam and I did with naturally occurring food recognition factors and enzymes. All those lines of thought, and others, are part of the thinking on which my current beliefs and convictions about bait, and how to use it, are based.

The above list may read like a confusion of a number of lines of thought about bait. Right. There have been times when I have been confused. I've been focusing on bait and its uses for over 25 years and have lived through most stages of development, and each change of direction in thinking, or change of emphasis. When it comes to bait you need to mould all the available knowledge floating around out there to your own thinking and adapt it to your own carp fishing approach. You have to rationalise your own time scales for bait application, and understand the evolution – and devolution – of the effectiveness of not just each bait concept, but each individual bait you use.

My own bait thinking is built around my own concept of carp fishing. I want the best possible food source so I know the carp will go on eating the bait, no matter how much of it is introduced, over a period of time. I want to get the fish addicted to the food source as soon as possible. I want the bait to be as appealing as possible without risking making it unacceptable to the carp in terms of taste, flavour or additive overloading. I want to fish the hookbait in an acceptable – preferably irresistible – preoccupation situation in which the carp's natural anti-capture resistance may be lowered.

I'll come back briefly to those avenues of thought, but I would make the point that they are all concepts that have stood the test of time. In the early 80s we were told that all you needed to catch carp was a pound of soya and semolina, a fair few mils of irresistible flavours, and a few glug-glugs of sweetener to mask the bitterness of the flavours. The concept caught carp, but from the off I felt that at best it was a temporary solution. Condiments will mask the quality of bad meat, but they don't make it an acceptable food source. Carp eat food – or what they have been deceived into believing is food – not flavours.

Ready-mades were an extension of the attractor bait concept. They are a great convenience, but however good they are within their own category I feel that because of their attendant cost limitation exercise there are competitive angling and feeding situations in which their effectiveness as a food source will be limited. Why?

Angling pressure has an influence on carp's feeding habits. Baits represent a classic good news/bad news scenario. They are recognised as food, so carp will eat them. Then they get caught on them, so they gradually become wary of them. At some stage in the pressure cycle the next bait they get caught on has to be different to, or more appealing than, the previous one. But there is a limit to the number of stages of "more appealing". There comes a point when the food quality has to be more fulfilling, and the bait represent a better food source.

Go to a big unpressured water in France and many of the carp will feed on baits which simply smell like food. It has always been my experience that better quality food sources are more consistent catchers than cheap ready-mades, but no one can deny the effectiveness of cheap and cheerful baits for unpressured fish. But don't go to France thinking that all the fish over there are going to feed avidly on the cheapest ready-mades. Capture pressure and lack of nutritional fulfilment soon start to make carp more discriminating.

Rod Hutchinson, prime mover in a number of areas of bait development and a champion of instant baits.

Pressure, not nationality, builds up capture resistance in carp. Some carp react unfavourably to pressure much quicker than others. Some natural carp appear to have a better built-in instinct for what is food, and what is window dressing.

I'll not go through the full bait cycle. It starts with attraction. Nutrition is always an aspect, but it grows in importance as pressure increases and discrimination grows. Preoccupation is invariably a valuable bait weapon. The aim of preoccupation is to take the carp's mind off what it is doing and make it more catchable. Attraction, nutrition, preoccupation. The three main bait principles.

Establishing a food source with the right bait is aimed at extending that list to create addiction. Think of an addiction then think of trying to create that need in the carp you are fishing for. It's worth aiming for.

If you've got a problem with how attractive your bait needs to be then think of it in terms of the opposite sex. However happily married you are there is a woman somewhere who can capture your attention to an extent that might complicate your life. That's the bait concept you are aiming at. "I don't really want to know about this but I'm just going to have to have it!" The more happily married or permanently attached you are the more extraordinary the temptation may have to be to get you off

Kev Knight (centre) of Mainline Baits in the winner's circle again. Match anglers turned carp angler are always dangerous, and Kev knows his stuff about bait development, too. Rob Tough and Rob Hughes make up the cast list.

the straight and narrow. The more pressured and capture-resistant the carp are the more extraordinary or firmly established the bait will have to be to grab their attention. (If you are one of those red-blooded guys with your brain situated somewhere below your belt then in carp fishing terms you are probably a mug fish!)

Nutritional baits have evolved. I see the odd criticism of Fred Wilton's brilliant nutritional bait theory, first proposed in 1968! Critics seem to forget just how revolutionary and incredibly successful Fred's baits were at the time. And yes, of course we have moved on from the ingredients available at the start of the 70s. Carp baits would be the only area of the civilised world to stand still for forty years if we hadn't. But Rod Hutchinson reckons that bait sales reflect a swing back towards HNV baits. Fred talked in terms of the best available food source. That covers availability, content and quality. HNVs; fishmeal baits; Mainline's new-age baits, which Kevin Knight has written about in his chapter. They have all evolved from Fred Wilton's original nutritional bait concept – and his original classic HNV ingredients still work. (Fred experimented with enzymes, but didn't make his thoughts or conclusions public.)

So what is the bait cycle in terms of quality of food source? Given the best possible make-up of each type of bait I would list them in ascending order as follows: "Continental" ready-mades; home market ready-mades; 50/50 bait mixes; birdfood baits; all-season baits; HNV baits; fishmeal baits; active new-age baits. The baits in each category will vary in effectiveness. "Birdfood baits" and "Fishmeals" cover a whole host of different ingredients and end products. Two or three years ago "new age" would have been a reference to Mainline baits, but a number of highly effective baits have now appeared which fall into a mysterious "unknown basis" category. If it works in mysterious ways and I can't categorise it then I've chucked into the new-age category! Sorry about that bait-makers!

The best bait is the one that works best on a water at any given time. The season and the pressure cycle dictate that the type of bait – and the best individual bait within each category – may well vary from water to water. Kev Knight makes the point that the best baits go on catching. That is fair comment when applied to some fish, but certainly not all of them. Exactly how carp

Two of the Mangrove's big fish of the 90s. Conan would fall for the same bait on a number of occasions, but Scaley seemed to sense danger more quickly and would rarely fall for the same bait twice.

associate smells with danger we don't know. On the Mangrove Conan will go on getting caught on Activ-8 or Big Fish Mix forever. Scaley associated baits with captures a great deal quicker than that. The unpredictability of this previous-capture aspect will hold true for target fish from other waters, which is why many of us like a change of bait every two years or so.

Every two years? Some of you like a change every two hours! So while my approach is based almost exclusively on established food source baits many of you prefer the instant type of baits. I have caught plenty of fish on instant baits in the past. When I had my inventive bait head on one of my great joys was coming up with a new attractor combination which had the indicators jumping irrespective of the quality of the bait. The potent combination of Richworth's Blue Cheese flavour and Garlic and Soya Oil (from Garlic Perles) was my own recipe. It brought me a terrific result at Waveney D Lake, and worked well for many other anglers through the 80s. Garlic Mint – a user-friendly version of Garlic Oil – was mine. Nutrabaits' Fruit Special was a mix I put together to win the first "British Championships" at Horseshoe in 1991. And while I hesitate to mention it I think Betaine was mine, which isn't quite true because I found it (underlined) in a book on fish olfaction kindly given to me by none other than Fred Wilton!

Rod Hutchinson was always my role model on attractors. His knowledge of what catches carp always was, and still is, extraordinary. I would guess that everyone selling baits today owes something to Rod's input somewhere back along the way. Nowadays Martin Locke of Solar is just as well versed in what turns carp on and has an impressive list of instant baits and highly effective attractors.

But there are now so many excellent bait companies that it is perhaps unfair to single out a handful. Find your own approach, your own line of thought on bait, then refine it. Talk to your chosen bait company about what you are trying to achieve. Understand it. Understand that a bait which works instantly might quickly start to lose its effectiveness, while a bait that is slow to work may go on working over a longer period. Understand that certain types of bait and combinations of attractors are more suitable for a big fish campaign. All bait companies have a range of baits because they understand the different approaches carp anglers have.

Don't overlook the obvious. The carp captures in *Carp-Talk*. The remarkable successes recorded in Mainline's "What's Occurring?", Nutrabaits News and Nashbait's Whisky or Formula One News.

When you are away from the water selecting your bait is the biggest step you will make towards successful carp fishing. While you are on the bank using your chosen bait to its greatest effectiveness – which covers location, application and presentation – will make the difference between success and failure. Never underestimate the difference the right bait, used correctly, can make.

The weekly Carp-Talk *is a mine of information if you want to keep abreast of what's catching, and which baits are producing the bigger fish.*

Bait Choice by Design

It is difficult to generalise about baits, but in an attempt to explain what different baits are likely to achieve we have to. We can't look at every bait available to carp anglers and assess their strength of attraction, value as a food source and likely life as an applied bait. Experience and logic suggest that generally speaking the higher the source of attraction and the lower the food value the shorter the life of the bait. Some ready-made manufacturers may feel uneasy with that sweeping assessment, but it is how many experienced users of bait feel about boilies.

Such an assessment is not a dismissal of attractor baits. If you are fishing one night a week and don't have time to go to the lake to bait up then you need a bait that is going to capture the carp's attention pretty instantly. If you are going on a week's trip to a distant water with no freezer facilities then preserved baits may be your only option. If you are going to a big overseas water with a limited pressure record then instant appeal baits may be the most effective option. Just be aware that preserved ready-mades have their limitations and, if possible, avail yourself of alternatives.

Observation and experience suggest that an over-flavoured attractor bait

Instant food bait success in the first big Horseshoe match in 1991. The attractors I put in my Hi-Nu-Val bait were later used to form Nutrabaits' Fruit Special. Prior to the match – which I won – I figured that Richworth's Tutti-Frutti baits would be in use, so Tutti figured strongly in my bait!

has a two or three-day life in a given swim *per application*. This will vary from water to water but with a flavour-based bait that works instantly expect results to decline rather than escalate. You're fishing with sweeties, not food.

The *Carpworld* Fishabil trips reinforced the lesson about the declining effectiveness of preserved ready-mades time after time. We started on Sunday and for a while the fish would go quiet after the setting up and the initial bait bombardment. Results would tend to be at their best from Monday through to Wednesday. After that we would start to struggle and how we applied and fished the bait became an increasingly important element in getting takes. Those of us who took the precaution of taking a back-up supply of food baits with us continued to catch for the rest of the week, but the lesson was clear. The ready-mades we were using weren't good enough baits to represent a food source to the carp over a seven-day period. Flavour saturation? Disillusionment with the food

In action on a pleasure trip to Fishabil. Regular use of ready-mades gave me the impression that most versions started to lose their effectiveness after three days' continuous use.

Making your own is still an option. John Lilley churning out the Big Fish Mix in his garage some years back. Good recipe, too, by the look of it! Some anglers work as bait teams to speed up bait making, and to ensure a regular flow of bait into their target water.

value of the bait? I would think a combination of the two. Carp's reaction to quality baits can be surprisingly quick, so I guess it's possible that they can quickly react adversely to a poor quality food bait, too.

I'll emphasise the lesson learnt about the value of the bait *per application*. If you always fish short sessions and don't have time to bait up then attractor baits may be the right bait for you. Try ready-mades. Make a bait based on ready-made flavour combinations but with added caseinate, liver powder and liquid foods. If attractor baits are the route you choose to go down then study attractors and experiment with combinations and bases. The beauty about attractor baits is that you're looking for instant action, so if you don't get it you can try something different. You are appealing to the carp's most basic feeding instinct, not its long-term feeding instinct.

It's when we start looking at baits as a food source that we start to raise doubts in many carp anglers' minds. Most want a bait they cast out and which then catches carp. The best food source baits may not do that. To

This made me stop and think! This is Graham Chapman who fished in the next peg in the first Madine Carp Classic. He almost won, and his "biggest cheapest bag of ready-mades I could find" outfished my proven Activ-8 by five fish to one!

lengthen the life of the bait the attractors may have to be kept below instant appeal levels. To get the best out of a food source bait, the bait may have to be introduced over a period of time.

When you are prebaiting you can't risk using a bait that is going to fail either on the basis of poor food value or overloaded attraction.

We are dependent on our food sources. All creatures are. Carp are no different and the best food source bait is established to the point that the carp are at least familiar with it, at best dependent on it, even better, addicted to it. Availability is as important as the make-up of the bait.

The best bait isn't necessarily going to catch most carp on any given water. A good bait applied and used well will out-score a better bait

Another surprise. My air-dried Trigga baits arrived at Raduta a week late during the October 2001 session, and produced this 55lb 4oz mirror and a 45lb 8oz common on the first night I used it.

Second-day ready-made success at Raduta. Returning a welcome 46lb 4oz common which fell for the Mainline Fruit-tella ready-mades which were the main bait for the trip. The baits went on catching, but the big fish action on them slowed down.

applied and used badly. Think of your bait and how you have used it this season. How close has it come to being established as a food source? Fewer than one per cent of us can claim to have established our bait as a readily accepted food source on our own water. Yes, we may have cashed in on an established bait. "Get on the 8-ball!" Food source established! Yes, many of the baits are now so good that when carp are feeding strongly they will accept them as part of their diet. But to catch a target fish you may have to establish your own bait, in which case application may be as important a consideration as design.

Catch reports in *Carp-Talk* give a marvellous insight into the baits that are catching carp, but there are two things the reports rarely tell us. The first is the degree to which the bait has been applied prior to the capture. The second is the attractor levels. I would guess that the major differences between those who use bait well, and those who use it badly, lie in these two aspects, attraction and application. I know I like steak and that it does me good. I don't need to be attracted to each steak that Mary puts before me. It is a food source. The same is true of eggs, fish and milk products. Food sources. If I asked Mary what was for dinner and she told me "Strawberry flavour" I would think she was losing the plot!

But I had to learn that steak, eggs, fish and milk products are valuable food sources. You have to educate your carp that the bait you are going to catch them on is a food source.

Attraction can be instant. Dependence has to be built up.

How instant can food source baits be? I face this problem when I go overseas for a week. Almost invariably the bigger fish each session are caught late in the week. I know this and start out with an 'in yer face' baiting: at least 7 or 8 kilos of food source baits first night, with no expectations of catching instantly at that level of application. I want as many carp as possible to get a taste for the bait as quickly as possible in the hope of building a short term dependence.

I very often do catch first night and by the second night the bait is really starting to kick in. OK, it's difficult to take a "new" bait anywhere, but I think I was the first to take Nutrabaits' Trigga to both Chalet Lake and Domaine de Boux in recent years, and both caught prolifically after an early dousing of my area of the lake.

Using attractor baits I would expect a reverse result, with the majority of the fish coming at the start of the week. If I did a session based on attractor baits I would be ready to change baits by Wednesday and start over again.

How far can you go with attractors to give optimum attraction without causing overload? I think you are going to have to ask each individual bait company about their products on that one. I've experimented with baits. I've designed bait. But I'm now in a situation where I just want to go to a venue with a bait I know will catch carp if I use it right.

It is a mistake to think of all additives used in carp baits as flavours. Enhancers, essential oils, food oils, liquid foods, sense appeals, flavours... There is a growing

South African common of 39lb 7oz. This fish fell to a bait supplied by local carp angler Johan Hierons, the proprietor of The Edge Bait Company. The edge is that these baits are preserved in the packaging, giving fresh baits with a two-year shelf-life. An essential concept for the travelling carp angler of the future.

list of carp bait additives, some of which invite overload, others needing to be used sparingly. If in doubt about levels check with the bait company. These guys are real experts and understand their own products far better than any of us can hope to.

I've used a range of baits over the last few years. My first choice has always been a food source bait, and it's become obvious over the years that bait design made massive strides through the 90s. In the 80s a quality food source bait needed a pre-baiting exercise to get the best from it. Pre-baiting still helps but some bait companies have managed to achieve a remarkable combination of instant attraction and long-term food bait. I took Mainline's Activ-8 to Madine in 1999 and caught a fish of 37lb 12oz within a couple of hours of casting out a single hookbait. I took Nutrabaits' Trigga to Lake Raduta in Romania, and caught a brace of fish of 55lb 4oz and 45lb 8oz the first night I used the bait.

The gap between instant appeal and long-term nutrition has closed, and one of the biggest developments in carp baits over the next few years will be that the gap will close still further. The one problem bait companies haven't come to terms with is producing a long-term preserved bait that is as effective as its freezer bait counterpart. Taking quality baits abroad is still a problem that has to be overcome by air-drying, or finding local freezer facilities. Progress is being made on this front though. There is a new bait guru called Johan Hierons of The Edge Bait Company in South Africa who appears to have overcome the preservation problem.

It's only a matter of time before there are baits available incorporating the convenience of shelf-life ready-mades, with the instant appeal of the most successful attractor bait, and the nutritional value of the most effective long-term food source freezer bait!

Preoccupation

"Momentary lapse in concentration."

Long-term carpers will remember the impact the results of the Redmire anglers had on carp fishing in the 70s. In those days Redmire had an impossible tag and results achieved there were very influential. To read *Quest for Carp* is to understand the difficulty of Redmire in those days. In 1969, the first year of the syndicate, leader Jack Hilton fished the famous pool for 16 full weeks – for just one 23lb fish!

Small baits became the cornerstone of success at Redmire, and the bulk of the catalogue of particles and seeds we use today was written by the inventive minds of members of the Redmire syndicate. Successively maggots, casters, and sultanas achieved some success. Anything small and edible became the next possible carp bait and various seeds, beans, peas, pet foods and items of seafood were tried, some with great success, others without troubling the silver paper indicators. Then sweetcorn started to rewrite the record books (eventually quite literally, for Chris Yates in 1980 and Terry Glebioska in 2001!) and open the eyes of even the most sceptical of carpers to the possibility of small baits.

Kevin Clifford at Redmire in the mid 70s with a sweetcorn brace of 20lb+ fish from a remarkable week in which he landed no fewer than nine twenty-pluses.

But to me the defining result which put preoccupation top of the list in my carp catching armoury was Rod Hutchinson's extraordinary Redmire results on hemp. In an era when a fish from Redmire was news Rod aspired to a number of carp in one morning more than once – after he finally brought himself to start fishing the hemp he had been introducing to the water for some time.

The Redmire methods and baits spread and achieved success on numerous waters, but eventually the impact of the principle of preoccupation was diluted somewhat by the growing reputation of specials, then boilies. For the last twenty years boilies have had a fascination all of their own. They **are** fascinating and they tend to be the principal carp fishing line of attack. I'm no different to anyone else in leaning heavily on their use. I know how difficult it is to achieve preoccupation with them, but they are selective, easy to apply and fish with, and their use **can** be harnessed to the principle of preoccupation, which we will come to later.

But preoccupation is king, and it isn't easy to achieve with boilies alone.

Quest for Carp, a riveting book which spells out the difficulty of fishing Redmire in the late 60s and early 70s.

Hemp is as effective now as Rod Hutchinson taught us it was in the mid 70s. Why? Because carp love it, and hardly anyone ever fishes it as a hookbait! It isn't easy to use as a hookbait, so even if results over hemp aren't what we want them to be the hookbait tends to be a bait other than hemp itself – even when we have a mass of bubbles in front of us telling us that the carp are preoccupied beyond our wildest expectations! The same can be said of a number of baits which preoccupy carp, but are never used as a hookbait. How many of us have used pellet hookbaits, for instance? Was there ever a greater carp pre-occupier than some of the pellets commonly in use in carp fishing?

There are two forms of preoccupation, short term and long term. Long term is achieved by prebaiting, gradually making the carp dependent on the bait you are using. Short-term preoccupation is the type of fishing most of us want to take advantage of. Create a feeding spot, get them feeding strongly, then catch one, or some, or lots of them.

Even by splitting small baits into a number of categories it isn't easy to do justice to the subject of preoccupation. For the balance of this section I'm going to look briefly at harnessing preoccupation to catching carp, then in successive sections examine

One of Rod Hutchinson's remarkable Redmire hemp catches in the 70s.

the main categories of small baits available to us.

Although preoccupation is a powerful weapon harnessing its use can be difficult. I well remember the plaintive comment of John Pooler at Birch Grove at the start of the 90s. He had a bed of hemp five yards out and it was a seething mass of bubbling carp. You could

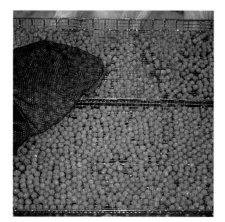

Small baits have been my first choice for pressured waters and difficult times of the year for well over ten years.

All you ever wanted to know about pellets and carpet feed – and all other aspects of bait – courtesy of the Nutrabaits Bait Club.

define the area of the hemp by the area of bubbles on the surface. After a day and a half of this frustration someone asked him how he was getting on. "Well put it this way; if this was a boxing match the referee would have stopped it in favour of the carp a long time ago!"

I smiled, but suffered a similar frustration in the next swim the following morning. Two tiger nut baits in the middle of the bed of hemp with a scattering of tigers as back-up. Again the area of the hemp was defined by the area of bubbles, and again there wasn't a single bleep at the rod end. In my case the frustration was compounded by what followed. The carp's feeding resulted in a scum forming on the surface – which they continued to feed on as it drifted down into Micky Sly's swim to my right!

So how do you stack the odds in your favour to increase the chances of a take with carp preoccupied on a bait you aren't actually fishing on the hook? I've got two lines of thought. One is that if needs be I am going to have to fish a hookbait to match the groundbait, and I carry some hemp and pellet hookbaits around with me.

PVA bags, a superb method of achieving preoccupation and drawing the carp's attention to the hookbait.

At one time I had these specially made for me by Ian Russell of Heathrow Bait Services but they are now available from a number of bait companies. The second, and standard, line of attack is to extend the preoccupation from the seeds, pellets or groundbait to the bait I'm using. Most of my pressured fishing is done with small baits – small meaning 8 or 10 mm. If I'm using baits of 14mm and upwards then chopped baits are included in the spod material or the PVA bag to gradually step up the size of the feed they are preoccupied with from tiny, to larger, to the hookbait.

PVA bags are, to me, the ultimate preoccupier, particularly when they are used in a spod situation. However well you spread your spodding the groundbait is going to be in patches. The carp become accustomed to feeding on small patches of tiny baits. They can become quite greedy for them. The PVA bag becomes another patch of bait, and with the correct set-up the hookbait becomes difficult to avoid. A mix of pellets and chopped baits, with the buoyant hookbait on top. When the carp sucks at the patch

Boats are a convenience, but there is a danger of over-baiting, and baiting too infrequently. Constant use on a water can make it difficult to introduce an element of surprise in the baiting situation.

the hookbait can be the first bait to go in there. If the presentation isn't spot on the carp can avoid the hookbait.

I think it is important not to over-bait in an intended preoccupation situation. If you are using a catapult limit yourself to ten pouches of tiny baits, then play it by ear. In a spod/PVA bag situation start with five spodfuls, then keep refreshing the swim both with fresh PVA bags and topping up with the spod. Baiting from a boat can be difficult to monitor because we all tend to over-bait and apply baits too infrequently. Remote-controlled boats can start to lose their effectiveness when you settle for the one patch of bait, rather than area baiting and getting the carp moving from one patch to another. Tiny bait situations are difficult to monitor because they are cleared by fish other than carp, and success is dependent on having bait in the swim. Let your mind go back to your maggot and float, or swimfeeder days. Swim building on a little and often principle, aiming for preoccupation. Better still, go and watch top match anglers in action. A fresh introduction of bait with every cast. A little and often. Keep them feeding and sooner or later the mistake will come.

When you are using small or tiny baits as groundbait be clear in your mind what you are trying to achieve. Preoccupation is designed to achieve what Roger Smith described as "a momentary lapse in concentration" on the part of the carp. That is the ultimate objective of the small bait syndrome – or any baiting situation for that matter. The longer you can keep the fish in your swim, or the more often they revisit your feeding area, the greater the chances are of that lapse in concentration occurring with your hookbait. It is far easier for carp to clear a swim of bait in a boilie-only situation than it is in a two or three-dimensional baiting zone.

Some groundbaits fill carp up quicker than others. On a prolific big fish water you may need a background of particles to extend the feeding period. On another water a particle and boilie situation may result in too much bait in the swim and reduce the chances of a take on the first couple of visits from the carp. So it isn't just a question of choosing a boilie and a groundbait, you need to build some understanding of the pluses and limitations of each groundbait you

Two-tier preoccupation led to the capture of this rarely caught Cassien mirror of 57lb. Four days' steady baiting with Trigga and a pellet and chopped baits 'dinner plate' was the formula for this South Arm capture.

consider. The objective is to catch carp, not just feed them, and the best baiting situation is the most effective one, not the biggest! To catch you need to walk a fine line between feeding them and keeping them hungry, the aim being to achieve that "momentary lapse in concentration" that describes the moment of a take so well.

You build preoccupation, and then you focus the carp into a capture situation. If I'm not using PVA bags then I'm using stringers of chopped or small baits. The idea behind achieving and extending preoccupation is to catch in situations where the carp aren't willing to throw themselves on the bank – as Rod Hutchinson and his contemporaries did at Redmire in the seventies. And of course the more desirable the tiny baits are to the carp the greater your chances of achieving preoccupation.

Preoccupation – Pellets

In the mid-70s I was a naive keenie taking my first tentative steps into the big wide world of carp fishing. From the first season at Snowberry bait was a major item to me. Maggots, flake, crust, luncheon meat, a flirtation with particles in the shape of tic beans and maples, then the seduction of specials, the predecessor of boilies. Unless you were part of some inner circle you tended to be a few years behind the times in those days. When I first started using specials, boilies were already in use on some southern waters and Fred Wilton's recipes were already known to some, but weren't generally available.

My first special was pellet-based. Trout pellets. Now a bait looked on as the great preoccupier, but in those days what you did with trout pellets was make specials of them, in much the same way you make method baits with them now! In fact it wasn't until trout pellets resurfaced in the 90s that their usage changed from being the basis of specials to being used in their original form as a small food source. Some enlightened anglers will have seen their potential as a groundbait long before their general rebirth, but I'm making the point about their change of usage to illustrate the change in emphasis of bait principles over the years. In the 70s they were a source of

The Bait Company is another source of highly effective preoccupation-achieving goodies. They advertise regularly in Carpworld *and* Crafty Carper.

nutrition and attraction. In the 90s they became the epitome of baits offering nutrition, attraction and preoccupation.

In his *Carpworld Tapes* some years back Rod Hutchinson referred to pellets as being the fastest working carp bait available. Where the carp are "on" pellets they can become obsessed with them. I know carp matches aren't everyone's cup of tea, but believe me, when you walk onto a water to fish a carp match you need to know two things. What time do they feed and what are they feeding on? Go on a water where pellets are working and there is only one line of attack. Get them feeding on pellets and take it from there.

I like mixes of pellets. So few anglers use pellet hookbaits that there is little likelihood of pellets blowing, but carp being caught in situations focusing on one particular pellet may cause alarm bells to ring and a resistance to build up. I

Trigga pellets. I like a mix of sizes and breakdown rates in my pellet mix.

Pop-up over breaking-down hemp pellets.

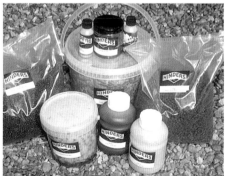

Part of the fascinating range of products available from Hinders.

can only write about the pellets I have had success with so don't limit your choice to my recommendations, but what I can say is that my choices are based on pellets that have been responsible for the capture of numerous carp, including some very big ones, and many of them in pressured match situations.

My preference is for natural pellets rather than flavoured ones. Because pellets are such tiny food particles there tends to be a strong smell release from them anyway. To use pellets incorporating an

Preparing for kitchen trials of a range of pellets.

artificial flavour can cause smell saturation of the swim and undermine the attraction of the bait itself. To overcome this you have to limit the quantity of flavoured pellets used. My pellets are foods and I want a background smell of food in the swim. The bait itself needs to be the strongest smell of food, or most identifiable source of attraction. In theory I like the concept of pellets flavoured to match the smell of the bait, but with highly flavoured baits I think pellets of this type need to be used sparingly.

My first choice of pellet is Hinders' 3mm mini Hi-Betaine pellets. They have proved deadly on waters as diverse as Cassien, Raduta, Birch Grove, the Motorway Pond, the Mangrove, Madine, Etang de Boux, Fishabil and Tyram Hall. Mini-Betaine pellets are my first choice, but I always use a mix of pellets, my other favourites including Mainline's Activ-8 Response pellets, Nutrabaits' Trigga pellets, Rod Hutchinson's Formula Majic toasted particle pellets, Hinders' Slicker pellets, and the Bait Company's rapid-breakdown Betaine pellets.

Rod Hutchinson has a range of pellets based on natural smells and flavours. I particularly like his Formula Majic pellets, based on dried, crushed hemp, maples, sweetcorn and nuts. Formula Majic pellets introduce a natural food smell to the baited area. If I'm using a strongly flavoured bait I'll use a scattering of one of Rod's flavoured pellets in my pellet mix, Monster Crab pellets as a background to Monster Crab baits being my favourite combination. Monster Crab pellets are based on capelin fishmeal, soya, cereals, crushed hemp and Monster Crab flavour.

Other pellets worth considering, some of which I've used without coming to any firm conclusions, include Dynamite Baits' Swim-Stim, Nutrabaits' Corn Steep Liquor pellets, Mainline's and the Bait Company's hemp pellets and tiny koi rearer pellets.

I'll emphasise that my experiences with pellets have been limited to a small percentage of the wide and effective range available from the bait trade. Feel free to take confidence and guidance from the selection of pellets I use, but don't let your thinking or experimenting be limited to my choice. I know what I use works. What I don't know is if there is something even better out there! If you live within striking distance of Hinders a trip there to check out the range of baits and pellets they have available might well

Formula Majic pellets are a bit special. Check the activity they create when they are breaking down. Ideal pellet mix and PVA bag additions.

pay dividends. Bryan Jarrett of Hinders is an excellent, successful carp angler and it was he who put me onto the mightily effective mini-Betaine pellets.

Mixes of pellets have at least two big pluses. One is that you have a mix of smells rather than one possibly identifiable source of attraction. The second is that some pellets break down, while others remain intact. I like both principles, the disappearing food source and an existing one

The next stage on? I've caught over these specially-made Mainline Crumball pellets. The match fraternity have groundbaits that achieve this sort of effect, but we seem to be a bit slow in catching on.

encouraging preoccupation: a mix of the two principles gives the best of both worlds. If you can add a range of sizes of pellets to your mix then the end result can be a combination of preoccupation and confusion.

A big advantage pellets have over other sources of preoccupation is that they can be used in PVA bags without any additional preparation. Seeds and particles have to be dried out before they can be consigned to bags.

I don't think I can leave pellets without discussing them as a basis for Method feeder fishing. Extending preoccupation on a bed of pellets to a Method feeder can result in a frenzied reaction to the bigger ball of bait. I carry a bag of Sensas PV1 binder with me on all sessions. This ingredient will rapidly stiffen pellet feeder mix to the extent that you can add hemp, pellets, chopped tigers and chopped baits to the mix, and make it hard enough to be cast up to 100 yards with the right rod and reel set-up. Frank Warwick's excellent chapter on the Method deals with this subject in greater detail.

I'll close this section with a couple of bits of advice. The first is not to be half-hearted about using pellets. Look at the alternatives available. Try to find out if pellets are working on the water you are fishing, or intend fishing. Then, once you start using them, remember that you aren't using them to feed the fish, you are using them as a means of catching carp. Harnessing any source of preoccupation to produce takes can be the hardest part of the battle.

Returning a Raduta margin common of 42½lb which fell to an attractor snowman set-up fished in a bag of pellet mix.

When you do come up with a choice of pellets chuck a few of each type into a bowl in the kitchen just so you can find out how they react to water, how long they take to break down, and whether or not they produce any desirable side effects, like continual breakdown, colouring up and so on. And if you are using pellets and other baits in PVA bags do go to the trouble of checking out your presentation in water before committing it, unseen, to the bed of the lake. After a day's experimenting in the kitchen a couple of years back I completely altered my approach to PVA bag presentation and have had tremendous results on the altered set-ups since.

Preoccupation – Seeds

As with pellets seeds are among those baits that are used a great deal in carp fishing, but rarely used as a hookbait. Hemp has been in use as a carp attractor since Rod Hutchinson started advocating its use in the seventies. Kevin Clifford's experiments and successes with red dari seed followed, and the principle of seed as a carp bait was firmly established – again through the efforts of the inventive Redmire anglers. Rod, Kevin and others actually used their seeds as hookbaits, but since that time most anglers have used them as a bait to fish over, rather than to use as the actual bait itself.

As with pellets the history of the use of seeds is a stop-start one. For a great many years the effectiveness of the hair, boilies, then tiger nuts made groundbaiting for carp as a general principle unfashionable, pellets and seeds later being re-examined and

You have to watch the reaction of carp to tiny seeds to understand how deadly they can be.

'rediscovered' as pressure on the carp increased and alternative baiting situations became necessary. Hemp has always been around. Wheat was a popular alternative, although I never had any successes which I attributed to the use of wheat, hard as I tried at one time. But the continuing success of hemp resulted in alternatives being sought and in the late 80s groats achieved some outstanding successes in the North-West, and its use gradually became general. When I won the first major carp match at Horseshoe in 1991 I fished over a heavy bed of hemp and groats, a popular combination of the late 80s and early 90s.

The combination of hemp and groats was the forerunner of the mega successful seed mixes of the 90s, which have brought the use of seeds back into focus in a big way. I was quite startled by the carp's reaction when I saw Hinders' Partiblend in use for the first time at Fishabil in the mid 90s. I felt I had an edge on bait and swim knowledge but Roddy Porter's Partiblend in the next swim cancelled out any edges I had! The carp on the North Bank wanted Partiblend, and were willing to eat Roddy's boilies as part of the feast.

Dynamite Baits have a stunning, growing range of seeds, particles, groundbaits and hookbaits on offer. Quality products these and ideally packed for carrying around with you "in case".

Seed mixes have become so effective that when we think of seeds now it tends to be as a collective mix rather than in terms of individual types of seeds. Hinders' Partiblend and Haith's Red Band with Aniseed are seed mixes I have used with success and which have proven track records. The mixes of tiny and larger seeds can result in instant preoccupation on the part of the carp and I've found seed mixes easier to fish over than hemp can be.

I've got a very soft spot for hemp though and I always fish a mix of seeds and additional hemp when I'm using seeds as a groundbait.

Again don't be limited in your choice by my own experiences. A glance through the Bait Company advert reveals a range of seeds and seed mixes, with the old faithfuls hemp, tares and groats still receiving individual billing and seed mixes in the form of Combi Mix, Combi Mix and Aniseed and Supa Combi and Aniseed on offer. Other bait companies will be well aware of the effectiveness of seed mixes and will have their own versions available. Check them out.

The ageless hemp. One of my favourite groundbaits, effective all year round, and attractive to big fish. Don't overdo it though. Carp seem to eat this seed in small quantities.

Haith's of Grimsby have been supplying Rod Hutchinson since the mid-70s, and are now advertising their products. They have an excellent range, their Red Band seed mix being a proven carp groundbait.

As with pellets I find seed mixes instant. In fact they can be so instant that they are difficult to fish really effectively in terms of application. Like pellets they are a target for other species of fish when the carp aren't feeding, which means you are never quite sure what you've got in front of you. Like pellets they need introducing on a regular basis to ensure that the feeding situation is as you want it. On the other hand they can be well worth the effort in that they can get pressured fish feeding on bait at times when boilies alone just aren't producing. Seed mixes work. Believe that. What's more they work well on first introduction, which can be a major plus on distant waters you have travelled to for a week's fishing.

But beware! There is an interesting contrast developing between English and French venues. Boats are in use on most French venues, which means that pellets, seeds and other methods of preoccupation can be practised by everyone, including the laziest of anglers who can't be bothered to work at swim building at home. Where boats are in common usage the carp soon develop a resistance to groundbaiting situations and the buckets of seeds and pellets you take to France with you may just become excess baggage.

On the other hand there are many home venues where the principle of preoccupation hasn't been fully explored, simply

A seed mix from the now defunct Essex Bait Services helped Crowy to a four fish catch from Orchid during a British Championships qualifier. We look pretty pleased about the result! A happy picture which sums up the camaraderie of carp matches.

because the anglers can't be bothered to spod. Have a walk round a new venue and check how many marker floats and spod rods are in evidence. Very few? None even? In that situation you can be pretty certain that preoccupation is going to be an absolute winner. Forget about markers and spods scaring carp. Yes, they may spook pressured fish in some of the big fish venues, but if you are fishing such a water then you don't need to be reading this! When you go on the circuit waters you have to invent your own tactics as you go along.

But for the rest of us how do we fish seeds, pellets or particles at ranges of greater than 10-15 yards if we can't use a remote-controlled bait boat, or a boat? By means of a spod. In fact I'm quite happy using a spod on remote-controlled boat waters, simply because remotes are rarely used to achieve a groundbaited patch: they tend to be used as glorified PVA bags. They are useful, they catch, but they create a predictable baiting situation which in time can build up a resistance in the carp's feeding.

Bryan Jarrett of Hinders emphasises that all seeds should be soaked then boiled before use for maximum effectiveness. At the risk of repeating myself I'll emphasise that I always carry a pressure cooker with me on sessions where I'm using seeds. An overnight soak then two boilings per day means I can carry seeds and particles dry, boil them up on the bank immediately prior to use and have fresh baits for use on an ongoing basis. I've seen some

To fish seeds, pellets or particles at range you need to become proficient with a spod. Don't be afraid of them. I find them to be carp attractors rather than carp scarers. Spodding is covered in a separate chapter.

very conflicting opinions about the use of hemp but I prefer to use it freshly cooked, and I think that goes for all other seeds and particles.

Of course the ultimate use of seeds is to fish them as groundbait **and** hookbait. Hemp over mixed seeds is a starting point. Paddy Webb uses black foam as his hemp hookbait. Hutchy used to thread uncooked hemp onto hairs, tied to the hook. Kryston's Bogey has achieved popularity as a binder of seeds. Seeds superglued to cork balls or rig foam is another avenue to be explored. Where there is a will there is a way, and if you choose to fish a seed hookbait you will invent the best way of doing it for yourself.

To me seeds are the ultimate natural. They are natural baits and achieve a natural feeding environment – tiny items of food on the bottom of the lake. They have a natural appeal which I don't like messing around with by the introduction of artificial flavours. Seeds are attractors and preoccupiers in their own right. If you can realise their potential they can give you a big edge, particularly on waters where their use hasn't been fully exploited.

Tiny seeds seem to get cleared quickly. Learn from the match anglers on this one and keep introducing seeds on a little and often basis. Sandra Halkon-Hunt impressively showing us how it's done during a Fishabil open match.

Preoccupation – Particles

The original in-depth particle material was written by Rod Hutchinson, first in 1975 for *Angling* magazine, then updated in 1980 for *Rod Hutchinson's Carp Book*. Rod's thoughts on particles were then further updated in 1988 for *Carp Now and Then*, a treasure trove which includes the 1975 and 1980 material, plus Rod's late 80s thoughts on the subject. Rod groups all manner of food items under "particles" including his beloved hemp, which we talked about in the previous section.

In an age of pressured carping only the best particle baits seem to have survived to be in regular use. To achieve preoccupation you have to get the fish feeding avidly, and any bait they associate with danger becomes increasingly difficult to use successfully. So some of the particle baits with a history will produce an adverse feeding reaction in the carp, while others seem to have survived the test of time, and still work.

I'll start by listing the particles I have had success with, go on to those I know to have worked for others, then list the ones that I know still go on working. I am aware that in the minds of many carpers "particle" now means "tigers". Happily they are sadly misinformed!

A treasure trove of information and advice on particles and their use.

I have caught carp on maggots, casters, maize, sweetcorn, maples, brazil nuts, broad beans, almonds, soya beans and tiger nuts. These baits still work, the only oddities being broad beans, which seem to have a very short – but quite dynamic! – life, and almonds, which soon start to rot in water and can only be used on a very limited basis.

Particle baits I know to have been successful but haven't caught on myself (despite using a number of them quite conscientiously) include sultanas, cockles, prawns, chick peas, black-eyed beans, mot beans, peanuts, cashew nuts, hazel nuts, aduki beans, haricot beans, garden peas, pinto beans and lima beans.

Cockles, one of the many effective particles which are not in common use.

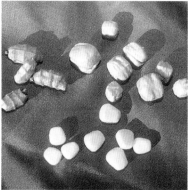

Artificial hookbaits have made the use of particles much more convenient. Carp seem to be particularly drawn to artificial maize, or sweetcorn.

Haven't caught on peanuts?! No. I think my attitude to peanuts is well known in carp fishing, although perhaps not to newer readers. I won't use them because they are dangerous to carp. Birdfood-grade peanuts are carcinogenic (can cause cancer) while peanuts of any quality can cause a vitamin E deficiency if used to excess. Tigers, too, can be a problem to fisheries if used to excess, which is why there are nut bans in force on many carp waters.

Hazelnuts require some comment. I've recently seen them described as one of the most successful of particle baits, but they are difficult to fish.

They contain an air pocket, which makes them float. When Mark Summers used them on the Tip Lake he used to sit and prick them with a pin to make them sink. I don't know if the current crops of hazels exhibit this frustrating trait but it's as well to check before you fire a load out into the lake!

Some brazil nuts float. I guess brazils are of a size that takes them above a true particle, but they are a natural, and a useful alternative to boilies on occasions – in particular where poisson chat, crayfish, eels or nuisance fish render your boilies unfishable. I've caught on brazils, but have had no big fish successes on them. I fish them as a boilie, using them as a scatter bait with boilies when I do fish them. Again check the buoyancy of

My mate John Lilley with a Madine margin-caught carp which won us the Carp Classic team title in 1999. Tigers fished next to an isolated potamogeton bed did the trick. John's partner is Dominic Martin.

any you fire out or put on the hook. Some brazils float, which makes them ideal as buoyant, sinking hookbaits.

Maize I had enormous success with when I first used it, and again at Birch Grove in the mid-90s. It never struck me as a big-fish bait, but I've heard of recent big fish successes on it so perhaps I misjudged it. Mike Wilson's famous Baiting Pyramid theory (*Carp Fisher 1* and Rod's *Carp Strikes Back*) was based on a prolonged campaign using maize (aka Reding Protein Mix at the time!) so perhaps this is a bait that requires extensive prebaiting to get the bigger fish on it.

Looking back my successes on particles have been limited because I fished them badly. I've tended to whack them in by the bucketful, rather than by the pouch, spod or handful. Particles fill carp up quickly, so a little and often is as important a principle in particle fishing as it is with most other baits. Preoccupation is a state of feeding you have to build up to. Find the level at which the carp become most active and competitive and keep topping up to that level while you fish. In Rod's later writings on particles he sets great store by Roger Smith's advice to treat each particle as a separate bait, as you would a boilie, rather than whaling them in by the lorry load, as has been known to happen with small baits.

Most particles require an extensive soaking then boiling. You may think that boiling is sufficient, but it's not the same. If I haven't had the chance to soak my particles then I pressure-cook them twice to

The first fish I saw from the Mangrove, June 1983. The angler is Dave Preston who wrote about his method of making chopped-up baits from big balls of paste boiled in foil. The innovative Dave is head of his own Preston Innovations company.

get the best out of them. Tigers in particular need a great deal of cooking to get the best out of them. Carp's recognition of them is instant, and the longer they are cooked the more the natural recognition-aiding juices flow. You may get away with uncooked tigers where they are being introduced in numbers but in the long term you are doing yourself, the carp and the other anglers no favours by introducing badly prepared particles.

Not all particles are big fish catchers. Sweetcorn always has been, and still is. I find it a difficult bait to fish as a hookbait but the new artificial buoyant sweetcorn hookbaits from Partridge and other companies make presentation of corn a great deal easier. Tiger nuts are also big fish catchers. Simon Crow had an electrifying multiple thirties and

Making my own "tiger nut" in the mid-90s. The idea resulted in two exceptional winters on the Mangrove and Birch Grove.

forties catch at Madine in the Dream of Madine videos on tigers and they have accounted for numerous carp in this country and abroad. Sweetcorn apart, the more visible particles tend to encourage sight feeding from smaller carp, maize in particular having a reputation as a prolific small carp puller. When I used the strange bait soya beans at Snowberry back in the 70s I caught loads of carp on it, but no doubles.

My own favourite particles? Maggots and casters, fished with hemp in winter. Tigers as a scatter bait with boilies at any time of the year – on any water where their use is permitted. Maples, a very attractive feed to carp but a very difficult bait to fish successfully. I think maples are an excellent "holding" bait where fish are in shoals and you want to hold them in your swim long enough to catch more than your ration.

To me tigers are the greatest particle of all, and were the reason I changed to fishing small boilies in the eighties. The initial impact of tigers on most waters was electrifying – but everyone soon knew that and all the other anglers on the water were in on the act. That put me on enquiry. What if I had my own tiger? A small boilie that was as attractive to the carp as tiger nuts, but I was the only one fishing it.

I put that into effect, and with the help of Mainline Baits I came pretty close to finding my own tiger with 8mm Grange baits on the

Biggest of 19 Birch winter fish in six weeks, the common known as Red Eye at 32lb. 8mm Grange Reds were my personalised particle, or "tiger nut", for this campaign.

Mangrove in winter in the early 90s, and then again with 8mm Grange Red baits in winter on Birch Grove a few years later. The choice of the Grange was important. It struck me as the most natural bait I'd ever fished. I feel the natural aspect of particle baits is an important consideration in their success. You can use them in numbers without saturating the swim with artificial flavours. I've gone down other routes since, but establishing my own tiger nut brought me brilliant winter results on the Mangrove, Birch Grove, and more recently on overseas trips.

If you want your own tiger nut – small boilie – don't ignore the obvious. Some years back friends of mine expressed envy that I had access to a supply of 8mm baits. At a Horseshoe presentation ceremony Tim Fromant made a comment in his closing speech to the effect of: "Perhaps we can even get a supply of 8mm baits now!" – aimed at their bait suppliers Mainline I guess. I smiled. Tim and Mike Winstone are among the best spodders and PVA bag users I've seen in action. Once you get to use 8mm baits you can forget your throwing stick and catapult (other than in the margins). You put the baits out with a boat, PVA bag, spod or bait rocket – which means the baits don't have to be round!

Dave Preston taught us about big balls of paste, bagged, boiled then chopped up, in the early 80s. Paste rolled into sausages, chopped then boiled. I can't remember the source but some time ago I read a method of microwaving pastes, then chopping them to produce small boilies. When you go small and can't afford to go to a bait-roller then forget round. Just think of the effectiveness of tigers and imagine a season fishing your own tiger. Worth a few hours' hard work in the kitchen I think! I find a pound of small baits to be adequate for a two or three-day winter session, and all my baiting up as I leave the water is done with bigger baits to make life more difficult for nuisance fish.

Most bait companies make small baits available now. Most mixes are on offer in 10mm. At scratching time, and in the winter, fishing very small baits can mean the difference between success and failure. There is no hindsight here. Many moons ago there was some sort of protein bait versus particle bait debate. The comparisons were meaningless. I made the point then that if you could take the most successful bait recipe and fish it in the most successful bait format – i.e. hemp size –

A few alternatives...

then you would be getting near to the ultimate bait. Hemp-size boilies are still some way off. Or are they? Anyone out there achieving preoccupation by fishing their favourite bait as crumb?

Dedicated New-Age Carp Baits

Kevin Knight

The partners in Mainline are carp anglers Steve Morgan and Kevin Knight. In the early 90s, following a range of base mixes, ready-mades and flavours, they launched a carefully researched, designed and field-tested bait called The Grange. Containing Corn Steep Liquor (Parts 1 & 2) it was named after the difficult Essex syndicate water it was designed to be used on. Results on the Grange – particularly in winter – were hard to ignore. In the autumn of 1994 I rang for some. I fished the Grange on the Mangrove that winter and had my best cold weather results ever – far beyond any expectations I had for winter fishing. Since then I have had exceptional results on the Grange, Grange Red, Activ-8 and Assassin-8 PT10. I've asked Kev Knight for a piece on new-age carp baits because that's how I look on these complete baits. Dedicated baits is Kev's term for them. New-age is how I refer to them. They have pointed a way forward and opened the door to a new age in dedicated food source baits which others are successfully following. It goes without saying that what is actually in these baits and how they work are closely guarded secrets. I would add that I've included this chapter because I think Mainline have harnessed a principle that I know from experience is very difficult to incorporate successfully in a bait – enzyme activity.   Tim Paisley

When Mainline Baits was founded it was a natural progression to look at the highest quality ingredients possible. The best bait is fundamental in a pursuit where success revolves around carp and their feeding habits. Mainline's contacts in the food and meat industries presented us with a whole wealth of opportunities in terms of research and product availability both at home and abroad. We knew that we wanted to create a totally new concept in baits that were attractive to fish, nutritious and digestible. Having a wealth of food industry knowledge at our fingertips we spent a long time researching ingredients and talking to nutritionists who were able to point us towards the most beneficial products to achieve this concept and our ultimate goal.

We quickly discovered that there was much more to an effective and usable food source than the old accepted thinking of high protein levels. If an ingredient has a protein-rich profile, for example, is that protein readily available to carp? If so is it available all year round, in all temperatures? Designing carp baits in a logical yet scientific way opens up a whole new can of worms, but the end result can be a bait that proves to be something very special. The principle has been established and continued

Overseas big fish for Kev while putting a new mix through its pre-launch paces.

through a succession of Mainline baits and it is no coincidence that these have proven to be amongst the best the carp world has seen. Lab results or theory are one thing; success on the bank is an entirely different matter. As all anglers know theory alone has never put any carp in the bottom of the net.

Our initial research and design involved the use of expert nutritionists, extensive tank tests, and a network of top-level field-testers. Logging results on prototype baits supplied to our field force allowed us to see how these experimental food sources performed against the best alternative recipes available. Each new bait is tested for at least a period that includes all four weather seasons before being released to the shops, and so in turn to the public. This trial period enables us to answer all questions regarding the bait's effectiveness and performance in all weather and temperature situations as honestly as we can, whilst monitoring the effectiveness of the product.

Ingredients, design, tank testing, field-testing... We know all our competitors are capable of taking all these steps towards the best possible bait. We also knew that the two most difficult areas of mass bait production lay in producing and repeating a hardened finished product (boilie) from the raw materials selected, and doing so in a cost-effective way. Careful research and testing produced a bait we were proud of – The Grange. This was designed to tackle a difficult Essex syndicate water and succeeded beyond all our expectations. But if this bait was to be as successful for others then we knew the recipe and the preparation had to be precise. The answer lay in producing what we refer to as a dedicated bait formula. No variables. We would measure the ounce of this and ounce of that of the ingredients, which were an essential part of the recipe. Corn Steep Liquor was – and still is – an integral ingredient in the success of The Grange. Corn Steep had been around for some time. Feedback on it was mixed. We researched this aspect and felt that we managed to pinpoint the problem. The hit-and-miss results on Corn Steep were eliminated by means of adding a second profile in the form of the 'Part 2' to protect and modify the tone of the original, and for the reason explained below.

When you pass your own precious bait formula to unscientific bait-makers who are going to subject the finished product to extreme temperatures you have another area to consider. Boiling can render some of the best carp attractors and foods less effective and, in some cases, even ineffective – but it goes without saying that boiling is a vital part in the process of boilie production. You can make recommendations for abbreviated boiling times but you know

Mainline user and prolific catcher of carp, Ian Chillcott, with Yateley Car Park Lake's Single Scale at 43lb 12oz.

they aren't always going to be followed to the letter. So part of our research programme was to find buffer ingredients which would protect the properties of items that could be denatured against high temperatures. Our nutritionists managed to identify and harness some ingredients to do this job for us, and this aspect has become a vital area of the design of the succession of the successful Mainline 'Dedicated Bait Concept' baits.

Arriving at cost-effectiveness in a bait is a problem all bait manufacturers are faced with. Our food industry ties and our rapid growth meant we were able to combine research with bulk buying to keep costs to a minimum and to enable us to buy top-quality ingredients at prices unavailable to others; therefore we were able to produce high-quality products at a competitive price. Successively the Grange, Activ-8 and Assassin-8 have taken increasing advantage of our unique design aspects, our ability to buy the right ingredients at the right price, and a marketing policy based on exceptional field-testing results.

We knew from the launch of The Grange that we were onto something special and with repeat captures of some of the hardest fish in the country – many as often as ten times in a season – on the same bait there was no arguing that the food sources we were offering were very acceptable to the fish. To our delight the balance of initial recognition of the bait as a food source and acceptance of it over a period of time had been harnessed to a remarkable extent!

So what's in a Mainline dedicated bait? Instead of relying on the cornerstone ingredients used by and available to every other bait firm we looked further afield. Whilst milk proteins, birdfoods and fishmeals are all valuable ingredients (which we use) there were plenty of others that didn't fall into quite such convenient categories and had amazing potential in terms of both attraction and nutrition. Correct levels of these ingredients – both liquid and dry food sources – are essential in order for the baits to perform to their optimum. Put bluntly some interplay of ingredients can produce baits that are constantly changing in both attraction and nutritional profile and get the bobbins flying like never before. No longer does a bait that has been immersed for 24 hours need to be considered less attractive or acceptable than one recently introduced. However, one wrong move in the mixing process and the advantages can be easily lost. I'll emphasise the point already made. The simplest way to ensure a perfect bait is produced every time by an angler in the kitchen is to take the measuring and weighing of ingredients away. The principle of the dedicated bait mix has been born. Making our products available in a freezer range has been a further stage in ensuring that the bait has been prepared correctly for optimum effectiveness.

It goes without saying that we are reluctant to give too much away about our hard-earned secrets and the basis of our successful concept. Taking this one step further, and with a new train of thought as well as new ingredients, the second of our dedicated

Kev with the big fish from The Grange syndicate water weighing in at 44lb 8oz.

Keith Jenkins with Jack from Horton during an exceptional year on Mainline which earned him the Angling Times *'Angler of the Year' title.*

mixes was born in the shape of the Activ-8. During trials we noticed a greenhouse effect occurring, with sugars being formed surprisingly early on the surface of the bait as a result of the active ingredients held within. Again the problem of protecting the more delicate ingredients was surmounted and the projected activity within the bait harnessed to occur when it is most needed, when the bait is being used for angling purposes! It is noticeable that both the Grange and Activ-8 are often at their most effective when they are apparently 'turning', which is actually part of the interplay of active ingredients rather than a deterioration in the quality of the bait. Due to the 'working' and active ingredients within the baits, our research proved that the best method to suspend this activity was by freezing them as opposed to any other method of short or long-term storage.

Then came the Assassin-8, the next bait in line. We found some new ingredients we wanted to incorporate in a bait to take our concept a stage on from Activ-8. The problem we had here was not in the bait design, but in cost. Again with the help of our extensive contacts within the food industry, we managed to achieve the right balance between nutrition, attraction and cost-effectiveness. Assassin-8 proved to be as successful as its two predecessors, and then some!

But the one that has made the news on a weekly basis recently, and the newest member of the total concept club, is the NRG. This has been on trial for the past 16 months and the results have surpassed even our own expectations. With a slightly stronger smell and lighter appearance, the NRG has caught well from its first usage on all waters, including some of the hardest circuit waters in this country.

We pride ourselves on our products. All the hard work has already been done by Mainline, all you need to do is accurately mix the eggs, base mix and liquid. Not only does this principle make things easier in the kitchen, but it does away with a list as long as your arm of ingredients, additives, palatants, flavours and enhancers for inclusion in the bait. The cost is kept as realistic as possible for anglers who want to use our products.

An interesting aspect of features built around our design concept is that the baits are clearly fish attractors, not simply carp attractors. We have had record barbel plus countless specimen tench, bream, chub and roach reported on a regular basis. All fish seem to recognise and benefit from the valuable food sources within the baits, and on many carp waters that have been baited by teams it has been noticeable that carp weights have gone through the roof.

Many carp anglers are wrongly under the impression that as baits catch carp they automatically lose their long-term effectiveness. Mainline's dedicated baits question that philosophy. Being such outstanding food sources the more they are used on waters the better they seem to perform, as results in the angling press week after week, and season after season, will testify. We see little need to sell a magic new recipe every season when our baits have been shown to perform better during the second season of widespread use than the first. The nation's most famous carp fall for them time and again.

Anyone can string words together to convince the bait-buying public that their products are the best, or use fancy advertising claims. At Mainline we are proud of our achievements both at home and abroad since the introduction of the dedicated bait concept. This approach has seen Mainline Baits set new records each and every year, since 1997, including a world-beater of 73lb 13oz for Tim himself. And as everyone knows, a picture never lies.

Dave Lane with a trio of English fifties on Mainline: the late Mary from Wraysbury at 50lb 8oz (Dave also caught the great fish at 49lb 15oz!), the Two Tone Mirror from Mid Kent at 54lb, and the elusive Eye from Sonning at 55lb.

Special Hookbaits

Whatever bait or baiting situation you use in your carp fishing all captures have one thing in common; the carp has to take the hookbait into its mouth and give a strikeable indication (hopefully a run) for you to catch it. The starting point for my carp fishing confidence comes from the bait that I'm using. I need to feel sure the carp will eat what I put in front of them. Then I need added confidence from knowing I am using a hookbait which will increase the chances of the baited rig being sucked into the carp's mouth.

Almost all my carp fishing is done with specially prepared hookbaits. My main focus is on using rock-hard baits with a suitable degree of buoyancy.

When I'm travelling to distant waters I never know when I'm going to need very hard baits to withstand the attentions of crayfish and poissons chat. On the big waters where you may be landlocked for a day or two rock-hard baits are the minimum requirement. My starting point is a supply of hard hookbaits as similar as possible to the free offerings I'm using to gain the carp's attention and confidence. There are a number of ways of achieving hardness, or protecting the hookbait, which we will discuss in detail later.

My second requirement is a degree of buoyancy in the hookbait. Buoyancy is an essential ingredient to me. I want the hookbait to be lighter than the free offerings. I'm not hung up on critical balancing. There is a degree of freedom of movement to the free offerings. A carp eating a succession of free offerings employs a certain degree of suck. Many of the rigs we use restrict the freedom of movement of the hookbait. Hookbait buoyancy is to minimise the carp's suspicions during a cursory "examination" of the hookbait – which can take all sorts of forms! If the carp fans the hookbait with its fins, or rolls it around with its nose, then I want a degree of movement. When it sucks at the hookbait I don't want it to be too obviously tethered by the hooklink. It must go into the carp's mouth at the suck stage – which is why I like the combination of longer-than-normal hooklinks and buoyant hookbaits.

As with hardness there are various ways of achieving buoyancy, and we'll look at these in some detail, too.

For me specially prepared hookbaits are the icing on the bait confidence cake. This picture goes back over ten years. I'm still at it!

High-viz pop-ups from Frank Warwick and Dynamite Baits, part of the special hookbait armoury.

To talk about hookbaits we've got to give some thought to presentation. Pressured carp can become increasingly nervous in their feeding and our hookbait presentation has to keep pace with the carp's learning curve. In match fishing anglers scale down in breaking strain and hook size. There is a limit to how far down the scale a carp angler can go. Most of our fishing is done with comparatively crude gear, and doctoring the hookbait to induce a take may be our main line of attack.

I carry a special hookbait carrier with numerous hookbait alternatives in it. Because a great deal of my fishing is done over seeds or pellets I rarely use pop-ups – although I always carry them. Bottom baits, buoyant bottom baits (slow sinkers), soaked baits, attractor baits, Frank Warwick's High-viz baits which he discusses in the next chapter, and pop-ups in at least two or three alternative baits. I always have these variations with me.

Why do I rarely use pop-ups? For two reasons. One is that I am a heavy baiter, whether it be in terms of prebaiting a nutritional bait, or applying beds of hemp and pellets – or other sources of potential preoccupation. My aim is to get the carp feeding on the bottom, long term and short term. I don't want the possible preoccupation spell to be broken by the bait being on a different plane to the free offerings. A carp grubbing round for seeds or pellets may have to work hard for its meal. A handful of freebies in among the groundbait will extend the preoccupation to the boilies I'm using. When the carp encounters the hookbait I want it to be lighter than the free offerings so the carp can suck it in with a minimum of resistance. The hookbait needs to at least counteract the drag of the hooklink and hook, preferably with some margin for error. I find this concept appealing with beds of tiny baits, PVA bags, and stringers. I find it less essential when I'm fishing a bigger boilie hookbait over a scattering of boilies – although even in that situation I prefer a degree of buoyancy, hoping the lighter bait will be sucked in further and will result in a better hookhold.

I think my slightly negative feelings about pop-ups have come about through spending so much time fishing over silt. When I'm fishing over silkweed, in Canadian pondweed or hornwort, or over debris (tree lines in late autumn, for instance) I may use pop-ups. In those situations it's a more practical presentation, and I have confidence in the idea that the carp is accustomed to finding free offerings on different planes in the weed; that the hookbait off the bottom may be more natural than in weed-free waters. If you use pop-ups then you have the required built-in buoyancy and it is a question of weighting the pop-up to your own required degree of buoyancy. There are two schools of thought here: an overweighted pop-up which pricks the carp as it picks up the bait, or a critically balanced bait which the carp can easily suck into its mouth. Discussion of the preparation of pop-ups is included in what follows.

Hookbait Buoyancy

The science of buoyant hookbaits has moved on apace over the last few years. Until the mid 90s the alternative methods of production were cork or polystyrene inserts, baking, microwaving or panning/ frying. Because I have always wanted the hookbait to be as similar as possible to the free offerings I have,

Baits inserted with foam or cork are a popular way of preparing pop-ups and buoyant bottom baits. Some foam is more volatile than other versions. I prefer fly body or Fox foam for stability during boiling.

until recent years, preferred inserted baits made from the same paste as the free offerings. For many years I froze these and took along as many as I thought I might need for a session. Then Danny Fairbrass of Korda Developments revealed that he was air-drying his inserted hookbaits (as many other successful anglers do, including Terry Hearn), and I followed his lead. The number of cork balls advertised suggests that inserted baits are still a very popular form of buoyant bait, so here's a few thoughts on making them.

For **inserted baits** make a ball of paste based on the freebies recipe. When I was going down this route I added an ounce per pound of Nutrabaits' Nutragel for added hardness and experimented with boiling times, usually boiling for up to twice as long as the freebies. (I see Egg Albumen recommended as an additive but this isn't as good as Nutragel.

Egg Albumen leads to a thick skin, whereas Nutragel can give a harder bait right through.)

Because of the extended boiling time I increased the attractor levels by up to 50%, to allow for some loss in boiling. If I was using a fishmeal or birdfood base mix I used to sieve the mix (Paddy Webb tip) to give a more watertight buoyant bait. I used different sizes of cork balls to achieve different buoyancies. Most hookbaits I used for fishing on the bottom rose very slowly in the jar during testing. These would sink with the weight of the hook and hooklink. Experiment with the quantity of paste required round a cork ball to achieve the required buoyancies.

A word on presentation. If you are using a mix that takes on water you may need to tie the hookbait on with an overhand knot. This was never my favourite form of presentation, partly because much of my fishing was done on waters with eels in them. Mischievous creatures eels... I always carried a supply of normal large-eyed darning needles (still do) for threading inserted and rock-hard baits. The normal

Microwaving is favoured by many to arrive at their specialised hookbait.

Microwaved baits reabsorb liquid and leave room for experimenting with increased attractor levels.

needles pierce the hard skins of special hookbaits better than baiting needles, and leave the cork ball or polystyrene insert intact. You need a large-eyed needle to make threading the eye of the needle with braided hairs easier. If you are using light nylon hairs then a normal sewing needle is ideal.

Microwaving is a very popular way of making buoyant hookbaits. I've used the method a great deal but never had the same confidence in the finished baits as I had in inserted baits. Others swear by them. Again work from a modified paste (not from boilies), roll into balls, then experiment with the number of baits to be cooked at a time, microwave levels and cooking times. On our microwave I got the best results by working with a number of cookings of 12-16 baits at a time. Level 6 – one minute. Turn the baits. Level 6 again for another minute. Turn the baits again. 30 seconds at a faster level to finish them off. Others work with longer

Lee Walton of Nutrabaits with a big mirror from Birch Grove. Lee's description of his method of preparing pop-ups by panning is very revealing.

cooking times at the Defrost level, again half cooking, then turning, and then cooking again. Some mixes may take different times to those suggested here. Experiment, but the low-level, split-times idea proved far more successful than one cooking at one level. Until I started splitting the cooking periods I tended to finish up with burnt offerings which bore very little resemblance to the free offerings. Using the method described above gave me baits I had more confidence in – but still not enough!

Panning is a favoured method I have little or no experience of. It's the favourite pop-up preparation method of some of the best pop-up makers so it obviously has its advantages. In addition to being a method favoured by many panning can be effective when you need emergency pop-ups on a session and only have boilies to work from. Having little or no experience of this effective method of preparing buoyant baits I asked Nutrabaits hookbait star Lee Walton to give us some insight into how he goes about preparing pop-ups by means of the panning method. What Lee had to say turned out to be very revealing! Over to Lee Walton:

"A great deal of the basis for the success of pop-up baits is at the preparation stage. I use a combination of the Nutrabaits Pop-up Mix and the base mix for the bait the pop-ups need to match. The Pop-up mix is based on milk proteins so there are two points to watch with it. The first is that it will produce pop-ups lighter in colour than baits from the undiluted base mix. The second is that it dries out quickly once the paste has been made, which we'll deal with at the mixing stage.

I work with one-egg mixes. Panning subjects the baits to great heat so I need an exaggerated attractor and colour level at the mixing stage. For instance if the normal level of flavour and colour is 5mils and ¼ of a teaspoon respectively per pound of bait, then I will use 10mils of flavour and a teaspoon of colour in the one-egg pop-up mix. This may sound excessive but I've been experimenting for years and these are levels which produce

Lee Walton demonstrates his technique with panned hookbaits.

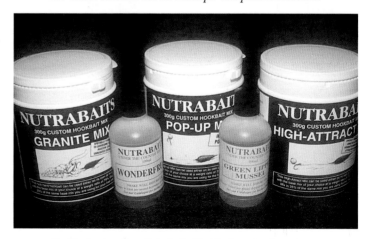

Hookbait mixes from Nutrabaits. Most bait companies are now producing their own specialised mixes.

baits which look and smell like the original baits, and catch carp! I steer clear of using liquid foods in panned baits, even when they are present in the baits themselves. They tend to burn, and the smell of burning is detectable in the finished pop-ups. You may get away with using Trigga liquid in pop-ups, but otherwise liquid foods are risky additives to use in panned bait preparation.

For normal pop-ups I work 50/50 with the pop-up mix and the base mix. For super buoyant pop-ups – which some anglers prefer – I may go up to 75% pop-up mix to 25% base mix. The more of the light-coloured Pop-up Mix you use the greater effort you will have to make to match the colour of the pop-ups to the baits. Make your one-egg mix – which will smell and look very exaggerated. Work with a softish paste because pop-up mixes are prone to drying out. Put the mix in a plastic bag to slow down the drying-out effect.

I roll out the pop-ups using a bait table one size smaller than the required finished baits. The baits will swell at the cooking stage. For example for 14mm baits I use a 12mm rolling table. To avoid flattening of the baits I have a 14mm table standing by to stand the baits in prior to cooking. This way they retain their shape. Roll out the one-egg mix then get ready for the cooking stage.

When I'm panning I have a few freebies from the bait mix close by so I can match the panned baits to the baits from the mix. We have an electric cooker at Nutrabaits which I find ideal for this process. Use a non-stick frying pan over a gentle heat source, and warm the pan through before introducing any baits. Cook 15-20 baits at a time. Roll the required number of baits off the rolling table into the frying pan and keep shuffling them round in the pan by rotating the pan with the handle. Keep the pan over the heat, but don't let the baits stand still, or overheat.

The total cooking time is about 4-5 minutes. After two minutes of panning the baits will swell up and start to lighten in colour. This means they are about half-cooked. Keep going for the full four or five minutes (exact time will depend on the mix and you may have to experiment a bit to find out the ideal timing for your bait). Finish the cooking, roll them out of the pan onto a towel or tea towel, and leave them to dry."

I use Lee's pop-ups in a great deal of my fishing. They smell right, look right, and catch fish. Thanks for that, Lee and Nutrabaits – very enlightening.

The discovery of new materials means that in recent years the science of buoyant hookbaits has progressed enormously. There are ingredients available which can be mixed with your chosen base mix to produce paste baits, and can be boiled to produce buoyant baits very similar to the free offerings. I have experimented with the Richworth Pop-up Mix, Richworth Fishmeal Pop-up Mix and Mainline's new Polaris mix, and have found them to be very effective. I treat the pop-up mix as just another ingredient and add it to my base mix at a rate of 50%-60% for pop-ups, 25%-33% for buoyant bottom baits. The required levels will depend on the consistency of the original base mix, but those percentages are a good starting point.

Ignore the Richworth instructions that suggest you make this mix with water. Use eggs in the normal boilie-mix way, although you may have to add Nutragel or an alternative effective binder with higher percentages of Pop-up mix. If you want your hookbaits to look exactly like your free offerings you may have to experiment with adding colour to achieve something like a match, brown for fishmeals, red for some birdfoods and brighter colours to match orange and yellow baits. The tough finish I achieve using the Richworth Mix allows me to trim my hookbaits with scissors to the precise buoyancy I require!

Hookbaits made with the Richworth mixes are my favourites. When I first used Trigga buoyant bottom baits made in this way I was careful to use them from frozen, taking new supplies out of the freezer or cool box every couple of days. At the end of the successful Birch opening to the season in 2001, when I had ten thirties from the water in ten days of fishing using these baits, I had half a dozen thawed-out hookbaits left and dropped them into the tackle box. They were still there when I was fishing at Raduta in October. I was running low on pop-ups for my snowman hookbaits, felt that the dried-out, unappetising-looking Trigga hookbaits were worth a try, and put one out on one rod. I landed a fish of 41lb on that rod within an hour of positioning the end tackle! All five of those hookbaits accounted for good fish. I've since come to the conclusion that there is something special about Trigga/Richworth hookbaits and now always use them air-dried. They finish up rock-hard and need a sharp drill to prepare them for threading on the hair.

Ian Russell of Heathrow Bait Services is able to produce brilliant pop-ups to match the mix you are using. These are boilies which are uncannily similar to the free offerings (subject to slight colour variations), very buoyant, very easy to use and very confidence-giving. I carry pop-ups in three mixes, buoyant bottom baits in two, pellet pop-ups and bottom baits and hemp pop-ups made by Ian, all part of the armoury that may help me outwit the carp on a day, or session, where takes are hard to come by.

The baits produced by Ian don't have the same finish as that I achieve with the Richworth mixes (which means either a different ingredient or a different method of preparation) and a number of other bait companies are catching up with the natural pop-up concept. Kevin Nash and his Airball pop-ups, and the new versions and mixes from Nutrabaits and Mainline are just a couple of pop-up improvements we can all take confidence from. It may well be that the bait company you are using can now supply pop-ups to match their base mixes. Check this aspect out before you land yourself with the task of taking over the kitchen and committing yourself to producing hookbaits which may well turn your indifferent season into a successful one.

(I should make it clear that almost all bait companies supply pop-ups to complement the boilies they sell: but there does appear to be a variation in quality and buoyancy, which often means some effort on the angler's part to come up with really effective buoyant baits that match the free offerings.)

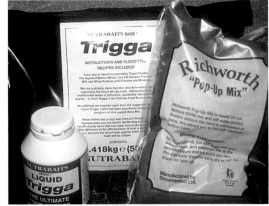

My favourite home-made hookbaits are prepared from a mixture of the base mix, liquid additive and Richworth Fishmeal Pop-up mix. One-third Trigga to two-thirds pop-up mix has produced hookbaits which have been responsible for some remarkable results.

Buoyancy Aids

I go to great lengths to have a variety of hookbaits with me to cover all possible contingencies, then occasionally find myself in a position where I need to improvise because I haven't go the specially prepared hookbaits quite as I need them. I use foam or cork in my bankside balancing set-ups. When I'm making individual boilies more buoyant I use

Aids for achieving buoyancy on the bank.

The stack rig using three 8mm Grange Red baits and a cork ball. This set-up is very effective, and very easy to balance.

foam, either fly body foam which comes in blocks and is cut to the required size and shape, or the Fox foam (pictured above), which is very buoyant and very dense.

The Fox Nut Drill and Cork Sticks, Cork Plugs and the Boilie Punch and Foam are invaluable tackle box aids for achieving buoyancy on the bankside. Fox also do cork balls, which are available from a number of other sources.

The Fox Punches come in three sizes; 6mm, 8mm and 10mm. In terms of bait sizes I find 14mm is the smallest boilie you can drill and insert satisfactorily. I would work to under half the diameter of the bait for the diameter of the drill, using 6mm foam for 14mm baits, 8mm for 18mm and 10mm for bigger baits. Drill the baits carefully, extracting about ¼in of core at a time – to avoid splitting the bait. I drill about 9/10 of the way through the bait. If you need to add as much foam as possible and need to drill right through the bait go three-quarters of the way through, then push a needle through the hole to show where the exit hole will be. Then, to avoid splitting the bait, drill from the opposite side to finish off the drilling. (If the engineers could achieve an exact meeting halfway under the Channel then you should be able to manage it with an 18mm boilie!)

There are four colours of foam available from Fox; red, yellow, orange and brown. During a session at Domaine de Boux a couple of years back I was dropping the odd fish, didn't have any specially prepared hookbaits in the bait I was getting action on and started drilling and inserting. I was short of brown foam to match the baits and started using yellow – an effect the fish seemed to like. So foam can be used for added buoyancy, and to come up with a high-viz bait variation on the hookbait theme!

With particles and very small boilies I use cork balls or shaped foam to achieve the required buoyancy. My second capture of the Domaine de Boux fish at 58lb 14oz in October 2000 came to a balanced tiger nut set-up, using Fox shaped brown foam as the middle 'nut' in the set-up. This is my usual tiger nut set-up and can be adjusted to pop-up or buoyant bottom bait status depending on the amount of foam used.

When I fish cork balls with small boilies or particles (small tigers or maples for instance) I fish three or four-bait stacks with the cork ball next to the top of the stack. In terms of sight and scent I prefer to have an actual bait at the top of the stack. I don't find the stack overbalances with this set-up. Balance is easy to achieve with these set-ups. You simply trim the cork ball with scissor points until the required balance is achieved. Once you have a cork ball of the right buoyancy it tends to balance each successive hookbait set-up and there is rarely any need to balance the rig each time you rebait. The stack rig is deadly and has brought me some super fish in difficult conditions. Having the confidence and belief to actually fish it can be a problem with this set-up. Just rationalise that once the carp sucks it in it has a great deal of difficulty getting rid of it and your belief in it will grow.

One other form of buoyant bait to look at, and these are the artificial maize/sweetcorn, tiger nut and Chum Mixer baits now available from a number of sources. At the time of writing my experience with these is limited, but it is about to grow! During a recent difficult Birch Grove session three of my four takes came on imitation sweetcorn fished over hemp with just a scattering of sweetcorn added. I was fishing prebaited quality baits on all rods to start with, and finished up with the artificial corn on three rods out of the four. Corn can be a difficult bait to fish as a hookbait so this was a real eye-opener and an area for further experiment during the year ahead.

The Dipstick, a bait-hardening system from Gardner Tackle.

Hookbait Hardness

Hookbait interference can be a nightmare. I've suffered it on the meres through eels, and on overseas waters through interference from eels, poissons chat (or poison shits as they are unaffectionately referred to by Simon Horton!) and crayfish. Disappearing hookbaits undermine everything you are trying to do. The interference comes at non-feeding times, and by the time the carp's feeding time comes round you don't know if you're fishing effectively or not. This may be irritating – but manageable – on small waters where you can keep checking, but we can all live without that sort of interference. On the big windswept waters it may not be possible to get the hookbaits back out there anyway.

New-age hookbaits now available from a number of sources. The maize/corn version is particularly useful, as sweetcorn can be a difficult bait to use as a hookbait.

Friend Micky Sly with a Birch mirror of 34lb 12oz caught on an artificial corn hookbait fished over sweetcorn and hemp within a few hours of Micky first using the artificial bait!

So rock-hard hookbaits can be an essential requirement, but one you may not be prepared for on a first trip to an unknown water, or a first trip abroad.

The anomaly here is that most pop-ups tend to be rock-hard, but I haven't found them to be as effective as bottom baits on the majority of the overseas waters I've fished. You need to go prepared with a rock-hard hookbait version of your main bait.

A practical tip first. The snowman set-up can be highly effective, and I'm not the only angler who sees it as my first choice for most of my fishing. The pop-up part of the snowman set-up is often harder than the bottom bait, particularly when the bottom

112

The Mistral range of liquid soaks and additives. The Beef, Oceanic and Neutral versions are effective bait hardeners.

The Mainline Hookbait Enhancement system being used to enhance and harden hookbaits.

Micky Sly meshing hookbaits with the Tackle Box special mesh.

bait is a freezer bait. Ian Poole has made the point that the ready-made version of most freezer baits is usually harder and has a higher attraction level than the frozen version. So if you're using a freezer bait it's an idea to carry a small pack of the ready-mades for the bottom bait on the snowman set-up.

I find snowman set-ups to be an effective way of fishing attractor pop-ups when I don't want to fish a popped-up bait. Simply use a standard bottom bait with the high-viz pop-up as the top part of the snowman. I watched Rob Hughes fish like this at Raduta, using about twenty different alternative "top-knots" for his baits to keep ringing the changes in trying to come up with a hookbait combination the carp showed a liking for. If the snowman proves to be over-buoyant because of the buoyancy of the pop-up then weight it down, or fish the combination as a pop-up.

There are special mixes and special liquids for achieving bait hardness. I've already mentioned the effect achievable through mixing Richworth's pop-up mix as a percentage of your base mix. A number of companies now market hookbait mixes which will be worth experimenting with to come up with the desired end product. Rod Hutchinson sells the Clawbuster Mix, originally specially designed to withstand the attentions of crayfish and ensure that Rod had hookbaits he could leave out for days on end if necessary on the big waters. Nutrabaits have a Granite Mix to achieve the same end result. Keep an eye on the advertising from other bait companies to find out what specialised hookbait mixes they have on offer. We've never had it so good in this area – and it will only get better!

There are liquids which harden baits, and special containers to harden them in! The Gardner Dipstick system is for hardening baits in liquid. From Mistral we have Beef Amino, Oceanic Amino and the Neutral Hookbait Hardener, all three of which harden baits soaked in them. At one time Lee Jackson's favourite bait soak was Mistral's Oceanic amino, a combined attractor and hardener. The Mainline Hookbait Enhancement system is a range of bait hardeners in addition to being effective bait soaks.

Meshing Baits

If you find yourself on a crayfish/possions chat water with no hard baits then meshing the hookbaits will get you by. This is a commonly used practice demonstrated by Simon Horton during a difficult hookbait-interference session in France. Tackle Box sell a terrific hookbait mesh, but if you find yourself on a distant water with no mesh and disappearing hookbaits then ladies' tights are the answer.

Meshing sounds messy and ineffective. It is simple, and it works. I saw Simon catch two super fish to mid-forties using meshed hookbaits during the session mentioned above. To mesh a hookbait cut a small area from the mesh or tights. Practice will soon teach you how much material you need. Stretch it round the hookbait, pull tight into a bunch, and then tie off the bunched area. Thread on the hookbait, or tie it on in the usual way. You may start off with little confidence in the concept, but a couple of nights of disappearing baits will soon convince you that it is worth trying on at least a couple of rods.

Conclusion

The ideal answer is to take specially prepared hookbaits with you on every trip. My specially prepared balanced bottom baits need a drill to prepare them for the hair, and withstand the attentions of all water dwellers that I've encountered. Mainline, Nutrabaits and Tails Up all provide me with the hardened pop-ups I need for pop-up and snowman set-ups, while the combination of Richworth Fishmeal Pop-up mix and my chosen base mix means I can make hookbaits that give me confidence in every angling situation I encounter. My high-viz hookbaits are taken care of by Dynamite Baits and Frank Warwick; any other specialised hookbaits I need come from Ian Russell at Heathrow Bait Services.

To me having the right hookbait, or the means of producing it, is the icing on the confidence cake.

Session stubble and a stunning mid-forty mirror for Si Horton. The fish was caught from a Champagne syndicate water on a meshed hookbait during a session when interference from the poissons chat made normal boilie fishing impossible.

Raduta margin common of 42½lb, my biggest fish to date on a snowman attractor top-knot bait.

Ian Russell of Heathrow Bait Services with a beautifully scaled mirror. Ian is one of the best hookbait-makers in the land.

High-Attract Hookbaits

Making a hookbait especially effective for use on its own with few or no free offerings is a specialist subject in its own right. Achieving consistent success by deceiving carp into accepting a hookbait fished in isolation is more complex than first meets the eye. With this type of presentation a truly irresistible bait and highly effective rig become even more critical than when you are fishing amongst free offerings of one kind or another. Free offerings will often entice a carp to investigate and hopefully create a feeding situation in which your hookbaits may well be noticed, and picked up. The carp's attention will be focused by the availability of food items in the vicinity of the hookbait.

"So why not fish over free offerings all the time?" I can almost hear you asking. Well here are a few scenarios where fishing singles might be necessary.

The first that springs to mind is the situation where carp are showing at extreme distance and where putting out free offerings is simply not possible. I can cast a single hookbait further than I can put out a boilie rocket, or introduce free offerings with a throwing stick. Plus, of course, there are those situations where carp will be less spooked by just a couple of hookbaits being cast to the area than repeated splashes caused by free offerings being introduced. This point can apply to carp at any range. Let's face it, there are always going to be pluses and minuses here. Take for example those times

Frank Warwick

when carp have been present in the chosen swim and have moved on within minutes of the first free offering hitting the water. I know it can certainly work the other way and carp will respond well to bait, even feeding as the spod is hitting the water, but in my book I much prefer to open the session on single hookbaits, small stringers, or PVA bags and take the opportunity of catching any feeding fish present in the swim before risking spooking them.

Another ideal single situation is the short session where time is at a premium and baiting up is not really likely to be worthwhile. In this kind of situation single hookbaits are a good option, particularly in the colder months, and especially in winter. Fish are usually harder to find in the winter so by fishing singles you can actively search for the carp by moving swims and casting on a regular basis. This is the sort of situation where, if you introduce bait, you are stuck

Short sessions are perfect for utilising single hookbait tactics. This carp came within a short space of time after quietly casting out two hookbaits.

with it in a number of ways, not least of which is being loath to move off it in case you miss something.

The other obvious point to consider with single-hookbait fishing is that you never risk overfeeding. Gauging how much bait to put out is always a dilemma but with singles it doesn't even enter into the equation.

As well as being a valid tactic in its own right when fished in isolation an attractor hookbait can certainly be rewarding when fished over other bait. Whether it be pellet, particle, Method mix or boilies, over the years I have caught many carp by utilising this tactic. In fact when I think about it the use of a high-visibility attractor bait fished over darker free offerings has usually been at least as effective as using a hookbait that is the same as the free offerings in use at the time, sometimes markedly better.

There have been exceptions where the more understated natural hookbait has worked better and it would be wrong not to admit that, but by doing a direct comparison whilst fishing a pattern will soon emerge. It has to be said from my findings that the bright attractor bait will usually more than hold its own when fished against other hookbaits in a direct comparison. On the other hand, when most other anglers on a water are using hi-viz singles then their effectiveness can be diluted. But if you are the first to really get to grips with their use on your water the rewards can be superb.

So how do I define an attractor bait? Well the

My biggest ever winter brace, the Birch Grove Video fish at 35.04 and the common Red Eye at 35lb 14oz. Both fell to a single attractor balanced bottom bait fished one rod length off a baited area.

visual aspect is massively important and not to utilise this aspect is a big mistake. The way the carp's attention is firstly drawn to the bait is visually. Carp have been proven to have very good colour vision and a single hookbait, to be really effective must be obvious enough to capture the carp's attention. During the colder months from trees I have observed carp actually spot a bait and go down to investigate. No doubt a dark, less visual, bait would have gone unnoticed, especially when carp are not moving near the bottom of the lake, which is most of the time, unless they are actively engaged in feeding activity.

When I have tried fishing a highly visual single bait against a bland natural colour – brown for example – where both baits have had identical additives included in their make-up I have found the visual version blows away the darker version completely. In fact it became so obviously better it almost seemed like a waste of a rod using the dark-coloured bait but I find that to stay on top of the situation I must still do the comparisons to make sure the results are consistent. Reassuringly they always seem to be.

The case for the visual aspect is further endorsed by the important fact that the bright hi-viz singles catch virtually nothing at night. I know it sounds unlikely but I can count on two hands the number of carp on hi-viz singles in many years of trying them in the dark – unless they were fished over bait of some sort. In the light of this I would suggest that you make single attractor hookbaits a day-only tactic and fish over free offerings at night, or at least use stringers or PVA bags of some sort. The only time I will fish attractor baits at night is when I want them in position ready for the following morning's first light feeding spell and I don't want to risk spooking carp by recasting at such a productive time.

A lovely linear from Zyg Gregorek's Anglers Paradise Main Lake. I have found single attractor baits to be excellent on that water.

This tactic has paid off handsomely and many times I've been woken by a carp screaming off at first light on an overnight hi-viz single.

Interestingly enough the only way I can get the odd run in the dark on singles is by using day-glo white versions, which suggests that these can be seen more easily than other colours. I discovered why this might be when I watched a programme on TV called "Supersense" narrated by David Attenborough. The programme looked at aspects of various creatures' vision and, interestingly, they highlighted the fact, with proof, that cyprinids see in the infra-red spectrum.

If I'm not doing it I'm thinking or talking about it! Taking part in an experts' panel at Carp Show 2002. Mike Kavanagh is doing the talking here.

White is the colour that best reflects any light in the infra-red spectrum that is available via moonlight. With this in mind I made it my business to try white hookbaits in the dark, both in single fashion and fished over bait, and interestingly enough I caught on both. Through a great deal of use I know that using white does increase your chances of a pick-up at night. I do many talks around the country for the Carp Society and have mentioned this in my talks. The feedback from anglers who have listened to me and have tried white with good success leads me to believe I have definitely stumbled across something positive here.

The colour of single attract baits is a big subject. You should have no preconceived bias against any colour; in fact it's dangerous to have one. Colours don't necessarily have to be loud and bright to be visual, it simply depends on the situation. If you are fishing over a sandy or light gravel bottom a black, green or blue bait can be easily seen, and have the added bonus of under-use. On many waters as well as pitting your wits against the carp you are competing with other anglers, too. By offering the carp a bait a completely different colour to the norm you can swing the odds heavily in your favour. I can say for definite that the carp in your lake will not associate black,

Playing one in January whilst fishing singles at very long range.

green or blue baits with danger. I can say that with complete confidence knowing that those colours will probably rarely, if ever, have been used – or, if at all, only for a short time before these baits were given a proper chance to establish just how effective they can be.

Here's something important to think about! Any bait you choose to use fished as a single will be more likely to work well if the carp are accustomed to finding baits of that smell and colour introduced regularly. For example if you prebait sparingly with a certain colour and flavour of bait, like for example a Blue Cheese-flavoured blue-coloured bait, then it follows that when you actually fish with the hookbait it will be more likely to be readily accepted when a carp

This is one of five carp on my special attractor baits in three hours on a freezing February winter morning. The rods on bait remained quiet on that occasion.

encounters it. The best season I ever had on my local water, Redesmere, was when I fished with two of my mates as a team. We chose a bait that would be very different from other baits – so other anglers wouldn't duplicate it. My two friends liked fishing over decent quantities of bait, whereas I preferred fishing singles at range. During, or at the end of, each session I would put bait out, fishing on baited areas at night and fishing singles during the day. Between the three of us we were introducing considerable quantities of bait and because of this the singles fished at very long range were much more readily accepted. I had an absolute bonanza, much better, I think, than would have been the case on an unfamiliar, unprebaited, single hookbait attached to a rig.

I should clarify that in this instance

when I suggest prebaiting I mean scattering high-viz baits around over a fairly broad area with a throwing stick. Don't put them out as a tight bed of bait. From my experiences the carp don't seem too keen on a tightly baited area of bright baits, so I suggest you avoid this. Just get them used to finding single bright free offerings, that's the best tactic.

I should also make it clear that when you introduce high-viz freebies matched to the hookbait you should reduce the levels of attractors and flavours you use in the freebies by at least 50% to give the bait a more palatable taste. This is an important point. The hookbaits can be more potent because the carp don't get to eat those! You can get away with higher levels of attraction in the hookbaits to give extra pulling power. It's important that the bright colours of the hookbaits and freebies are a match in this method of fishing.

People often ask me what the best colour is for singles. This is an impossible question to answer. Preferences can vary from water to water, with the time of the year, and from season to season. What I can say with confidence is that white baits are the best in the

Redesmere – this is where my love affair with attractor baits started in 1982.

dark, or where they are rarely used, but fairly quickly go off the boil when overused. Green baits are a brilliant option for hookbaits; and, for that matter, if you make up your own bait try dyeing the free offerings green. This can give a well-used bait a whole new lease of life. It is a very different option and sets you apart from those anglers who use the same old brown bait year in year out.

Blue baits require a leap of faith by the angler to use them and give them a fair go. Rod Hutchinson has written that

Redesmere in winter, the setting for some of my earliest successes on single hookbaits.

blues show up better in deep water, and I know this is correct. When I first used white baits in the early 80s they were brilliant but as soon as their effectiveness slowed I changed to sky blue. This kick-started action all over again and was a real eye-opener – in fact much better than I had foreseen. To a human blue baits just don't look like food and that's what stops us from using them. Your main problem with blue baits will be finding a shop that stocks blue colouring!

For some strange reason red baits are particularly good on weedy waters. This has been confirmed by friends of mine who have used them to great effect, and their findings have mirrored my own.

I have to say that yellow baits have worked

everywhere I have ever tried them, particularly on waters where people are using hemp, corn and maize and the carp are used to finding small yellow items of food. On one such water I rolled 10mm-sized baits and flattened them to make almost perfect imitation maize/corn lookalikes, with the bonus of added attractors included. Simply outstanding results were experienced where plain old round baits were much slower, with less predictable results.

This leads me on to a point about attractor baits in general. Something as simple as changing the size and/or shape of the bait can bring quick results. Reducing the size of the baits to 8-12mm can be very worthwhile, and changing the shape to small barrels, squares or discs is a good move.

Orange-coloured baits can be one of the best options and these can work well on most waters. I always carry some baits made up in this colour and where three rods

This carp came as a result of roving tactics in winter. I cast singles fairly frequently and cover a lot of my swim until I either get a run or a liner to reveal the carp's holding/feeding area.

are allowed I have at least one rod fishing orange baits. This is a colour that anglers often overlook as a bit obvious but it is one of the best.

Much has been said about the pink baits I specialise in, and with good reason, because they are wonderful! I have to say that part of their initial success was down to the fact that for a long time I was one of the few people in the country with the correct dye to achieve that ridiculous day-glo pink colour that I make. When I first used it the carp had quite simply never seen anything like it before, so thought it was safe. Talk about visual! I've had anglers make some strange comments when they have seen me using that colour of bait, such as, "You've got to be having a laugh!" My Belgian mates said the same thing but soon changed their tune when they saw the results I had very quickly on their syndicate lake where bright baits had never been used before.

If your attractor baits give off a good food signal your results will be better. As with the Method mix Tuna oil is an especially good additive in warmer weather when using single baits. I leave my hookbaits soaking in the Tuna in Sunflower oil.

I like to fish single attractor baits over baits like these. Pellets, groundbait, hemp, and corn – preferably in the margins at night.

OK, I've covered the colour and shape aspect of high-visibility, high-attract single hookbaits, and I can't emphasise enough how important both aspects can be in arriving at a bait which will catch carp on a regular basis. Let's now move on to other aspects of the jigsaw of attract baits.

Most carp when given the choice will select food items that first of all look good, and then smell good, the final part of acceptance being taste. Therefore taste is the final

120

process before carp either consume or reject a food item. I am quite sure carp are able to monitor taste to a certain degree before a food item has entered their mouths. The more soluble a food item is the more pronounced this capability appears to be. The old assumption that taste is of little importance because a carp is not actually getting to eat the high-attract hookbait is a mistake.

There is a lot to be said for a carp angler keeping carp in an aquarium at home to do tank tests on. For many years I kept carp up to 5lb in weight in a huge tank at home. Some of the tests I used to conduct were fascinating, even though some may argue that those kind of tests can give a false picture due to carp in a tank not being under angling pressure. That is immaterial really. Preferences are preferences, simple as that. Some of those findings set me on the right track with additives that really do switch the carp into feeding mode. Some that spring to mind are as follows:

N-Butyric Acid   Carophyl

Nestles White Chocolate (ground down)
Chicken Oil (made and extracted from chicken meal and which is over-sprayed on Chum Mixers to induce feeding)
Turmeric   Milk B Enhancer

Liver Powder (Solgar Argentinean human grade from good health shops)

Worm Extract	Sea Salt
Iso Eugenol	Honey
Onion Oil	Brewers Yeast
Malt Extract	Betaine
Beta Carotene	Anchovy paste

Ambio and Minamino from Boots the Chemists
Coconut and desiccated coconut

Typical single attractor bait conditions.

Those are some of the items the carp showed a marked response to and which I used in various attractor baits as a result of those experiments. By testing you can soon identify and dispense with additives which don't attract, or even repel carp, which can save you plenty of wasted rod hours and valuable time.

I've made no reference to synthetic flavours in that list of attractors so I'll cover them separately. Once a carp has located your hookbait and decided to have a closer

Yet another big upper-thirty caught on a single.

look the food message given off by that bait will often be the deciding factor as to whether the carp picks it up or not. Flavourings certainly play their part in attracting carp. In recent years there has been a swing away from the use of synthetic flavours for use in carp baits. After all they have been heavily used for many years – abused even some might say. But they still work, and I know they always will, so despite my best efforts to find more natural effective attractors to give a good edge I have yet to find any that will hold their own against, or outfish, a bait that contains at least a percentage of the most effective synthetic flavouring in its make-up.

Certainly you can enhance the effectiveness of a bait by blending natural liquid and powdered additives into a flavoured bait, but most ingredients used in the make-up of a base mix for use in a visual bait are usually milk proteins, soya protein, whey powders etc. and they naturally taste and smell bland, hardly giving off any food message at all. So if you're the sort of angler that dislikes the use of synthetic flavourings think about this aspect. I have found from experimenting that an unflavoured, visual bait may very occasionally work, but not very well at all in my book.

One bait that certainly will work without artificial flavours added is a good fishmeal bait. I used to make up my own base mix and it was customised to use only the paler fishmeals in its make-up, such as cod meal, sardine meal, and white fishmeal. I omitted capelin and anchovy meals as these are dark in colour and make the resulting base mix too dark. Then I found that by adding a substantial amount of day-glo white dye to the mix the end result was that I had achieved a highly visual fishmeal hookbait. The bait worked superbly in its own right but with the additions of extras such as Squid Octopus Koi Rearer flavouring and Shellfish Sense Appeal, Halibut Oil and sea salt the highly visual attractor fishmeals were outstanding, and worked well in winter too.

This beauty fell to flattened 8mm minis shaped like maize and flavoured with Mainline's brilliant Milky Toffee flavour.

For many years I tried to isolate and pinpoint just what it was that could be the common denominator in the very best flavourings, and the only ingredient with a recurring theme seemed to be Iso Eugenol. This one item appeared to be included in the make-up of most of the best flavours. This was duly obtained and laboriously tested; and yes, it does work, but the dosages required were very small indeed or else carp were somehow put off. But used very sparingly it certainly did work. My results just went to show how easily a potentially good additive can have a fine dividing line between attractor or repellent. In the end I resigned myself to the simple fact that when a flavour keeps working that's good enough. "What more do you need to know?"

Then something cropped up that introduced a whole new ball game in identifying just what really did make some flavourings and additives more potent than others – pH. I had a strong feeling that the message given off by the liquid additives within the bait interacted more positively if they were different from the water's background pH. When I obtained a professional pH testing kit and tested all my flavours and key additives it really proved to be an eye-opener.

What became apparent was that the more instant additives and flavours were either of a high alkaline pH, or were of a very low acidic pH. I also noticed that most of the flavours and additives I could use at really high dosages without any adverse effect on the bait's effectiveness were of a high pH, usually of over 8.5 right up to nearly 11. On the other hand acidic flavours had to be used more sparingly if they were to remain effective. Some of the best flavours had a pH as low as 3.2. It struck me that there had to be a relationship between the pH levels and the optimum inclusion rates which I had ascertained through many years of trial and error.

For example you could easily ruin a single attractor bait and render it ineffective if you were to go blindly down the over-flavoured bright bait avenue and unknowingly used an acidic pH flavour as your choice and then went heavy on the dosage – for example using 5-10 mil per egg when ½-1½ mil might have been more appropriate.

On the other hand, with an alkaline flavour it would appear that you can go very high on inclusion rates, much more than you may ever realise, without overloading the bait. For instance I have used Solar's Squid & Octopus Koi Rearer flavour which has a pH of 10.2-10.8 at as much as 25 mils per egg in single

A selection of pop-ups and balanced bottom baits in different colours that I always carry with me when I go fishing.

hookbaits. The baits just keep working much better than if you were to use a more modest, apparently sensible amount such as 4 mils per egg.

My mate Lee Jackson waiting to net a carp hooked on one of my Pineapple Specials.

So what about flavours and attractors which have a neutral pH of 7? In my experience these tend not to be as instant but will catch carp. But they might be more suited to a balanced less obvious food bait where simply a label for that bait is all that's required. It may also be the case that this neutral pH additive could be much more palatable when consumed in quantity.

There can be very few single hookbait attractor combinations that are not improved by the addition of an essential oil. By their nature essential oils will remain in the bait and give a more prolonged source of attraction, long after an artificial flavour's has burned out and run its course. This could be an important factor depending on the type of water you are fishing, especially on the sort of venue where you might need to leave a hookbait out for long periods of time, for example on a big understocked water where it may take a considerable time for any carp present to encounter your hookbait. The same considerations apply to fishing big open waters overseas when storms can stop you going out in the boat to reposition baits for a period of days.

Some of the better essential oils I have personally had success with are Bergamot, Ylang Ylang, Garlic, Black Pepper, Nutmeg, Onion, Sassafras and Rod Hutchinson's RH1 oil. In my case these were all used not as the main attractor but merely to complement the main attractor used. I would suggest that you always err on the side of caution with essential oils because of their potent nature. Start with low dosages and see how they work out first. As a rough guideline try 4 drops to a one egg mix, but in the case of the more potent essentials like Onion Oil and Garlic you will need to work to lower dosages than that.

Pop-ups or not?

Whenever I talk about attractor baits, single hookbaits in particular, a lot of people automatically assume I am talking about pop-ups. It's almost a built-in foregone conclusion. In fact nothing could be further from the truth. I would say that I catch most of my carp on carefully prepared balanced bottom baits, or wafters. In other words baits which slowly sink the hook and rig and rest gently on, or close to, the bottom.

Pop-ups obviously catch their share of carp but it certainly pays to be versatile and ring the changes by experimenting and finding out which presentation the carp are most likely to fall for. I personally hate using pop-ups which are ridiculously buoyant and require one or two BB shot to sink them – or worse still swan shot, or shots. Just think of how inefficient and clumsy the rig is with all that bulky clutter on it. I can almost imagine those bulky shot catching on a carp's bottom lip and impeding a good hookhold. I go to great lengths to make sure my pop-ups only take one number 4 or 6 shot to sink them. This is achieved by adding a heavy-ish HNV mix to the pop-up mix to reduce its buoyancy and regulate it. By doing this in various quantities I can achieve virtually every conceivable variation between a standard pop-up and a bottom bait, like a slow sinker, a fairly quick sinker, a critically balanced very slow sinker and so on. I make up many one-egg mixes and make a note of percentages of ingredients used and label the finished bait accordingly. For a quick, cheap and speedy way of adding weight to off-the-shelf pop-up mixes, instead of using HNV ingredients you can simply add a good old 50/50 mix. Depending on how much you put in this will regulate buoyancy.

That's about it on high-visibility, high-attract hookbaits. In conclusion I must confess that I must be one of the big bait companies' worst nightmares. Over the years I have written about, promoted and encouraged anglers to try the bright attractor hookbait route. I have never suggested dropping food baits and changing completely. All I have suggested is that anglers don't overlook the single high-attract hookbait tactic as an option. I always travel well prepared with both food baits and attractor hookbaits so I cover all the options.

Having said that, I wish I had a pound for every time I have given a special hookbait to a fellow angler and seen them quickly rewarded, and opened their eyes to the effectiveness of hi-viz, high-attract hookbaits.

Another area of my carp life; filming at Orchid Lakes for one of the successful Gardner Bait and Rig videos. In shot from left: Chris Ball, Richard Gardner, Martin Bushell, Marsh Pratley and Len Gurd.

Rig Clinic

One of the most remarkable aspects of carp fishing during the last few years has been the sheer quantity and variety of ready-tied rigs that have been made available to carp anglers and – even more remarkably – are being purchased by carp anglers! I'm not sure what the real explanation for this explosion of ready-tied rigs is. Does it mean that rigs are a mystery to carp anglers? That, like me, they find tying them boring? Or that they have no confidence in tying their own terminal tackles?

Ready-tied rigs have their place. There will be some of you who will be physically incapable of tying rigs. Some of you will consider yourselves to be walking disaster areas and just don't trust yourselves to tie rigs. Some rigs are complex and it is perhaps worth forking out just to have them with you. But I think the majority of ready-tied rig users just don't have the confidence to design and tie a rig, and then have the necessary belief that it will hook a carp, and put it on the bank. This chapter is designed to give such people confidence, and explain rig tying and rig design.

Now I do not like tying rigs. It bores me. But I tie my own. Not because I don't trust a rig-tier to do the job right. As it happens I do. I've flirted with Carp 'R' Us ready-tieds and ready-weldeds, and I always carry a range of ready-welded fluorocarbon booms for possible use in my combi-rig and hinged set-ups. I am impressed. The ready-tied rigs available from Carp 'R' Us, Fox, Nash, Gardner and others are well thought out, tied up with excellent materials, and are impressively executed – but... I've got three reservations about ready-tied rigs:

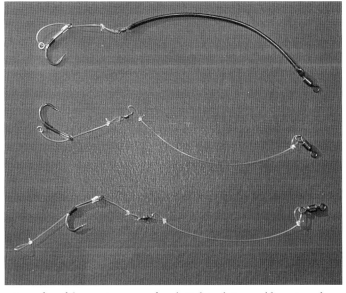

Just a few of the growing range of ready-tied rigs being used by carp anglers.

1) Ready-tieds are expensive compared to buying the raw materials. Of course they are. You are not only buying the raw materials, you have to pay a skilled and trusted rig-tier to tie your rigs for you. What happens during fishing when the hook point becomes slightly blunted? I'm ruthless about changing hooks. It's not just a question of possibly changing the hook after every fish. It can be necessary a lot more often than that. A hook point can catch on gravel, or a snag, or it can just lose its fine point for no apparent reason.
Have I always changed hook when I know I should do so? No. Sometimes the hook will 'touch up' with a sharpener. On the odd occasion I've thought, "It'll do," when I knew it wouldn't. And later I've reeled in and changed it. Now while a ready-tied rig is more convenient to use, it is also a lot more expensive. The thought of the cost can stop an angler changing the hook – and rig – when he knows he really should change. The cost of the hook should not be an issue when it comes to efficiency. With a ready-tied rig it can easily become one.

2) Most ready-tied rigs are too short. That's not a criticism of manufacturers. Most rigs are too short! Manufacturers are simply following the market trend in rig design. Many anglers have a problem visualising what happens when a carp picks up a bait. They have some concept that the hooking has to take place as the carp straightens up. Too short a hooklink means that the bait may not be sucked in far enough. If you suffer the odd loss you can't lengthen

the hooklink, which is the first measure I take if I lose a fish. My first priority with a rig is that the fish can suck the bait well in. Rightly or wrongly I feel that the further the bait goes in – particularly with an element of stiffness in the rig – the more difficulty the carp has in ejecting the bait and hook.

3) Most ready-tied rigs discourage versatility. A rig is a rig is a rig. OK, you can carry a variety of ready-tied rigs around with you, but unless you carry a range of materials, and know how to use them, you are stuck with other people's rig concepts and designs, people who have never been on the water you fish, or tried to catch the fish you are fishing for.

But my main concern about ready-tied rigs is the first point, the possible loss of effectiveness your fishing might suffer because of the cost element. On some sessions I've changed four or five rigs in a day – without hooking a carp! Bream and tench can blunt modern rigs. Hooking up on a branch or other snag can. I've heard Terry Hearn talk about a silty water where the hooks went blunt overnight of their own accord! I've experienced the same sort of thing but hesitated to mention it till I heard Terry refer to the syndrome.

How much do ready-tieds cost? I've seen some at £1.49 each. Others at £1.99 each. £1.99? Eight quid to change four rigs on four rods? A tenner to change rig five times? That's not quite a fair assessment. If you tie your own rigs you have to buy the raw materials anyway. I've worked out that on average they cost of the order of 60 pence per rig, at most, depending on the choice of hook. So you are probably paying a quid or so for someone to tie your rig up for you. How many rigs do you use in a year? Or how many rigs would you use in a year if cost didn't enter into the equation? Doesn't bear thinking about, does it? Save your hard-earned money for bait.

Learn to tie your own rigs so you can afford to fish efficiently with needle-sharp hooks all the time.

OK. Some of you will be wondering what all this business about changing hooks is about. Which leads us to the obvious question of how sharp a hook should be. I think Derek Ritchie refers to the necessary sharpness as "sticky sharp". Good description. Some hooks grab hold of you if you as much as touch them, and are difficult to shake off. At one time Kevin Nash had his hooks sharpened by a jeweller to achieve the necessary sharpness. Ouch. My main criterion is that the point has to hurt me if I test it against my skin. Really hurt, instantly.

I'll promise you this. A high percentage of you reading this spend a great deal of your carp fishing life fishing with hooks that simply aren't sharp enough. Carp don't readily hook themselves. If they sense a problem they try to get rid. Sticky sharp hooks make it difficult for them to achieve this. The sharper the point the better the chance of the hook penetrating beyond the point of no return – till the carp is on the bank, that is.

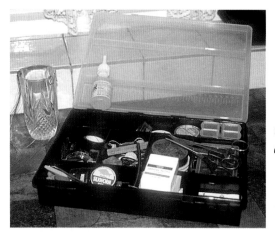

Rig-tying session in progress. When I'm using line aligner set-ups I tie rigs at home, but most of my rig-tying is done on the bank.

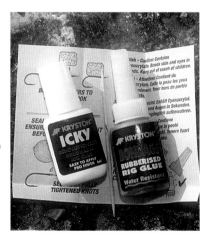

Rig-tying aids. Kryston's Icky (superglue) and Bondage. I'm a reliable knot-tier but I like the added confidence that using glue on my end tackles gives me.

Convinced? If the answer is "Yes", then read on. If it's "No" then get saving up... But either way change that hook or rig as soon as it loses its maximum effectiveness.

Rig-Tying

You need hooks, line, swivels, scissors, superglue, and forceps. Possibly silicone tubing. With some rigs you need rig rings, but we'll not complicate matters at this stage.

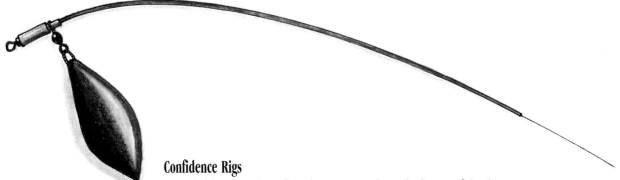

Confidence Rigs

So called because they allow the carp to pick up the bait confidently, move on to continue feeding, and hook themselves. All my fishing is done with tubing, and a semi-fixed running lead. I've demonstrated that bit. There are other arrangements. Many of you will prefer shop-designed helicopter rigs. It isn't difficult to find or design a set-up which enables you to present a hooklink on the end of your line. It's the terminal tackle part that seems to present problems. Let's look at set-ups from the reel-line swivel forwards, the sharp end of the rig business.

For a confidence rig you want a reliable, supple, tough mono, or a reliable, soft, tough braid. Decide how long your hooklink is going to be, and cut a length of line 6-8 inches over-length off the spool. You need an over-length piece of line to allow for the knots. You'll quickly learn from experience how long the starting point piece of line has to be to arrive at the desired length of hooklink.

The Knotless Knot

You have a length of line. First stage is to tie a loop on one end by means of an overhand knot. Do that, and then decide how long the hair is going to be. On most set-ups these days the hair is simply an extension of the hooklink, achieved by tying the knotless knot. Which we will now do. The beauty of the

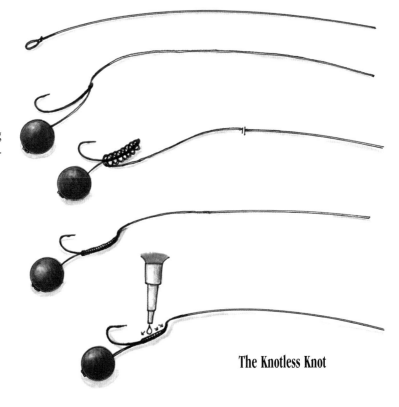

The Knotless Knot

knotless knot is that the starting position of the line against the hook, and the allowance for the hair, doesn't alter with the tying of the "knot".

You pass the untied end of the line upwards through the back of the eye, from back to front. Now trap the hair to achieve the correct length. If necessary actually mount a boilie on the hair to start with so you can accurately assess the required hair length. Leave at least half an inch between the top of the bait and the bottom of the hook knot, ideally slightly longer. The top of the boilie wants to be level with the bend of the hook, or below it.

Now with the long end that has been passed through the hook eye whip down the shank of the hook in tight, snugged-up coils for the required distance. A favourite length for this whipping is to take the turns down the shank to level with the point of the hook. Once you've done that trap the turns with your weak hand and pass the loose end of line back up through the eye of the hook – again from the back – then give the hooklink a sharp tug to bed in the coils.

I "varnish" the whippings of the knotless knot with superglue to fix the hair in the right position on the back of the shank, and also glue the hooklink where it leaves the eye of the hook. With braid my intention is to stiffen the hooklink for half an inch to create a line-aligner effect, and also to fix the position of the line coming out of the eye. No need to stiffen the line if you are using mono, but I still prefer to glue the exit point of the line in position as a safeguard against the line rubbing against the eye when you are playing a fish.

Many patterns of hook benefit from the addition of a silicone tubing or shrink tube line aligner. The line aligner improves the hooking power of the rig and reduces losses through hook pulls. Add the line aligner – if required – at this stage, by means of a small darning needle. Thread the line through the front of the tubing with the needle. In the case of silicone work the tubing over the eye and shank of the hook until the line exit point from the tubing is about a third of an inch above the eye of the

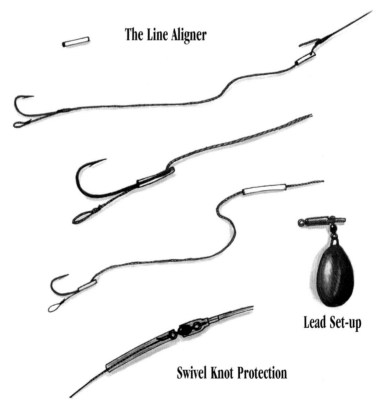

The Line Aligner

Lead Set-up

Swivel Knot Protection

hook, on the point side. With shrink tube, position the tubing in the same way, and then shrink it. When you are shrink-tubing prepare a number of hooks, then immerse them in boiling water to achieve the necessary shrinkage.

You now have a finished hooklink with the hook set-up on one end and a loose end at the other. I carry my pre-tied rigs like that, reusing empty hook and swivel packets time and again for storage. There's no need to tie a swivel on the loose end at the rig-tying stage. Carry the rigs loose-ended then tie them to the reel line swivel to the length required when you are fishing.

Many anglers protect the swivel knot with silicone tubing. I use a tail rubber. Either way slide the protector onto the hooklink before you tie it to the swivel, then work it over the swivel.

Don't make the mistake of tying

confidence rigs too short. 12-15" is a minimum. When the carp picks up a bait on this type of set-up it is feeling for a resistance. The further it moves before it feels the resistance the greater its growing confidence, and the greater the impact of the hook-point when it makes contact with the fish. This is the moment of no return, for the angler or the fish. If the hook does its job there's no return for the fish – till it's had its photo taken. If it manages to get rid of the hook and bait it won't return to your baits!

I carry enough pre-tied rigs to get me started on a session, then tie enough each day to keep me going through the day and night. On busy sessions I'll use ten or more rigs in a day, which would be a pretty expensive exercise at £2 a throw. A Raduta session could cost me of the order of £200 just for rigs!

Tying a supple hair

If you want a fine line hair rather than the hair as an extension of the hooklink, tie the knotless knot with a reduced number of turns, 6-8 is enough, and without a loop on the end. Tie the hair onto the shank with a whipping knot, then complete the gluing and line aligner set-up, as required.

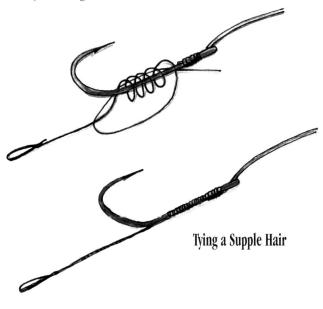

Tying a Stiff Link

There are special hooks with offset eyes for tying stiff rigs. I'm not sure how valid they are. To me they are in defiance of good hooking mechanics. I prefer to use a straight-eyed hook with the knotless knot for stiff rigs. The angle of the line through the front of the eye looks awkward, but it's a good hooker, and works along the lines of a line aligner set-up.

Tying a Supple Hair

I think there is a difference of opinion among stiff rig users regarding the most effective form of hair. Some prefer a supple hair to achieve a degree of natural movement of the bait at the inspection stage. Others simply use an extension of the hooklink to form the hair. If you are using small baits a stiff hair might not be ideal – because it may split the baits. In that case add a supple hair as for the set-up looked at above. If you choose to tie your baits on you want a rig ring on the end of the hooklink line prior to starting the knotless knot.

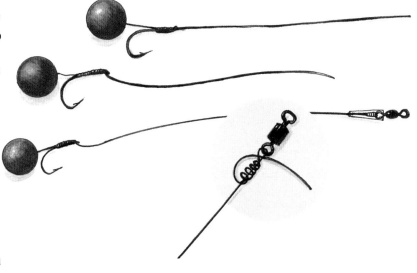

The stiff link was originally designed by Mike Kavanagh to be fished at around 4" in length. When you are using this length you need a hinge effect at the swivel end. Tie this by means of an overhand loop, and carefully tease the loop down to the required length. Pull this as tight as possible, then superglue it. The finished effect is a pivoting hinge at the swivel end.

If you are fishing a long stiff link then I don't see a need for the hinge. At best it is optional. With this set-up I fix the hooklink. Tie the whole thing up as for a mono confidence rig, but at 9-10" in length.

My favourite material for stiff links is black Amnesia. It's tough, stiff and user-friendly. There are various breaking strains; the best compromise between a material that is easy to work with, and one that does the job as a stiff rig, is in the 15lb breaking strain version. If you have trouble with knots for stiff materials try keeping them wet as you tie the knot, then suddenly pulling them tight. In a recent article Jim Gibbinson recommended Lip Salve for lubricating difficult materials when bedding down knots. I've been experimenting with it and it works well.

Pop-up Rigs

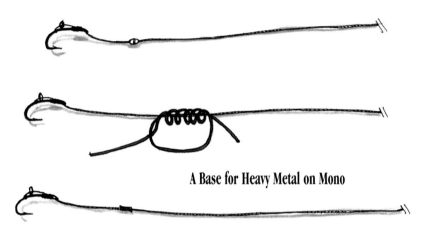

A Base for Heavy Metal on Mono

I wince when I see shot demonstrated on mono pop-up hooklinks. There must be a danger of shot damaging mono line. To create the necessary anchor weight start out by using a stop-knot or a rubber float stop. Thread the float stop onto the hooklink before you tie it to the swivel. Put a dab of superglue at the desired spot for the anchor weight, slide the rubber onto the glue, then mould Heavy Metal round the float rubber. Alternatively tie a stop-knot with thin power gum, then mould the heavy metal round that.

I think some of the current metal putties can be moulded directly onto the line, which is a bonus. All those I've used so far have needed some sort of base to hold them in position, as described here.

Mechanics

The essential element in tying a rig is to achieve good mechanics, and a reliable finish. I've described the basics here. If you want to tie more sophisticated rigs then study the rig books, or buy the rig you want to copy – then imitate it! Use sharp hooks. Use reliable, tough line. Tie your knots carefully, bed them down properly, then superglue them. In a recent article I read a leading writer boasting that he doesn't superglue his knots. Good for him, but is that really useful advice for aspiring anglers trying to imitate their role models? I superglue all my knots from the reel line swivel forwards. I never had a knot go on me before superglue arrived on the scene, but the glue gives me added confidence, so I use it. In fact I'd feel nervous casting out a rig not treated with superglue or rig glue now.

Does superglue damage line? Read my description of how I fish the snags at Raduta! Not in my experience, and I've been using it for some years now. I should add that I have little or no experience of supergluing mono (other than Amnesia), though.

When you are first tying rigs work to higher breaking strains than you may think necessary. I use 30lb Amnesia and 25lb Silkworm in my combi-rig set-ups. If a carp gets into a nasty spot then the hooklink is the part of your set-up most likely to come in contact with snags and sharp edges. Working with heavier materials means you have something in hand if your knots reduce the breaking strain of the material you are using, too. For instance I find the only satisfactory knot with 30lb Amnesia is the four-turn blood knot. I don't think this is a particularly strong knot, but working with 30lb line I've got about 50% of the strength of the material in hand! And I superglue it...

How do you...?

I get asked how I tie the rig I use for most of my fishing. There are two possible problem areas. One is in achieving a satisfactory finish with the 30lb Amnesia. The second is in tying the braid end length short enough.

I use a four-turn blood knot for the Amnesia. The problem is in tightening the knot, particularly at the rig ring end. I carry a drill which just fits through the rig ring, and fits comfortably through the spare eye of the swivel. Take the four turns then pass the line back through the loop. Drench the knot with spit, or smear it with Lip Salve, pass the drill through the swivel or rig ring, then pull suddenly and hard on the two ends of the Amnesia to bed the knot down. This one really needs supergluing.

I use the clinch knot for all my braided knots. To achieve a 1½-2" end tag you need to tie the hook set-up first. I have a supply tied up ready for quick changes when the hook point loses its potency. Pass

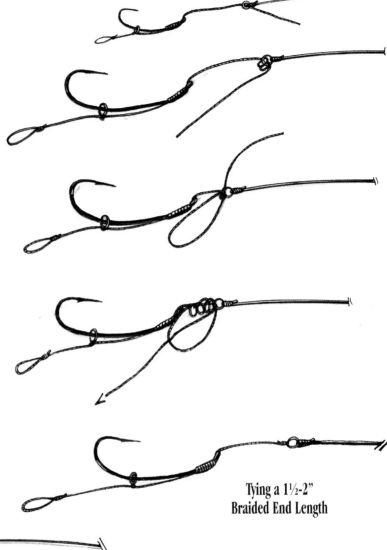

**Tying a 1½-2"
Braided End Length**

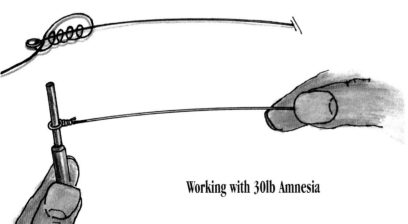

Working with 30lb Amnesia

the loose end through the rig ring twice, and ease down to about half an inch in length. Tie the clinch knot, dampen, then ease tight. Once it's tightened up I hook the hook onto the handle of the forceps and pull really tight to bed down thoroughly. Then I superglue...

Sliding Rig Rings and Silicone Tubing on the Hook

You incorporate a sliding rig ring or a silicone rubber sleeve at the start of the hook tying stage.

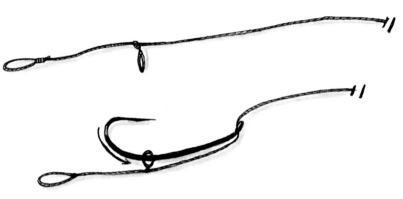

For the rig ring tie the loop for the hair, then tie the line to the ring with the hair at the required length. Bring the ring over the point of the hook, round the bend, then pass the free end of the line through the back of the eye as the start of the knotless knot procedure. Position the ring, then take six turns round the shank and pass the line back through the back of the eye of the hook. I use a 1½mm or 2mm rig ring and position it level with the point of the hook. The smaller ring is less likely to be repositioned inadvertently, but still blows back up the shank efficiently when required. If you fish barbed hooks 2mm rings will be the smallest size you can thread onto the shank.

When I use silicone tubing on the shank of the hook I thread it over the line, then thread the point of the hook upwards through the silicone. Slide the silicone round the bend of the hook to the required position, adjusting the length of the "hair" while you are doing so, then start the knotless knot procedure with the free end. If necessary put a small cut in the silicone to make it easier for it to blow back up the shank of the hook on an attempted ejection.

In both instances finish off the knotless knot and the hooklink set-up as described earlier.

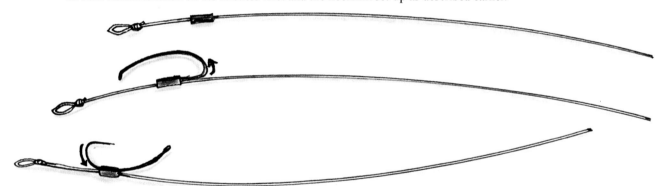

Conclusion

This isn't intended as a guide to rigs, it's a guide to starting to tie your own rigs. Reliable materials, sharp hooks and strong knots produce effective, reliable rigs.

Rig design? Well I've perhaps been a bit hard on ready-tied rigs at the beginning of the chapter. You can learn a lot from them. Some of the more sophisticated ones you can imitate. Those that are a real pain in the neck to tie you may have to buy and carry around with you. But do you really need to pay someone a quid to tie you a simple rig consisting of a hook on the end of a hooklink? Make the tying of simple rigs your starting point. As you gain confidence you can move onto imitating the excellent D-rigs, blow-back and extending rigs that are designed to trap very wary, very pressured fish.

If you start your carp fishing chasing pressured fish with sophisticated rigs you will leave yourself nowhere to go but back to real life!

Whatever set-up you use always fish with hooks that bring the tears to your eyes when you test them against your skin for sharpness.

Realities of Rigs

I've used the word "rig" in the chapter heading as a focus. In reality a rig is what you tie up, hold in your hand, and attach to the end of your line. Presentation is how you use your rig out in the lake.

Almost all material about rigs is written on a one-dimensional plane. Running or rotary? Braid or mono? Stiff rig or supple? Pop-up or bottom bait? Most magazine and book drawings of rigs are for illustrative purposes and may give a false impression of how a rig actually lies after it is cast out. You look at a drawing and see a lead, an extended hooklink, and a baited hook on the end. These drawings are to explain the make-up and mechanics of the rig. They don't always deal with the reality of how it presents the bait.

Some time back I was chairman of a forum on which Ray Dale-Smith of Carp 'R' Us was one of the panellists. The first question I put to the panel was: "What is your starting point for a rig on a water you haven't fished before?" Ray's immediate answer was: "First thing I need to do is discover the nature of the lake bed." Obvious, I suppose, but massively significant for all that. You need to assess the nature of the lake bed. It can influence the choice of lead, the length of the hooklink, the choice of bottom bait or pop-up, the design of the rig, and your actions immediately after casting.

One other very important influence to consider when we are looking at how the rig lies is the weight, or buoyancy, of the hookbait.

What we are looking at in this chapter are some of the aspects of rig make-up and the variations on a theme which can be achieved, accidentally or intentionally, when you cast out. Many anglers express anxiety about fishing over silt. Others are afraid of weed. So we'll start with the obvious point Ray-dale made and look at the nature of the bottom and the problems that can be encountered on different lake or river beds.

Nature of the Lake Bed

I fish a variety of waters and in the course of a season's fishing I find myself presenting a bait over, or in, silt, silkweed, weed, sand, clay and gravel. Sand and clay are a firm base so can be included with gravel. Weed is a law unto itself and needs separate consideration in the Snag and Weed Fishing chapter. So the three main categories of lake bed which are of prime concern in rig design and presentation are hard bottoms, silt and silkweed. All three are quite fishable. All three may hold the carp's natural food supplies. All three can throw up quite different problems of presentation.

On panels and in print rig guru Frank Warwick has made it clear that he will go to great lengths to discover exactly how his rig lies after he has cast it out. I've read other writers who have suggested they never give it a thought! I'm with Frank on this one. How the rig lies is an important aspect of its presentation. As an example let's look at the performance of one quite arbitrary choice of presentation, a stiff rig of about 9" fished in conjunction with a 3 or 4oz lead and a straight bottom bait hookbait. This is just an illustrative starting point to get you thinking so don't get impatient if this isn't how you fish – because for the most part it isn't how I fish, either!

Ray Dale-Smith of Carp 'R' Us talking up a rig storm at a carp show. "Start by discovering the nature of the lake bed." Sound advice.

The buoyancy of the bait makes a great deal of difference to the way the rig acts as it lands.

1) Gravel or other firm bed. No problem. You just cast out. Or do you? How does a 9" stiff hooklink with a straight bottom bait lie after it's been cast out onto a firm bottom? If the stiff link is tied with a loop at the swivel, as many are, then it can fall in any direction. The weight of the bait will depend on the size of the bait, but with an 18mm straight bottom bait the hooklink is unlikely to drop straight and flat, which I think is the ideal presentation with a stiff link. With the loading of a straight bottom bait of 18mm upwards (bigger bait or double bait) I feel this rig needs straightening out after the cast to achieve the most effective presentation.

With a lighter bottom bait, or a shorter hooklink, the link may well

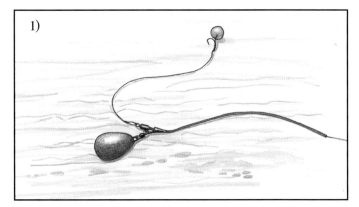

fall flat. With a buoyant bottom bait it will certainly do so, although it could still fall in any direction in a 360° arc. Knotting the stiff link at the lead swivel, and possibly reinforcing the knot with a tail rubber or a length of silicone tubing, will cause the stiff link to fall straight, away from the lead.

If I'm fishing a straight bottom bait over a hard bottom I simply straighten out the hooklink after the cast to achieve the presentation, or lie of the rig, I require.

You want a straightened-out hooklink but don't like pulling back? Then fish a lighter, or more buoyant, hookbait.

With material other than stiff links there is room for experimentation. Supple braids will fall in a heap, as will supple monos. The stiffer the material and the lighter the hookbait the straighter the hooklink will fall.

2) Silt or other soft bottom. A minefield. What is "soft"? How far does the lead penetrate the lake bed? It will vary from lake to lake, area to area, and even in spots within a few feet of each other. I'm quite sure that a bed the lead penetrates can give presentation problems with stiff rigs. If the lead has penetrated to no further than its own length then you have a super presentation. The lead will be hidden and the hooklink will be on the bed. Using a buoyant

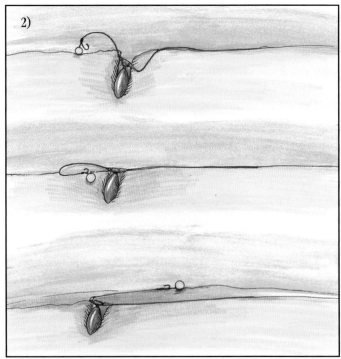

A panel of rig experts talking to a big audience at the Carp Show 2002. From left: Mike Kavanagh, Frank Warwick, Terry Hearn and Martin Clarke.

bait the link will slowly fall straight, and the carp is pulling against the weight of the lake bed when it pricks itself.

If the lead buries itself more than 2"-3" into the silt then you have a problem. You've shortened the hooklink, which will loop up from the hole in the silt. In this situation I don't know how far into the lake bed the lead has gone, how long the hooklink now is, or how clumsy the actual presentation is. I don't feel confident with this set-up.

A stiff link doesn't tangle, so when I'm penetrating silt I simply pull out to ensure that the rig is lying flat and straight. Some writers express nervousness about this tactic. I've done it countless times over the years without running into problems.

Fishing my stiff/braid comb-rig I have an added difficulty with very soft silt. If the lead penetrates too deep the rig pushes back on itself and there is a chance of the braided end-length tangling when I pull out. I pull out anyway. If the lead feels to have been in too deep I reel in and recast. If the lead comes out easily, then I know from experience the presentation will be OK and I leave it.

Silt rigs were, as their name suggests, designed to cope with silty bottoms. Helicopter and rotary rigs are not necessarily silt rigs. Most of the rotary rigs I see available in shops lock the hooklink at the lead. With a silt rig the hooklink can either travel on the cast to a stop on the line, or be temporarily* fixed at this stop on the cast. The stop may be as far as 2' up from the lead on this type of set-up. The lead penetrates the silt but the travel allows the hooklink to rest on top of the silt. I don't like presentations with the lead on the end of the line for both hookhold and safety reasons, but a silt rig can be the only really satisfactory way of presenting a very short hooklink on silt.

(*Temporarily in this context means that the hooklink pulls back down to the lead when you are playing a fish, and the link must be able to release from the line in the event of a breakage.)

12"-15" supple rigs of mono or braid are suitable for silt fishing. The line drops in coils on top of the lead and can be left as it lies. The only worry about fishing in silt is when the lead is known to be penetrating beyond its own length. Up to its own length is fine, but beyond its own length means that all the rig is not above ground and may not be lying as you intended. Chances are it looks nothing like the neat rig drawings we all know and love.

Many anglers seem to have a fear of braided hooklinks so I've covered their performance as a separate entity, shortly.

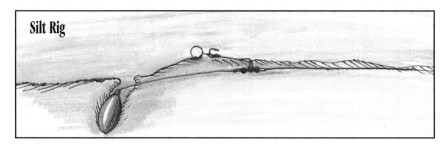

3) Silkweed bottom. I like fishing in silkweed but you've only got to look at silkweed growing in the edge of a lake to understand the presentation problems it presents. The beauty of silkweed is that it

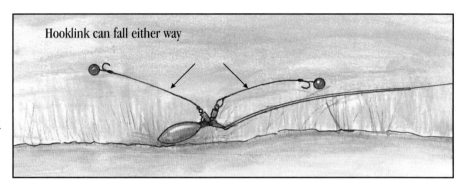

Hooklink can fall either way

can be full of carp food, so carp feed there. It is short enough to fish in, or on, but it is also patchy and irregular. Feeling the lead go down with a bump simply means that the lead has hit a firm patch. It doesn't necessarily mean that the hooklink has dropped flat on the bottom. Solar's Hookbait Foam allows you to mask the hook to ensure clear presentation, or even pull back if you really protect the bare hook.

If you want to guarantee a one-shot cast then use the Foam or, ideally, a PVA bag if range allows. You may have to redesign the hooklink to make allowance for the fact that it could be lying over weed. There are plenty of viable alternatives to stiff links and again, if there is a real problem here, the answer may well be longer hooklinks of supple mono, braid, or one of the coated hooklinks.

I don't like fishing a straight bottom bait in silkweed, but some successful anglers seem to have confidence in the presentation so don't be put off by my nervousness of what may be a perfectly successful arrangement. I'm uneasy about any situation where the penetration of the hook may be hampered by weed round the point, not because I feel the fish may have difficulty finding the bait.

Presentation and Hooklink Materials

Carp change with pressure. They become conditioned to sets of circumstances. One type of rig tends to work for a while because it is different to what's gone before. Then the carp recondition their thinking and build up a defence mechanism even to the most effective rig, and the angler has to think it out again. I don't know where your carp and carp waters are on the pressure-go-round. What are your carp conditioned to? No writer knows, unless he is fishing your lake. So you can either imitate the successful rigs of the other anglers on your waters, or think your presentation out for yourself.

Here are the common choices of hooklink materials. They all have their uses. I carry all of them with me when I'm fishing, and while I have a first choice of rig I'm always on the edge, waiting for signs that what I'm doing may need rethinking, and the presentation modifying or redesigning.

1. Supple mono hooklinks of up to about 12lb b.s.
2. Stiff mono or fluorocarbon hooklinks of 15 b.s. upwards.
3. Braided hooklinks.
4. Multistrand or multiple stranded hooklinks.
5. Coated multistrand or coated braided hooklinks.
6. Combinations of two or more of the above materials.
7. Secret hooklinks I don't know about! (Enlighten me...)

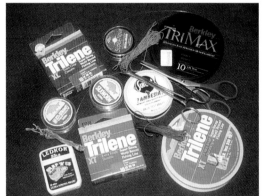

Match the hooklink to the situation, not to some carved-in-stone prejudice.

We've never had it so good in presentation terms. Five or six hooklink materials giving hundreds of possible rig and presentation permutations. What are they for? Where and when are they best used?

The starting point is the nature of the lake bed. You have a preferred rig, or a starting point set-up. Rationalise its use. How will it lie if I just let it drop? Am I in a situation where I can afford to straighten out? Rig fashions change rapidly. This is one area where a book can quickly be out of date, where it pays to keep abreast of the rig columns in the carp magazines and any new rig books that are published.

It is up to each angler to analyse his/her own angling situation. Assess it in terms of their usual rig, and ask themselves if changes are necessary. Silt and silkweed can be two of the most awkward mediums to fish over. And long, supple hooklinks can be the answer to this difficulty. Many anglers are nervous of braid, so we'll discuss it in some detail.

Braided Hooklinks

The simplest answer to some of the presentation problems we face is the much-maligned braided hooklink. We'll take a look at the advantages and disadvantages of this type of set-up, and the situations where they are likely to be at their most effective. Many of the comments that follow can be used with reference to supple mono hooklinks, which are favoured by many anglers. My main dislike with supple mono is that it often lacks the abrasion resistance and natural knot strength of braid, and I've seen big fish lost through mono hooklinks parting. But mono is getting stronger and more abrasion resistant for its diameter, which means it is likely to find increasing favour as a hooklink material in years ahead.

Dave Chilton of Kryston Products, hooklink supremo who knows what carp anglers need, and how to catch carp on the products. Dave's a terrific carp angler.

To suggest that all braids are similar is like suggesting that all boilies are the same. Back in the 70s and early 80s, before effective braids were generally available, we tried all sorts of alternatives to mono in an attempt to find a more effective hooklink material. Achieving softness and suppleness was the objective. Black Spider was the first braid I used. It was supple, black and about twice the thickness of the current braids. Braided lines have come a long way since then. What we have available now are braids designed and manufactured as carp hooklink materials. Supple, camouflaged, matt finish, natural. Undetectable? Many anglers swear by them. Others won't give them time of day. I've got colossal faith in them, in their place. I've used them extensively over the years and in certain situations they are still my first choice of hooklink material, including two of the problem areas we looked at earlier, thick silt and silkweed.

Let's look at the old wives' tale that braid tangles before discussing the advantages of the material. I've fished braid as a hooklink material on and off for twenty years and I'm fairly well acquainted with its drawbacks.

When you cast out a supple hooklink the hookbait drops on or slightly behind the lead. That's certainly true of braided hooklinks. They fall in a heap, with the coils above the lead. When you cast into silt the action of pulling the lead out of the silt into the coils of braid can cause a tangle. The hooklink wasn't tangled on the bottom, it was coiled and fishing effectively. You caused the tangle when you started to reel in.

If you don't believe that check it out for yourself. A cast-tangle is caused by the line wrapping round the tubing, lead core or reel line **behind** the lead. It can't wrap round the lead itself, which is what happens when you pull out of the silt. Most genuine cast-tangles occur as the lead drops through the water. The lead spins and the hooklink and reel line try to wrap round each other. Tangles of this type are easily identified on the retrieve. Tubing is the best anti-tangle material.

I know braid gives the appearance of being tangly but virtually all the braid tangles I've suffered in my fishing have been caused when I have picked the lead off the bottom for the retrieve. It is most likely to happen when the braid is at its lightest on the first couple of casts with a newly tied braided rig. I dip the hooklink into the water to soak a braid before casting, and when I'm casting into silt I'll have a couple of casts before leaving the end tackle in place. Tubing and dipping remove all chance of back-tangles with braids.

Because there can be a problem in straightening out a braided hooklink I use them in situations where I prefer to let the end tackle lie as cast. Unpredictable, patchy silkweed and deeply silted lake beds are ideal for braided presentations. You can let the lead and hooklink lie as cast in. With silkweed the braid will take up the contours of the weed. With silt it doesn't matter that the lead may be buried up to six inches in the silt. Over the years I've got into the habit of fishing braided hooklinks of 12"-15" over silt and silkweed. A lead six inches in the silt gives me a hooklink of 6"-9" with the full weight of the lake bed for the fish to pull against for self-hooking purposes.

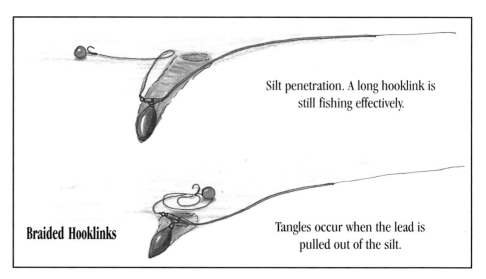

Silt penetration. A long hooklink is still fishing effectively.

Braided Hooklinks

Tangles occur when the lead is pulled out of the silt.

Even when I'm fishing stiff or combination rigs I often have a braided hooklink rod standing by in case I need to whack out a stringer at short notice. I have pulled back with stringer presentations but I'm happiest letting a stringer drop close to the lead and allowing the carp's investigation of the disturbance and greed to take over.

For most of my braided fishing I use Kryston's 25lb Silkworm. It is tough, reliable, and catches carp. That is simply a personal preference. There are now dozens of excellent, proven braids to choose from. With PVA bags and Method set-ups I shorten the braided hooklink to 6"-7". With these tactics you are trying to achieve on-the-spot preoccupation, which may reduce the chances of the fish moving off and hooking itself on a longer hooklink.

The Performance of Leads

When you are casting onto a difficult lake bed it goes without saying that the lighter the lead the fewer your presentation problems are likely to be. The lighter lead isn't going to penetrate silt or silkweed as deeply. But many anglers are casting distances that require a heavy casting weight, and many prefer a heavy lead to increase the efficiency of their semi-fixed lead as a hooking aid. So the remarks that follow are mainly with regard to leads of 3oz and upwards.

Types of leads

Here are the main categories of leads we will look at here.

1. Pendant leads, by which I mean leads that hang down from a swivel.

2. In-line leads, meaning a lead with a hole through the middle through which the line, lead core or tubing is threaded.

3. Specialised leads, which may be pendant or in-line leads. I've separated them from the main groups to make reference to them easier.

There are all sorts of considerations to take into account when you are choosing the lead for the job. I've got enough leads in the garage to refurbish a church roof...

Pendant leads

There are three main aspects to look at: the length, shape and weight distribution. All three influence the casting performance, the extent to which the lead penetrates the lake bed, and the efficiency of the lead in getting the best out of the rig. As I first cast a heavy lead into silt at Roman Lakes in the mid-70s, and have been doing so at a range of silty venues ever since, I think that what I have to say about lake-bed penetration is valid. But open to debate!

The longer the lead (within reason) the further it is going to cast. The dumpier the lead the greater the loading it puts on the rod tip – with a reduction in potential distance for most casters – but the more efficient it may be as a hooking set-up. I put it like that because different shapes of leads of the same weight feel as though they are different weights when you are casting with them. Round leads feel heavier and are difficult to cast. Elongated leads feel lighter and cast much easier. For long-range leads designers

Zipp-type pendant leads are my first choice for most of my fishing where casting is involved.

look to combine the best casting properties with the best hooking arrangement. So the lead needs to be a compromise between dumpy and long, which the four most popular shapes of distance leads pictured here incorporate into their dcsign.

It is only possible to assess lake-bed penetration in terms of the effort it takes to extract the lead! Round leads are a nightmare in silt. They cast about two-thirds of the distance of a long-range lead, and when I first cast one out at Birch Grove in the early 90s I couldn't pull it out of the silt from the bank and had to go out in the boat to do so.

Here's an anomaly. The longest lead in the centre of the picture also proved to be very difficult to extricate from silt. Greg Fletcher and I used this design in our quest for greater distances at Roman Lakes in the early 80s. We had to hand-line them out of the silt to retrieve them. Korda and MCF leads weren't around in those days, and at that time the best casting shape, most acceptable silt penetration and hooking-aid compromise was with Arlesey Bombs and Zipp Leads.

When you look at the different designs of lead you would expect the MCF lead (top right) to penetrate deepest into the silt. As it isn't difficult to pull out the problem associated with extrication may not be the depth of penetration but the way the silt folds back over the lead. The streamlined shape of the MCF and Zipp-type leads permits penetration and extraction while the weight distribution and shape of the dumpier leads and round leads makes it harder to retrieve them. Frank Warwick confirms that the silt closes in over a round lead, making it much harder to 'unplug'. When Frank did some tests on leads by casting them to the far margin, ball leads and dumpy leads always displaced silt, which seemed to close in, really trapping the lead much more than the streamlined and Zipp types. In addition the ball leads tend to really drag along the bottom on the retrieve with virtually no inherent lift at all.

The distance lead's plug-in is one problem underwater photography would not resolve because silt disturbance would make it impossible to take pictures in the silty environment.

In-Line Leads

There is a wide variety of in-line leads, just a few of which are illustrated below. There are many more available. I'm not a great user of in-lines but they can have their advantages, and there are certain situations where I will use

Round leads are not a good casting shape and are unsuitable for fishing in silt.

them. The problem with in-lines is that unless you are using Kevin Nash's Safety Leads it is difficult to come up with an entirely safe in-line set-up – i.e. a hooklink that the carp can pull clear of the lead should a breakage of the reel line occur.

In-lines don't cast as far as pendant leads, but because they are effectively 'attached' to the line front and back they don't penetrate silt or silkweed as deeply either. I like the hooking properties of the Essential Products' Comet Lead with its bulbous nose, and this lead is often my choice for PVA bag fishing where I'm casting with the lead in the bag.

I hesitate to say this but I find in-line leads tangly, which is one of the reasons I tend only to use them with PVA bags. Yes, you can cut down on tangles by using a tail rubber behind the lead, but then you are limiting yourself to the Nash Top-liner design. With most models the tail rubber reduces the chance of lead-release still further.

In-line leads seem to be extremely popular, and I'm not sure why. They don't cast great distances, you can't use a

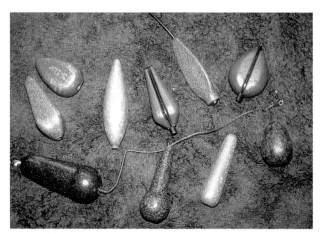

In-line leads. I have no idea why they are so popular – although I often use the Essential Products Comet Lead in PVA bag set-ups.

running rig with them, they can result in tangles behind the lead, they drop nose-down when I want them to drop flat, and with most designs it is almost impossible to come up with a really safe set-up.

The Kevin Nash Top-liners (middle and top right) are safe to use, they cast reasonably well, and the fact that they are in-line leads and flat means they may be ideal for overcoming some of the problems associated with fishing in silt and silkweed.

I've just studied the picture and the sight of the MCF Dumpy In-line lead (bottom right) has jogged my memory. These leads don't cast at all badly. I watched an angler use them at Fishabil many years ago. They cast a long way, and in terms of takes they were one of the best hookhold leads I've seen in action. They lose marks on the safety aspect though.

Specialist and Flat Pendant Leads

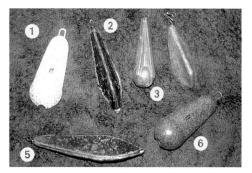

There are a number of designs here which overcome problems with silt, and help overcome lake-bed snags, although I'm not sure of the casting potential of some of them.

Leads 2 & 5 are different views of the same lead, the famous fluted leads much loved and used by Rod Hutchinson and others. These zigzag down through the water, reducing the angle of descent and softening the impact with the bottom. They sit on the silt and the difference in feel when you start to reel one in compared to an orthodox pendant lead of the same weight is remarkable. Their application is not just on silt and silkweed but for bottom snag situations where the lead can be lifted up cleanly off the bottom rather than dragged along the bottom and possibly into a snag. Richworth market a version of this lead which should be available from many of their stockists.

Specialised slow-sinking leads which drop more gently on silkweed and silt, and pick up off snaggy lake beds quicker than more orthodox shapes.

Leads 1 & 6 are the flat Big Fish Adventure leads which are available as pendants or in-lines, and incorporate a safety aspect. I'm told they cast well and descend through the water at a sloweddown rate, although I haven't experimented with them.

Lead 3 is from Birmingham Angling Centre, is a good casting shape, and gives a slowed-down descent, which again results in a minimum penetration of silt and silkweed.

I haven't used them but Gardner market a Tri-Lobe or Riser lead made by Anchor Leads. When you use the 4oz version of this lead

Riser leads from Gardner, a variation on the slow-drop, quick-lift theme.

you certainly don't have problems hooking carp. It performs well and although not very aerodynamic you can still whack it a long way. Its advantages certainly outweigh any disadvantages, or any slight loss of distance in casting.

While we are on specialist leads it's worth repeating that Korda make a brilliant flat lead in weights up to 5oz (also covered in the chapter on boats). I've got a shedful of these for rowing out baits on the overseas waters. Korda have recently added some circular, flat, pendant, dimpled 'Watch leads' called Big Grippas to their range in weights of 5, 6 and 8oz. These are ideal for long-range work in heavy weather on the overseas oceans. There are situations in which it can be very difficult to hold bottom and these latest specialist leads are designed to cope with such situations. These are invaluable for some of the swims at Raduta where you can find yourself fishing on slopes over a slippery clay lake bed.

I've used flat leads for a great deal of my fishing in recent years and my feeling is that they act like a fluted lead when you start to reel them in, and they lift off the bottom quicker than the casting designs.

5oz flat pendant leads from Korda (left), ideal tools for fishing in river currents, on sloping lake beds, and for rowing out baits.

Korda's Big Grippa leads (right). Available in weights up to 8oz. Ideal for holding bottom in difficult situations.

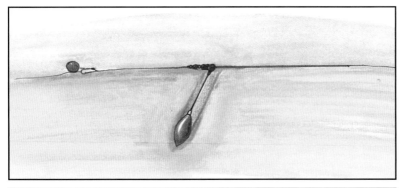

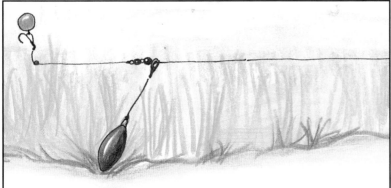

Whatever happened to lead links?

Specialist leads can soften the problem of fishing over silt and silkweed. But until the early 80s lead links were in popular use. I used long lead links on silty waters and shorter links on hard bottoms. When the bare hook rigs came in lead links became obsolete, because the full weight of the lead was needed to exaggerate the initial pricking effect of the hook.

Now lead links seem to have been forgotten, even in situations where

they would help solve presentation problems. How about a slow-sinking bait and a lead link over silkweed, for instance? Or over dead leaves, or thick silt.

Swan-Link Leger

I rarely, if ever, see this one illustrated these days, but it's an extremely useful set-up. You simply tie a piece of line to a swivel or leger bead and add swan shot to the required casting weight. This set-up was normally used with up to four swan shot but there is no reason why it shouldn't carry more, or have the weight increased by the addition of Heavy Metal. Don't pinch the shot on too tightly then they can pull off in the event of the link getting snagged or weeded while you are playing a fish.

Conclusion

I can draw few really firm conclusions in a chapter of this nature. There are so many variables that it's only possible to point out the possible problems and suggest practical solutions, rather than try to give definitive answers. Hopefully it will make readers give some thought to what happens to their rig when it disappears beneath the surface, and give some guidance on what it's possible to do about it. And although there are problems associated with the lake beds we've looked at so far, those problems are multiplied when we need to present a bait in a really weedy water, an area that is covered in the Snag and Weed Fishing chapter.

Anti-Eject – Sophisticated Rigs?

We need a starting point. What are sophisticated rigs? To my mind they are rigs that add a dimension to the simple concept that a carp picks up a bait, pricks itself, swims off in alarm, and hooks itself, or gets itself hooked. The added dimension is to achieve a situation in which a carp that picks up a hookbait has difficulty ejecting it. There are various ways of achieving that extra dimension, which we'll look at shortly, but as many of you will be thinking that you are fishing for carp which don't need sophisticated rigs, let's go back beyond the starting point of the discussion. Is there a need to complicate matters further than fishing a simple stiff, mono or braided hooklink with a hook on the end – or no need?

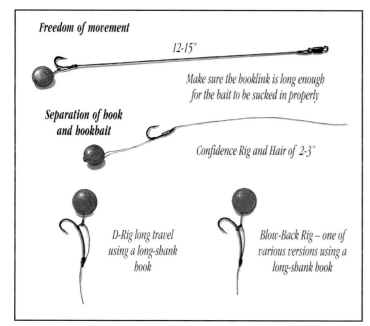

Freedom of movement

12-15"

Make sure the hooklink is long enough for the bait to be sucked in properly

Separation of hook and hookbait

Confidence Rig and Hair of 2-3"

D-Rig long travel using a long-shank hook

Blow-Back Rig – one of various versions using a long-shank hook

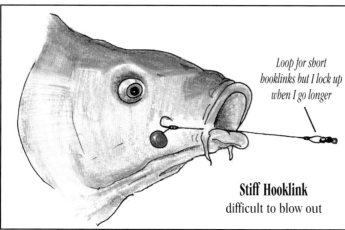

Loop for short hooklinks but I lock up when I go longer

Stiff Hooklink
difficult to blow out

Let's start by considering some rig and presentation principles which can reduce the chances of the carp ejecting the hookbait. You're not going to eliminate the possibility but there are measures you can take to increase the chances of converting a pick-up into a carp on the bank.

1) Ideally there must be some freedom of movement of the bait in the presentation to help it pass any pre-pick-up examination by a suspicious carp, and to ensure it can easily be sucked in when the carp decides to take it on.

2) The carp can only focus on the bait, therefore the further the bait is from the hook – or the more independently of the hook the hookbait acts – the more difficulty the carp has getting rid of the hook. Most successful anti-eject rigs are based on long hairs, or a degree of separation of the hook and hookbait at the attempted ejection stage.

3) The stiffness of the hooklink is an accepted anti-eject principle. My reservations about simple stiff rigs are that they minimise the natural movement of the hookbait, and they can be suspect hookers.

4) The more baits the hookbait consists of the more difficulty the carp may have in getting rid of the hookbaits and hook. Many anglers are nervous of experimenting with multiple hookbaits but carp will often have a go at these set-ups. In much of my fishing I use a snowman, or double hookbait, and

when I'm fishing small baits I fish up to four baits in a stack with great confidence. I feel that carp have a real problem ejecting stacks.

5) Effective pop-up set-ups may be more difficult to eject than bottom bait set-ups, particularly where a good degree of separation of hook and hookbait is achieved. The anchor weight itself may add an anti-eject dimension to pop-ups rigs.

6) The hinged effect introduced by Terry Hearn adds an anti-eject dimension to stiff rigs, introducing a surprise element of movement to these set-ups.

You can come up with variations on a theme but I feel those are the main principles in the thinking behind the design of anti-eject rigs.

Mouth like the Channel Tunnel, the feeding and rig-testing end of a very big carp.

We've got another problem to address when we are talking about sophisticated – or complicated – rigs. For many of you they will involve making changes. Changes are tough. If you find it difficult to make changes don't worry about it. Join the club. I agonise over changes, as I'm sure many other carpers do. Better the devil we know... We only make changes when we are desperate, or when we are fully convinced that we are missing out on something. When it comes to considering changes be objective. Assess your results. Consider the results of others. Don't dismiss the successes of others as being down to luck, or having more time than you, or resulting from bait sponsorship. Assess, analyse, and if you come to the conclusion that you could do better, then make changes.

When you are toying with the idea of a rethink bear this thought in mind. When Lenny Middleton first cast out the revolutionary hair rig on Darenth Big Lake he was agonising over his new brainchild and was far from convinced about its potential effectiveness. "If nothing happens in forty minutes I'll reel back in and change back to the old side-hooking set-up." Fortunately for us something did happen within the forty minutes. He caught a carp on the new set-up. But even when the hair became publicised as a new, super-effective carp-catching weapon many anglers had difficulty making themselves fish the hair, even though they **knew** how successful it was.

Sophisticated rigs? There will never be a bigger leap in moving from one dimension to another than the invention and early use of the hair.

I'll make it clear that there have been periods when I've doubted the need for sophistication, or the added dimension. By achieving long or short-term preoccupation I was able to keep catching my share of the carp. Perhaps I wasn't catching my share of the bigger carp, but I guessed that was down to being in the wrong swim, or that old enemy bad luck, or not having got the bait exactly right that season, or just not being there when the bigger fish were feeding. You know... The land of self-delusion we all live in when things aren't going quite right and we can't understand why.

Winter fishing started to change my mind about rigs. Carp aren't as active in winter, therefore I could rationalise that an added dimension to the terminal tackle could be a definite advantage. If the carp was just going to sit there sucking and blowing suspect hookbaits then perhaps I could improve my chances by making the sucking easier and the blowing more difficult. Either that or settle for catching very little during the months of cold-water conditions.

To start with I added a dimension by using very small baits and varying the number of baits in the hookbait trap – making the winter snack more appealing and more confusing – with the aid of PVA. Small baits, a degree of preoccupation, multiple stringer set-ups, then, later, stack rigs. They were all added dimensions that kept me half a step ahead of the carp and improved my winter results quite dramatically. Then, when I went to Orchid Lake a few winters back, I found myself in situations where I had to rethink the actual rig. I couldn't fish my favoured multiple stringer set-ups because of silkweed and range and had to give some thought to the anti-eject rig concept I'd last fished in the early to mid-80s!

The D-rig was the added dimension I used on Orchid, and with some success. The Orchid fish are pressured, and I was there during a winter when the fish didn't really get their heads down, but using the D-rig shook me out of my long-standing rig lethargy and made me rethink my year-round attitude to anti-eject set-ups. Had I been deluding myself?

The difficult area to come to terms with here is the question of just how easy is it for a carp to eject a hookbait? Thinking back I had watched carp with baits a few times, way back at the Mangrove and more recently at Birch Grove and Horseshoe. Conclusion? There are times when they are very cautious in their approach to any bait, even free offerings during the unpressured close season. The experiences of other anglers suggested that carp have little problem ejecting a suspicious bait. There was a letter in *Carpworld* 129 from Bob Gansbuehler of Essex who told us all that over the years he had watched carp toying with bait tied to a range of hooklink materials on numerous occasions. In his experience a carp always knew when it had picked up a wrong 'un – no matter how fine the hooklink material used – and wouldn't swim away until it had shaken the hookbait out of its mouth. Mmmm. No doubts in Bob's mind. It was very difficult to fool them. For him the rig answer was undoubtedly a set-up

Orchid pop-up set-up, the design of which owed a great deal to the thinking behind Terry Hearn's pop-up rig.

Terry Hearn. His big fish successes from the early 90s onwards made everyone stop and think.

they had difficulty getting rid of. Such a rig wouldn't be 100% successful, but it might give a better conversion rate of pick-ups to takes.

I'll throw a couple more thoughts into the debate. In the 90s Terry Hearn came along and made catching big target fish look comparatively easy. Not **easy**, but compared to what anyone else had achieved, or was achieving, Terry's results were quite outstanding. Terry made his rig public. It was very sophisticated; the hinged stiff pop-up rig. The non-believers among us put Terry's success down to witchcraft. That rig looked an awful lot of trouble to tie up!

Then we've had the hooklink revolution pioneered by the great Dave Chilton of Kryston. Each new wonder hooklink material from multi-strand through to the coated materials Snakeskin, Snake-Bite and Mantis have sold by the warehouseful! Publishers of rig books can't keep up with the demand. So the great carp fishing public does believe in very sophisticated hooklink materials, but they're not as convinced about rigs that need some thought and a degree of effort to tie up.

I'm not criticising anyone here. I'm describing my own reactions to the increasing sophistication of rigs during most of the 90s! No need. So why wasn't I catching more big fish? It couldn't be as simple as the concept that big fish have very big mouths and therefore find it much easier to eject suspicious hookbaits – could it? Later, rather than sooner, I decided there was great significance in Terry Hearn's rig and that it was time to climb on the anti-eject bandwagon.

Terry's rig was a starting point, but I'm not a fan of pop-ups, and I don't like what I consider to be the suspect hooking power of stiff rigs. On the other hand, stiffness as an anti-eject principle clearly has a lot going for it. I changed direction on rigs from confidence set-ups to anti-eject by designing a stiff to braid combi-rig based on a stiff boom and a braided end-length. I first used it at Fishabil during a difficult week when the

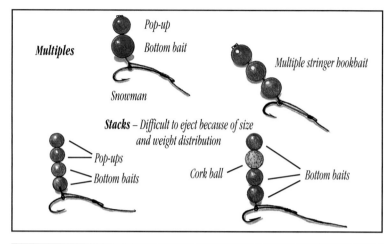

A popular version of Terry Hearn's successful pop-up rig which has accounted for a number of his big fish

fish weren't feeding (which they weren't because no one was catching). But I believed in the mechanics of that rig, stuck with it, and when the fish came on the feed on the final afternoon it proved effective. Six fish in a few hours including a brace of thirties at 38½lb and 33½lb.

The hinged stiff rig became the basis of most of my fishing. It proved effective and started to account for plenty of fish, including the odd bigger fish. The big Domaine de Boux fish which I caught in October 99 at 59lb 2oz and 58lb 14oz fell to the rig twice in two days. On one of the captures the Amnesia boom disappeared into the great carp's huge mouth, with the hook lodged 4-5" back in the middle of the roof of the mouth. The 43½lb fish I caught on the last morning at de Boux was hooked in just the same way. Yes, I can explain those captures as luck, or being in the right place at the right time, but the nature of the hooking of those fish suggested that they had encountered the hookbait, and just sucked and blown. They were confident they could get rid of suspicious baits, but had fallen foul of the rig. The rig had worked as I envisaged it would, which gave me a great deal of confidence in my own thinking on rig design. No need for sophisticated rigs at Fishabil, or Domaine de Boux, but perhaps there were times

An unusual view of Terry's rig. When we were taping material for his Carpworld *series I took this shot of his rods standing made-up in his carp room.*

when they helped...

I think this idea that the carp will take on a suspicious bait confident that they can get rid if they have a problem is important. The more confidence they have in the bait the more willing they are to take on a possibly suspicious bait. I don't think we ever really fool them. They are always aware of the presence of tackle. We can preoccupy them to the point that we achieve the sought-after momentary lapse in concentration. We can confuse them with PVA to the point

that they aren't really sure just where the point of danger lies. But the bottom line is that there are fish which are perfectly capable of avoiding every one-dimensional rig they encounter. And many of these are the very fish we most want to catch.

Two points about big fish. One is that they tend to be big eaters, so they have to become practised at avoiding end tackles or they would spend half their lives on the bank. The second point is that they have a mouth like the Channel Tunnel, which makes sucking in and ejecting baits much easier than if they had a small eating orifice.

The version of the hinged stiff rig I started fishing in the late 90s was very effective, although at some stage I became nervous of short-shank hooks for waters with very big fish in them. I started looking at longshank hooks – for two reasons. The first was that I felt longshank hooks may be better hookers than short-shanks for very big fish. The second is that when you are using a D-rig, or a rig ring sliding on the shank, a longshank hook allows a greater degree of movement and separation of the bait than a shorter-shanked hook. After using a variety of longshank hooks during 2000 I finally settled on the Carp 'R' Us Longshank Nailer, which I've used successfully in size 6 at Cassien and size 4 at Lake Raduta with an absolute minimum of hook pulls.

I now use a sliding ring on the shank of the hook when I'm fishing longshanks. There is an element of anti-eject in a sliding ring set-up, but only an element, and I think carpers get too tied up with moving and sliding bits. Separation of hook and bait by means of the D-rig, a sliding ring or a long hair are important anti-eject aids, but in their own right they don't necessarily constitute anti-eject rigs. The length of the hooklink, the hooklink material, the design of the hook and the nature of the hookbait(s) all contribute towards the success of a rig.

33lb 12oz and 31lb 8oz, two of ten thirties in ten days in June 2001 from the riggy Birch Grove, fishing anti-eject rigs and a mix of Trigga and Grange Red baits.

Designing an anti-eject rig

The more anti-eject principles you can successfully incorporate into one rig, the more questions you ask the carp when it has a go at your hookbait. I use this expression "has a go" because that is how I look on it. There is an evolutionary process at work here. Or perhaps I mean devolutionary. Anyone who goes back to the old paste bait moulded round the hook era knows that the carp became quite bold with their examination of hookbaits. Bleeps, twitches, half-way ups. They could suck and blow with impunity. What caused a take was never entirely clear!

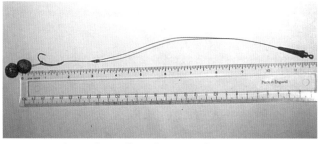

My bottom bait stiff/supple version of Terry's concept.

Immediately prior to the development of the side-hooking and hair set-ups twitcher hitting was given increasing prominence. Then the new age of run-inducing rigs dawned and twitcher hitting mercifully faded into history: the practice was not good for your nerves or your health. Side-hooking took advantage of the carp's willingness to suck and blow – to have a go. Removing the bait from the hook to the end of fine line hair moved the goalposts quite dramatically. The carp could no longer suck and blow with impunity. For some months it became a question of every suck (or blow) a coconut! You could argue that it would be fair to substitute "years" for "months" in that last sentence but my recollection is that carp quickly realised there was something seriously wrong and on most waters the initial mind-blowing level of success was soon moderated. Carp fishing has always been easier since the dawning of the hair, but never as easy as the initial moving of the goalposts made it.

It's worth reflecting on the original concept of the hair as its inventor Lenny Middleton fished it. His hooklinks were confidence rigs of 15" and more. The bait was 2-3" off the hook. He fished the hooklink straightened out. His rig was more than a bare hook rig. It was an anti-eject set-up, and a set-up that is still favoured by many anglers.

But the main principle latched onto by the carp scene generally was the bare hook concept. And for long

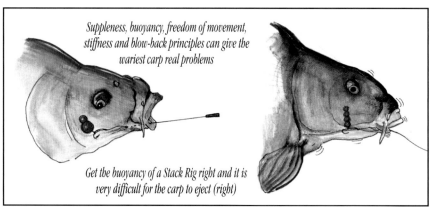

Suppleness, buoyancy, freedom of movement, stiffness and blow-back principles can give the wariest carp real problems

Get the buoyancy of a Stack Rig right and it is very difficult for the carp to eject (right)

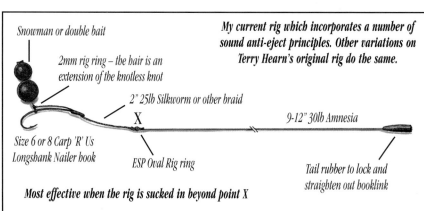

Snowman or double bait

2mm rig ring – the hair is an extension of the knotless knot

My current rig which incorporates a number of sound anti-eject principles. Other variations on Terry Hearn's original rig do the same.

2" 25lb Silkworm or other braid

X

Size 6 or 8 Carp 'R' Us Longshank Nailer hook

ESP Oval Rig ring

9-12" 30lb Amnesia

Tail rubber to lock and straighten out hooklink

Most effective when the rig is sucked in beyond point X

148

enough it has done the job. But the idea of taking the bait closer to the hook and making the hooklink shorter has made ejection easier. The arrival of the bare hook rigs meant that the carp had to avoid the hookbait altogether, become more adept at sucking and blowing successfully, or learn to get rid of the hook when they were pricked – which some are more adept at doing than others.

In other words 20 years on from the hair achieving general usage the carp are reverting to the 70s syndrome. They are willing to take on a suspect hookbait because they know they can test it by sucking and blowing. Anti-eject moves the goalposts again, with the long fine hair still being used in its original role. The D-rig dates back to the early 80s when Roger Smith invented it at Savay as a follow-up to the hair. Mike Kavanagh's invention, the stiff rig, dates back to the early 90s. The blow-back rig the early 90s. The multiple hookbait set-up is also a Savay invention and was first used (or publicised) by Albert Romp. Albert figured that where stringers were in common use carp would be accustomed to sucking in groups of baits, and he was proved right.

Why were all these concepts brought into use if there is no need for sophisticated rigs? Because some carp are less catchable than others.

Some anti-eject rigs are simpler to tie than others. The long, fine hair with the moveable anchor point on the bend of the hook to increase the effectiveness of the blow-back element has been publicised by Kevin Nash, Chris Haswell and Jim Gibbinson, among others.

If you don't like tying up complicated rigs try this simple concept, fished on a longish supple braid or mono hooklink. Fished as shown here this is a difficult one for the carp to eject once they've sucked it in. The set-up accounted for a string of good fish from Birch in the winter of 98/99.

The hinged stiff rigs are usually shown as incorporating a D-rig or sliding ring on the shank of the hook and feature four anti-eject elements – some movement of the bait, stiffness of hooklink, the hinged effect, and the separation of hook and bait.

The D-rig is popularly used in conjunction with a variety of hooklinks, including mono links, stiff links, hinged stiff links, and stiff/braid combi rigs. Again you can incorporate three or four anti-eject elements into these set-ups.

My current rig is based on a stiff/braid combi-link. The 1½"-2" braided end piece and ½-1" hair hinge allow for some natural movement. The stiffness of the 30lb Amnesia boom discourages ejection. The blow-back effect of the rig ring on the shank allows for a degree of separation. As a rule I fish this set-up with a snowman or double bottom bait hookbait, firstly to increase the problems of ejection,

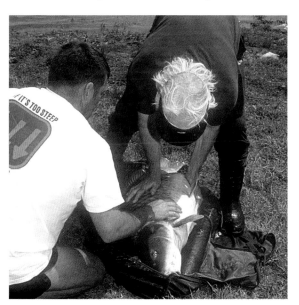

The big common from Raduta. This great fish was hooked in the top right-hand side of its mouth, suggesting that it was sucking and blowing to test the bait when it fell foul of the rig.

and secondly to give more impact to the hook point when the carp blows the baits back along the shank. As a rule this happens when the carp has pricked itself: I feel a heavier hookbait set-up acts as a better "hammer" to aid penetration and reduce the chances of the hook being shaken out by a cute carp.

Practicalities

Each to their own. It's a question of how much trouble you want to go to. A friend of mine, Choppy Walton, from Barnsley, uses the somewhat vulgar expression "Can't be arsed..." for people who can't be bothered. I think we're all a bit like that about certain aspects of carp fishing. I can't always bring myself to change swims when I know I should do so. It's the same with rigs. A great many of you will be half-convinced that your rig could be made more effective but can't be bothered to take the extra trouble that may be involved. Others are just nervous of change.

Sometimes the only way to make changes is gradually to convince yourself that they may be necessary, then keep nagging at yourself and rethinking the principles involved until you actually do something about it. I've been there and done that, too. And oddly enough it's rig changes that I have most difficulty talking myself into. Don't fret if you can't bring yourself to change things overnight. Just keep revisiting possible changes in your mind until you are finally convinced that it is the way ahead. Then do it. You may not get it right first time. Find a starting point, then rethink it and modify it as you go along.

Recent experiences have convinced me that the big fish are big eaters and avoid regular capture through their instinctive or learned ability to avoid getting hooked. In other words the fish we most want to catch only become catchable if the bait, the baiting situation and the rig are right, and for most of us it is the rig that is the missing link.

One final point on this subject. Many years ago Rod Hutchinson made the point that carp don't have hands. They can push baits around, and waft them about, but they don't really seem to know if there is a problem or not until they have taken the bait into their

Domaine de Boux 43½lb mirror. The stiff boom of my combi-rig actually disappeared into the carp's mouth when I landed it. One of the most important elements of an anti-eject rig is that the carp can suck it well into its mouth. Many rigs fail through being too short.

mouth. The further it goes in the less chance they have of getting rid. The starting point for any anti-eject rig is that it is long enough for the carp to be able to suck it well in. Don't come up with the ultimate anti-eject rig, and have it fail because it's too short for the carp to take it well into its mouth!

Finding Fish, Features and Feeding Spots

I once asked Rod Hutchinson how much time an angler should spend exploring a swim to try and get a clear picture of the underwater terrain. His answer was simple. "You can't know too much about what's underwater in front of you." His reply was a relief, because that's exactly how I feel about building a picture of the unseen environment beneath the surface. The featureless level playing field of the surface of a lake hides a mysterious world. Learning to "read" the lake or river bed and its features can help you with location, patrol routes and feeding spots.

In a separate chapter Terry Hearn talks about observing the lake bed when you are able to use a boat. I deal with using a feature finder in a separate part of the book. Here I'm going to look at finding out about your swim from the bank by means of a marker float, and a fishing rod.

Marker floats. I've seen the odd comment assessing them as "carp scarers" in recent years. They can be. But they are also an indispensable angling aid. The only time I don't carry a marker float rod is when I know I can go out in a boat and use a feature finder. Even then I will often use a marker float to explore the close-in territory when the baits are in position and I'm waiting for the next possible feeding time to come round.

What I will emphasise is that when you find it necessary to find out something about a swim you are not familiar with the

Rod Hutchinson – "You can't know enough about what lies under the water in front of you."

timing of any possible swim disturbance through exploratory casting is all-important.

I regularly fish 48-hour matches. Carp matches are one of the most pressured situations in carp fishing. Round the venue are too many highly successful carp anglers. To win you and your partner need to catch more carp than anyone else. Likelihood is that you are in a swim you know nothing about. You need to find out as much about it as possible, and spook the carp as little as possible. Carp matches invariably start around midday. An early-to-late afternoon feeding time is a distinct possibility. This means you need to limit the initial swim exploration to the absolute essentials. It's surprising how much you can find

Fishing the British Championships final at the weedy Horseshoe Lake with Simon Crow. In a 48-hour match you need to know as much about the swim as possible, in the shortest possible time, without risking spooking the fish.

Fish movement pin-pointed the position of the carp here. Partner Steve Briggs in action in the European Championships at Fishabil in spring 2000, an event we used to warm up for the World Cup a couple of months later.

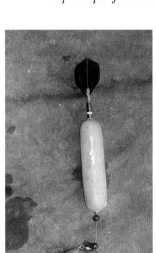

Marker floats. Carp scarers? They can be if they are abused, or used at the wrong time, but as far as I'm concerned they are invaluable angling aids.

out with a marker float in twenty minutes or half an hour.

When Briggsy and I fished the 2000 World Carp Cup at Fishabil we drew a favourable peg. Pre-match baiting and swim-exploration time allowance was 15 minutes! Because it was in a normally out-of-bounds area I knew very little about it, other than that there were underwater snags in front of us somewhere. I guessed 40 yards from observing carp in the area in the past. We had two casts with marker floats. One landed in the snags and we lost the end tackle. The second cast landed slightly shorter, and was short of the snags. That was the line Steve fished and we hardly lost a fish in what was potentially a fairly hazardous area. Neither of the pairs either side of us fished the short line for the first day and a half, incidentally!

What do I look on as the absolute essentials of feature finding? You need to locate and identify any hazardous or meaningful snags. If the water is weedy you've got to get a picture of the extent of the weedbeds and the location of the fishable areas. You need a rough picture of the depths, from as far out as you can cast back to the margins under your feet, and along the bank to the left and right. Roughly mapping weedbeds can involve more casts than you want to make. Checking the depths takes very few casts.

OK, I'm setting the picture, but I'm getting ahead of myself, too. I'm presuming you all understand how to set up a marker float rod, and how to use it. Some of you may not be familiar with the set-up. Others may not be getting the best from their marker rod. So let's begin at the beginning, with the essential marker floats and marker float rod.

On the way to winning the World Carp Cup 2000 with Stevie Briggs. Half a dozen casts with the marker float told us what we needed to know.

When all else fails you can only watch. Ritchie MacDonald weighing up form during a charity event at Yateley Tri-Lakes, about 1990.

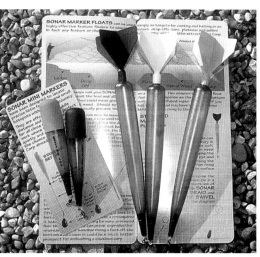

The ESP Sonar marker floats. A small one for discreet feature finding; a larger one for extreme range work.

Marker Floats

Unless you have specialised requirements most marker floats will cast out into the lake, and rise to the surface when required to do so. Some are tougher than others. Flights coming adrift and swivels pulling out of the bottom of the float are a real irritant. Problems like this make the carrying of spare marker floats absolutely essential.

Specialised marker floats are extra-buoyant versions for fishing in thick weed, super-aerodynamic ones for casting very long distances, and small, drab coloured ones to minimise any possible carp-spooking effect. (I'm not sure about that last point. When I'm using a marker float I'm most concerned about the line rising from the bottom to the float, rather than the splash or the float itself. When you're floater fishing carp occasionally try to eat controllers, which suggests that they have no great fear of such objects!)

The distance a marker float will cast is a definite limiting factor in terms of exploration of long-range swims from the bank – and visibility. The longest-casting float I have used is the ESP Sonar Dart. This casts huge distances, is extremely buoyant, and very visible at range. At the time of writing its breakage record is still a demerit, but the markers fly so much further than any other model I've used that there are situations in which the Sonar still has to be my first choice. (I don't know why but these models tend to break at the narrow neck. If you are a DIY or model-making buff it may pay you to strengthen this area of the float. They are the best, but not when they break!)

I'm not going to single out any others. I've

A range of marker floats of varying aerodynamics, castability and buoyancy. Always carry spare marker floats with you in case you find the swim you are assessing turns out to be snaggy.

153

included pictures of a range. It's worth getting hold of one of the major retail tackle and bait catalogues each year as a reference point, and to find out which models and makes of a range of items of tackle and bait the retailers are favouring. I look on the Tackle Box, Dartford catalogue as a brilliant guide when I want to make a choice from a range of items, but Leslies of Luton, Chapmans and other big retail shops produce very detailed catalogues which are well worth collecting. (Retail catalogues are often given away free with *Carpworld* monthly magazine.)

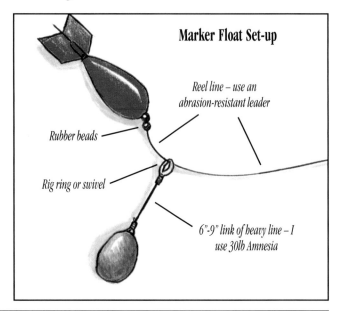

Marker Float Set-up

Reel line – use an abrasion-resistant leader

Rubber beads

Rig ring or swivel

6"-9" link of heavy line – I use 30lb Amnesia

Marker Float Rod

Some of you will fish puddles. Some of you will fish inland seas. When you are fishing very small waters any old rod will do as a marker float rod. On waters where there is a need to explore to distances of 100 yards and more by casting from the bank then the nature of the marker rod increases in significance.

You don't need to play fish on a marker rod. The action only matters to the extent that the rod is a casting tool. A marker rod required to cast a heavy, bulky load long distances must have a powerful action, and be built to stand abuse. Fully exploring a swim when you are not actually fishing can take repeated long-distance casting. 4 or 5 ounces of lead plus a highly visible marker float is not a subtle casting load. Use a rod that is up to the job. There are rods specially built for marker float work now. Get yourself one, or use a tough long-range rod of 3-3½lb test curve. Make sure you choose a rod you are comfortable casting with and which will do the job.

I use big reels for virtually all my fishing. For marker rods they aren't really essential, but I do like to use a reel with a baitrunner facility to make checking the depth

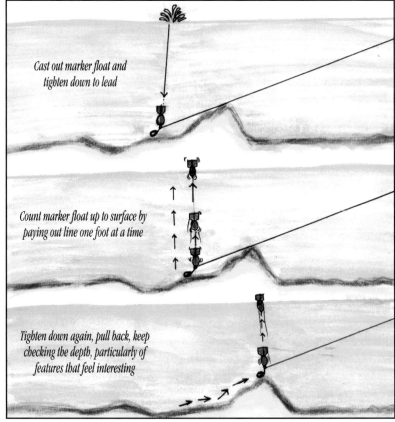

Cast out marker float and tighten down to lead

Count marker float up to surface by paying out line one foot at a time

Tighten down again, pull back, keep checking the depth, particularly of features that feel interesting

When positioning end tackles then reeling the marker float in, bear in mind the position of the marker rod to the fishing rod lines

easier. A good line clip on the spool which doesn't damage the line is also an important characteristic of the marker rod reel.

You need a strong, tough mono shock leader (mono to keep finger damage to a minimum and to make the float as free-running as possible), but the reel line only needs to be strong enough to enable you to retrieve the marker. In weedy waters you will need a stronger reel line than in open water. Braided line is becoming increasingly popular for feature finding. Your reel-loading should be designed with the nature of the fishing you are likely to encounter in mind. Short-range heavily weeded waters, heavier line. Long-range open-water fishing, lighter line. If you fish a range of waters then carry a light line and heavier line spools.

The drawing explains the marker float set-up. A heavy lead is tied to a strong lead link of 6"-9". A swivel or rig ring is tied to the other end of the link. The line is threaded through the swivel or ring, passed through two soft rubber beads, and is then tied to the marker float swivel. So the marker float is on the end of the line, with the swivel of the lead link resting on the marker float buffer beads prior to the cast.

Cast out to the required spot. Sink the line and tighten the float down to the lead link. Knock the baitrunner into free-spool mode. Pay off line one foot at a time until the marker float pops up on the surface. You've counted the depth in feet. In non-weedy waters you can reel in a few yards at a time and check the depth at various distances from the bank on the basis of a single cast. This very quickly gives you a feel for the shape and nature of the lake bed. Have you encountered any obstacles as you pulled the lead back along the bottom?

If I find a significant feature as I reel in and need to explore the area further I pay off some line, clip the line on the spool, reel in, recast to the clip, then re-explore the spot. Paying off some line and then clipping ensures that you recast beyond the area you want to explore. Recast. Re-investigate. Check the depths left and right and across the interesting spot.

You've found a spot to fish? Leave the marker float in position for a little longer and cast just beyond and slightly to one side of it with one of your unbaited end tackles. Drag slowly back to check for weed or snags. Feels good? Then clip that rod to the distance, or mark the reel line immediately with a fold of very sticky electrical tape. That's one rod taken care of. If you want two rods in the area then repeat the process with a second rod.

If that's your main spot then make a cast with the spod rod and clip that line to the distance, too. You've got two

This early February Orchid mirror of 35lb 8oz came as a result of a combination of feature finding, observation, and determination.

155

The silty Mangrove. To us the lake bed is about as heavily featured as the surface! But the fish know where the food sources are. Fish observation and accumulated experience are the keys to open-water success on waters of this type.

When you find a productive open-water spot mark the line with tape so you can recast accurately in the dark, or without repositioning the marker float.

fishing rods clipped and marked to the spot. I make my initial casts with baited rods using the marker float as a precise location aid. One rod long right. One short left. Or one on the marker, one well behind it. Mark both lines with tape.

A word of warning if you are not familiar with casting to marker floats. Most anglers point the marker rod tip well under water (I jam the tip against the bottom if the rod will reach) to keep the line from the rod to the marker as far out of the way as possible. But bear in mind that the marker line is there and position your end tackles accordingly. And bear in mind the position of the float and lead in relation to the already-positioned end tackles and lines when you come to reel the marker in. I describe the embarrassing and undignified pitfalls of marriages between fishing lines and markers in Paul Selman's book *Carp Tales 2*. I'll not repeat them here!

If necessary mark the marker rod with tape to pinpoint the spot, particularly if you are going to have to unclip to explore different areas to position another rod. Bring the marker float in as soon as possible – but before you bring it in make sure you have an exact bearing on a skyline feature which you will be able to identify for recasting in the daylight and in the dark.

Weedy Waters

Finding fishable spots in very weedy waters can be an absolute chore, particularly in matches and on short sessions where time is of the essence and the spooking factor most significant. Three of the waters that Simon Crow and I have fished in matches in this country are very weedy – Orchid Lake, Tyram Hall and Horseshoe Lake. You know you can only make a limited number of casts. You

"They'll be on the shallows in the sunshine at this time of year," said Rod when we were taping for Carpworld *one March. The following day I went to the Mangrove, followed his advice, and landed this 22lb common within quarter of an hour – from a spot I'd never even considered covering previously!*

Birch goes down to 18ft at its deepest. So where did this lovely 31½lb winter common come from? A known summer hot spot in four feet of water. Fortunately fish movement put me onto the spot and it produced another 30lb+ common three days later.

need to be sure your end tackle is fishing efficiently. I've fished swims at Horseshoe and Orchid where I just couldn't find a spot I was 100% happy with. Very often you have to settle for fishing over silkweed. On these types of waters you need to make the initial exploration with the marker rod, then make a number of casts with your fishing rod to check the nature of the bottom adjacent to the marker. The weed round the lead and on the hook are the tell-tales to determine if the nature of the bottom you are going to have to fish on or into is suitable. Learn to recognise silkweed. Fish love it, and some of it is absolutely crammed with natural food. Martin Clarke recommends using a pike treble to refine this part of the exploration, although I've never gone to those lengths. But who's to argue with Martin's results?!

Swim exploration on a weedy water can be tedious. On occasions you need to make far more casts than you want to just to satisfy yourself that you've found a fishable spot, let alone an ideal one. In two British Championship finals on Horseshoe I've had to settle for "good enough" for both my rods, when on a longer session I would have accepted temporarily spooking the fish, and spent far more time exploring the swim to come up with better spots.

The weediest waters I've fished for sessions have been Motorway, Horseshoe and Orchid. Swim exploration can be more leisurely and accurate. Make sketch maps of any swim you fish. Some Horseshoe regulars reel-clip the line to the clear(er) spots then pace them out on the bank. The Tackle Box sells a super device, the Shakespeare LCM-1, which

Wherever I'm fishing I'm reluctant to take my eyes off the water for a second. The fish can tell you more than any marker float, lead or feature finder.

you clip to the rod butt after casting out, pass the line through, and reel in. The device tells you the distance to the spot! Line up against a skyline marker, mark the distance and the nature of the spot on your swim chart, and you start to build up a picture for future reference.

Weedy water regulars set great store by identifying clear spots by means of "the donk". I pass on this advice from others because it isn't one of my more refined carp fishing accomplishments! When you cast out have your index finger hovering over the spool, as though you are going to pull the line down under the wind the moment it hits the water. In this instance you are trapping the line so you can feel the action of the lead. If you feel a clear, sharp "donk" as the lead hits bottom you

157

have hit a clear (enough) spot. If the lead lands with a muffled feel, or you don't feel it drop, then you have cast into weed.

The late publishing editor of *Coarse Angler* magazine, Colin Dyson, used to read the depth of water in front of him in this way, by counting down from the instant the lead hit the water to the instant it hit bottom. I think a foot per second was his formula, but I guess the weight of the lead is a determining factor with this method. It may be worth casting next to a marker float at a known depth and seeing if you can come up with a "count down" formula.

If you can become accomplished at counting-down, reading the "donk", reel-clipping and line-marking you may be able to dispense with the need for a marker float altogether!

Reading Silt

For many anglers silt causes the sort of paralysis of the mind I feel when faced with a manual of instructions for a camera or household appliance. Most of the waters I fished through my formative carp fishing years were silty. You couldn't escape the stuff, so you had to learn to understand it, and fish in it, or on it.

Carp observation can provide a lot of answers, including where they feed, how they feed, and what they feed on.

When you are faced with feature finding on an unknown water, particularly one which you look on as a strange and hostile environment, your starting point is to ask yourself this question: "Where do the fish feed?" Read Hilton, Hutchinson or Hearn and you understand that their minds revolve(d) around the four 'Fs': Finding Fish, Features and Feeding spots. On silty waters some areas are more productive than others. The most productive spots are natural food larders and margins. Margins are more identifiable than feeding spots! Ignore them at your peril.

Here's a salutary tale. We had the Mangrove netted for eels in 1990. Eel men use fyke-nets. The netting of the Mangrove was very successful, but the guy who did the netting commented that one area of the silt was full of methane gas, and the eels in the net at that spot had died. He gave a rough indication of the area. It was known to be a very unproductive one.

Watching carp isn't strictly feature finding, but in the case of finding feeding spots on silty waters it can be. To me a fish head and shouldering is a feeder. I fish spots carp mark in that way, not just on a single-cast basis, but for a session or two. I've found some very productive spots on the Mangrove by fishing head-and-shoulder spots.

Some silt pockets are deeper than others. In winter the deeper stuff seems to be most productive. If you are fishing over seeds and/or pellets deeper silt may be best because you are encouraging the carp to grub in the bottom, as with silkweed. For single hookbait or boilie-only fishing, where the stimulation from the bait may be needed to induce feeding, then firmer patches of silt may make more sense.

Natural food is a clear indicator of a potential feeding spot. We all get excited when we reel in a hook or lead with bloodworm on it. Martin Clarke's treble feature finder may be useful here. **But...** I think natural food is only high in the silt at certain times of the day or night, which may or may not be the carp's feeding times. So don't flog away at the wrong time and dismiss a spot as a non-larder – because you may be trying to read it at the wrong time.

Smelling the bait or the end tackle when you reel in may be an aid to finding the 'nicest' silt. If it smells repugnant then you may want to explore other spots in the immediate area. The quality and depth of silt seems to be very patchy, and natural food hot spots very localised.

Wind Direction and Depth

Wind is a feature. I'll not add to Terry Hearn's comments on wind. I learnt from them, as I'm sure many of you have. But any feature – including wind direction – has to be considered in terms of depth of

Silt featureless? A partially drained Domaine de Boux reveals one of the features that it is very difficult to identify, even with the aid of a feature finder. The disturbed area in the middle of the picture has been dug up by the carp in the course of their feeding. A natural hot spot if ever there was one.

water. Carp in all waters have their preferred depths, and at times they seem unwilling to move, irrespective of conditions.

One of my favourite stories about conditions as a means of feature finding came about from putting together the

Yateley Match Lake during a Stoney & Friends fund-raising weekend. Half an hour with the marker float at a non-feeding time told me enough to enable me to position three hookbaits effectively. Key here was a deeper area round the left-hand edge of the island on the right. The spot produced the famous Scaley at 35lb 8oz!

Rod Hutchinson Tapes for *Carpworld* some years back. We were coming out of winter. The sun was shining. "They'll be on the shallows in these conditions at this time of year," commented Rod, wistfully looking out of the window. It was early March, I was starting a session on the Mangrove next day and Rod's comment was large in my mind when I arrived. Sunshine and a mildish south-easterly. Not exactly my favourite Mangrove conditions because it meant going in Reed Warblers, many people's favourite Mangrove swim, but not mine – apart from a brief period during the very early days.

Rod said they would be on the shallows in those conditions. The pads weren't up, and I cast a PVA-bagged bait into a spot I had never covered before. The shallowest, sunniest, on-the-end of the windiest spot in the swim – in the margins of the bay round to my right. I had a middle-of-the-afternoon take (a Mangrove rarity) within quarter of an hour of casting out! Thanks Rod. But if the water had been ten feet deep would the spot have produced? Sun, wind and shallows can be a potent combination for much of the year – and among my favourite carp-catching conditions – but I was surprised to find the mixture producing as early as March.

Depth can be the determining factor. The favoured depths vary from water to water so I can't even give meaningful guidelines. In this country I'm happiest in depths of 5-8ft, but there are so many exceptions to that depth that I only treat it as a guideline when I've got nothing else to go on. I set little or no store by the idea of deeper water in winter. It may apply to some waters, but not the home waters I fish.

Mark the clear spots, and the features, and the depths on your chart. Take in Terry's advice about fish being high in the water in high pressure. Conversely they are going to be deep in the water in low pressure, and I think low-pressure periods are when silt-living natural food is at its most available to the carp.

Understanding

Feature finding and the location of feeding spots and patrol routes tends to be based on a build-up of experience, knowledge and understanding. That big, big word 'understanding'. Further back than I care to remember I read a comment by Jack Hilton to the effect that "the feeding hot spot may be no more than a foot square." My mind went into reverse at that point. That concept was way beyond me at the time. Now I find myself looking for that precise spot, be it through observation, studying the feature finder, or working the lake bed with a marker float and fishing rod.

I'll give an example of the process of narrowing down to a precise spot. When you work a featured area by means of a marker float, clipped-up rods and a skyline feature, treat the position of the marker float as the bull's-eye and keep casting to slightly different spots on the dartboard. Even within that tight little area of the lake the carp will have a spot, or spots, where they are more likely to pick up a hookbait. You gradually learn those spots from fishing your own water over a long period of time. Travelling to distant waters for seven-day sessions, or 48-hour matches, teaches you that there are times when you need to accumulate a lifetime's knowledge in anything from half an hour to a few days.

The famous Jack Hilton, a major influence in the early 70s. As a beginner I was blown away by Jack's comment: "The feeding spot may be no more than a foot square", but it makes a lot more sense to me now.

How successful you are in achieving that can make the difference between success and failure!

Spods and Rocket Science

I use small baits and groundbaits in a great deal of my carp fishing and find the use of a spod an absolute necessity on waters where the use of a boat is not permitted – which in this country means most waters. I carry a number of spods and at least one spod rod with me at all times.

I'll start by describing the spods in common use, because the type of spod you use can dictate the nature of the rod you need. There are numerous spods and rockets available now but they tend to fall into four categories. Until you are familiar with spods you may not understand why there is such a diversity in design, and may find yourself on the bank with a type that isn't suited to the use you have in mind.

Pocket Rockets

These are an excellent, comparatively recent innovation and have made spodding a comfortable exercise for anyone. At the time of writing Gardner and Fox make rockets of this type. They carry a light load, but are aerodynamic and in most conditions will cast a long way using a normal rod of 2¾-3lb test curve.

These spods are best suited to pellet, seed and particle loads. You can use them for boilies provided you top up with

I use small baits in a great deal of my home fishing and always carry a range of spods with me to suit the conditions. Here I was introducing bait downwind and the Pocket Rocket proved ideal.

liquid before casting, but are at their best with denser loads. With the right loading you will find that you can cast a Pocket Rocket as far as you can cast 3 or 4oz of lead.

Drawbacks with Pocket Rockets are that they underperform into the wind and in a big cross-wind, and they carry a modest load with each cast.

Big pluses are that when you cast with them clipped up at the reel you can minimise the splashdown, and you can use them successfully for casting floating baits, which release every time from this model, but not from most others.

The Gardner Pocket Rocket, the spod that brought spodding to the masses! No need for a specialised rod with this type of spod. The only spod I've used which will drop floating baits successfully.

Bait Rockets

I'm using this expression to describe a range of rockets similar in design to the Pocket Rocket, but of larger carrying capacity. Because they are of bigger size they carry a bigger load than the Pocket Rocket, which, in turn, means they are harder to cast, and require a stronger rod. A tough 12ft rod of around 3½-4lb test curve should be adequate for these rockets.

Bait rockets are very aerodynamic, and very versatile. They can be used for seeds, pellets, particles and boilies. If you find seeds and pellets are overloading the rod don't fill the spod to the top.

When using with boilies you need to top up the spod with liquid or water. I simply lower the spod into the edge of the lake prior to casting to achieve this. The liquid gives added weight and greater casting stability. There are versions with load-retaining caps which release on contact with the water. Casting with boilies you do tend to lose some of the load. Either use a capped spod, or top up with seed for the last inch or so.

With these rockets 100 yards-plus is a comfortable cast for big chuckers. 80-90 yards is more realistic for more modest casters. These rockets tend to penetrate deep into the water which increases swim disturbance. They can plug in the silt in shallow water.

I like the load these Rockets carry, and their casting weight. Most of my swim-building donkey work is done with rockets of this type. At the time of writing Gardner, Fox, MCF and Giant make excellent Bait Rockets.

The Gardner XL Rocket, one size up from the Pocket Rocket. Ideal for medium to long-range donkey work, and suitable for all types of feed.

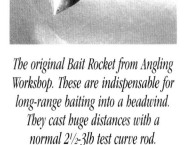

The original Bait Rocket from Angling Workshop. These are indispensable for long-range baiting into a headwind. They cast huge distances with a normal 2½-3lb test curve rod.

Particle Spods

The original spods were snub-nosed jobs drilled with holes to make reeling in easier. These are still available but have been largely superseded by rockets.

Spods are at a disadvantage over rockets on two fronts. You can't use them for casting boilies because they don't retain liquid, and they don't cast as far because they aren't as aerodynamic. They are useful for casting dense loads like seeds and particles up to about 80 yards (further if you are a bit of an animal).

A big plus is that they don't penetrate the water as far as rockets, which can be an advantage where swim disturbance is to be kept to a minimum. They require a rod of 3½-4lb test curve, perhaps even stronger for the bigger models.

Spods are available from most rocket makers and at the time of writing are still produced by one or two cottage industry manufacturers, most notably John Bryhn of Bankside Products.

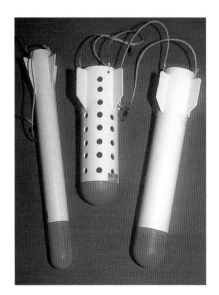

The MCF range of spods and rockets.

Boilie Rockets

For some reason these are largely ignored by spod users, but I wouldn't be without them, and always carry a couple of spares in the tackle bag. Boilie Rockets are the long narrow version of bait rockets. They cast prodigious distances very straight using a normal rod of around 3lb test. I can cast Boilie Rockets 20-30 yards further than any other rocket or spod.

The big advantage of boilie rockets is the distance and accuracy you can achieve with them into the wind. Although they are designed for boilies I use them for all my long-range spodding in very windy conditions. Most

Teamwork. Pip and Jemima in action during the 1999 Madine World Carp Classic. They won the Ladies' title the following year.

The Fox four rocket range comes complete with statistics of loadings and suitable rods.

carry 8 x 18/20mm boilies, or 12/13 x 14mm baits. If you are worried about bait spillage, underload by one boilie and top up with seed, or stop the top of the rocket with Solar Hook Foam.

At the time of writing Angling Workshop, MCF, Fox and Giant make boilie rockets.

Loadings

The Fox range of spods and rockets is worth additional mention because they include a payload rating for each model in their 5-language instruction packs and in their catalogue. This, in turn, gives some indication of the strength of the rod you will need for using the Fox models, and similar types from other

manufacturers. At the time of writing former British and European Carp Match Champion Andy Murray is part of the Fox set-up and I would guess that expert spodder Andy had some input into the design and rating of this range of spods. The reader can relate the payloads to the spods and rockets illustrated here.

Fox Rocketeer	with bait 175gm	bait and water 210gm*
Fox Bait Rocket	with bait 165gm	bait and water 200gm*
Fox Boilie Rocket	with bait 85gm	bait and water 130gm
Fox Stubby Spod	with bait 85gm	bait and water 115gm

* These ratings are for models filled to the top. If you struggle with that kind of payload then fill to third or three-quarter level when using denser payloads like seeds and pellets. With tiny pellets there is usually no need for additional liquid to achieve the necessary casting weight.

Spod Rods

I think carp anglers used to be discouraged from spodding because of the weight of the spods and the stiffness of the rods required to cast them! The ratings on the previous page give a clear indication that boilie rockets and Stubby Spods, or Pocket Rockets, can be cast with a normal rod of 3-3½lb rating. "Normal" refers to rating. Spod rods tend to get abused and you are safer shopping around for a purpose-built spod rod designed and built to withstand constant casting with very heavy loads.

For the heavier work there is a growing range of spod rods available. Fox make two models: the Excel Spod Rod with a rating of 5½lb and the Rocket Rod, rated at 4½lb. At the time of writing both these rods are priced at under £100!

Century have three spod rods, all adorned with a large-chested topless lady from which the range takes its name – Big Bertha. (Big girl!) Century rate their spod rods as DD for the 12oz casting weight model, C for 8oz and A for 6oz. *Carp!* contributor Frank Warwick is a Century consultant and has had considerable input into the Big Bertha range.

In action with the Bait Rocket during the 1998 Madine World Carp Classic.

Other popular rocket rods include two models of the Bruce Ashby Rocketeer (available through the Tackle Box, Dartford), the Free Spirit Launcher and Launcher Big Spod rods, and two models of Alan Young's Spodnik rods, designed by Alan (who makes most of my rods) and built on Harrison blanks.

Most specialist carp shops carry spod rods these days. The important thing is that you get a model that suits the rocket or spod you are most comfortable with. I'm a reasonable caster but I struggle with the higher-payload spods and the higher-rated spod rods needed to cast them. Don't dive in and equip yourself with a set-up you can't reach the marker float with!

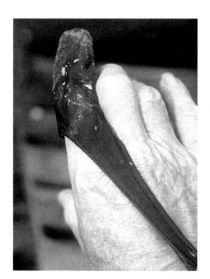

If you are likely to undertake prolonged spodding carry a supply of finger-stalls with you to minimise personal injury. This is the Hinders version.

Using Rockets and Spods

First requirement is a rod capable of casting your chosen rocket or spod. Second requirement is a strong, tough shock leader! A loaded spod can weigh 6oz or more. Don't attempt to cast that sort of load without a shock leader. I use 27lb Pro Gold for my leaders, but there are tapered versions, and any tough reliable line of adequate breaking strain will do the job. I prefer mono leaders for spod work. Quicksilver leaders are very tough but they do slow down the initial impetus of the cast, and make the use of a finger-stall mandatory.

Don't go too light on your reel line when using spods. I find some rockets cause excessive line twist, which is exaggerated with lighter lines. I find a reel line of about 10lb to be the minimum I can get away with without causing a build-up of line twist, and an eventual frap-up round the butt ring, followed by the inevitable crack-off. This phenomenon seems to be exaggerated when I'm using boilie rockets. Because of the lighter load the line isn't laid as tightly on the retrieve. It can be a chore but always remember to position the shock leader knot at the back of the spool when you reel in. This will help minimise disasters.

Don't be put off by this possible problem. I can go full sessions without a crack-off, but I always carry spare rockets with me – in case. The heavier the rocket or spod on the retrieve the less trouble there seems to be with line twist build-up and frap-ups.

When you are using boilies always remember to top up the rocket with liquid. A boilie load doesn't cast half the distance without the added weight and stability of the liquid load.

Many anglers are fazed by bait loss, particularly where boilies are being cast out. This aspect doesn't bother me at all. So there is some free bait dropping in an unfished area out there? Then the carp have got a free, unpressured meal. Much of my fishing is designed around the free meal concept anyway. I don't want them to be under pressure from end tackle every time they encounter my baits.

The bucket of spod is by the rods during the 2000 World Carp Cup at Fishabil. Steve and I used a clipped-up Pocket Rocket to reduce swim disturbance, and backed up our PVA bagging by introducing five spods of hemp and pellet every hour.

Paddy Webb refers to this spillage area as the drop line, and will often position a single hookbait there to take advantage of the scattering of bait. If you watch the spillage it always tends to be at around the same distance. Put a bait there, or thereabouts, and find out if the carp are feeding there.

Casting

You see different styles of casting with rockets and spods. Most of my casting is overhead, although I will move the rod to over my shoulder when I'm casting a heavy load. I tend to vary the drop from the rod tip to the spod depending on the type of spod or rocket I'm using. The lighter the spod, as with bait rockets, the longer the drop I will use. With a

Tiny seeds. Deadly for carp, but how do you introduce them at range if you don't use a spod?

Chopped baits. One of my favourite groundbaits, best mixed with seeds or pellet for spodding purposes.

Mixed hemp and chopped tigers, a proven big fish groundbait. Hinders mini-Betaine pellets work well with this mix.

heavier load a shorter drop seems to work better for me.

I always carry finger-stalls with me for spodding. Even a modest baiting-up where you are having to give the rod a big whack can start to cause injury to your casting finger. Hinders of Swindon sell casting stalls, and it's possible the type you can buy from chemists for protecting injuries may be suitable. Don't be without them. My casting finger used to finish up in an awful mess before I started using a stall.

Spooking Carp

Get to know your carp and what they will stand for. It is not my experience that carp are scared of spods. The more they want what comes out of the spod the less fear they have of them.

I've learnt some important lessons about spods through fishing around. Horseshoe anglers are great spodders. I was taking pictures towards the end of the first Carp Society Fish With the Stars event, and local Horseshoe star Kev Mildenhall and his partner were in the running for first place. I watched Kev land a fish, then looked on in horror as he picked up the spod rod and put a couple of spods of hemp out over the baited area. No! But the guy knew his fish, and they carried on feeding. They were hot for the hemp and were dashing around feeding on it, increasing the chances of one grabbing the hookbait in the induced feeding frenzy.

You file occurrences like that in the memory bank. A couple of months later I was fishing the Hull & District's Motorway Pond, a shallow, weedy water with spooky fish in it. Feeding time was around eight till ten in the morning. I did a bit of spodding into a hole in the weed at about six o'clock, cast a PVA bag into the spot, and waited. I knew there were fish around and expected action early in the feeding spell. The first take didn't come till nine, and I suffered a cut-off.

The Motorway Pond. Spooky carp, but curiosity led me to spod over their heads in a shallow, weedy swim, and I had a take within quarter of an hour! If in doubt, find out.

I'd got a problem. The fish had been feeding on the baits for an hour prior to the take. Had they cleaned me out? I remembered Kev Mildenhall's tactic at Horseshoe and decided I'd got nothing to lose by trying it. Five Pocket Rockets of pellets into the hole in the weed, casting clipped up to mark the distance and to minimise the splash and water penetration, PVA bag on the spot – and I had a take on that rod from a carp of 26lb within quarter of an hour of the recast!

When Steve Briggs and I won the 2000 World Carp Cup at Fishabil we weren't sure whether to spod the short line Steve was fishing or not. Steve was PVA bagging, and I was fishing over a scattering of spod and freebies further out. I was comfortable building up bait on the long line, but we didn't want to spook the short-range fish. In the end we settled for five casts of hemp and pellets with the Pocket Rocket every hour or so, and the tactic worked brilliantly. Steve picked up fish steadily on the bags from the short line over the first couple of days, while I was getting occasional fish from longer.

On the final day I experimented with putting a boilie rocket of boilies over the long line hookbait every now and then. It worked, and I kicked myself for not trying the tactic earlier. They were going down and picking up the contents of the rocket within minutes of them being cast out, revisiting the hookbait while they were doing so. A succession of fish from long during the final day put the icing on the cake.

Tactical Spodding

There will be times when you need to introduce a lot of bait, usually with a view to attracting fish into the swim, and/or holding them there when they do turn up. When you need to indulge in heavy baiting, work to a plan. There is a tendency to put out the marker float, and attempt to hit the marker with every cast. It's a valid tactic and it's worth fishing one rod, or maybe even two, over a tightly baited situation. When you are fishing to holes in the weed you may be forced into this tactic.

But as a rule when I'm heavy baiting I look on the tightly baited area as the centre of the dartboard. The bull's-eye. Then I work out from the bull's-eye to spread bait over as much of the swim as possible. A spread of bait will intercept and catch the attention of more carp. Not all the carp that come into the swim will be willing to feed in a heavily baited area. They may be more comfortable moving from one patch of spod-bait to another. If you are using PVA bags this spread of patches will be particularly effective. The PVA bag is just another patch of the bait for the carp to feed on.

The bull's-eye rod – or rods – may turn out to be the most productive, but giving yourself alternatives may turn up bonus fish, and at times it can turn out to be the more productive tactic of the two. When I'm partnering Crowy or Briggsy in matches we always fish alternative methods, one fishing tight, the other fishing spread. And we spread the spodded bait at different ranges to find out just where the fish are moving through the swim.

When you do feel the need to bait heavily do your main baiting away from feeding times. I fish waters all over Europe and almost invariably the quietest time in terms of likely feeding spells is late morning to early afternoon. That's when I do the bulk of my feature finding and spodding. If you are on a strange water try to find out when the feeding times are and plan your session and spodding accordingly.

Masters of bagging and spodding. Tim Fromant and Mike Winstone in action at Horseshoe Lake. Their win in the 2000 British Championships was one of the most outstanding carp fishing results of all time.

Baiting Levels

Inexperienced anglers, and those not accustomed to using a spod, tend to associate spodding with swim-building. Rationalise what you want to do when you have a spod with you. How many pouches of bait would you put out with the catapult? How many handfuls if you were out in the boat, or if you were baiting the margins? What will the carp in your water stand for? If in doubt I tend to settle for occasional spodding. I've got a baiting level in mind, and I try to maintain it. Little and often. I think carp are curious and investigate most splashes. I won't push my luck by constant spodding immediately prior to or during a feeding time, but I'm not averse to making the occasional cast right over the baited area to freshen

This Birch Grove 31½lb mirror fell for the tactic of introducing a spodful of bait over the hookbait. The spod rod was clipped to the required distance in advance, and the take came as I reloaded the spod for the second cast!

Landing a fish hooked over spod at Horseshoe during the 2001 Fish With the Stars event. The take came with just ten minutes of the match to go.

things up and perhaps persuade the carp to have a fresh dig around for bait.

If you're in doubt about using spods think about this. Not introducing bait with a spod is more likely to cost you fish than using one intelligently. Whatever happens don't be guided by "rules" and "don'ts" when the opposite might apply to your fish and your fishing. I break all sorts of rules in my fishing, often on the basis of just finding out, and I catch numerous bonus fish as a result.

Special fish. Horseshoe 26lb 12oz mirror, a venue personal best which won me a tenner off friend Ian Chillcott, and the section prize and biggest fish of the weekend award for my partner Roy. It was my first Horseshoe fish in five matches at the water – and my fifth lousy draw on the trot!

I've watched fish disturbed from bait introductions many times over the years at Birch Grove in the close season. On occasions I've chucked handfuls of boilies on top of feeding fish just to see what their reaction will be. They always disappear! Then, within ten minutes, they come creeping back, and within another five minutes they are feeding as though nothing has happened. I think of that syndrome when I am having to top up with a spod, or recast into a swim when I know the fish are present. Yes, I'm going to spook them, but it will be a very temporary state of affairs, and when they do return I've increased the level of food available to them, and, hopefully, the chances of them making a mistake with the hookbait.

A spod can be a tactical weapon as well as a swim-builder. Always have a range of models with you, and think long and hard about how you are going to use them to get the best from your swim. Don't ever worry about the splash they make. We get instant takes after casting out a heavy lead. I've had the indicator pulled out of my hand twice in one morning after casting out a loaded PVA bag. I've had a take from a big fish immediately after finishing an hour's spodding on the Mangrove. I've seen tactical casting with spodded hemp or pellets induce feeding activity and immediate action.

Spods mean food, and carp know it!

Orchid February 26lb common. I wasn't sure how much bait there was left in the swim so I freshened up with ten spods of Mainline's Grange Crumball, to top up the smell of food without adding to whatever bait might be left. The take came within minutes of putting the spod rod away.

Snag and Weed Fishing

I was fishing one of my favourite swims, Little Social on the Motorway Pond near Hull. Out front Little Social Bay was full of hornwort, Canadian pondweed and features. To my right was a line of pernicious snags. During the course of the day I hooked and landed a couple of carp, biggest 27lb. After the second fish the carp angler in the next peg walked down for a chat. He was fishing the swim along to my right and was clearly finding the water a bit of a struggle. In fact at that time I don't think he'd had a fish from the water. His opening gambit of a brief conversation was:

"I'm off next week. I think I'll come in here for a couple of sessions."

"Yeh, it's a good swim."

There was a pause as we both looked at the good swim.

"You'd think Hull and District would do something about all this weed, wouldn't you?"

I felt he was missing the point, somehow! Carp are where the weed is!

Little Social Bay on the Motorway Pond near Hull, a good training ground for coming to terms with carp in weed and near snags.

"Weed" is a bit all-embracing. I regularly fish in, on, or around five types of weed and I don't necessarily adopt the same approach for all of them. Canadian pondweed, hornwort, potamogeton, silkweed and lily pads. Simon Horton will undoubtedly have added some more in his chapter. I encounter those five weeds regularly in my fishing at home and overseas.

There are at least three lines of thought to look at when you are considering fishing in weed. Presentation starts with the rod, reel and indicator set-up. Then you've got to give a great deal of thought to how you are going to get your fish out after you've hooked it. And as a rule the end tackle has to be modified to make allowance for the fact that you are casting into weed, and to make playing the fish easier.

Bankside Set-up

You see some stupid fishing in weed and around snags. Carp anglers have this concept that carp run, therefore it is necessary to let them run. Even when the bait is on the edge of snags or heavy weed and the angler is tucked up in his sleeping bag and is going to take upwards of thirty seconds to get to the

Solar's Pozi-Boss set-up for getting as much tension as possible into the line. I was fishing across weed and a big wind here, a combination which makes drop-back indication very hit-and-miss.

169

rods? Make that upwards of a minute in some cases! Recipe for disaster, unless the carp obligingly swims away from danger. "I lost three..." seems to be some sort of badge of honour with carp anglers. "It was through the snags/weedbed when I picked up the rod!" Yeh.

In other words, "I fished like a plank", and didn't deserve a thing.

The starting point in the approach to difficult angling situations is the rod set-up, and what's on the reel. In snag and weed fishing my reels are simply shut down tight, fishing off a solid goalpost set-up, battened down rod-pod, or immovable single

Fishing rock-solid and locked up at Orchid Lake.

banksticks. Indicators are Solar's Quiver-loc tension arm indicators. The superb Pozi-Boss indicator set-up allows me to adjust the tension of the indicators to give more direct contact with the end tackle. When you're fishing a fraught situation you're in trouble straightaway if the first indication you get is the buzzer howling a one-noter at you. That's enjoyable – and welcome! – in open-water fishing, but not when the end tackle is in weed or near snags. Almost all my takes, even in open water, start with a couple of warning bleeps, which are as likely to be by way of slight drop-backs as the carp picks up the lead as tightenings of the line. I'm fishing tight to the end tackle and the carp has difficulty taking line. You need the heaviest lead you can get away with using this set-up so you don't move the end tackle as you tighten up.

I've fished with braided line at close quarters in weed and I'm a bit nervous of it close in. I've caught fish at long range using it, and to be honest I think it is a must for the sort of fishing I'm describing here. Mono is described as having around 25% stretch, which could just make the difference between a carp finding sanctuary and not with a rock-solid set-up. If your budget runs to braided reel lines they can increase the effectiveness of your snag and weed fishing. I used Rod Hutchinson's Sinking Sabrebraid on the Motorway, and it did the job impressively. I've recently spooled up with Shimano's Antares Special Dyneema braid for extreme-range fishing on overseas waters. If in doubt about braided lines ring Lee Jackson at the Tackle Box. Lee's given me confidence on a number of occasions when I've needed to make changes and wasn't sure about the product I intended to change to. Tackle Box sell a range of braided reel lines, as will many well-stocked specialist shops.

Braided main line, a big plus when you are fishing tight to snags or in weed and need immediate control of the fish.

Whether you use braid or mono be sure it is strong enough for the job – minimum 15lb breaking strain – abrasion resistant, and in good condition. Always check the line after you've landed a fish, particularly if there are zebra mussels or other sharp obstructions in the water.

I'll make one other point about braid over mono, and hopefully this is a situation you will never encounter. Two days running on the Motorway Pond I suffered cut lines after – or during – takes. I was using mono. On the first occasion I thought I had a line problem, and respooled the reels that night. The next day it happened again, with the new line. This was in sunny weather, the line was running through patchy weed to the end tackles, and there are pike in the water. After the second occurrence I came to the conclusion that the problem must have been pike striking at the shiny line as it moved through the water. So I respooled again, to braid, and had no further problems with cut-offs.

So, yes, carp run, but here we are talking about situations where you daren't let them run. Your whole set-up should be geared to getting the earliest possible warning of a take, ensuring that the carp doesn't find trouble before you even pick up the rod, and giving you instant control when you do pick up the rod.

Have a think about the set-up you are using at the moment then give yourself marks out of ten for early warning and instant control. Ten out of ten is about acceptable in most snag and weed fishing, because a take can mean that your troubles are only just beginning! Less than ten out of ten – which is the way most of us fish snags and weed most of the time – means your fish-landing potential is less than favourable from the moment you cast out.

Immovable Set-up

Your rod set-up should be immovable. I fish goalpost set-ups most of the time in my open-water and snag fishing. There are buzzer bars with screw fittings at each end to fix the bars at two or three points. Solar sell buzzer bar adaptors for turning their three or four-rod buzzer bars into goalpost set-ups. Don't attempt to fish locked-up with a buzzer bar that can spin. A take on a locked-up rod can be seismic (although sometimes you just get a polite tap-tap request to pick up the rod!) and there must be no weaknesses in the set-up. If there are any the carp will exploit them.

Get into the habit of fishing with the butt ring behind the buzzer head. I have mine tight against the head. I have the rod tips slightly in the air to give me a start in getting the rod up quickly. The clutch is set so the carp simply can't take line.

Some of you may be imagining that the carp will break the line on a take in a locked-up situation. It can't! A great deal of a carp's power comes from its weight and momentum. If it doesn't have the chance to gain momentum then a lot of its initial power is taken away.

When you get a locked-up take near snags your bottle twitches. You need a strong rod to help you gain control, a strong heart which stands up to the stress of not being able to give line – no matter how frightening the pull on the rod may be – and tackle which will withstand all the stresses an unhappy carp and the underwater furniture can put on it.

I hardly need add that if you are fishing weed or snags you should be glued to your rods. Leaving rods to fish for themselves is a non-starter. In snag and weed situations it is indefensible. A chance you aren't in a position to convert is bad fishing and a serious set-back to any session.

Presentation

It's easy to underestimate weed – as I have done on a number of occasions in the past – and not take all the necessary precautions to increase your chances of landing hooked fish. All my weed problems have come about through not using a breakaway lead set-up. I've never had much trouble with carp in lily pads so when I started fishing hornwort and Canadian pondweed I presumed they would present me with the same sort of problems as lilies. Not so. Fishing the Little Social swim referred to earlier gave me a much healthier respect for – and a more realistic attitude to – carp in weed than I had previously.

Fishing in heavy weed I thought in-line leads would be a suitable precaution. I was wrong! I'd read some advice by experienced weed angler Gary Bayes about tying leads on with a rotten bottom for weed fishing, but disregarded the advice. I didn't think I needed to go that far. (Actually the first reference I saw to rotten bottoms was in a Rod Hutchinson article in the 70s.) After ignoring the advice about tying on the lead had cost me a good carp I made the necessary adjustment and found that a breakaway lead was the solution. I started tying on using 4lb or 6lb line and landed the rest of the carp I hooked during my brief spell on the water.

I should explain that I waded in to free a couple of weeded fish in Little Social Bay. (I had two fish weeded-up on different rods at the same time, but that is another story, as they say!) The lead was definitely the problem. With the lead caught up in the weed you lose the necessary direct pull on the fish, with a great loss of power. I've noticed in the past that a fish that feels really solidly stuck is often "snagged" by the line being quite lightly hooked up on the edge of a branch or obstruction. In that situation a bent rod doesn't exert much power at all.

It's remarkable how much difference the presence of a lead makes when you are playing a fish. When the lead breaks away the carp come up on top more quickly, and it's much easier to play them in. So a lead tied to the set-up instead of actually being part of it is essential in heavy weed, or where the carp might find weed.

If you are using a rotten bottom – or weak link – give some thought to the relationship between the weight of the lead and the breaking strain of the link, otherwise you can easily crack off on the cast. At close range most of my weed presentation is by means of a PVA bag, with the lead inside, which eliminates the problem. If you are having to cast a distance which would break the link then add a PVA link to the set-up.

When you start tying leads on you imagine you aren't going to be able to reel them in and are likely to go through tons of them. In fact they reel in surprisingly easily, even through heavy weed, so for the most part you only lose them when you need to lose them, when you are playing a fish.

Sounds like a lot of trouble to go to all this, and mentally it can feel that way at times. Been there... After the filming of the Dream of Madine videos a few years back I got the chance to move down to the potamogeton beds that Simon Crow, Steve Briggs and Rob Hughes had their impressive results from. The weather was the hottest I'd been out in but I drove myself to up-camp and move

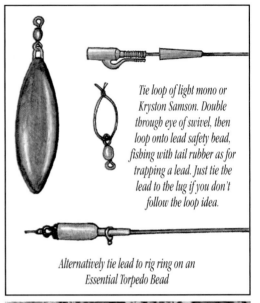

Tie loop of light mono or Kryston Samson. Double through eye of swivel, then loop onto lead safety bead, fishing with tail rubber as for trapping a lead. Just tie the lead to the lug if you don't follow the loop idea.

Alternatively tie lead to rig ring on an Essential Torpedo Bead

Motorway hard-fighting 26lb mirror, the fish that convinced me that I had to fish with weak lead-links to make playing weeded fish easier.

swim – for just the final night's fishing. Had the guys been fishing weak links? No, and they'd managed to land all their fish OK. So I didn't bother.

"Didn't bother" is an accurate description, because the idea was niggling at me. The only take I had came mid-evening, from the back of the pot beds. Out in the boat, over the fish, snagged solid. I lost it. Madine is over 500 miles from home. I'd fished the week through in a heatwave, reluctantly moved swim in a heatwave, and was an inch short of

Lesson learnt? Not 100%! The potamogeton beds in the background which featured in the Dream of Madine videos. After the guys had left I moved down and lost a fish in the weedbeds – through not tying my leads on! Incidentally French potamogeton appears to be more attractive to carp than our version of the plant.

What a difference a weak link makes. Even in heavy weed, when the lead breaks away the fish is forced to the top much more easily. Motorway 27lb+ caught when I started tying leads on with Kryston's Samson.

going the full nine yards, simply because I'd run out of effort and couldn't be bothered to tie up a weak link! I would have loved a forty from Madine but I still haven't had one, and I'm not sure I'll go back there now.

Anyway, lesson finally learnt. When I'm fishing difficult situations weak links are always a part of my weed set-up now. Don't find out the hard way that you should really have been using one.

End Tackle

Let's look at some of the aspects of presentation peculiar to weed fishing. One is the chance of your hook fouling the weed on the cast. The rig, or overall presentation, has to be designed to overcome this problem. I may be unnecessarily neurotic about fishing in weed, but I'm cautious about taking some of the advice I see in print about casting into weed, some of which is from extremely successful weed anglers, I hasten to add!

Holes in weed can be very productive. I invariably use a PVA bag for that situation. When not using a PVA bag I practise feeling the lead down and being reassured by the bump as it hits bottom, but then I wonder if the hookbait has

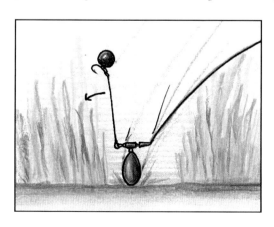

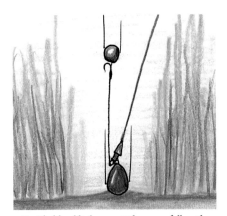

Braided hooklinks or supple mono follow the lead straight down and drop adjacent to it.

exactly followed the lead down, or has it strayed slightly on settling and perhaps caught a stray weed stem or leaf? Plus I imagine that feeling the lead down with your finger can pull the lead back in an arc in deeper water, again with the chance of swinging it back from the hole into the weed. Silly me, I know, but sitting behind rods for hours on end is an act of faith, and if you have no faith in the unseen end tackle situation you have just created you aren't fishing effectively, or confidently.

Solar's Hookbait Foam is invaluable in weedy situations, but you still have to rationalise the rig itself. Stiff rigs can keel over against weed, even when the lead hits a firm bottom. I'm not confident fishing my self-straightening hooklink/buoyant bait set-up, which may result in the hook snagging as it drops at an angle. In this situation the shorter the hooklink the less chance there is of a problem occurring. Using a material which follows the lead straight down, as with braid or supple mono, means that a clean-feeling lead touchdown results in a hookbait lying clean.

All the end tackle presented in a PVA bag is the safest way of casting into weed, and an effective presentation. I've experimented with stiff links with bags but prefer a 5-7" braid hooklink, often with the hookbait popped up 1-1½".

Playing Fish in Weed

Hornwort and Canadian pondweed are the worst weed mediums I've experienced for fish losses, and where these weeds are present you can't take enough precautions to minimise losses. You need to be on the rods as quickly as possible, get the carp's head up, and keep it up. Don't pussyfoot around with carp in this type of weed. Get control and keep control, and keep heaving until the carp is in the net, or until it is clear of danger.

I hate that form of fishing. A take isn't a moment of glorious expectation. It is what you are fishing for, but there is an element of "Oh no!" about them when they occur.

Lily pads are different. I'm comfortable with carp in lilies. The fish will help you. The lily pad surrounds at the Mangrove were a good training ground. They frightened me to death when I first saw them because you are playing fish in towards and through the pads. But I've found that the secret with lilies is a good hookhold, and patience. This is a situation where you don't just keep pulling their heads off. If you can keep them on the move all the way in, then do so. If they get stuck and feel immovable, lower the rod tip slightly. You'll feel them move. Get the pressure back on straightaway. While they are on the move keep the pressure on. If they go solid, slacken off slightly.

If they get stuck in weed, put the rod down and wait. Patiently. Weed isn't like snags or lilies. There is nothing for

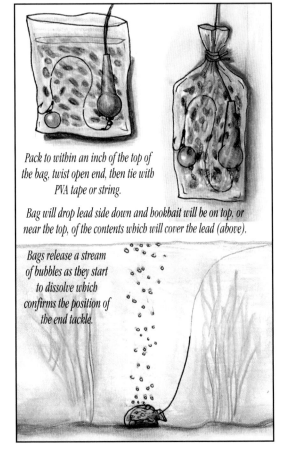

Pack to within an inch of the top of the bag, twist open end, then tie with PVA tape or string.

Bag will drop lead side down and hookbait will be on top, or near the top, of the contents which will cover the lead (above).

Bags release a stream of bubbles as they start to dissolve which confirms the position of the end tackle.

174

them to work the hook loose on. If I have to go out to a fish in a snag I don't expect it to be there when I find the end tackle. In weed I don't expect them to get off.

Snag Fishing

I've done a fair amount of successful rock-solid snag fishing. A margin spot at the Mangrove where I always fish like that. Some of the margin spots at Birch. Fishing in weed at Motorway, Orchid, Domaine de Boux... The list goes on. But the true test of all your ideas and beliefs comes when you go and fish the snags at Lake Raduta in Romania! You understand then that much of the carp fishing you do along the way is by way of education – accumulating experience and acquiring confidence in your methods for the big examination.

I was nervous of the idea but I fished locked-up solid with the rod tips high in the air with the snag rods at Raduta. Some of the fish in there are so big and powerful that a screwed-down clutch doesn't actually mean a carp can't take line. But it certainly slows them down, and gradually stops them, and it makes landing them possible, which is the object of the exercise.

A take on a rock-solid set-up can result in one of two things. The rod pulls down and stays down, or it pulls down, then straightens up as the fish changes direction and comes back against the pull. Was it Jim Gibbinson who described the initial "zizz, zizz, zizz" of the line being dragged off a screwed-down clutch? Heart-stopping stuff.

Provided the tackle and the set-up is right, what does not

Partner Simon Crow poised by the rods while snag fishing in the British Championships at Orchid lake. Si landed four fish from four takes in this snaggy corner, putting us through into the final.

Beautiful 38lb common caught on the Method at 30 yards range from one of the hornwort beds at Domaine de Boux. Experiences at this water and the Motorway Pond convince me that carp have a special liking for hornwort.

happen is that the rod doesn't break, the line doesn't break, the rod doesn't get pulled in, and the innards of the reel aren't mashed. In fish playing terms you redefine the meaning of the word 'bottle' when you pick up the rod at Raduta. The old cliché of the slow-moving sandbag on the other end of the line can suddenly become reality, and all your dreams may be about to come true. As mine did in just such circumstances – as if you need reminding!

But if the fish is sitting in the middle of a snag

Rock-solid at Raduta with the clutch screwed up tight. The bent-over tips show how hard I've wound down to the leads. Nerve-wracking stuff!

getting rid of the hook then all you will have will be regrets – be it at Raduta, or Selby Three Lakes, or the little pond down the road. Two possible big fish I lost at Lac de Madine are still as vivid as many I've landed since.

Snag Leaders

For normal fishing I prefer mono leaders, but there are some situations that demand the specialised leaders made by Kryston. Quicksilver is available in three breaking strains – 25lb, 35lb and 45lb, and the toughest of the lot, Ton-Up, in 85lb breaking strain. Qucksilver is adequate for most situations, and comes on 25-metre spools, which makes very long leaders possible where required. Ton-Up is spooled in 10-metre lengths.

Rock solid mirror of 44lb 12oz from Raduta. This fish was mental and tested my tackle and bottle to the limit.

Don't confuse snag leaders with shock leaders. All a shock leader needs to do is run onto the reel for a few turns. On the other hand, snag leaders have to withstand all sorts of abuse, even when you are fishing locked up. When you are playing a fish you don't know what the line may be brushing up against or running through between you and the end tackle. I fish the snag leader as long as possible, although you may need to compromise when you are casting. At Raduta my set-up was 27lb Pro Gold reel line, 36lb Pro Gold leader, topped off by a 10-metre Ton-Up leader.

Rock-solid at Cassien. Tree stumps on the lake bed are the problem here, and a lead bouncing around the bottom the danger. Fishing locked up seems to confuse the carp and gives you the chance to get into the boat and out onto the water.

Snag leaders. Kryston's Quicksilver and Ton-Up. Ton-Up is the toughest, but when you are fishing from the bank and have to cast Quicksilver is the best possible compromise.

Sea fishing shops sell some very impressive bulk spools of abrasion-resistant leader line. Stu Wallis was using a very abrasion-resistant, soft-feeling line when I fished with him at Raduta in October 2001, so it may pay to shop around for the right leader material. The beauty of the bulk spools is that they allow you to fish extra-long leaders for added protection.

I've seen some very fancy knots illustrated for shock/ snag leader knots but I use the double grinner all the time and it's never let me down. I use four turns on the weaker line and two turns on the stronger one. Wet the line thoroughly when you are tying this knot, and bed it down with great care. If you feel it strangle too sharply as you pull tight test it close to destruction to make sure you've got it right. If it's not right it breaks very easily. If it's tied right it's as good as any leader knot I've tried.

Returning a Cassien South Arm 46lb 4oz mirror landed from the boat.

Buoyancy Aids

Like tied-on leads this is another aspect of specialised fishing that seems like an awful lot of trouble to go to – until you lose a fish because you didn't go to the trouble. The only two waters I've fished where this applies are Raduta and Cassien, but there are numerous waters in France, and some in this country, where snags in the lake bed present a problem. As a rule these are tree stumps that were cut off and left when the area was being prepared for flooding. In Cassien and Raduta they can be small bushes. The difficulty here is that there is a chance of the reel line dropping into one of these snags, which means that your line is

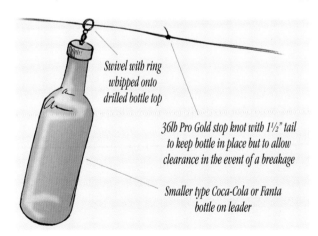

Swivel with ring whipped onto drilled bottle top

36lb Pro Gold stop knot with 1½" tail to keep bottle in place but to allow clearance in the event of a breakage

Smaller type Coca-Cola or Fanta bottle on leader

through the snag and the fish beyond it. When you put pressure on the fish all you do is pull it back to the snag, and the end result is a prayer for help, or a lost fish.

The precautions you need to take will depend on the severity of the problem. At Cassien you have the problem of tree stumps, or a very stony or rocky lake bed. The ground is running away from you, which means the line can be on the bottom for some distance. I've got round this at Cassien by tying buoyancy aids into the set-up about 8ft from the lead with a weak link. The larger version of the Fox Pike Bait Poppers are ideal for the Cassien lake bed. It is the final twenty or thirty yards of line you are trying to keep off the bottom, and I've found that the Bait Poppers make the difference between being able to reel in or losing your lead in a couple of the swims I've fished there.

I don't know how the buoyancy of ping-pong balls compares to Bait Poppers. I'm told that a popular way of running line across more severe bottom snags is to use a series of ping-pong balls clipped on the line on the surface. I've seen it done from a distance at Madine, but I haven't tried it myself.

177

On my first Raduta trips the rods I moved to the left-hand side of my swim when I was looking for new productive spots turned out to be a real problem. The lake bed was dropping away to 8-10ft beyond extensive shallows with underwater snags on them. When I got a take on these rods the line was snagged halfway out. I'd no buoyancy aids with me so I finished up adapting Fanta bottles for the job. Rod tip way up in the air, with the line running to a Fanta bottle, fished on the surface short of the end tackle. Not aesthetically pleasing, but the set-up proved very effective.

In this instance I wanted the buoyancy aid to slide back up the line (because the 5oz lead wouldn't sink it). I drilled a hole through the top, bound a Gold Label ring/swivel onto the bottle top, threaded the line through the ring, then tied a heavy line stop-knot with a long

Raduta mirror of 47lb from the snaggy 500-yard spot. I successfully landed four forties and a 55lb+ from the area, all on the locked-up methods described here.

tag-end left on it to act as a stop at the top of the long snag leader. This set-up worked brilliantly. Fishing tight the line was up out of the bottom snags, and the hooked fish couldn't pull the bottle under!

Conclusion

Where you find weed or snags carp won't be far away. Weed holds food and carp love to lie up in it, often having their own individual hole they will return to day after day in a spell of hot weather. Successful weed and snag fishing isn't easy and at some venues it sorts the positive carpers from the nervous ones.

In heatwave conditions carp can be hard to track down, and even harder to tempt. At such difficult times weed comes into its own and can make carp location very easy. But to make them catchable from snag or weed areas you may have to go to far more trouble than when you are fishing over a nice clean bottom with no snags within a hundred yards. Go to that trouble. Nowadays when I've got to go to more trouble than I want to with tackle arrangements my driving force comes from the thought that the next take could be from the fish of my dreams. To lose such a fish – any fish – through lack of effort is bad fishing, and the loss will keep coming back to haunt you. Just do it.

Snag fishing at over 500 yards at Raduta. The tough Cortland braid enabled me to have more line on the spools, and kept me in touch with the distant fish. Thanks to Rob Hughes for the assist here.

Big Waters, Boats and Feature Finders

I prefer the expression feature finder to fish finder. Carp on big waters are highly mobile. Locate the carp with a fish finder (if the carp-like images on the fish finder are in fact carp) and you may need to spend your sessions fishing from a boat to keep in touch with them! My big-water fishing tends to be based on focusing on likely holding areas, patrol routes, or transit camps, making enough bait available to turn the area of the swim into a feeding area, then trying to pinpoint likely feeding spots on my patch. I find feature finding on big overseas waters just as vital as on smaller waters back home.

The loneliness of the long-range, big-water carper.

Lac de Madine in eastern France was the first really big carp water I fished. 2,500 acres, but with limited bankside access. Fishing the water taught me that the big overseas waters are a totally different proposition to anything we have at home. Not to put too fine a point on it, I was out of my depth. It's all right theorising from this end about what you are going to do out there, but once you're on one of these huge waters you soon realise that a boat and a feature finder are essential if you want to fish effectively. I had a number of fish to 39lb 12oz from Madine on that first session, but I lost what I thought was a big fish through not having a feature finder and not knowing enough about the underwater terrain in front of me.

I thought I knew what was out front. I had a bait in 8ft of water out by the marker buoy in swim 8 on the road bank. It was late in the session and I'd already landed fish from the swim. I was on the phone to Mary when I had a

Back at Madine, tooled up for the job, and still out of my depth!

steady lift to a single tiger. I rang off, and hit it. I was under the impression that as long as the fish kept clear of the buoy I was all right. The line swung left across the front of the buoy. A slow plodder. Nice. My first forty was on the end – I hoped! Then the line fell slack. Cut off and gutted. On the following session I had a feature finder and was able to explore the spot. There was a sharp drop-off from 8ft to 16ft short of and to the left of the buoy. The terrain was rocky. The spot needed fishing with long Quicksilver or Ton-Up leaders, which I wasn't using on that initial session.

You learn some painful lessons the hard way,

and that was a painful one. Since that experience I have been obsessive about understanding as much as possible about the lake bed in front of me. I came back and told Mary we needed to raid the piggy bank. A boat and a feature finder are essential for fishing the big venues.

Cassien was the next big water I tackled. 1,200 acres we're told. Much bigger than that some people say. At least ten times as big as our huge Wraysbury One is the reality! Most anglers are highly mobile on Cassien. The fish are on the move, and so are the anglers. I'm getting too old for all that – although on one eight-day session I did move swims an unprecedented number of times for me – twice. I was trying to get to know something about the South Arm, and wanted to build up a picture of the Arm to narrow the sprawling venue down to an area I wanted to fish.

Swim 8 on the road-side at Madine. Bland-looking surface hiding some real surprises. 8ft of water to the right of the buoy; a steep, rocky drop to 16ft on the left.

The second move I made on that session was an important one. I'd fished two swims up towards the top of the arm. I liked both swims, but I didn't like what the feature finder told me about the underwater topography of the areas. Not enough variety. I moved down to the area of Gerard's. I spent all day Saturday looking for meaningful areas on the feature finder. I needed to get in a swim I felt confident in, one which I felt sure had enough variety of features that I

My biggest Madine fish being returned. 39lb 12oz. I loved the place but found the carp fishery management of the water to be frustrating.

could be confident the fish would visit the area regularly. Three hours of searching and I went back to Carp HQ, disappointed. I'd already discussed the area with then-chef Charles, and I needed more guidance.

"I can't find what I'm looking for."

"You went on the small island. There are good features you can reach there." The lovely man gave me more detail and the necessary insight and confidence to settle on a swim in the area. The feature finder did the rest and I salvaged a messy, very hard-working session with three days of peace and a March mirror of 46lb 4oz. I'd found the stretch of Cassien I wanted to fish and was in no doubt when I went back in November 2001. For the latter session I knew what I was looking for, had enough belief in what I was doing to enable me to stay put in my chosen swim, and landed fish of 35lb 12oz, 42lb 8oz and 57lb during what was a slow period on the venue.

When you first see the bed of a lake through a screen you realise how little you know about the lakes you spend your life on. Feature finders are a revelation. You realise that with a marker float you are able to obtain a very sketchy picture – at best. On the big overseas waters your swim is likely to be bigger than some of the waters you fish at home. You need a feature finder to get any sort of underwater picture when the fish may be anywhere from the margins to 500 yards out. You'll never find meaningful **fish** images on the screen when they are moving out of your way whenever you get near them, which is what happens in shallower water.

So you tackle this huge expanse of water, accept that at some time during your stay the fish are going to move through, or move in, then set about finding the likeliest spots to catch them from.

You start with the similarities to fishing at home, by looking for the features you are already familiar with. Snags, weed, plateaus, troughs, holes and so on.

When in doubt always try to come back down to the lowest common denominator – where do they feed?

The snags in Cassien and Raduta are covered in mussels, an attraction to the carp and a danger to the angler. Very often you can actually see weedbeds. In deeper areas they may be submerged. When I find a submerged one I put an end tackle through it (from the boat if necessary) to find out what sort of weed it is. Carp seem to be attracted to most types, but I'm more confident near (in order of preference) hornwort, potamogeton and Canadian. I'm aware that other anglers have different preferences to me, and I tend to be influenced by their preferences, rather than disagreeing with them. If they've had rewarding results from fishing their weed preference then the carp must like it, so their choice is an addition to the features I have confidence in.

I'm more attracted to indentations in the lake bed than to bars and plateaus. I feel troughs, channels and holes are more likely to be food traps, or may even have been dug by the carp. Holes are something it is very difficult to detect other than visually or with a feature finder. I first noticed them at Etang de Margot, and have since seen them in the silt at both Chalet Lake and Domaine de Boux. In this country I've noticed them in Birch, where the carp can dig absolute craters in their search for natural food. They will be present in most silt, loose gravel, clay or sandy lake beds but finding them is not always easy.

Carp feed in silt, but there is an interesting anomaly here. A number of very successful anglers have commented that they like silt, but prefer to fish a hard spot near silt, rather than in it. I can't argue with the logic of that. However you look at it, silt is

I had a number of fish during the making of the Dream of Madine videos, this chunky mirror of 34lb being the biggest. By this time I was using 45ft Quicksilver leaders to cope with the line-cutting features in the swim.

Your home and your session supplies travel with you at Cassien, making a substantial boat a necessity. This is one of the boats which can be hired from Lee Picknell's Cassien Experience, or from Gerard's.

Some of the snags at the 2,500-acre Lake Raduta in Romania. You don't take liberty with zebra mussel-covered carp refuges like this.

a food trap and a feature to be reckoned with, rather than crossed off the list. The better feature finders will let you read the lake bed to the extent that you can identify the difference between hard patches and silt.

Depth

Depth is significant in all waters, but the depths the carp are attracted to in overseas fishing move the goalposts as far as all our previous experiences are concerned. Here are a few examples. Madine – 6-8ft, with a strong leaning towards weedbeds, particularly the French version of potamogeton, which is a brownish

Cassien. At first glance it doesn't strike you as a "big" water because of the narrowness of the arms, but at 1,200 acres and extending for miles it fishes big. The view from the top of the South Arm looking down towards Gerard's about half a mile away, with Pierre's a further half a mile beyond.

broad-leafed variety. Etang de Margot – 3½-4ft, and even shallower much of the time. Domaine de Boux – 8-9ft, but with a strong leaning towards the shallow margins, and a very strong attachment to the extensive hornwort weedbeds that are in evidence some years. Raduta. I've had action down to 24ft, but only occasional fish, and nothing of significance. Most of my bigger Raduta fish have come from depths of 8-14ft. I've read a recent comment by Ken Townley that his favourite depth in France is 28ft.

Cassien throws up the sharpest reminders of how little we know or understand about carp. When I first went there with Steve Briggs he suggested I try different levels to find out the depth the fish were feeding at. I soon started following this advice. "I always have a bait at 25ft," Steve told me. I've had fish from depths of 12ft-51ft from Cassien, the two biggest, mirrors of 57lb and 63lb, coming from 51ft and Steve's preferred 25ft respectively.

But the depth is simply a guide. It gives you a starting point for the level at which to seek the spots that are likely to be attractive to the carp. I spend two to three hours each day looking for "carpy" spots with the feature finder. If you've got a big, uninteresting-looking expanse of lake bed in front of you then the slightest irregularity may be of interest to the fish. In more featured areas it may be a question of trying to select the most significant-looking. Is there a reason for the carp visiting that spot to feed? If you can't find such a spot, then a feature the carp are likely to visit will be the priority. I keep scouring the swim at non-feeding times because I'm never happy that all three or four rods are fishing in meaningful spots. Until they are in the four best spots available to me – which they never are – then they aren't fishing to their full potential.

Conduit-tubing marker in place. This one's in shallow water at Fishabil. In Europe you can buy extending pole markers in sections which screw together and have a battery-powered light source in the top. If the line snags the marker it pivots down then returns to its original position when the line pulls clear.

Intriguingly all my very big fish captures have come from new spots that I've just introduced the patch of bait and end tackle into for the first time that night, or that day, even when I've been fishing the swim for some time. This may be a coincidence, or it may be a sign that the bigger, wiser fish are steering clear of the obvious pressure areas other fish are being caught from. Either that or I've finally found the right spot after a few days of fishing spots that were good enough, but not the right ones.

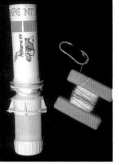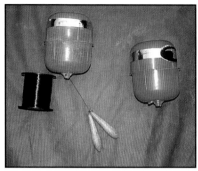

Above left: Two markers which find their own depth. The Gardner H-Block, and the European Fox (not our Fox) self-fixing marker, which finds the depth, cocks when the chamber at the bottom fills with water, and has reflective tape round the top for ease of location in the dark. The self-fixing element is a problem in rising water levels, as often happens at Cassien.
Above right: Steve Briggs' home-made ballcock markers which self-adjust with changes in water level. Note the reflective tape for easier location in the dark.

Markers

The image on a feature finder screen is a fleeting, constantly changing one. When you find something of real significance that you want to investigate further you need to mark it instantly, otherwise you may not find it again. It's surprising how quickly you can completely lose a feature that stood out like a sore thumb on the screen only seconds previously. Even going back to smallish waters with features you have fished before it can take you half a day to locate the favoured spots again. It's very difficult to find and keep your bearings or maintain a perspective of distance when you are on the flat, featureless surface of a water.

I carry three or four Gardner H Block markers in the boat with me. These are very buoyant plastic markers in the shape of an H, with the securing cord wrapped round the centre of the H. When you throw them into the water the cord unwinds and the marker sets itself to depth.* The instant I see something of real interest on the screen I throw an H-block over the side as a reference point. The first image you see may not be the best in that localised area, or you may finish up not using it, but mark it straightaway, then investigate around it until you have a clear picture of the area. When I'm spending an hour or two out in the boat looking for features I spend the period throwing H-blocks over the side, then retrieving and moving them, until I've found the most meaningful spots, and built up a

Above left: Ideal Fish Finder for the travelling carper. The Eagle Fish-Easy is a self-contained unit powered by eight type-D batteries. The transducer is fixed by suction pad.
Above right: The Eagle Ultra-Classic, powered by a rechargeable battery and with a transducer that needs fixing to the boat.

* *With use the cord on the H-blocks starts to stick and very often the situation will arise where the cord doesn't unwind fully and the H-Block starts to drift. This is a real frustration. Be prepared for it happening and either treat the cord with a lubricating liquid, or replace it with a more suitable line.*

picture of that little area.

When you find an obvious hot spot you have the difficult decision to make as to whether to use a permanent marker or not. Some spots are so good that I just have to mark them precisely. When I have a couple of spots in one small area I use one marker at a reasonable distance from the spots and use it as a reference point for picking up the features on the screen each time I position the end tackle. I talk about markers some more later in the chapter.

Relocating exciting localised features can be extremely difficult. The first time I fished Cassien I spent eight days in the Bridge Swim fishing the margins and out to the plateau. Briggsy had gone on about fishing a bait at 25ft, but to start with I just couldn't find a really meaningful spot at that depth, which wasn't for want of trying. Eventually, on the fifth day of exploring the area, I found what looked like a stunner. A small clearing in a circle of weed about six feet across. It took me ages to absolutely pinpoint the small spot with an H-block and position a scattering of bait and the end tackle in the circle. Next morning the feature produced Half Moon Scale at 63lb!

Steve Briggs returning a good common to the expansive waters of Raduta. The 700-acre "bay" behind Steve is just a small part of the huge, sprawling lake.

That night a fish kited down from the top of the plateau and moved the H-block marking the weed circle. I'd lost the feature! I spent hours trying to relocate it, but without success. The area of water 25ft deep wasn't extensive, and I must have spent hours investigating that depth prior to and after finding the weed circle. It had done the job for me, but I would have liked another couple of nights and mornings with a bait positioned there. In a fortnight's fishing I'd

Rob Hughes and Stu Wallis teaming up to make rowing baits out easier in World Record Bay at Raduta.

spend one and a half nights with a bait in that spot, and it produced a fish of 63lb.

Incidentally at exactly the moment I had Half Moon Scale, Briggsy, who was fishing 400 yards to my left at the bottom of the North Arm, caught a fish of 51½lb, also from his favoured 25ft!

Get a bait in a feeding spot at the right depth and at the right time and the job is half done for you.

Steve Briggs has designed and made his own markers for fishing Cassien. They are particularly useful for waters with fluctuating water levels so I've asked Steve to describe the markers here. Over to Steve:

"Most of us who have fished abroad

for any length of time come to accept that markers form one of our most essential items of tackle. What those markers are made of, and what their uses are, vary from person to person. I've messed about with all sorts of shapes, sizes and methods, and have ended up with a way of making markers that suits a range of different uses.

The markers I use for most of my boat fishing are simply the oval-shaped ballcocks that you can buy cheaply in most hardware stores. My reasons for liking these are that they are about the right size and buoyancy, plus the fact that because they are bright red in colour they are easily visible without having to modify them. I normally add a piece of reflective tape to the top of the marker to make it visible at night with the aid of a headtorch.

The main modification comes in the way that I attach the marker. At the bottom of the ballcock I drill a hole through the plastic threaded section, which protrudes by an inch or so. The important thing is that the line passes through the hole and is able to run freely rather than

Simon Horton running out to drop two end tackles in the same area. When you are fishing on your own, or are looking for features, taking the rod out with you is the best way of rowing the bait out.

being tied to the marker. The line is then cut so that the length of line used is deeper than the water you will be fishing. Having done that a heavy weight is tied to one end of the line, and to the other end a much lighter weight is added. Normally I use an 8oz lead as the heavy weight and a 2oz lead for the lighter one.

The reason for setting up the marker in this way is that as soon as you are above a spot you wish to mark you can position the marker and release the heavy weight, which will sink straight to the bottom at the desired spot, while the lighter weight will balance the marker and ensure there is no slack line between lead and marker. You soon realise the importance of being able to position a marker quickly and accurately when you're out in the boat on a windy day. It's surprising how far you can drift in just a few seconds without realising it is happening and lose the feature you are trying to mark.

The other advantage of using a marker that is set up in this way is that it is self-adjusting. Many waters, especially the large reservoirs, tend to have fluctuating levels, and a marker that is tied on, or fixed, is liable either to sink or float away if the level rises, or, if the level falls, the anchor line can slacken off and you no longer have an accurate marker. But with this method the marker is constantly able to adjust itself to the changing level, and there's no need to retie it every time you try a different spot." *(See picture on page 183.)* **Steve Briggs**

Fish Finders

I may refer to them as feature finders, but the popular Eagle range of models are actually called Fish Finders! The range is available from the Tackle Box, and other well-stocked retail outlets.

The most convenient one to carry and use is the FishEasy Portable. This operates off 8 Type-D batteries, which makes it easy to have spares available on a long session. This size of battery is universally available, which means that you can buy spares if existing supplies are exhausted.

The other convenient feature of the FishEasy is that the transducer is attached to the boat by means of a suction pad. This is an asset when you are travelling abroad and need this easy means of attachment. The FishEasy is my first choice when I'm travelling to Raduta.

When you're travelling by car the weight of an additional battery to power the fish finder is no big deal, and on these trips I use a rechargeable battery and an Eagle TriFinder, which has more features than the FishEasy. The TriFinder seems to be better at identifying underwater weedbeds than the FishEasy, and the longer battery life is a convenience, but for the most part the FishEasy will do most things the majority of us want from a fish finder.

Whatever model you take make sure you have plenty of battery life, or replacement batteries, with you. On waters like Cassien and Raduta you are very dependent on the fish finder to enable you to keep your end tackles clear of the underwater snags present in both venues. Raduta in particular would be near-impossible to fish effectively without a feature finder.

Using Boats

You take boats and the use of them for granted until you actually have to use one! Then you discover that they are an angling aid. They don't make it easy, and they aren't easy to use, particularly if you prefer fishing on your own, as I do.

What kind of boat? Very often the choice is limited to the type available at the water you are going to fish. As a rule these are far more substantial than a boat you can carry around with you. Of the waters I've fished the boats supplied, or hired, at Cassien, Raduta and Fishabil have been excellent, stable and well maintained. At most other venues I've visited I prefer to have my own boat with me.

If you are buying do you go for a hard shell or an inflatable? Mine's an inflatable, but a substantial one; a second-hand Avon Redbreast Four-man dinghy with separate buoyancy chambers so the whole boat can't deflate if anything goes wrong. John Lilley recommended this type of boat and I found one at a local boat-yard. Cost at the time second-hand was around £500. New these boats cost in excess of £1,000. This sounds over the top for an inflatable but this is far tougher, more substantial and better suited to big-water conditions than the smaller inflatables available.

Bear in mind that when you are selecting a boat for big-water fishing it must be capable of carrying you and all your equipment for a session to your swim, in addition to being suitable for rowing out baits or landing fish in adverse conditions.

The Sevylor range of inflatable boats available from Tackle Box, Dartford, and other big tackle shops are suitable for small and calm-water fishing. At the time of writing the three Sevylor Fish Hunter models cost around £110, £150 and £250, lengths and maximum capacity being 6' 10" and 360lb, 8' and 600lb, and 9' 2" and 700lb respectively.

Simon Crow tight-baiting and dropping an end tackle using an H-block marker at Raduta, a useful strategy when you want a permanent or temporary marker.

Tackle Box also sell two models of the Bic Boats, a design which is popular with anglers and looked on as being very stable. The Bic Sportyak is the smaller model with a length of 7', a width of 3' 9" and a weight of 42lb. I would look on this model as a small-water boat. The Bic 252 is more suitable for big-water fishing. It is 8' 3" long x 3' 10" wide and weighs 99lb. The Bic Sportyak costs £210 and the Bic 252 £399.

I would look on the Bic 252 as being of the minimum size for big-water carping. Most of the boats provided or available for hire on the popular big-fish oceans are more substantial than any of the models covered here.

The problem with owning a boat is finding a compromise between suitability and convenience of carriage. This is why top-of-the-range inflatables are so popular with carp anglers. They are suitable for packing into the smallest possible space, have a fair degree of stability, and will carry a reasonable amount of gear.

While the boats available on the bigger waters tend to be eminently suitable for carp fishing, those on offer at the smaller waters tend not to be! Many of the holiday-type venues are casting only. When I fish waters like Domaine de Boux, Etang de Margot and Chalet Lake I always take my own inflatable. Before you go to a distant water find out what the rules are about the use of boats, and what sort of boats are available at the venue – and how many. If you fish as a pair with a friend one boat between two is acceptable. When you are fishing as a party spread round a lake, or fishing on your own, then ideally you need your own boat, one which will cope with all the conditions the trip will throw at you.

Electric Outboard Engines and Batteries

This is beginning to sound like an awful lot of gear to lug round, but as a rule when you are using a boat and the full monty with it, you are able to drive down to the waterside and take it from there. On the big inland oceans a boat and an electric motor are essentials, and if you are using an engine then more than one battery is a prime requirement, too. You can run a battery down just finding a suitable swim at Cassien!

Tackle Box, Dartford, include boats, engines and batteries in their comprehensive catalogue. They sell a range of Minn Kota Electric Engines, with a thrust ranging from 30lb through to 50lb. Prices range from £150 to £467. Batteries required are heavy-duty versions, normally used for caravans or lorries. You need at least two with you.

My electric engine is a Shakespeare Sigma 12-volt of 37lb thrust, which is probably a minimum power requirement judging by the Tackle Box list. I bought this in the first flush of enthusiasm for overseas fishing three years back and haven't used it yet. I row on the smaller waters and tend to row or use the lake equipment on the bigger ones. If I were buying now I would be guided by the experts at the Tackle Box. Steve Briggs is another expert in this area. Steve has been using boats and their accessories on long sessions for many years and I've used a great deal of his know-how and experience in my big water approach.

Life Jackets

Always have a life jacket with you on trips where the use of a boat is likely to be involved. In summer on a small, shallow water when I'm lightly dressed and shod I will often go out without the life jacket on. On waters like Cassien and Raduta I always wear one. In winter when I'm likely to be wearing heavy clothing and footwear I always wear one.

I wince when I see pictures of people standing up in boats, or watch anglers stand up to apply bait. Don't do it. Accidents do happen. Anglers have been drowned as a result of falling out of boats, or the boat capsizing in rough conditions. It wasn't going to happen to them... Storms can come up from nowhere. Rough weather can be very frustrating on a big water when the fish have turned up in the swim, but keep a sense of proportion. Think of the wife and kids back home. No carp is worth losing your life for.

Always carry a suitable life jacket with you and if there is any element of risk attached to a trip out on the water, wear the jacket.

Rowing out Hookbaits

Rowing out hookbaits may entail rethinking the shape, type and weight of your lead, particularly where you are fishing at range. Tightening down across a wide expanse of water in a big wind can result in the lead being moved out of position. My preferred leads for this type of fishing are Korda's flat swivel leads, or their recent introduction, the circular Big Grippa leads. For this type of fishing I look on 5oz as being a minimum weight. 6oz or more may be necessary on the clay lake bed of Raduta, particularly if you are positioning the end tackle on a slight bank-facing slope, or using one of the buoyancy aids described elsewhere.

You think 5oz is overkill? On a recent trip to South Africa I rowed a hookbait out about 150 yards while a friend held the rod. The bait was positioned in 3 feet of gin-clear water on a clean gravel patch. I was fishing over hemp and chopped tigers, with just a light scattering of freebies. I dropped the end tackle and signalled for my friend to tighten down, then watched in horror as the end tackle disappeared from view! Just the simple act of sinking the line and tightening to the end tackle had moved the end tackle off the baited area. We had to start over again, but it was a lesson in just how easy it can be to move the end tackle if you don't take all the necessary precautions. From time to time I've tried to reel an end tackle in and found it stuck in a snag. At the time I wondered what had happened. Now I know!

Before I started using a boat I presumed that the best way to row out hookbaits was to leave the rod on the bank and take out the end tackle. It can be if you are fishing with someone, but I very rarely have that luxury (by choice). So I've had to come to terms with rowing out hookbaits on my own. And the easiest way to do that is to take the rod out with you.

I learnt to row-out from Rob Hughes and Simon Horton. Take the rod out. Introduce the free offerings, if any, drop the end tackle, lay the rod down in the boat with the tip over the back and the handle on the seat. You need the reel close to you, with the bail arm open. Row back in as straight a line as possible. Keep an eye on the spool to ensure that line is paying out throughout the row-back. If the line is tending to stick then scoop some water over the spool to keep the line flowing. Whatever happens don't move that carefully positioned end tackle, and don't accidentally close the bail arm. It has happened to all of us!

If I'm fishing two rods close together on a marker then I will sometimes position two rods at a time. Rob Hughes' method for doing this is to leave one rod in the rests and take out the end tackle: the second rod goes out with him for an end tackle drop and row-back. Simon Horton's method is to take out two rods, drop the end tackles, and row back. I prefer this

The biggest fish I've landed from the boat, the Domaine de Boux big mirror at 59lb 2oz. I caught this huge fish two days running, and had Frank Warwick to thank for the netting on both occasions. We were both stunned when we saw this huge beast lying on its side just beyond the reach of the net!

188

approach, but it's only possible in reasonably calm conditions. You can achieve an acceptable spread of the end tackles by flicking one to the left and one to the right, but you can only do this when you are fishing two end tackles close together. You can use Rob's method when you are fishing end tackles well apart.

If I find a producing area at range and the weather is very changeable, with big winds around, then I will position more end tackles in the one area than I would normally. This is a safeguard against the possible frustration of not being able to take an end tackle back out to a productive spot following a take in adverse weather conditions. During a session at Raduta in October 2001 I finished up with four end tackles in one area of the lake. I was having to wait for occasional calmer weather to take the baits out, so when it did calm down enough I spread as many end tackles around the area as possible. I was fishing at about 500 yards which meant there was a fair amount of rowing involved, but as the area produced five 40lb+ fish to 55lb in six nights it merited the coverage I gave it. On one stormy, productive night I finished up with just one of the extreme-range rods fishing!

If you are fishing near a feature and don't want to leave a marker in position, but want very precise baiting, use an H-block on a temporary basis. H-block in position, introduce the bait, drop the end tackle, row back to the bank, then retrieve the marker on your next run out, or when you have finished positioning the end tackles. There is an edge to be achieved with this method of precise baiting. When you are using hemp, seeds, or pellets introduce the groundbait after you have positioned the end tackle. It may reduce the spooking effect of end tackle in the swim.

The sectioned tubing markers obtainable in Europe. The light source in the top section gives off a sexy red glow and is powered by three AAA batteries, recharged by solar power during the day.

In calm conditions, or where the water is shallow enough for you to use an anchor, it is far easier to position end tackles and free offerings than in deep water with a strong wind blowing. I started using the temporary marker approach in difficult circumstances and find it a very effective way of coming up with precise bait and free offering open-water placement in adverse conditions.

In a big wind getting the boat in position to actually make the drop can try your patience. Manoeuvre until you have the boat pointed towards the swim, and the drop point straight behind the boat. Drop the end tackle, quickly put the rod down and start rowing before you get blown off line, or before there is too big a bow in the line. Off you go in the required direction, ensuring that line is paying off the spool smoothly, and that the leader knot doesn't stick as it comes off the spool. (Position the leader knot at the back of the spool before rowing out.)

Rowing back to base with the rod can be a problem with this method of positioning. You need to row back in as straight a line as possible to make sinking the reel line easier. Line a far-bank marker up against a point on the back of the boat and keep the two points in line. Keep glancing over your shoulder to make sure you are still on track. Be aware of the position of the other lines when you are getting close to the bank. Tighten down as gently as possible to ensure that you don't move the end tackle, even when using the heavy leads recommended earlier.

Rowing Baits Out at Night

Always wear a life jacket at night. If there is anyone else on the water tell them you are going out. Be prepared for trips out at night and don't let darkness impair your carp fishing efficiency, particularly on waters where most of the feeding takes place at night.

First requirement is a marker you can find in the dark. Easy? Don't you believe it! If it is difficult to find your bearings during the day, it is nigh-on impossible at night. Familiarise yourself with the far bank skyline, and any lights, in relation to the area you are fishing. Learn to recognise lake-bed features on the feature finder that can act as signposts in your patch. You have no sense of distance in the dark and homing in on a known depth can be one of your best guides to the marker area in the dark.

Use a marker with a light, or with reflective tape, that lets you home in on the spot. There are some excellent European markers made by a company called Fox (not our Fox) which are self-adjusting, self-cocking, and have a wrap of reflective tape. I tend to use these as an area marker, and pinpoint the spots I'm fishing with H-blocks, which you can only find in the dark when you get close to them. Some European companies also sell screw-together conduit-tubing markers with an AAA battery-powered red light in the top section. There is a solar-powered light sensor on the top of the light unit to save on battery power during the day. As it gets dark the light starts to glow a fascinating ruby red. These markers can be used for depths down to 24ft, and while they can be awkward to

My Avon Redbreast "Four man" inflatable. Separate buoyancy chambers make this model one of the safest of the inflatables.

assemble for deeper spots they are the best night-time markers I've used. One other word of warning about these markers. The light unit makes them a bit top-heavy, and you need to make the top section more buoyant to counteract this characteristic. At the time of writing conduit-tubing markers are not available in this country, but it's only a matter of time before they appear. There is a market for them.

The new LED headlights are superb for swim work, but not as effective out on the water. I take a couple of battery headlights and a bright beam torch out with me at night. I've learnt from experience that finding a marker at night isn't easy, and now take all sorts of extra precautions to point me in the right direction.

A feature finder with a back-light is an eye-opener at night. I'm not a great believer in fish images being meaningful, but I can't ignore what I see over the baits through the echo sounder at night. Where does that lot hide during the day?

Once you've rowed out and dropped the end tackle you need to row back – of course. But you need to have thought of that before you went out! If you don't leave a light by the rods, or near the bivvy, you will be lost at sea. I leave an orange, clearly visible light near the rods at the spot I've selected for landing. This takes into account the position of the other lines. Be aware of the other lines both on the way out, and on the way back. Repositioning one rod and wiping out three others on your return is a tad counter-productive!

For fishing at up to a couple of hundred yards range the Carp-Tech Rig Lights are ideal for marking the swim for the return trip. You can clip them to the rods, they are light on batteries, and they show you the way home without damaging your night vision. Beyond two hundred yards you need a brighter 'return home' light than the Rig Light.

Playing and Landing Fish

Finding out what is between you and the end tackle is an essential part of feature-finding on snaggy waters and dictates how you go about playing fish. If possible I land my fish from the bank.

To me the essential element in landing fish successfully is being able to keep them under pressure. On snaggy waters I fish locked-up solid and don't allow the fish to run, or only let them take under heavy pressure. If the nature of the lake bed dictates that I go out in the boat I leave the rod locked up until I'm ready to go out, then stay bent into the fish as I reel the boat towards it. That way I'm pulling on the fish all the time and reducing its chances of getting its head into trouble.

Most of the boats available for hire at distant waters are sturdy affairs. This is one of the Fishabil boats.

The reality of the travelling big-water session fishing angler. Big-fish and big-water star John Van Eck's boat loaded up and ready to go at the Orient. The picture says it all. How can you learn that lot in one or two sessions?

You pull yourself out until you are over the fish, then keep as much pressure on as possible, to tire the fish and keep its head up. You can't exert as much pressure from a boat as you can from the bank. In addition to which you are directly over the fish, which to me gives a worrying angle of pull on the hook. So keep a balance between heavy pressure and overdoing it. And take your time until the fish has tired.

If you are on your own try to organise yourself prior to the fish being ready to be netted. You'll give yourself anxious moments if you're still trying to position the net when you've got a big fish lying there, beaten. Frank Warwick and I went out in the boat to net a fish of 58lb 14oz from Domaine de Boux. I played it for quarter of an hour before it came up on its side, looking gigantic. It looked far bigger than its actual weight and we couldn't believe what we were looking at when we first saw it!

It righted itself and decided to go for a further five-minute swim round, which was a very anxious five minutes indeed!

When I've netted the fish I simply hook the landing net over a rowlock, or some other protuberance, and row back to the bank. The fish will turn the right way to go with the flow. I prefer this method to risking standing up to heave a big, heavy fish over the side of the boat, then possibly having them flapping around in the bottom of the boat on the trip back in.

Don't forget the light by the rods when you go out to play a fish. Don't forget the landing net. I've done that, at Cassien, in the middle of the night, and had to row back with the rod laid in the boat and the clutch set so the fish could take line in an emergency. Eventually I successfully landed a fish of 37lb 12oz.

My two biggest fish, the Cassien mirror of 63lb and the Raduta common of 73lb 13oz, were landed from the bank. I knew there was very little trouble between me and the fish and preferred to keep the pressure on and keep them moving rather than risk jumping in the boat and possibly losing control long enough for the fish to get into trouble.

The deciding factor for me as to whether I go out in the boat or not is the nature of the lake bed between me and the fish. In many of the swims at Cassien you need to use a boat because of the steep drop-off – covered in tree stumps in many places – between you and the end tackles. I've made the wrong decision once at Cassien and lost what may

Shoes Jones baiting up from the smaller version of the Bic boat at a wintry Birch Grove. Suitable for small enclosed waters this model, but not for big, windswept venues.

have been a good fish thirty yards from the bank when it hit a snag as it came up the slope. It isn't a mistake you make twice.

Team Work

For the most part I'm a carp fishing loner, but rereading this I have to come to the conclusion that for big-water fishing with a boat you are better served fishing with a reliable mate as a team of two. Fishing at range with a boat is very, very hard work. Even when you are fishing at a modest 220 yards, bait placement involves a round trip of a quarter of a mile. Get a bit of action and the miles soon start to add up.

Swim selection and successful feature finding are the keys to big water success. You cannot know enough about what lies in front of you under the surface, and the longer you stay in the swim the more you can learn about it, and the greater the chances are of having the baits in exactly the right place when the fish show up.

The alternative method of big-water fishing is to find the carp and keep moving to stay with them. I leave this approach to the new kids on the block, like my friends Simon Crow, Briggsy, and Alijn Danau. I admire their energy and their dedication, but I'm getting too old for chasing carp around a lake – unless I feel I absolutely have to!

Simon Horton and Frank Warwick playing a fish from the boat at Domaine de Boux.

The Method – Why Bother?

Frank Warwick

Is it just my imagination or do many carp anglers consider the Method to be a small-carp, match-based, half-hearted approach to proper carp angling? I definitely get this feeling when I look around and see how infrequently the approach is used on many of our lower-stocked big-fish waters. And, to be honest, more modest waters, too.

As tends to be the case, until you have actually witnessed or sampled for yourself just how devastatingly effective the technique can be it's easy to dismiss, and in doing so throw away what is in my opinion a monster edge. I well remember taking part in a series of carp matches in the mid-90s called the Sony Carp Challenge. These matches were really the first of their kind and attracted all manner of competitors. Quite a few of the chosen venues were smallish carp waters, and it was on one of these venues that I first saw the Method in action. In fact it became a talking point among the more seasoned carp anglers taking part in those matches, just how unbeatable the Method could be when fished against more traditional carp fishing approaches. Having been suitably inspired a number of the participants went away from those matches and used the Method for some spectacular results – John Hofgartner being one who springs to mind. To be fair most of us knew about the Method for many years prior to the Sony Challenge, but it was really those matches that exposed its true potential, certainly in my case at least.

I reasoned that some of the more difficult waters would surely respond to the use of the Method, albeit with some fine-tuning. I was not to be disappointed! Initially Redesmere was to be my test-bed water. Redesmere has quite a reputation for being a moderately difficult venue so it fitted the bill well. As you may know the Method works well when frequently rebaited and recast – particularly on fairly well-stocked waters – working the swim up and creating a strong feeding response, and hopefully creating competitive feeding among the carp. The hefty noise made by a baited Method feeder hitting the water is a tad off-putting but once the food has been encountered the carp don't really seem to mind it, with takes often occurring minutes after the loaded feeder has hit the water. But on less densely populated big-fish waters the question was how to apply the Method effectively?

Moulding the mix round a Birmingham Angling Centre 2oz Method feeder.

Initially the Method often attracts other species, so the starting point is just casting out two feeders and catapulting out balls of free offerings, then sitting back and waiting. Wondering how often to recast and rebait is the difficult part to assess. Take Redesmere for example. One take in a two-day session using more conventional tactics is generally classed as a result. I know from experience on that particular water that on average anglers will only recast two or three times a day, obviously some more, some less, than others. That's the trend, but with the Method utilising food items that break down and are consumer-friendly to other species, casting out and just leaving Method feeders does provoke that nagging doubt that you have possibly been cleaned out and have not been alerted to the fact. Sometimes you will pick up a bream or a tench, but by no means every time the bait is eaten.

So what's the answer? Simple. Recast freshly baited feeders regularly; that way we know that we have at least got bait on offer next to the hookbait. Only introduce more balls of groundbait when you have received action; that way you avoid over-baiting the swim.

Who said Method fishing is for small carp?

For the initial quantity to put in, a good deal of trial and error is required to find out the optimum amount. I tend to ball-in quite a lot of bait in one chosen part of the swim and fish one rod on that baited area. The other rod – or rods if more than two rods are being fished – are fished over no groundbait in other areas of the swim. The interesting thing is that on waters where the Method has been used quite frequently the rods fished with feeder-only over no loose feed whatsoever tend to be more productive. If you are one of the first anglers to use the Method on your water you will usually catch more over a baited area. However it pays to hedge your bets and find out for yourself which tactic the carp

Two pieces of dissolving foam prevent tangles and enable the use of longer hairs and light hookbaits in weedy swims.

My favourite catapult for Method balls is the Whopper Dropper.

respond to best on any given day.

The disturbance of quite a few balls of loose feed hitting the water can be the deciding factor regarding which tactic to use. What I can say without any reservations whatsoever is that two or three rods fished with just a decent-sized Method mix ball on the feeder only will catch very well indeed.

A good starting point with this approach is to recast every four hours on all rods, with a bit of restraint at known feeding times, like early morning. Recasting at feeding times can really blow your chances. I much prefer to have the swim settled down from recasting the feeders, with the mix nicely spread and part broken-down from the feeders in an appealing manner, which tends to happen on my Method mix in around 20-30 minutes. Conduct tests in a clear margin and see for yourself. See for yourself how long it takes for the mix to swell and break away from the Method feeder, and then break down into an effective meal.

Get this part right and the fish will come for sure. I can honestly say that my results on the Method have been so good in recent years that I could really kick myself for not using it much more in the past. On the regular occasions when I fish the Method against more conventional set-ups it just keeps blowing them away. Head and shoulders better in fact.

Anyway, enough of my introduction! Let's get down to the real nitty-gritty. What to use on the feeder, and as a hookbait, kit needed, tips and edges. Here goes.

A selection of feeders. Experiment and find out which type suits your requirements.

My Method mix helped along by the addition of juice from fermenting particles.

Conventional maize hookbaits and my own specially prepared boilie-mix flavoured lookalikes for colder temperatures.

Rods, Reels and Line for Method Fishing

It is a plain fact of life that Method feeder angling will give the rod a very thorough work out indeed, and any rod not man enough for the job will soon be found out. I find a rod of at least 2¾lb test curve is required for Method fishing. Anything softer tends to flatten and feel threatened. When you consider the weight of a loaded Method feeder can be anything up to 6oz or more it's not surprising to find anglers shying away from Method fishing, especially if their rods aren't up to the job.

I find a through-actioned rod better suited to Method fishing. Fast-tapered rods are adequate but tend to have a habit of casting the Method ball off the feeder unless the feed has been made much stiffer to withstand the extra force exerted on the cast, which can defeat the object slightly. I also find a long rod better for casting Method feeders, the cast being a progressive overhead thump/lob, making the rod do the work rather than the angler. In fact a rod that casts a deadbait a long way will also be good for Method fishing. I have been working with Century to build the ultimate Method rod based on the need to handle big weights yet have a through action. Here's the interesting bit; the rod is going to be 14ft long to give more leverage and progressive power.

If you don't have heavy enough rods then don't be put off the use of the Method on that account; simply scale things down a tad. Match the feeder and the ball of Method to your gear. I know it's nice to be able to have the tackle to cover more distant areas of the swim, but generally most of my Method carp have come from more modest distances, many of them in the margins.

Reels? Nothing special here. What you normally use will be fine. I tend to use my Shimano 8010 Baitrunners most of the time though! I have recently been using Shimano's new 10000 XTE Baitrunners – these are superb – only changing to the bigger Daiwa Emblem Zs or Shimano Big Pit reels when maximum distance dictates the need – which is relatively rarely.

Main line. I have to confess that so far I have only used nylon main line for Method feeder fishing, my choice being 12lb breaking strain GR60, which seems to be a nice compromise. 15lb is thicker, which makes it harder to cast the required distance without having to hit the rod harder and risk casting the bait off, although I use it in weedy and snaggy conditions without hesitation. On the other hand, in most situations 10lb main line is fine, but I like the extra insurance the 12lb GR60 gives. In tests on the bench 12lb GR60 consistently breaks at 15-

Preparing to cast a single Method ball to a bubbler.

16lb, which is impressive for its diameter.

For casts of up to 80 yards with the Method feeder you can get away with not using a shock leader, but for trouble-free casting at greater ranges I would advise the use of a 35lb or 45lb Quicksilver leader.

Method Feeders

There are a number of Method feeders available. At the time of writing my personal favourite is the Birmingham Angling Centre

On the rods in autumn – still a good time of year for Method fishing.

(BAC) version. They are available in 1oz, 2oz and a heavyweight 3oz version. Of importance is the fact that they are very well made and of sturdy construction. Having a range of a choice of weights allows you to change weights to suit conditions. What has become very apparent to me is that with some feeders the lack of weight enables the carp to lift the feeder without hooking themselves properly. Using lighter feeders I used to get quite a few strange twitchy indications and aborted takes. Using the 2oz and 3oz versions of the BAC feeders cut out a lot of these indications and made me realise the importance of the feeder's weight and design for getting the best from this approach.

This beauty came 35 minutes after the feeder hit the water, cast at some slight movement from a carp.

Interestingly enough, to a man, all the anglers I have persuaded to try the BAC feeders have noticed improved indications and results. This is not an advert, by the way, just an honest opinion of a very nice product which is right for the job. Well done, Terry Eustace and Eric of BAC. Dennis MacFetrich of MCF has recently brought out his own quite similar version which is mega carp-friendly. Excellent.

On some waters I have used feeder leads which I think John Bryhn designed for use at Horseshoe Lake. These are useful where you require a quick change of tactics from conventional in-line lead to Method fishing. The John Bryhn-designed feeder lead can be simply loaded with Method mix and off you go – without having to retackle, which can be unnecessarily time-consuming on a short session. The Method leads are less conspicuous in close proximity to the hookbait for those who are paranoid about concealment of the feeder. I know there are quite a few anglers who are concerned about how a Method feeder looks once it is exposed as the mix is either broken down or attacked by carp. I must confess I did at one time worry about this aspect myself but as I have used the Method more and more I have come to attach far less importance to this aspect than I used to. In fact as an experiment I have cast an empty feeder with just a hookbait attached to a rolling carp and caught soon afterwards, so I feel the presence of the feeder may not be of great significance to the carp in most circumstances.

I have to confess that I prefer a 2½-3ft length of leadcore behind the Method feeder rather than anti-tangle tubing. I like nailing this part of my tackle to the lake bed out of harm's way, and the leadcore does the job admirably. I use the ESP or Kryston version in 40lb b.s. both for concealment and as a carp care requirement. I don't like the thought of bare nylon or Quicksilver having the chance to rub the carp's flank during the fight. I attach the leadcore to either the nylon main line or the Quicksilver leader by means of a needle whipping knot. Keith Moors' knot is very good for connecting leadcore to nylon in the 10-20lb range where a heavier shock leader isn't required.

Baits for Method Fishing

This is a fascinating subject in its own right. The Method allows you to be very individualistic about ingredients and additives. I think this is why I've enjoyed fishing the Method so much. In addition to the blinding results, you can experiment to your heart's content, which makes the results so much more pleasing when they come.

I was around carp fishing in the 70s so using home-made pastes and specials was the norm in my carping for many, many years until the advent of the boilie. Consequently I have some good memories of some of the additives and ingredients that were very effective in the old days, so I simply used this knowledge and revamped it for my Method mixes. On the other hand, you may be the kind of angler who likes everything done for you. In that case you simply buy ready-made Method mixes in your local tackle shop. But with a little thought and effort you could make your own, resulting in more enjoyment and possibly more action in the process. Having said that I must admit that I know that some of the Method mixes offered by carp bait companies are very good. The less effective ones are made by "let's jump on the bandwagon" merchants. I'm sure you know what I mean.

From my own results and experiences I have come to the conclusion that a Method mix containing a mixture of different-sized items is preferable. Therefore I like to include a percentage of different-sized seeds, particles and pellets in the mix.

I prepare the particles separately at home about five days before my session. What I am going to say may startle some of you, but I think it is entirely relevant: I don't ever use tap water for preparing particles. I use either lake water or rainwater, which I collect in a water butt, which I keep in the garden. "Why?" Well in most parts of the country our tap water has been treated with fluoride – and possibly other sterilising and anti-bacterial treatments – in some areas resulting in a strong smell and taste. For instance I forgot to take some drinking water to Horseshoe Lake for one of the events there. I used the on-site tap water, and my mates and I all noticed it has a strong chemical smell. Depending on which part of the country you live in the water varies in taste considerably. We wouldn't drink tea made with the Horseshoe tap water, so what effect might it have on the carp? "What if?" Let's face it, if you use lake water from your chosen venue you aren't taking risks. Always remember that attention to small things can make a difference. Anyway, back to preparing particles.

I soak my particles in heavily salted lake or rainwater for 48 hours. My choice of particles is usually as follows;

This shot of Hardwick Lake on Linear Fisheries in Oxford shows carp's reaction to my Method mix. Exciting stuff!

hemp, maples and tigers in small quantities, groats and maize in quite a small amount, and finally a fair amount of a seed mix, ideally Dynamite Baits', or Hinders' Partiblend, or Haith's Red Band. For a guide to the amount of salt to use put in one heaped tablespoon of salt to one pound of dry particles. After I've soaked them for 48 hours I boil the mix for 40 minutes. If you are wondering why I use salt in particles it's because it's brilliant; a perfectly natural enhancer which the carp love. If your partner cooked your Sunday dinner and forgot to put salt in the vegetables for the boiling process your dinner would taste boring and bland. The same goes for your particles. Believe me; try it!

Let this little lot ferment in the water you boiled them in and whatever you do don't throw the water away. You will need it later at the lake.

You need to have appropriate tackle to cast balls this size a reasonable distance. If in doubt go smaller on the feeder weight.

Pellets

I use a mixture consisting of 6mm Mainline Activ-8 and Assassin-8 Response pellets in conjunction with Hinders' 3mm Hi-Betaine pellets and a small quantity of floating trout pellets and crushed Chum Mixers. The pellets and crushed Mixers are mixed together.

If you are wondering why I have included floating pellets and crushed mixers these simply help break up the Method ball and disperse the main feed around the Method feeder in a superb manner. The floating bits also break away from the Method feed and may catch the attention of passing fish higher up in the water.

Other Ingredients

Now we move onto my more personalised additives.

These include pork sausage meat, which you can buy from any big supermarket in frozen tubes. If you shop around they are not expensive. I recently paid 80 pence for a pound tube on a "buy one get one free" offer. Do the carp like this stuff, or what?! Some things never change!

PYM, otherwise known as Phillips Yeast Mixture, is an absolute cracker, obtainable in tubs from Haith's near Grimsby, although you may be lucky enough to find it in local pet shops. PYM was always a good additive in pastes – it was the main ingredient in one of the first commercially available base mixes, Hi-Pro – so using it in the Method mix goes down well.

I like tuna fish in my mix, straight out of the tin. The type in sunflower oil is the best. Use the oil in the mix. This turns them on as much as the tuna fish itself and also helps give a brilliant flat spot which hangs around on the surface for ages, helping you to bait up accurately, where necessary.

If you're feeling a bit flush you might like to include some fresh shellfish in the mix, such as cockles, shrimps, prawns, mussels or crabmeat. The last named is great on its own or mixed in the other items listed.

I include diced luncheon meat in odd particle-sized shapes or simply mashed up in the pellets and particles. Along these same lines you might like to include finely chopped Peperami.

One of my personalised additives is eggshell that has been toasted for a few hours in a low-heat oven. This is put in a bag, smashed up, then added to my mix. This is an old bream and tench anglers' trick from the 60s and 70s. The sound of the shell being crushed during feeding acts like a dinner gong when the sound carries underwater, attracting other fish to the spot. The small crunchy items encourage carp to suck and blow by sifting the food from the shell, making them more likely to make a mistake and get themselves hooked. Use with any mix. A good edge.

For convenience and because they are superb, the particles in Dynamite Baits' Frenzied Particle range, which are ready prepared, will save you lots of preparation time. Because they are cooked in the container they retain all those lovely juices. I recommend those.

Pilchards, anchovies, sardines in a tin in oil or tomato sauce. When liquidised this acts as a great binder and is very attractive in its own right, much the same as with tuna. Overlook this type of ingredient at your peril!

Another item I would recommend is Solar Tackle's Bag Mix, which is made up from insects and crustaceans. This is a pukka mix and can be used on its own or with other ingredients to very good effect.

One other possibility to cover is the addition of chopped boilies and liquid additives, such as Mainline's Corn Steep Liquor, which is a terrific additive and one which tends to give off a very strong signal to the carp. There are a number of other liquid bait ingredients you may like to consider including. Experimenting and trying to make improvements is part of the excitement of making your own baits, or Method mixes.

As you can imagine there are literally hundreds of possible ingredients, although I have only mentioned those which I can personally vouch for, items I have used and caught fish on.

Making the Method Mix

Here are some thoughts on putting your chosen mix together. This is what I do.

First of all you get a large plastic bucket or groundbait bowl. Put in a quantity of pellets, say 3 kilos. This may sound a lot but you can always take home what you don't use and save it for another time. Now pour the salted juice off your particles onto the pellets. Not too much. Just enough to damp them down and make them sticky. Leave them for a while, but stir them occasionally to make sure the juice is evenly distributed amongst the pellets.

Now add some of your mixed particles, bit by bit. Don't put in too many or your mix won't bind very well. Keep stirring and add your other chosen

As you can see I prefer fairly long booklinks for Method fishing for bigger specimens.

food items. For example two tins of tuna in sunflower oil, mashed up, chopped boilies, prawns, cockles, whatever you favour, and keep kneading the mix. Trial and error will tell you when the mix is ready. Keep trying it on the Method feeder till it sticks and feels like you could cast it out. Too wet, add more pellet, boilie base mix or Solar's Bag Mix. Too dry, then add more particle water, or liquid bait additive. You will soon get the hang of it.

One important thing I always try to do is to test a baited Method feeder in the margins where I can see it and time how long it takes the mix to break down. You don't want to be guessing on a vital aspect like that. 20-30 minutes is a good break-down time for me. The mix has usually spread out to the size of a saucer, or bigger, by then. If the Method

Tuna. This is without doubt my all-time favourite fish puller when added to the Method mix.

ball doesn't break down at all you should try to add more larger items which swell and crack the mix open. Floating pellets and mixers usually help sort out this aspect.

Personally I don't like pouring boiling water onto pellets as this tends to turn them into a smooth paste and ruin my idea of including bigger food items in the mix. But if you are in a hurry pouring boiling water onto the pellets is the quick way to get them to bind together.

Once you are totally happy with the consistency of your mix take note of what quantities of ingredients you used for future reference. On one occasion I recall omitting the oil from a couple of tins of tuna fish by accident and my results on that session were not as good as they had been previously. When I added the oil on the next session things went well again. Prior to that I had thought the inclusion of the oil was insignificant, but that experience showed me I was wrong. It just goes to show.

Rigs

No need to go ultra fancy or technical here. I am a fan of Kryston Snake-Bite. I simply use the 25lb version with the last 1½" of the skin stripped off to fish the material combi-rig-style, giving the bait some natural movement and increasing the hooking efficiency of the rig. I have used ESP Stiff Rigger hooks in sizes 5 and 6 and they have been excellent. Gardner Tackle have been working with me on a new hook, the Frank Warwick Incizor, which has performed well. As with any other aspect of carp fishing, if you are getting results on the hook you are using then there is no need to change it.

Most anglers perceive a short hooklink as the way to go when Method fishing, with some anglers going to the trouble of burying the hooklink in the Method ball itself. I could see the logic of this so I tried it myself. When I did so my number of hook-pulls and false indications were not good, to say the least, although I've been fishing for larger carp with the Method, and perhaps the bigger carp need more rope to hang themselves. Shorter hooklinks might work well with more competitive singles and doubles in hungry waters. But when I moved up from short hooklinks to links of 8-14" my fish losses virtually disappeared. I know some of you may not agree with the concept of longer hooklinks with the Method, but these observations are based on results and hard facts, which are difficult to ignore.

Hookbaits

There are so many to choose from that it's not easy to decide which is best but I have found without a doubt that maize, tigers, 20mm halibut pellets and the sausage barrel-shaped offcuts you find in bulk bags of Mainline baits are best for hookbaits. In fact any item which is included in the Method mix will work, such as maples, tares, chopped brazils, cockles, pellet hookbaits... Get your thinking head on and try unusual alternatives. I am seriously considering an old classic which is an underrated and neglected bait on the hook, namely broad beans. These were quite an instant bait and needed very little pre-baiting. Another is soaked sultanas, which swell back up to grape size when soaked. Black-eyed beans etc. The choice is endless.

As a sound bit of advice, though, give maize a go first as this is definitely a tough one to beat in Method fishing. Anything that proves better is going to be a hard act to improve on, that's for sure.

A good tip to overcome a possible problem is to be careful when using a relatively light, small hookbait such as maize. It can flail around and tangle quite easily on the cast, which is obviously not good news. To overcome this I have been using Solar's Hookbait Foam, which is a really useful, versatile product for covering the hook and preventing the hair and hookbait wrapping round the hook. Here's how I use the foam.

1. Take a piece of foam and impale it on the hook sideways, so the point is covered.
2. Take another piece of foam, lick it down one side, then lay it across the hair and sandwich the hook shank and hookbait between the two pieces of foam, which will stick together. These totally prevent tangles and after a few seconds in the water the foam will break away from the hook and pop up to the surface, making a very obvious target to catapult free offerings around. I never cast out without using hookbait foam when Method fishing. It's worth the extra effort to know the presentation is perfect.

Here are a few tips on Method fishing which you may like to consider

1. I have found the best Method ball groundbait feeder by a mile to be the Drennan Middy Trev Tomlin Whopper Dropper, with a metal frame and cable ties to attach the strong elastic. I cut the plastic hard cup off and attach a large groundbait mesh cup (as illustrated on p194). This set-up is superb and enables really big balls to be used at considerable range. I carry three of these catapults to cover all eventualities, i.e. boilies, particles and Method balls.
2. It's very easy to be put off Method fishing by whingers, who will usually take great delight in telling you that the noise from the bait going in is going to scare the carp, and also that it is not real 'hard-core' carp angling etc., etc. Ignore all this and really give it a go. Let them get on with their methods and you get on with yours. I bet I know who will be the busier!
3. I hate to say it but the use of a round thing – namely a boilie – for the hookbait will almost certainly slow down your catch rate. Think about being a tad different, and try to catch the carp with their guard down. Most carp have seen boilie-baited traps all their lives, so give the hookbait some thought and try some of my alternative suggestions.

Tight lines and drop me a line if you crack it on the Method. Good fishing.

PVA Bagging – Worth the Effort

I use PVA bags in a great deal of my carp fishing. It is one of my favourite tactics for breaking down the carp's defences. I have used it with great success in carp matches, on pressured home waters, and on huge overseas venues. To me PVA bags are one of the ultimate weapons for focusing the carp's attention to the hookbait, and at the same time trying to get the carp to forget that there may be a hookbait in the equation! Here's a nice little meal... Whoops. Photo time!

There are similarities between Method fishing and PVA bag fishing. I nodded my head in agreement with a great deal of what Frank Warwick has to say in his excellent chapter on Method feeder fishing.

The biggest disadvantage with bags is that you are limited to the type of contents you can use. The fact that water causes them to dissolve means that seeds and particles don't make ideal contents, for instance. But where bags have a massive edge over the Method is that you can stick some in the tackle bag, forget about them, and bring them into play when circumstances dictate their use. One of the pockets in my tackle bag is

Tim Fromant (centre) and Mike Winstone (right) receiving their trophy and cheque from Marsh Pratley following their amazing win in the 2000 British Championships at Horseshoe, all their fish falling to PVA bags.

Brilliant exponents of PVA bagging: Korda's Steve Spurgeon (left centre) and Chris Rose (right centre) following their second successive runaway qualifying win at Walthamstow No 1 in 2001.

Fishabil 36lb mirror, biggest fish of a 95-fish catch in under four days, most of the fish falling to PVA bags at 60 - 70 yards.

reserved for PVA bags and I carry upwards of 200 of them with me wherever I go. 200 over the top? No! When I went back to Fishabil for a four-day session in August 2001 I was thinking in terms of a few days' extreme-range fishing. In fact I finished up fishing PVA bags at 50-60 yards and enjoyed a 95-carp catch in just under four days. During the four days I used over 200 PVA bags!

There have been some remarkable catches and results

involving the use of PVA bags. Steve Briggs and I won the 2000 World Carp Cup at Fishabil, and bags accounted for about two thirds of the fish we caught. At the time the weight of fish that Steve and I caught set new world carp match records for FIPS-ratified events for 48-hour and 72-hour carp matches. Titles are more enduring than records! Later in 2000 Mike Winstone and Tim Fromant left the rest of the field out of sight when they won the final of the British Championships at Horseshoe Lake. They caught 374lb of carp in 48 hours, all on PVA bags. This wasn't a FIPS-ratified event, but a world record is a world record, and for such a weight of fish to be achieved in match conditions at Horseshoe represents one of the greatest carp catches of all time.

I can't mention carp matches without praising the carp fishing exploits of two of Korda Leads' employees, Steve Spurgeon and Chris Rose. Two years running they have won the British Championships qualifier at

Stevie Briggs with one of the many 'bag' fish he caught on the way to our World Carp Cup win at Fishabil in June 2000.

Walthamstow No. 1 with astonishing weights of carp. PVA bagging using Korda Developments' FunnelWeb system has been the cornerstone of their success each year, and it doesn't take a Nostradamus to predict that sooner or later they will win the final of the British. The best result Crowy and I have achieved in the British final was in beating the Korda guys by a place and finishing fourth during the Horseshoe Winstone/Fromant final of 2000. Mind you I think we had a

slightly better peg than they did. Star men these two, and brilliant exponents of PVA bagging.

You don't fish matches? Then you might be more convinced by PVA bag results at Birch Grove, or even Yateley Match Lake! Birch carp are pressured fish with honours degrees in end tackle avoidance. My first choice of tactic there is bagging, and currently my biggest fish from the venue, the famous Video fish at 34lb 2oz, fell to a PVA hookbait set-up. When I went to Yateley Match Lake for the Stoney and Friends Fish-in during September 2001, PVA bag set-ups were again my first choice. I hooked three fish, biggest landed being a famous fish known as Scaley at 34lb 8oz.

I'll mention one other result on PVA bags. I fished the daunting Lake Raduta in Romania during October 2001. The swim I chose had a deep margin, and I fished one rod 100 yards down this margin in about 10 feet of water throughout the two-week session. I stuck to PVA bags on this margin rod for the full session. I didn't know how many fish would visit the margin and didn't want to risk over-baiting it. So I kept a scattering

Birch Grove personal best on a PVA bag presentation, June 2001. The Video Fish at 34lb 2oz.

of pellets and freebies in the area, with the loaded bag recast into the chosen spot three or four times every 24 hours. The rod accounted for a number of fish, including commons of 42½lb and 44lb 4oz.

Why do PVA bags work? They score on a number of counts. They enable you to present a very focused quick snack to the carp. This concentration of the contents does two things. It increases the smell of food in the area of the hookbait, and enables you to present a mixture of food smells, limiting the chance of the smell of the bait itself representing a possible source of danger. The focus of bait can cause a brief element of preoccupation in the carp's feeding, causing it to suck the hookbait into its mouth. Whatever the reason PVA bags work dramatically well and are well worth the extra trouble involved – although, as with Method fishing, it is surprising how few anglers you see actually going to the trouble of fishing bags.

Provoking a feeding response is the key to catching with bags, and to get the fish feeding you have to have a clear idea of what really turns them on. In attempting to create any sort of feeding activity I look on small baits as a must, and while the reaction to certain baits varies from water to water there are some items which have proved so consistently successful wherever I've fished that I can confidently recommend them as being universally effective.

Unless you have watched carp feeding on pellets you can have no idea of their pulling power. Baggage limits permitting, pellets go with me to every water I fish. Which isn't to say that 'pellets' means any pellets. As with all things carpy some pellets are more effective than others. Given one groundbait to fish anywhere I would be torn between hemp and Hinders' 3mm Hi-Betaine pellets. Fishing PVA bags makes the choice an easy one, because pellets are dry, whereas prepared hemp is wet. But I prefer a mix of pellets, made up of the following:

Hinders' 3mm mini Hi-Betaine pellets; Mainline's Activ-8 Response pellets; Nutrabaits' Trigga pellets (in two sizes); Rod Hutchinson's Formula Majic particle/seed-based pellets; tiny koi rearer pellets; the Bait Company's quick-breakdown low fat betaine pellets. (I added the last pellet to my mix during a late 2001 Cassien session and had carp of 42½lb and 57lb the first night I fished over them!) There is such a confusion of food scents from this pellet mix that it will be difficult for the carp to relate to any single smell, or pellet, which to me is a safeguard against the use of a certain type of pellet blowing. I may be repeating myself there but I think it's an important principle on waters where you don't know what baits have been used and what smells the carp may have become nervous of. A mix of sizes and breakdowns helps add to the confusion here, too, and I like Nutrabaits' idea of supplying their Trigga pellets in different sizes.

Crumb is an ideal addition to a PVA bag set-up and there are an increasing number of bag mixes appearing from

Why do bags work? An appealing meal in a bag, with the hookbait difficult to identify, or avoid.

Bags a small-water presentation? At Raduta in October 2001 I fished one rod on PVA bags in the margin throughout the session. The rod accounted for a number of good fish, biggest being this super common of 44lb 2oz.

the bait companies. As with pellets I like the idea of a crumb based on the actual boilie I'm introducing and using as the hookbait. In addition to crumb I carry a range of attractor powders with me from Richworth and Nutrabaits for topping up bags, including Corn Steep Liquor powder, Green Lipped Mussel extract, and Betaine powder. I add a quantity of these to my pellet mix and give it a good shaking. Crumb I add by spoon as I pack the bag.

I've got to make mention of chopped baits. As with pellets they increase the level of attraction in the area of the hookbait without any need for added dips or soaks. Secondly they move the goalposts with regard to the buoyancy of the bag contents. A mix of different-sized and different-buoyancy pellets, plus a few whole baits and chopped baits, can make it difficult for the carp to select individual items from the mix. A good suck can have a fair percentage of the bag's contents flying into the carp's mouth. A buoyant hookbait may well cause the carp to take the bait into its mouth involuntarily.

Bear this in mind when you are tying up your hooklink. Frank Warwick comes down in favour of longer-than-normal hooklinks for Method fishing. I feel the same about hooklinks for PVA bagging. Make sure the carp can suck the bait well into its mouth. To my mind the further it goes in the harder it is for the carp to blow it back out – although we looked at rig design in more detail in the rig chapters.

When you are bagging use small boilies if possible, anything from 8mm to 14mm. Many of the bait companies make baits in 10mm size and this is an ideal size for bag contents and bag hookbaits. If the bait is small enough and good enough the carp don't seem to spend too much time figuring out that they've got a mix of boilies and pellets to go at. In fact during the Fishabil session I referred to earlier, where my boilies were a mix of Trigga and Activ-8 in 14mm, I had the line pulled out of my hand while I was setting the indicator twice in one morning following casts with PVA bags! Similarly some years ago, when I was visually convincing myself of the effectiveness of pellets at Horseshoe, I watched a carp grab a PVA bag and pellet contents immediately after it was introduced and before the bag had even had time to dissolve.

PVA bags are a tactic for all occasions. When I first started using them I looked on them as a weedy water approach, a way of getting the hookbait down to the bottom with free offerings in pads or weed. Now the only limiting factor is whether I can reach the carp with a PVA bag. If I can then it will be my favoured approach for presenting the hookbait on any water where I feel there may be an element of caution in the carp's feeding.

There is a growing range of bag mixes available now. This Bagmix from Solar is one of the most effective.

The Bait Company's hemp and quick-breakdown Betaine pellets, ideal additions to a pellet mix for bagging, spodding or loose feed.

How do you fish bags?

Some time ago I read that the remarkable long-distance caster Mark Hutchinson had cast a PVA bag over 200 yards! Wow. The possibilities behind a statistic like that are intriguing, but for most of us our casting objectives will be far more modest. But the greater your casting potential with a bag, the more fish you are likely to be able to reach. This means looking at the tackle used, the bags, and the bag set-ups.

I very rarely use a rod of under 3lb test curve in my carp fishing, with 3-3¼lb being my preference and 3½lb being my current upper limit. There is a degree of fish-playing compromise with rods of these ratings, but my main requirement is to be able to reach as many fish as possible.

When it comes to choice of rod most readers will be price-led. For bagging you want a tough 12-12½ft rod at the right price with a good track record for no breakages, or a good company name for breakage replacements (they can happen with the best of rods). The low price of some of the rods available now is remarkable, but don't jump for one which won't do the job for you. If your current rods are in the 2-2½lb range and you can't afford a stiffer set then try to get hold of at least one stiffer model for bagging and feeder fishing. A rod of 3lb test curve will enable you to put a bag or feeder out to the ranges you currently look on as a maximum cast for everyday fishing! Using one stiffer rod will give you the chance to get used to the feel of this type of rod without spending all the wife's housekeeping on a new set.

Pop-up over Crumball effect after the PVA bag dissolves.

Don't underestimate the importance of the casting action of the rod. I have a connection with Liverpool rod-maker Alan Young and possess a remarkable collection of rods. Then my friends Rod Hutchinson and his rod-maker Alistair Bond insisted on presenting me with a set of Dream Maker 3½lb test curve rods for Christmas. Apart from the fact that the Dream Makers are a real thing of beauty the extra yardage they give me in chucking out loaded PVA bags amazes me. You can feel the added strength in the middle of the rod and at times the extra 10-15 yards they will cast a PVA bag can be quite significant.

Incidentally, although I cover most aspects of spodding in a separate chapter I feel a spod rod is an indispensable complement to PVA bagging, a point I'll come back to later.

Reel and Line

As I rarely go below 12lb breaking strain reel line (plus a strong leader) I look on big reels as a necessity for most of my fishing. Having used a number of models of reels in recent years I've settled back to my old Daiwa Emblem Z 5500Ts, with Tackle Box baitrunner conversion, for most of the fishing I do where casting is involved. Initially I was enthusiastic about reverse-

You need a rod for the job for casting bags. Young Ben Hofgartner putting a bag into orbit at a Carp Society Carp School a few years back.

tapered spools but they seem to cause more problems than they cure and I now only use them for rowing out baits. The casting problems come in the form of line slap on the rod butt and frap-ups round the butt ring.

The new Shimano Super Baitrunner Aero 10000XTE reels from Shimano look to be a superb compromise in size for anglers wanting increased casting performance, but not wishing to adorn their rods with the big-spooled reels many of us favour. If you are in the market for a new reel check out the Aero 10000XTEs before you make a final decision.

The incidence of line slap and frap-ups appears to be peculiar to the big-diameter spooled reels, and varies from line to line. I suspect that line slap is caused by memory retention of the line, meaning the big coils coming off a reverse-tapered spool don't break down and allow the line to straighten out quickly enough.

My two current favourite lines for my idea of big casts are Gold Label's Pro Clear and Fox's Soft Steel. I've used the Soft Steel for some years now and have found it to be superbly reliable. (I'm a great fan of Gold Label's Pro Gold,

I prefer big-spooled reels for my fishing, particularly when I'm casting a heavy load like a bag or a Method ball. I find the orthodox tapered or parallel spool ideal for casting, and the reverse-tapered spool best for rowing baits out.

but I do find its casting properties to be suspect, especially after some use, and in hot weather. Pro Gold is one of my first choices for snag-infested waters where I am rowing out hookbaits.)

The majority of monos on offer now have good track records for reliability and abrasion resistance. If I need to go below 12lb bs for added distance I'm leaning increasingly towards the high abrasion resistance of Pro Clear. Line strength is rarely an issue. You can't break 8lb or 10lb line with a bent rod, but the lower the breaking strain the more vulnerable the line is when it comes in contact with any kind of snag.

Frank and I talk of 12lb bs lines because of the waters we fish abroad. For much of the fishing in this country 8-10lb bs is OK, provided it is reliable and has a good abrasion resistance rating.

PVA Bags

There was a time when I rationalised that the more loose feed I could cast out in a PVA bag the better the trap would be, simply because there would be free offerings in situ for longer. But through watching the most successful baggers in operation it has become obvious that there is almost a case of "the smaller the better" when it comes to bag presentation. I'm not just talking about casting distance, but about effectiveness, too. Maybe one mouthful is better than two or three mouthfuls, I just don't know, but I do know that I've had more success using smaller hookbait sized bags than I achieved with bigger versions.

I'm now happiest with bags in widths of 2"-3" and ranging in length from 4"-6". I'm familiar with bags from Kryston, Kevin Nash and Black Cat Baits in these sizes, and I can recommend all of them. Web PVA bags are very popular and I would be doing Korda a disservice if I didn't mention their FunnelWeb system, which is extremely popular and has been used to great effect in Chris Spurgeon's and Steve Rose's carp match successes. Anyone wanting an exact description of how these guys go about their PVA bag fishing can find a feature on the subject by them in *Crafty Carper* 49.

Whatever type of system you use carry a spoon with you for loading pellets and crumb or powder. A large teaspoon

Steve Spurgeon of Korda demonstrating his invention, the FunnelWeb system. The hook is simply nicked through the bag prior to casting. With this method you can have a number of bags ready for use prior to starting fishing.

Why I prefer sheet bags for much of my fishing. That first bubble will quickly be followed by a stream of them, which makes it easy to check the exact position of the bag on the bottom.

I spent a day experimenting with PVA bags in the kitchen a few years back, evolved to my present methods, and caught this Motorway Pond 30lb mirror the following weekend.

209

or small dessert spoon is ideal.

I prefer sheet PVA bags for much of my fishing. They have one big advantage over web bags when you are having to precisely position the end tackle in weed or against a snag – bubbles. Pack PVA bags tight to make them aerodynamic, and don't pierce them as I see some writers recommend. When a cast-out bag starts to dissolve it releases a stream of bubbles to the surface, which exactly mark the position of the end tackle. This can be invaluable when you are positioning the tackle in holes in the lilies or a weedbed.

A well-packed PVA sheet bag ready for casting. Whatever material you use pack the bag tight to reduce air resistance on the cast, and to accelerate dissolving in the water.

If you want to be sure of the precise location of the end tackle in longer-range fishing then add some hookbait foam or a brightly coloured pop-up to the contents of the bag.

The other aspect you can monitor with sheet bags is whether they are reaching the bottom intact or not. I've seen some interesting exchanges in carp magazines on the subject of free offerings not being tightly grouped around the hookbait. There's nothing

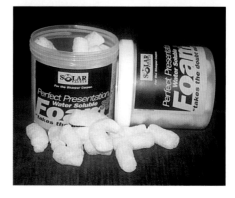

Left: Hookbait foam or a brightly coloured pop-up in the bag are other methods of checking exactly where the bag has finished up.

to say you can't use PVA bags in any form of fishing, including boating out. In deeper water the timing of the tell-tale bubbles will indicate whether the bag is reaching the bottom intact. If it isn't then add an outer bag, or use one of Kevin Nash's slower-dissolve bags. Problems are there to be overcome!

Loading the Bag

My first step with most of my PVA bag presentations is to push the hookbait down to the bottom of the bag, then push the hookpoint through the wall of the bag to the outside. This is to ensure that the contents don't mask the hookpoint, a real possibility where chopped baits are included.

I then add pellets to about halfway up the bag, topping off with a few freebies, some chopped baits, and a few more pellets to round off the bag. Pack to within about an inch of the top, then screw the loose material tightly round the hooklink line, tubing or leadcore and tie off with PVA tape. In this context tape dissolves OK. String doesn't.

Tim Fromant ties his bags differently. He ties them with mono, then ties the mono to the lead. The Korda boys have a supply of web bags tied up and simply hook one onto the end of the line, then cast out.

Having the bag hanging down from the lead limits your casting range. For optimum casting the lead needs to be inside the bag. Again I pass the hook through to the outside of the bag. The lead is then pushed to the bottom of the bag, the contents added, the bag packed as tight as possible and tied off with tape, and away you go. The lead inside the bag presentation is the best long-range set-up but it does limit your alternatives on rig design. If I'm fishing my anti-eject rig I fish the hookbait only in the bag. With the long-range set-up I prefer a braided hooklink of 7"-8".

My bag loading set-up, with the bucket of pellets living just inside the bivvy doorway.

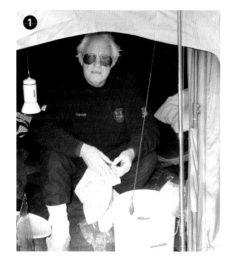

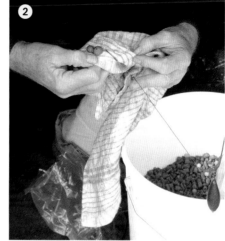

Dry off the baits and end tackle with a bait-smelling old tea towel.

Ready to go. I'm using Kryston Melt-Ex bags here, but all hookbait-sized bags are suitable for this approach. Just check that the bags you use dissolve at the prevailing water temperatures.

First step is to nick the hook through the wall of the bag to the outside so the point can't be snagged by the contents. Note the mixture of pellets in the bucket.

Spoon some tiny pellets into the bag first to pack it out round the hookbaits. These are Dynamite Baits' SwimStim pellets. Hinders mini Hi-Betaine pellets are my tried-and-tested first choice, but early results on SwimStim are promising.

Add the pellet and mini-bait mix...

continued overleaf

...and a few free offerings. I prefer to use small baits when I'm bagging to increase the chances of preoccupation.

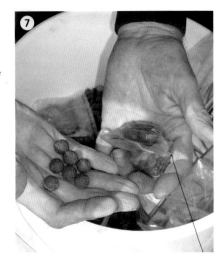

Fill to within an inch of the top of the bag with some more tiny pellets.

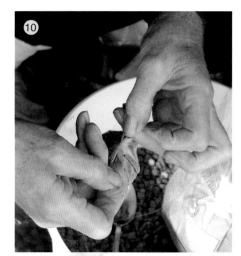

Screw the loose PVA really tight and tie off with PVA tape.

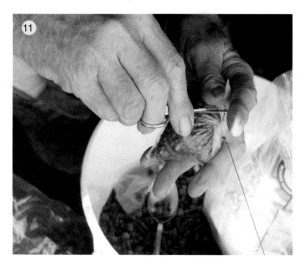

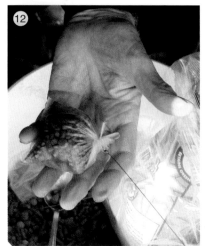

Trim off the loose tape and we're ready to go.

The mark is a spot 60 yards out where carp have shown occasionally for the last couple of days.

In terms of effectiveness there are arguments in favour of pop-ups and bottom baits. I prefer buoyant bottom baits, but I have had PVA bag success on pop-ups, too. A balanced hookbait sitting on top of a pile of pellets has a very appealing look to it, and you feel it must be very difficult for the carp to have a go at the pellets without finishing up with the hookbait in its mouth.

Preparation

The first big mental barrier to cross with PVA bags is to make yourself use them. We've all rehearsed a new method in our minds, equipped ourselves for it, gone to the water intending to fish it, then bottled it when we got in the swim and deferred it till another time. It's called human nature. There is also a lack of logic to it. Better the devil I know, even if it means yet another blank, than making a fool of myself with a tactic I'm not sure of – but which may well catch carp!

We make excuses for ourselves. "Don't really need them." "It looks like rain." "I won't be able to reach the fish with them." "Don't want to make a fool of myself." "No one else is using them so they probably don't work on here." The best one I've heard was when a questioner at a meeting was picking my brains for a way of catching carp. I asked him if he'd tried PVA bags. He assured me that the fish in his water were scared of them!

Part of the PVA bag equipment is a supply of suitable bags. Plus a spoon for loading the bags. A couple of tatty, bait-smeared old tea towels for constant drying of hands and end tackle without tainting the bait or end tackle with the smell of soap or washing powder (kiss of death).

PVA tape for tying off the bag.

Tactics and Spodding

Location of the carp is important of course. You are not just looking for fish, but fish within your casting capabilities with PVA bags. The fact that you can't see them doesn't mean they

"I'm aiming for the flat-topped tree," I told photographer Frank Warwick. His seasoned carp angler reflexes got it in one! The only fish of the session came from the far margin...

aren't there. I don't know if it's a defence mechanism but I rarely see fish show within easy casting distance of the bank. Not when there are anglers on the bank, anyway.

Pick a spot and cast a loaded bag to it. In open-water fishing with bags I tend to cover an area rather than a spot. If you want to cover one spot pick out a far-bank marker (a skyline marker so you can pick it out after dark). When the end tackle is in the right spot mark the reel line with tape so you can recast to the exact spot next time you reel in. This is like swim-feeder fishing as practised by specimen hunters. You keep dropping bait on the same spot, and the PVA bag is the swim-feeder.

Bear in mind that bags are particularly effective for fishing in weed, lily beds, under trees – where a lead in the bag set-up may actually cast through the branches – and tight to snags.

After the initial cast with a bag you can do one of two things; treat it as a long-term baited spot, or look on it as the start of a build-up of bait. On most waters I recast frequently with PVA bags. Every half hour or so to start with, then play it by ear on the basis of action, or the number of nuisance fish in the water. No take doesn't mean you haven't been visited and the freebies eaten. If you are aiming to bag-up then you need a build-up of feed in the swim, by recasting and using a spod. The fact that I've watched a carp go down for a PVA bag the moment it was introduced means that carp in feeding mode aren't fazed by the splash of a PVA bag. Those same carp won't be put off by the splash of a spod, either.

At the outset clip your spod to the distance you are fishing and fire out five or six spods of hemp and pellets. A scattering of seeds and pellets must be very hard work for the carp to clear. A PVA bag focuses the feed and gives the fish a meal that is much easier to feed on. Bagging and spodding can get the fish darting round on the hunt for food. When you can get carp competing for food in this way, catching them becomes a great deal easier.

The prolific Fishabil session I referred to earlier was revealing. Because the fishing was so hectic I used bags on two rods, and boilies over boilie free offerings on the other two. The bags outfished the hookbait rods by six or seven takes to one, and, interestingly, all six of the 30lb+ fish I caught fell to bags.

Bagging on prolific waters can be hard work. It wore Briggsy out when we won the World Carp Cup in 2000. It wore me out during my more recent Fishabil session. You need to keep recasting. You mustn't be put off by a succession of bream or tench. When the carp want it the rest are pushed out, but you may get plenty of action from other species on the way to catching carp, and when the carp take a rest from feeding.

The PVA bag approach for more sparsely stocked waters is different, although I still like an occasional recast to ensure that the hookbait has got some back-up goodies around it. As a rule you have a rough idea of the feeding times on slower venues. Simply make sure a fresh bag is in position half an hour or so before feeding time. At Raduta I was going two or three days between takes on the margin bags, but the two forty-plus commons made the effort of keeping that trap loaded well worthwhile.

I think most anglers want to catch lots of carp. PVA bagging is the most convenient and quickest route to results of this kind. When you really get carp in feeding mode you can almost visualise some sort of game going on out there. Splash. A number of carp home in on the fresh meal. If they are competing a take is almost inevitable, but you have to build up to the competing stage. It's easy to monitor the situation on the surface when we can watch their reactions. Less easy when it's going on out of sight on the bottom. That's when you have to try to get inside their heads and forget any myths that may be building up about spods, leads and PVA bags scaring them. They know a splash means food. I know they are going to eat what I am offering them. On a well-stocked water, if I haven't had a take within half an hour I think they've cleaned out the trap and I'll reel in and start again.

PVA bags make carp in waters of all degrees of difficulty more catchable. Don't ignore them because you look on them as being too much trouble!

50lb+ Captures of England

Chris Ball

Who would ever have thought – even the likes of someone like myself who has taken an active interest in recording the capture of very big carp in this country – that one day I would write a chapter for a carp book about the carp of 50lb and more captured in the UK. Well, the reality is that there have been many such fish banked over the last twenty years – though the great majority have come in the last five to ten years.

Some background

The giant leaps in the size of carp in this country have a history going back to before the last Great War. Take for instance the grand Mapperley mirror of 26lb captured in the summer of 1930 by Albert Buckley. This fish astounded the fishing world; even the likes of fisheries academics such as Tate Regan, a noted ichthyologist of the period, thought this was likely to be the ceiling, weight-wise, for carp in this country.

Albert Buckley's 26lb record breaker from July 1930.

Yet in little more than 20 years, a small pool hidden in the folds of the Herefordshire countryside took carp fishing by the scruff of the neck, shook it, and out came a string of tremendous fish that are still talked of half a century later. The impact of this tiny, almost insignificant piece of water – Redmire Pool – and its three record-breaking carp of 31¼lb, 44lb and 51½lb spanning a 28-year period, is possibly hard to imagine for modern-day carp anglers who are used to seeing news reports of 40lb – and even 50lb – carp nearly all the time.

Put simply, the arrival of Redmire Pool and its giant carp on the scene in the early 1950s was the equivalent of running a 3-minute mile today, or, more to the point, someone catching a 100lb carp from Savay!

But the happenings at Redmire didn't stop people from talking about other waters and the monster fish that they believed they held. Places that come to mind include Billing Aquadrome, Northants where a string of big carp caught in the late 1950s and early 1960s fuelled speculation that here was a water to rival Redmire, and perhaps even throw up a 50-pounder.

Other waters of prominence followed, all threatening to topple fish landed from the mighty Redmire. Ashlea Pool was one such place. Here noted carp angler Tom Mintram and his son Mike saw, in the mid-1960s, what they believed to be a tremendous fish, a record-breaker in fact. Boxmoor in Hertfordshire was another

Redmire Pool photographed by Richard Walker in the early part of the 1952 season.

The 'Redmire Leviathan' photographed in the mid-1950s by Eddie Price.

place where a monster was thought to live. This venue did produce a 40-pounder in 1966, but still the rumours of a bigger fish persisted. Close to where I once lived, a pit at Hollybush Lane near Aldershot, Hampshire, reputedly held several real whoppers. One particular fish around the 34lb-37lb mark was caught a number of times in the mid 1970s. And big-fish angler, Len Arbery, once told me that the largest carp he'd seen in his life swam in Hollybush Lane – an impressive statement, as Len was a Redmire Pool syndicate member at the time!

However the fact remains that none of these waters came anywhere near to producing a carp of 50lb; at best a small handful of 40-pounders was the result. This, I might add, in no way reflects against the waters or anglers mentioned, it is just a plain, simple fact.

Redmire again hit the headlines in 1959 with the capture of the second 40lb carp landed. This fish, captured by Eddie Price in the September of that year, proved to be one of the most famous carp ever to swim within these shores. During the next 21 years it was landed a further eight times, culminating in it becoming a record fish in June 1980.

But it would be a further seven years before the next forty was caught – then, like buses, two came along at once!

Pete Thomas with Dick Walker's legendary Redmire fish of 44lb.

First the Boxmoor fish at 40½lb in July 1966, then the giant Billing Aquadrome common at 42lb in September. This big common justified the long-held belief that Billing did hold huge fish, and much was made of the fact that the venue might produce a fish to topple Dick Walker's 44lb 'Clarissa'.

Again a period of time elapsed before we saw another forty on the bank. This time a fish from Kent was reported in June 1972 at exactly 40lb. Though shrouded in mystery, the fish was a genuine capture to a gentleman called Henry Weeks. Then it was Redmire's turn yet again! First John MacLeod with a 40lb mirror, and the following month the mighty Jack Hilton landed the same fish at 40lb 3oz. And still more was to come…

In August a 43lb 13½oz Redmire common was landed, a very fat spawnbound fish. However, the fact remained that Walker's record had been seriously shaken. I have a tale to tell about this particular fish. The captor was Chris Yates whose Redmire companion for the week was an incredible carp angler from Lincolnshire named Rod

Hutchinson. The pair, with eyes sticking out like organ stops, had some trouble in weighing Chris's beast. It was some time later when they agreed the record-nudging weight of 43lb 13½oz. I firmly believe that when Chris landed the fish it was a record, but in the interval between capture and eventual accurate weighing, a few vital ounces were lost. Not that anyone minded, but there was sadness when the fish was later found dead.

During the latter half of the 1970s many big carp started to be caught, some of them weighing in excess of 40lb. In 1976 a schoolboy named Martin Symonds banked a 42¾lb mirror; in 1978 a small Surrey water produced a 41lb mirror to Jonathan Leigh (a fish which he later caught again at 43lb); and in 1979 a 42-pounder was landed off the surface by Kenny Hodder from a little-known gravel pit on a complex called Yateley in Hampshire! The following year Yateley produced another (different) 40-pounder which in later years became known as Bazil, and another famous carp fishery not far from London Airport, Longfield, produced its first forty.

Jan Wenczka's capture of the Yateley North Lake mirror, later to be known as Bazil. Jan had to take to the water to land this impressive carp in the summer of 1981 when it weighed 41lb 10oz.

The first fifty

It is perhaps fitting that Redmire, still the UK's top carp water at the time, should yield this country's first genuine fifty-pound fish. The water had threatened to produce a fish larger than Dick Walker's Clarissa, the 44lb record fish from September 1952, for some time. Stories of monster carp, both commons and mirrors, have permeated Redmire's history since anglers first clapped eyes on the place and its fishy contents. In fact many, from Dick Walker and his close friends, plus guests, and later in the Jack Hilton era and beyond, claim to have witnessed truly huge fish swimming through Redmire's clear waters. Some of the stories, by respected carp men at the time, made your teeth curl! Could it really be true that Clarissa had been just one of the medium-sized ones…?

Yet it took close on 30 years before we saw a fish to beat Dick Walker's record finally put on the bank. It was a young, lanky lad from Epsom, Surrey, who took the title in what can only be described as dramatic circumstances. Fishing on opening day, June 16th 1980, the dream of a 50lb-plus carp became a reality in the shape of Chris Yates' 51½lb mirror. The battle, described so eloquently in Chris's *Casting at the Sun* book, showed that you didn't need all the latest tackle to master a monster. Chris typically used an old split cane rod and vintage Ambidex fixed-spool reel to master the fish of his dreams.

This carp had an identifiable past (Chris himself previously landed the same fish some seven years before) and had grown into a true leviathan; it was, at the time of this capture, around 48 years old. It firmly put Chris Yates on the map, and anglers everywhere have since benefited from this man's extraordinary talent with both pen and camera, not to mention that marvellous TV series *A Passion for Angling*.

It was perhaps Chris Yates more than anyone else through the late 1970s and early 1980s who perpetuated the Redmire monster myths. He gave the very biggest fish he saw names from a chessboard. His record carp became the Bishop; then there were the Castles, the Knights, and of course the Queen and the King. Though it has never been published, I have seen a page from the Redmire logbook (kept at the pool throughout the 1970s up to 1983) by Chris some time in 1979. The whole A4 page is taken up with a drawing of a Redmire leviathan. Every possible measurement is stated, i.e. size of eye 1 inch across, nostril width ½ inch, gill openings 10 inches and so on and so forth. The length, by the way, was stated as 42 inches from nose to the fork of the tail and it sported the proportionate width as well… it

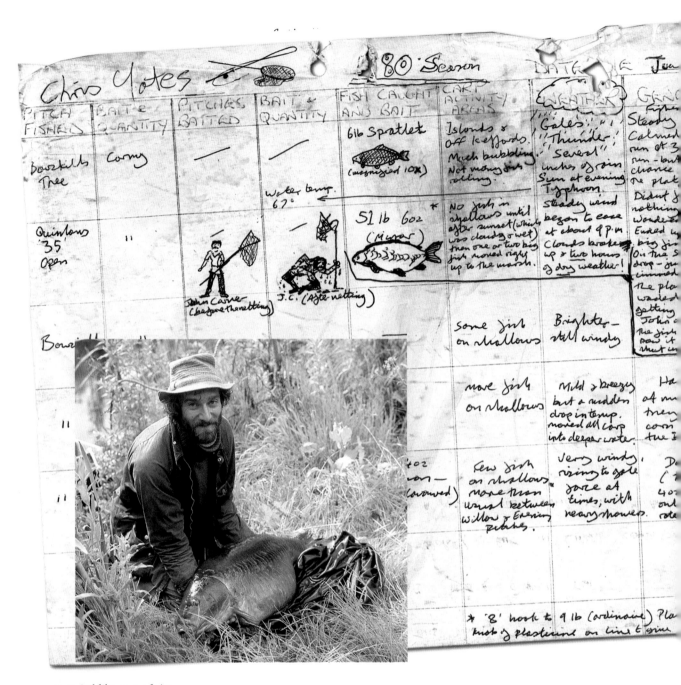

sounded like some fish!

While on this subject I'll mention that the circumstantial evidence to support claims of carp far larger than had been caught at Redmire Pool was strong – but actual proof scant. True, Dick Walker had reported in the mid 1950s rescuing a stranded spawning female fish which had beached itself in shallow water. He waded out, clapped his big net over it and brought it ashore. It was weighed roughly at a little over 58lb. He also mentioned that other than the large distended gut, the mirror didn't look appreciably bigger than his record fish.

Then you have the famous picture taken by Eddie Price at Redmire in July 1958 of a tremendous fish he found lying in weed off Ingham's pitch. It shows the head and shoulders of what might well have been a real monster. But we will never know for sure.

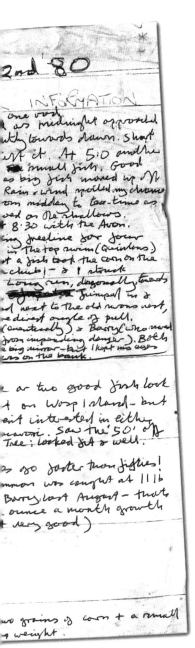

*Record of a record. Chris Yates'
graphic page from the Redmire Log
describing the capture of his
mirror of 51lb 6oz (later corrected
to 51lb 8oz).
Inset: Chris with his second capture
of the '38', this time at a weight of
51lb 8oz, shattering Dick Walker's
27-year-old national carp record.*

*The second 50lb+ carp caught in UK.
Dave Cumpstone with Wraysbury's
Mary at 50lb 8oz, December 1992.*

*Martin Locke with his Herts Club Lake
capture of the mirror known as Chop
Dorsal at 50lb 4oz in December 1994.*

…and the second fifty

It may surprise a few to learn that the
second 50lb carp banked in this
country also went on to become a
record fish – Wraysbury's much-loved Mary, which was landed by Dave
Cumpstone in December 1992 at 50½lb. This notable fish had acquired
a devoted following since it first became known of in 1991 when Peter
Springate landed what was then thought to be an unknown fish of 45lb
6oz. Later it was realised that Dave Cumpstone had already landed a
much smaller Mary at 28¾lb in June 1988.

I came within an ace of seeing the Cumpstone capture of Mary on a
cold December day in 1992 – had it not been for an important meeting
at work. Even more spectacular was the fact that only the day before
Dave had called me with news of a 40lb capture from Wraysbury, and
could I go and take some photographs? I picked up RMC Angling

*It was early June 1995 when young Roddy Porter
broke Chris Yates's long-standing record with this
spawnbound fish of 53lb 15oz from Duncan Kay's
Mid Northants fishery.*

manager, Ian Welch, on the way and together we found Dave looking cold and tired in the North Lake close to the NatWest Sailing Club.

This carp, called Mary's Mate, was in fine condition, and considering the circumstances, an outstanding capture. I remember asking Dave if he thought any more of the big Wraysbury fish were in the same area. He replied that he never put his bait back in the same spot, and anyway, if a carp was hungry enough it would find his bait!

Little did I realise that I would receive a call from Dave at the same time next morning. The conversation went something like this: "Chris, I've managed another one and it's bigger than the first!" I asked, "How big?" Dave returned with, "50½lb!" Unfortunately I couldn't get to see the fish and ultimately only Ian Welch had the good fortune to witness this amazing capture.

Under two years later and Mary was landed again, this time by big fish angler, Kevin O'Farrell – the same weight as before, 50½lb. Twice in 1995 Mary slipped up, then the following year an unprecedented five captures culminated in a very special capture – one that turned the fish into a record-breaker.

Not pretty, but a landmark capture. The Mid Northants fish known as Scaley weighed in excess of 55lb when Alex White caught it a couple of weeks after Roddy Porter's capture in June 1995.

However, before we take a more in-depth look at Mary, another potential record carp was caught twice in June of 1995, from Duncan Kay's Mid Northants fishery. The first capture, by Roddy Porter, was tinged with controversy, as it was the first year of the old close season being scrapped. The carp was caught a week before 16th June and weighed 53lb 15oz. Remarkably this was young Roddy's first carp in excess of 20lb! The controversy was short-lived, however, because shortly after (a few days after the 16th) the same fish was landed again, this time by Alex White at 55¼lb. The fish, heavily spawnbound, sadly died a while later.

The fish known as The Pet became Clive Tillotson's second 50lb+ capture when he caught the gutty mirror at 50lb 10oz from the Priory in September 2000.

Mary makes the top spot

It was a cold November day in 1996 that saw an extraordinary young carp angler, Terry Hearn, finally track down the fish he'd been after at Wraysbury. In tense circumstances, including the fish getting stuck on a snag necessitating the captor to take to a boat in a bid to release it, Terry finally heaved ashore a new record carp (he also landed a 40-pounder in the same amazing session).

The fish itself at this stage was just magnificent; its winter livery starting to show, plus a superb shape, made it the most desirable carp on the planet – and the carp world thought that too. Amid great excitement the record weight of 55lb 13oz was established – the scales were weighing 3oz light when I took them to be certified by Weights & Measures – which meant the great Mary and the name of Terry Hearn passed into carp fishing history for ever.

The same year other 50-pounders were reported. Emperor Lake, in the South-West, a secret syndicate water, threw up a 52lb 6oz mirror known as Smirk to Trevor Picton. This carp had steadily been growing

– the year before it was caught at 49lb 7oz by Paul Williams. Then there were the strange circumstances surrounding the capture of a carp caught from Hawkhurst, Kent. Pictures at the time, some claimed, showed it to be a magoi carp (a Japanese Black Koi carp). It weighed 51¼lb.

However, it was another common carp that really excited the carp world at the time. This monster fish came from one of the most unlikely places imaginable; a small lake with log cabins all around on a family holiday complex at Warmwell, Dorset!

This fish also provided the fairer sex with the largest carp ever to a woman. Angie Clayton, a seamstress by trade and a carp fisher by inclination, banked a fish that became known as Herman at 50½lb. Later in the year, just before Christmas, it was landed again at the same weight by Mark Holt. The Colne Valley threw up a whacker as well, though this mirror didn't come to light until a little while later. Caught in August 1996 by Phil Matthews, captor of a number of very big carp, he

Dave Mallin with a famous but rarely seen fish known as the Black Mirror from the Mere. Dave caught this great fish at 48lb and 51lb 8oz.

recorded the weight of the deep-bodied mirror at 51lb 1oz.

In the last five years

In 1997 Mary and the Emperor Lake big mirror, Smirk, dominated the fifties caught that year,

Pete Amey with Brucie at 50lb 9oz (Nov 98) and Smirk at 50lb 3oz (July 96) from the exclusive Emperor Syndicate Lake in the South-West of England.

though there were other captures by Paul Forward with the tremendous Herts Club Water's Chop Dorsal, at a massive weight of 53¼lb, and Trevor Willoughby with another huge Colne Valley fish of 52½lb. But it was in September that Terry Hearn again stamped his authority on the carp world by catching another massive carp, Two-Tone at 50lb 13oz. This particular fish from Conningbrook, a lake run by Mid Kent Fisheries, was destined for the top within a few short years.

Amazingly by 1998 you needed to catch a carp bigger than

The third fifty from Emperor Lake. Mark Woodball with a very gutty Sumo at 51lb 1oz, March 2001.

The Darenth complex in Kent has produced a number of slightly controversial fifties which are thought to have been imported as big fish. Here are three of them. From top: Paul Harris, 50lb 8oz; Rob Marsh, 50lb 15oz and Tony Lee 51lb 4oz.

50lb 2oz to get in the top ten captures of that year! Again the prominent fish caught were Mary and Smirk. But the Mid Kent fish, now a potential record contender, was in there too. Master Mid Kent Fisheries angler, Ian Brown, accounted for the Conningbrook mirror at 55lb 15oz. However, even this capture was eclipsed by Kevin Cummins when he landed Mary at a new record-busting weight of 56lb 6oz.

Into the last year of the decade and Mary still held the top spot. I was called out to take the photos for *Carp-Talk* of the fish caught at the start of the season by Darren Elks weighing 55½lb. Within touching distance of this weight the Mid Kent fish was landed twice in May. First to big-carp angler Dave Lane at 54lb and a little while later to Kent angler, Lee Watson, at 55¼lb. The Conservative Club in the Colne Valley produced another tremendous fish in the shape of a 52½lb mirror to Adrian Torlenni.

Two other most worthy fish were caught over 50lb in 1999; they both came from the Car Park Lake at Yateley. The celebrated Heather the Leather at 51¼lb to Steve Pagulatos; the other called Arfur landed by Tom Shaw at 50½lb. Yateley, for so long the home of big carp, had produced these two 50-pounders some 20 years after it produced its first forty!

The start of the new millennium saw a wealth of huge fish being landed. For once Mary was eclipsed for the top spot by Conningbrook's Two-Tone which was landed twice in June, first at 55¾lb by Rick Blakelock and a little later by Matt Lawrence at a staggering 56lb 2oz. It was also the year that saw massive fish from Ringstead and Darenth Big Lake – which first made the headlines as big forties – plus Acton Burnell (introduced as doubles) put in major appearances. And on top of all this was the huge common, Benson, from Bluebell Lakes, Peterborough.

This particular common had made several appearances at forty pounds in preceding years, but come May 2000 it went through the 50lb mark for the first time – at 51lb 2oz to Terry Pankhurst – and never looked back. In fact in October, Morgan McGlinchley recorded the common at 54lb exactly! Another notable that year was an amazing fish called The Pet, which was landed a number times at over 50lb, and of course the year 2000 saw a totally new whacker hit the headlines.

The front page of *Carp-Talk* May 2000 shouted out, "Unknown Monster", telling the angling world of a truly huge carp of 52lb caught from a little-known gravel pit, Sonning Eye, close to Reading, Berkshire. The angler concerned, Andy Dodd, held the carp world spellbound when the tale finally came out of a 32lb common, followed by mirrors of 41lb and finally the 52-pounder. Some investigative work carried out revealed that the big mirror had been caught some ten years earlier by Peter

Derek Bullock with one of the fifties Acton Burnell has produced. The common known as Bill, 51lb 4oz, September 2001.

The fish a Mainline bait was designed for...Brian Ives with his capture of the famous Essex Grange mirror at 50lb 1oz.

Geoff Crawford with a 49.10 from an undisclosed stillwater – the same fish was caught by Andy Beard at 50lb-plus in 2001.

Springate at 35lb! This carp was caught again by highly regarded carp man Steve Allcott in September 2000 at 52½lb.

The year of 2001 became a vintage year for captures of 50-pounders, with no fewer than 34 individual captures... and this didn't include the capture of the country's first 60lb carp! The top three places that year were taken by the Conningbrook fish, Two-Tone. First Terry Glebioska broke the old record held by Mary at 56lb 6oz when he banked Two-Tone in April at 59lb 7oz. Four months later Mark

Tolard caught the fish at 59¾lb and in October, amid much excitement, Nashbait's Gary Bayes landed the tremendous fish at 61lb 2oz – quite a moment in carp fishing history.

Not far behind came the Sonning Eye mirror known as the Eye at a new top weight of 57¼lb to that excellent carp angler, Chris Pearson. The Bluebell common was also recorded at its then highest ever weight of 57lb to Terry Buchan. Indeed it was such a year for massive carp that ten captures were recorded in excess of 55lb!

The remarkable Yateley Car Park Lake has produced two different home-grown fifties to Steve Pagulatous. Here the prolific big-carp catcher Dave Ball poses with Heather the Leather at 49lb (above) and Steve himself cradles the massive Arfur at 51lb 6oz.

Terry Hearn with his famous capture of Mary at a new record-breaking weight of 55lb 13oz in November 1996.

It should be placed on record that during 2001 celebrated big-fish man Dave Lane became the first angler to complete the capture of three home-grown English fifties when he banked the Eye from Sonning at a massive 55lb. Dave already had captures of Wraysbury's Mary and Mid-Kent's Two-Tone at weights in excess of 50lb under his belt.

Stephen Fudge recorded the Yateley Car Park's Arfur at 51lb; Derek Rowlands caught a whacker from the Herts club water in the Colne Valley; Mark Woodhall recorded a very fat mirror of 51lb 1oz from a South-West water; Andy Beard landed a

The famous CPs from Horton was named after the engaging Chris Pearson, here seen holding the Eye from Sonning when he caught the great fish at a massive 57lb 4oz in June 2001.

deep-bodied 50¾lb from St Ives Lagoon, Cambridgeshire, and Alan Taylor banked a monster common from Acton Burnell at 52¼lb. To top it all, John Cooper became the first man to land a brace of 50lb carp, both from Acton Burnell.

However, 2001 was the year that was also tinged with great sadness as some of the country's great old warriors passed away. These included the celebrated Mary from Wraysbury, Bazil from Yateley and Raspberry from Redmire Pool – great fish that will live on in carp fishing history.

2002 arrived and with it no let-up in the monsters being caught. As I write three fifties have been landed so far; Benson the common from Bluebell twice! First at its highest ever weight of 58½lb in early March to Nick Bycraft, and in mid-April by top carp angler Martin Locke at 54¾lb (caught on maggots). The other fifty was landed from Darenth Big Lake by Leigh Stewart-Day, a fish called the Leather at 51½lb. The list on the following pages contains a number of captures that were too late to be included in this commentary, including England's second '60', Two-Tone at 60lb 9oz to Brett White of Kent.

The English record carp capture at the time of going to print. Nashbait's Gary Bayes with the Mid Kent's Two-Tone at 61lb, October 2001.

Stop Press

When you write a chapter of this nature you half suspect that a record fish will be caught just after the book has gone to the printers. In fact Lee Jackson's very popular capture of Mid-Kent's Two-Tone, the fish of his dreams and one he had been pursuing for some years, occurred on the 29th August 2002, less than a week before print deadline. We have added Lee's capture of Two-Tone at 61lb 11oz to the big-fish list, although the weight is still subject to confirmation at the time of writing. Well done, Lee, from all of us, firstly for catching Two-Tone at a new record weight, and secondly for obligingly timing the capture for inclusion here.

50lb+ Carp Caught in the UK

Compiled by Chris Ball – Captures to 31st August 2002

The following is simply an historical record of the reported carp caught in this country at a weight in excess of 50lb. We have attempted to make a distinction between fish thought to have been born in this country (originals), and those thought to have been imported as grown fish (of uncertain origin). Some of the imported fish can be traced back to double-figure or twenty-pound-plus weights. Others suddenly appeared as big fish. There is no snobbery or elitism in this distinction, nor is it an attempt to cast doubt on the authenticity of any of the fish, or the captures. It is simply to make it clear that there may be different criteria to apply to the growth potential of the two categories of carp – and to make it known to future generations that at one time there were different categories. Thanks to Chris for compiling this remarkable list and to all those who helped with the information and the photographs. Our apologies to anyone whose capture has been omitted. If you feel you should have been included please contact Chris through *Carp-Talk* to ensure that you appear in future versions of the list. For the record the captures listed here refer to 30 different 50lb+ fish. **Tim Paisley**

Weight	Captor	Venue	Date	Origin
61.11*	Lee Jackson	Mid-Kent Fisheries	August 2002	Original
61.0*	Gary Bayes	Mid-Kent Fisheries	October 2001	Original
60.9	Brett White	Mid-Kent Fisheries	August 2002	Original
59.12*	Mark Tolard	Mid-Kent Fisheries	September 2001	Original
59.7*	Terry Glebioska	Mid-Kent Fisheries	April 2001	Original
59.2	John Cooper	Bluebell	July 2002	Uncertain
58.8	David Nicklin	Bluebell	June 2002	Uncertain
58.8	Nick Bycraft	Bluebell	March 2002	Uncertain
57.4	Chris Pearson	Sonning Eye	June 2001	Original
57.0	Terry Buchan	Bluebell	October 2001	Uncertain
56.8	Mike Redfern	Mid-Kent Fisheries	June 2001	Original
56.6*	Kevin Cummins	Wraysbury 1	September 1998	Original
56.2	Matt Lawrence	Mid-Kent Fisheries	June 2000	Original
56.2	Mick Davidson	Bluebell	September 2001	Uncertain
55.15	Ian Brown	Mid-Kent Fisheries	October 1998	Original
55.14	John Cooper	Bluebell	May 2002	Uncertain
55.13*	Terry Hearn	Wraysbury 1	November 1996	Original
55.12	Rick Blakelock	Mid Kent Fisheries	July 2000	Original
55.8	Darren Ward	Wraysbury 1	April 1997	Original
55.8	Bill Dawson	Wraysbury 1	May 1997	Original
55.8	Dave Mallin	Wraysbury 1	October 1998	Original
55.8	Darren Elks	Wraysbury 1	June 1999	Original
55.8	Les Watts	Ringstead	October 2000	Uncertain
55.4*	Alex White	Mid Northants	June 1995	Original
55.4	Lee Watson	Mid-Kent Fisheries	May 1999	Original
55.0	Dave Lane	Sonning Eye	July 2001	Original
55.0	Gary Fordham	Darenth Big Lake	October 2001	Uncertain
54.12	Martin Locke	Bluebell	April 2002	Uncertain
54.7	Andy Pickford	Bluebell	July 2001	Uncertain
54.2	Mike Kirk	Ringstead	October 2001	Uncertain
54.0	Paul Tolard	Wraysbury 1	July 1997	Original
54.0	Dave Lane	Mid-Kent Fisheries	May 1999	Original

54.0	'Hippy' Neil	The Priory	May 1999	Original
54.0	Nick Howard	Darenth Big Lake	October 2000	Uncertain
54.0	Morgan McGlinchey	Bluebell	October 2000	Uncertain
54.0	Gary White	Emperor Lake	July 2002	Uncertain
53.15*	Roddy Porter	Mid Northants	June 1995	Original
53.15	Nigel Stock	Wraysbury 1	June 1999	Original
53.12	Simon Cupitt	Wraysbury 1	December 2000	Original
53.12	Ken Dallow	Acton Burnell	July 2002	Uncertain
53.6	Lee Richards	Acton Burnell	June 2002	Uncertain
53.10	James Woods	Wraysbury 1	August 2001	Original
53.7	Jerry Hiscutt	Emperor Lake	June 1998	Uncertain
53.4	Phil Thompson	Wraysbury 1	August 1997	Original
53.4	Paul Forward	Herts Club Lake	November 1997	Original
53.2	Mark Tolard	Wraysbury 1	September 2000	Original
53.1	Clive Tillotson	Wraysbury 1	June 1998	Original
52.14	Aaron Lidstone	Emperor Lake	April 1998	Uncertain
52.12	Jim Shelley	Wraysbury 1	July 1999	Original
52.12	Paul Tolard	Wraysbury 1	September 1999	Original
52.9	Trevor Picton	Emperor Lake	October 1996	Uncertain
52.8	Jerry Stapylton	Wraysbury 1	September 1996	Original
52.8	Steve Allcott	Sonning Eye	September 2000	Original
52.8	Leon Bartrop	Darenth Big Lake	April 2001	Uncertain
52.4	Alan Taylor	Acton Burnell	October 2001	Uncertain
52.0	David Skelly	Emperor Lake	May 1998	Uncertain
52.0	Simon Scott	Wraysbury 1	August 1999	Original
52.0	Andy Dodd	Sonning Eye	May 2000	Original
52.0	Kevin Maddocks	Ringstead	May 2000	Uncertain
52.0	Tom Banks	Wraysbury 1	July 2000	Original
52.0	James Fox	Bluebell	June 2001	Uncertain
51.15	Matt Baines	Emperor Lake	May 1997	Uncertain
51.12	Derek Rance	Wraysbury 1	August 2000	Original
51.12	Tony Lee	Darenth Big Lake	July 2001	Uncertain
51.10	Paul Tanner	Bluebell	May 2000	Uncertain
51.10	Steve Ball	Strawberry Fields	June 2002	Uncertain
51.8*	Chris Yates	Redmire Pool	June 1980	Original
51.8	Peter Springate	Wraysbury 1	May 1996	Original
51.8	Jerry Stapylton	Wraysbury 1	June 1996	Original
51.8	Dave Mallin	Colnemere	May 1999	Original
51.8	Gary Hughes	The Priory	July 2000	Original
51.8	Steve Old	The Priory	September 2000	Original
51.8	Derek Rowlands	Herts Club Water	September 2001	Original
51.8	Leigh Stewart-Day	Darenth Big Lake	April 2002	Uncertain
51.6	Steve Pagulatos	Yateley Car Park	June 2002	Original
51.6	Martin Walker	Acton Burnell	August 2000	Uncertain
51.6	Martin Walker	Acton Burnell	June 2001	Uncertain
51.5	Aaron Lidstone	Emperor Lake	August 1997	Uncertain
51.5	Anon	Ringstead	September 1999	Uncertain
51.4	Chris Holliday	Hawkhurst	March 1996	Uncertain
51.4	David Skelly	Emperor Lake	September 1998	Uncertain

51.4	Les Watts	Ringstead	September 1999	Uncertain
51.4	Steve Pagulatous	Yateley Car Park Lake	October 1999	Original
51.4	Joe Bowler	Emperor Lake	December 1999	Uncertain
51.4	Tony Lee	Darenth Big Lake	December 2000	Uncertain
51.4	Derek Bullock	Acton Burnell	September 2001	Uncertain
51.2	Terry Pankhurst	Bluebell	May 2000	Uncertain
51.1	Mark Woodhall	Emperor Lake	March 2001	Uncertain
51.0	Stephen Fudge	Yateley Car Park Lake	November 2001	Original
50.15	Rob Marsh	Darenth Big Lake	November 2000	Uncertain
50.14	Neo Farrari	Darenth Big Lake	June 2001	Uncertain
50.13	Terry Hearn	Mid-Kent Fisheries	September 1997	Original
50.12	Jerry Stapylton	Wraysbury 1	September 1995	Original
50.12	Steve Mellor	Bluebell	May 2001	Uncertain
50.12	Andy Beard	St. Ives Lagoon	May 2001	Original
50.10	Clive Tillotson	The Priory	September 2000	Original
50.10	Lee Simpkin	Darenth Big Lake	October 2000	Uncertain
50.10	Ritchie Curtis	Colnemere	September 2000	Original
50.9	Pete Amey	Emperor Lake	November 1998	Uncertain
50.9	Kim Jobson	Emperor Lake	March 1999	Uncertain
50.8	Dave Cumpstone	Wraysbury 1	December 1992	Original
50.8	Kevin O'Farrell	Wraysbury 1	August 1994	Original
50.8	Kevin Cummins	Wraysbury 1	July 1995	Original
50.8	Angie Clayton	Warmwell	September 1996	Original
50.8	Mark Holt	Warmwell	December 1996	Original
50.8	Rod Killick	Mid-Kent Fisheries	August 1997	Original
50.8	Tom Shaw	Yateley Car Park Lake	June 1999	Original
50.8	Stuart Smith	Emperor Lake	November 1999	Uncertain
50.8	Martin Walker	Acton Burnell	June 2000	Uncertain
50.8	Kevin Maddocks	Acton Burnell	June 2000	Uncertain
50.8	Paul Harris	Darenth Big Lake	June 2000	Uncertain
50.8	Dave Ostapuik	Bluebell	July 2000	Uncertain
50.8	Anon	Darenth Big Lake	May 2001	Uncertain
50.8	Chris Thomas	The Priory	June 2001	Original
50.8	Billy Keefe	Darenth Big Lake	October 2001	Uncertain
50.5	Dave Lane	Wraysbury 1	April 1996	Original
50.5	Marcus Betts	Saddington Reservoir	June 2002	Original
50.4	Martin Locke	Herts Club Lake	December 1994	Original
50.4	Pete Amey	Emperor Lake	April 1996	Uncertain
50.4	Steven Scarlett	Darenth Big Lake	April 2001	Uncertain
50.3	Anon	Emperor Lake	February 1999	Uncertain
50.3	Kevin Blake	Darenth Big Lake	May 2001	Uncertain
50.2	Mark Woodhall	Emperor Lake	September 1998	Uncertain
50.2	Geoff Booth	Bluebell	April 2001	Uncertain
50.2	Terry Hook	Darenth Big Lake	May 2001	Uncertain
50.1	Brian Ives	Essex Grange	May 2000	Original
50.1	Graham Fowler	Darenth Big Lake	October 2000	Uncertain
50.0	Martin Young	The Causeway	June 2002	Original
50.0	Matthew Cammack	Bluebell	July 2000	Uncertain
50.0	Viv Dewsnap	Bluebell	October 2000	Uncertain

* Record capture at the time.

The Belgian Carp Scene

Alijn is one of the biggest names in carp fishing. Editor of the VBK (Vereniging van Belgische Karpervissers) magazine, author of two top-selling books, an angler with a string of big-fish successes to his name in his own country and beyond. To those of us from this country who know him Alijn is the Terry Hearn of Europe, and, like Terry, he is likeable and popular with it. He's also a very busy guy, so I'm delighted that he's managed to find time to put together this insight into the fascinating Belgian carp fishing scene.

Alijn Danau

Fishery Laws and Customs

In contrast to England where most of the big fish waters are run by individuals and professional fishery companies such as RMC Angling, most of the top Belgian waters are the property of the government. The government has several organisations, known as commissions, that have some participation in fishery policies relating to stocking and so on.

The VBK, the organisation which I work for, has several members in these commissions. Because of that we also have some impact on what happens to carp waters. Our impact is far less than we would like but most of our work is voluntary and the power of the green organisations is far greater than ours, and they are far better structured than we are. They have some political power, which we don't have.

Increasingly in recent years carp anglers have been forced into recognising the importance of securing fishing rights by the green organisations. The greens are subsidised by the government and are purchasing a great many waters On those waters there is no future for angling whatever. Because of that more and more people are trying to secure the fishing rights to their local fisheries. That is why in recent years we have had more and more syndicate waters appearing.

The VBK has secured several waters, and all those waters can be fished by VBK members only, but as anyone can join the VBK anyone can fish them, if they wish

Alijn and the Big Leather at 51lb.

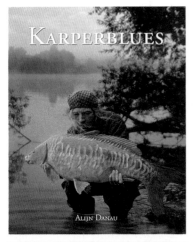

The three Belgian carp titles published to date. All three have a special place on author Tim Paisley's bookshelf.

to. De Blaarmeersen in Gent and Egelhemvijver on Hombeek are the two most famous waters we control. Both contain fish to over forty pounds.

The fishing rights on waters like canals, rivers and so on can't be secured for reasons I won't explain; it would take far too long! Because of that we have tried for years to change the no night fishing rule – up to the present day, unsuccessfully. Fishing is not high on the list of politicians' priorities! However, we keep on trying and we have never been so close to having night fishing legalised as we are at present.

Another new rule that is almost certainly going to be introduced concerns the retaining of fish. In future there will be no keep-nets or sacks. This is to discourage fish-stealing. Anyone caught with a carp in their possession will be fined. We don't want to see our top fish being caught in foreign waters. We have a much greater knowledge of what fish are in our waters than most French carp anglers have of theirs: Belgian carp popping up in foreign weeklies will undoubtedly be recognised.

We are currently working on introducing legislation which would allow us to prosecute fish thieves and penalise them with a much higher penalty than exists today.

Publications

Up to the present three Belgian carp books have been published, all in recent years. They are *Karperblues*, published in 1999 and now sold out, and *Tegen de Stroom In*, published in 2001, both those books being by me. The other book is *De Dunne Lijn...* by Luc de Baets, published in 2000. Luc was once the main man on the Belgian carp scene. He did a great deal to increase the general knowledge of the average carp angler through publications, slide shows etc. He gave up carp fishing in the mid-90s to become a very successful match and feeder-fisher. Thankfully a couple of years later he wrote his carp angling testament and gave Belgian carp anglers what they had been waiting for for over a decade, his book *De Dunne Lijn...*

The only Belgian carp periodical is the VBK magazine, of which I am the editor, although both *Karper* and *De Karperwereld* (both Dutch

Below: The VBK magazine Alijn edits and produces.

publications) can be bought in Belgium. The Dutch and Belgian languages are very similar so most of the time we are able to understand each other – although we have very different cultures when it comes to carp fishing.

Belgium compared to Holland

Belgium is only a small country compared to England or France, but we probably have as many big fish per acre of water as France, and far more than in England or Holland.

Carp culture plays a great part in this. All our top waters are stocked with mirrors and commons with good growth rates, and they are kept in balance. Most of our waters would probably sustain more carp, but the low stocks allow the fish to maximise their growth and weight. This is not the case on most waters in Holland. They have stocked a specially bred so-called 25% hybrid for three decades. When they started this programme in the late sixties/early seventies, the Continental carp world was heavily influenced by carp anglers who fished for wild carp. They found that wild carp were superior to the royale carp because of their fighting capacities. This led to the breeding of a strain of carp that had 50% wild blood. The OVB, which controlled the Dutch waters, stocked all waters throughout Holland with this type of carp for three decades. Only in recent years have they returned to stocking the same type of carp found in the waters of Belgium.

Alijn signing copies of his second book Tegen de Stroom In *at the February 2002 Carp Show at Zwolle in Holland. Alijn took delivery of 500 copies of the book in time for the weekend – and sold the lot!*

However, some angling organisations and individuals have been secretly stocking their local waters with fish they have brought in from Belgium or Germany. Especially waters near the borders. That's why some Dutch waters have bigger than average carp. Of course there are still a few big mirrors left from before the 25% hybrid stockings, but today they are few and far between. This is why Holland is a land of many carp, but with very few big ones.

Waters and Big Catches

Up to the present day Belgium has produced four different fish over 30 kilos (66lb) – two commons and two mirrors. Three of those fish reached their top weights during the same period of the mid-90s. Sadly none of those fish are still with us.

Skup, the big common, lived in a 50-acre lake near Geraardsbergen (de Gavers) and reached his highest weight of 30.5 kilos in March 1997 when he was caught by young local angler Pascal Vanderlinden. This fish was also caught by Ronnie de Groote at the end of 1996 at 30.3 kilos. The fish died in August 1998. Captures of Skup are well documented. As a youngster I lived near that lake. The first recorded capture of this fish was in 1986 at a

Belgian big-fish star Ronnie de Groote at a European carp show.

weight of 15 kilos. The fish was caught on more than thirty occasions during its life and still looked immaculate in its last years. The circumstances of its death are dubious to say the least.

In 1996 another big mirror of 30.9 kilos was caught by Filip De Meulder at a lake near the E-10 highway at a place called St. Job in't Goor. This particular fish, which was called De Knik, was also caught by an English angler, Michael Goodyear, at 26.1 kilos, a capture that appeared in *Carp-Talk* at the time. The giant fish was found dead, wrapped in line and tethered to a buoy, in 1997.

The Belgian record fish was caught in March 1995 by Phil Cottenier and has been well documented in the past. Its death was a bit of a mystery as the dead fish was never found. This fish used to come out several times each year and as it has not been caught for over five years there is now no hope left that it will turn up again.

Belgium's fourth carp over 30 kilos – a canal common – is still growing, and will hopefully grow even bigger. Unfortunately I can't give any details of this fish as I hardly have any myself.

Several other lakes around the country have produced – and are still producing – carp in excess of 25 kilos. The Big Leather from the 35 Syndicate in Hofstade, between Antwerp and Brussels, is one of the most famous. Its biggest weight so far has been 26.3 kilos when it was caught by Dutch angler John van Eck in October 2000, a capture which appeared on the front cover of the English *Carpworld* magazine. I caught the fish at a spawned-out weight of 23.1 kilos the following summer. This lake contains

Oliver Stevens broke the Belgian common carp record with his capture of Skup at 27.3 kilos in 1996.

Sven Hoebeeck with the late lamented big common Skup at 27 kilos.

another big fish in excess of 25 kilos which once appeared on the front cover of *Carp-Talk* when it was caught by Belgian ex-carper Luc Coppens.

Like many of Belgium's top lakes the 35 Syndicate lake is understocked and the fishing can be very hard. But then again most of the fish are immaculate, and of respectable weights, so they are worth putting in the time for. Apart from the two fifties there are another dozen or so fish in excess of 40lb in the water, depending on the time of year. There is

*Phil Cottenier helping VBK chairman
Patrick Bauwens with Jumbo.*

Patrick with Jumbo at 25.3 kilos.

a long, long waiting list for this lake, but members are allowed to invite guests on a limited basis.

A further known big fish, Clover 4, lives in a water near the French border. In 1997 it was caught at 27.2 kilos and in 2000 Dutch record holder Joop Butselaar caught it at 26.3 kilos. I was the next lucky captor, in May 2001, at a reduced weight of 20.2 kilos – again just after spawning! A mere three weeks later it was caught for the second and last time that year at an already increased weight of 23 kilos. This water is understocked, like so many others in Belgium, with a population of 20 carp living in 25 acres of water.

Jumbo was another of the famous Belgian whackers. Its top weight was 25.3 kilos for VBK chairman Patrick Bauwens in August 1998. This old warrior was found dead last year. I had the fish in the summer of 1997 at 21.4 kilos. Jumbo was also caught by several other big names, including Phil Cottenier at 24.2 kilos in 1998. The home of Jumbo was the cut of a stretch of river. Very weedy and very clear, and again with a very low stock of about twenty carp present.

The Long One was another very famous fish. This mirror lived in the same famous Kempisch Canal stretch as the record fish. It topped out at 28.8 kilos for Phil Cottenier in the spring of

*The home of Jumbo, understocked but holding a
small head of quality fish.*

233

1997, and disappeared after that. Rumours are that this fish is still alive but lives in another, private, stretch of the Kempisch Canal.

The Albert Canal is famous for its big commons but the fishing can be very hard. Locals don't hesitate to call in the police if they see you fishing at night. In fact you can only fish the water successfully if you live

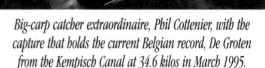

The prolific Phil Cottenier again, this time with the fish known as The Long One at 28.8 kilos. Rumoured to be alive and living in a private stretch of the Kempisch Canal.

Big-carp catcher extraordinaire, Phil Cottenier, with the capture that holds the current Belgian record, De Groten from the Kempisch Canal at 34.6 kilos in March 1995.

locally. This canal is in total contrast to, and very different from, the Kempisch Canal. It's much wider and the boat traffic is immense.

The canals have always dominated the Belgian big-carp scene. Canals like the Kempisch and Albert canals have produced big fish for decades. The Belgian record caught by Phil Cottenier at 34.6 kilos (76lb 2oz) in March 1995 still stands today and will probably stand for a long, long time. There are no fish around at present that look to be capable of going over that exceptional weight.

Both the Kempisch and Albert canals are extremely rich in mussels. Both have warm-water inlets which allow the fish to feed longer and grow longer each year. On top of that they are being fed by anglers all year round. Make no mistake about the impact of that aspect. The average Belgian angler is in the habit of baiting up between sessions and that contributes to the growth rates of the fish.

Rivers like the Maas have also produced fish in excess of 25 kilos, and there's no doubt that even bigger river fish are around. The Maas has unknown potential and it wouldn't surprise me if it turned up a very, very big fish. In fact a lot of the French-speaking south-east part of Belgium is still aqua incognita – an

That man Phil Cottenier again, this time with De Knik, a lake mirror which reached a top weight of 30.9 kilos before it died in tragic circumstances.

unknown quantity in terms of the potential of the waters in that area. In addition to that there is the language barrier, and the fact that carp fishing is still not as common in that area of Belgium as it is in the rest of the country.

The Changing Scene

For many years the Belgian carp scene has been inspired by English carp fishing. From the 80s till the mid-90s the influence was huge, stretching from Jack Hilton, Rod Hutchinson, Kevin Maddocks and Rob Maylin through to Terry Hearn in more recent years. The English carp magazines like *Carpworld* and *Big Carp* were consumed big-time here, although since the start of the Continental magazines and books that impact has faded. The new carp school seems to be less interested in what goes on in England. The same with bait companies and tackle manufacturers. Up to the mid-90s the English bait scene and companies dominated the Continental waters. Today there are countless European bait companies and their products are responsible for an increasing percentage of carp captures.

Methods

Belgian anglers have the habit of prebaiting before they go fishing. I

Alijn with Big Lynn, the first Integra fish to grow to over 25 kilos?

Another angler with the magic big-fish touch. Alijn's fishing mate Jerry Vandepopuliere with his capture of Big Lynn at 22.6 kilos in September 2001.

know of anglers who prebait several waters at the same time. It is not unusual to use 500 kilos of boilies per year. I'm sure this is one of the reasons why we have so many big fish.

Radio Integra, aka Negrita, is a perfect example of a bait-orientated water where the fish have grown to almost unheard-of proportions in recent years. There are several carp in there that have packed on five kilos in weight in two years – and that's the equivalent of 11lb in English terms! One of the current biggest fish, Big Lynn, even put on as much as 6.4 kilos in just fourteen months. From 16.2 kilos in July 2000 to 22.6 kilos in September 2001.

Another fish in there, the Big Tail Common, has come out only twice in the last four years, but look at the weight increase; September 98, 13.5 kilos, up to 18.6 kilos in October 2000. The fish wasn't caught in 1999 or 2001. In 1999 the water had just one fish over 20 kilos, the famous Hemp Fish, and only one other over 18 kilos (approximately 40lb). In 2002 there are 16 different fish over 18 kilos, and seven over 20 kilos. They keep on growing. We are hoping that the water will soon produce a fish over 25 kilos, and when that happens I bet my money on it being Big Lynn.

The downside of the prebaiting game is that some anglers claim swims, or the areas of the lake they prebait. On some big-fish waters they 'reserve' their swims from early January just to claim their rights. In some cases they might wait until May before they have a chance to fish. In most cases they only fish the weekend. You may arrive midweek with not a soul in sight, but you can't fish certain swims because they have been prebaited by the so-called owners. Personally I have an aversion to these habits, but on some waters it is so common that protection of an angler's swim or area has been

Radio Integra, the view from the West Bank. The buoys are used by the very annoying water-skiers.

turned into a rule! I try to avoid these waters as much as possible. I have been criticised in the past because I have a different opinion and because I have written about this practice, but then again I feel I have to speak my mind as it is a completely idiotic rule.

Radio Integra's Smokey at 19.3 kilos, one of the best-looking commons around.

I can honestly say that Belgium holds a lot of very talented carp anglers, but then again every country does... In our case maybe it has something to do with the variety of waters we have. Rivers, canals, big open pits, small weedy waters... Some of our top anglers you may never have heard of, but that's only because they don't publicise their catches.

Will our country produce another huge carp in the near future? We have a common moving in the right direction. We have the anglers capable of locating and catching big fish. We all have access to the baits and rigs which make catching big carp possible. I think it is only a matter of time before another huge Belgian carp is making the headlines in this country, and across Europe.

The Netherlands

The information I'm going to pass on has its limitations. We can't cover all the subjects relating to carp fishing in our country deeply enough to do them justice, but I hope to be able to give you an idea of how our carp fishing started, and how it is still practised today. Every chapter in a book written by a different author is a one-man show. Thoughts that are in a man's mind are personal and it is unlikely that these thoughts will be common to everyone. Carp fishing over the years has become very technical and to my mind the anglers and the carp are the main theme. We all fish in our own special way that brings pleasure – and of course carp – to all of us.

If you ever come to Holland don't let your dreams turn into a nightmare. Each country has its own rules and laws. Holland, the country with windmills, cheese and lots of water. If you fly over our country you can see that Holland is divided into many sections by ditches and dikes.

Erwin Vos

Below left: This is my favourite form of carp fishing. A beauty of 17 kilos from the canal.

Below right: My son Laurens with the first fish he caught in his life. That's how I started, too.

Water Types

We have a great many varieties of waters in our country in which we find carp, which makes Holland very attractive for us as carp anglers; but at the same time it can be very difficult. By difficult I mean that you have to be an all-round carp angler to fish our country. You may have to switch tactics, depending on the circumstances and the venues. We have lakes, canals, rivers, pools, gravel pits, and of course the polder country, and its waters. The polders are not very deep and the best approach here is a very active method of fishing, which most anglers don't like. Stalking with a float rod in your

hand is very old-fashioned, some would say, but to my mind this is the best way of observing carp and seeing how they approach your bait.

The biggest aid to locating carp is to have the opportunity to visit your water regularly. Over the last couple of years I have spent a great deal of time just visiting waters. Find your water, walk round it, go out by boat, and keep looking. There are some waters where carp follow the wind, and on others they ignore the wind. Carp seem to prefer different things in different waters, and their natural behaviour is likely to become modified by angling pressure. Just a couple of miles from my home there is a 12-acre lake where the best results come in a strong wind, but fishing the downwind end of the lake! I guess it is true of all countries that each water has its own idiosyncrasies.

Rivers

River Maas. In the 90s a record mirror carp was caught in this river. A year later Dave Thorpe from the UK caught a Dutch record carp, the biggest common carp up to that time. The area the fish was caught from was the Hollandsch Diep. It was 6th May 1994. The weight was 22.5 kilos, with a length of 115cm. Through the years a number of enormous carp have been caught from this area, but details of all these carp have not been published.

Dave Thorpe with his Dutch river record common of 22.5 kilos, May 1994.

In my area you'll find the River IJssel, a long river that runs from Arnhem to Kampen and ends in the Ketelmeer. This lake is directly connected to the IJsselmeer. This is the biggest lake in the Netherlands.

There are other waters which emerge into the Ketelmeer. From Amsterdam we have the IJmeer, Gooimeer, Eemmeer, Veluwemeer and Drontermeer. This is such a huge area with so much water to go fishing in that it has you wondering where to start!

The River IJssel and all the other rivers we have keep attracting anglers because of the secrets that lie below their surface. In the early days anglers from places like Zalk, Wilsum and Kampen had their own methods for catching carp. They used a stick with a sharp point on the end and

The River IJssel near Kampen.

speared the carp when they saw them swimming near the banks of the river. An alternative method was to use a stick with a metal wire loop tied on the end and snare the carp while they were hiding in the bulrushes. The carp they caught were taken home to feed their families. I'm speaking here about the period 1940-1960. (There are many places in the world where carp are prepared for eating. For example in the USA the state of Nebraska has a restaurant which is famous because of its recipe for carp, and diners have to make reservations to get a table for a meal. Each owner of this restaurant has become a millionaire before the age of 55. I just prefer a good home-cooked steak!)

From the IJssel several big carp have been caught. A number of 20-kilo fish have been reported. A huge grass carp 126cm in length and weighing 20.5 kilos was landed by Marcel Hemel in 1998. In 1990, near Zwolle, Dick Alberts

Wintertime and high water. Watch out for the barbed wire!

Cows exchange their land with the carp during the high-water period.

caught a silver carp weighing 24 kilos.

Fishing rivers has a certain magical atmosphere of its own. This is perhaps because we never know exactly what is likely to turn up in our net, or what potential the river has. Isn't that the feeling that keeps our heart beating in our search for carp?

A specific Dutch method of fishing for carp comes into its own at the end of the year and in the early spring. That's the time when the water level is rising so high that the rivers overflow and the surrounding countryside turns into a huge lake. Rainwater and melting snow runs downriver from the mountains of Switzerland and Austria, causing the abnormally high water levels. The small canals that are connected to the rivers are the first places the carp swim into from the rivers, and they then spread out across the grasslands where you would normally find cows feeding. The carp, including grass carp, search for food in the flooded fields. At these times you will find carp in water just 30-40cm deep. It's an amazing spectacle, and a time when I like to walk around with a camera in my hand, just trying to spot carp.

Why do the carp swim onto the grasslands? We don't know for 100% certain if the carp find these areas more attractive as feeding grounds, or for the reason that the river current is so strong that the carp are searching for places where the water pressure isn't as strong. During this period the carp will feed on all sorts of baits. On occasions dozens of carp show up at the same time. We tend to think that water temperature is important but

Bert Gorts during the high-water season. On the gate you'll see a white bucket with Bert's boilies in it. When he has a run he just walks out to the bucket and nets the fish.

239

even with water temperatures of 5-8°C they turn up on the flooded land and start feeding.

The best method for fishing at this time is simply with a pop-up. Pre-baiting isn't necessary. You just find the carp and wait for them to take your bait. You will have success with sweetcorn, boilies, pellets and worms.

When do you know that the water level is rising? Firstly by driving round to check if there is extra water coming into the rivers. Watch the Teletext page 720 on your TV. Knowledge of the area where you want to fish is a must. Take pictures during the dry season so you know where to place your bait when everywhere around you has turned into a lake. It's sad to lose fish on barbed wire fences! You have to fish with rods in a high position to make sure your line doesn't touch the barbed wire.

As soon as the water level starts going down the carp will leave the land and return to the river.

Bert Gorts with a fish you can only dream about. A linear from the huge IJsselmeer.

Lakes

Isn't it amazing that such a small country is rich with so many waters? You'll understand of course that I can't possibly mention all the lakes in Holland. I will just list the best known. These include;

Vinkeveense Plassen; Nieuwkoopse Plassen; Loosdrechtse Plassen; Friese meren; IJsselmeer, Zuidlaardermeer, Westeinderplas, Ketelemeer, Drontermeer, Veluwemeer, and so on...

So many nice places, and not just for the fishing but also for the enjoyment of the nature around you. De Nieuwkoopse Plassen; the Dutch water paradise? Later in the chapter you will find a list of the record carp that have been caught from this lake.

If we can talk about a problem with fishing these lakes I would have to mention all the birds. Especially during the wintertime all the birds gather in our hot spots and eat our bait. These waters aren't what I would call suitable waters for stalking with just one rod and keeping on the move. They are more suitable for what we call "the swinger method", and if you have a boat, then use it. Being successful in catching these carp you have to remain in one swim to attract the carp to your area, and hold them there. I should also mention that these lakes are rich in natural food and that sometimes it can take a long time to get the fish accustomed to eating our bait.

IJsselmeer: without a doubt one of Europe's biggest lakes. That miraculous things can still happen in terms of fishing in our

A fish from the river I treat with great respect. This old-looking mirror weighed 14 kilos.

Sometimes you have to be creative. When using a boat you can reach the better spots on the lake.

country has been proved by the few anglers who have discovered some marvellous areas on this lake which they prefer not to make public. They have discovered at IJsselmeer a few fishing grounds that go beyond our imagination. These men fish mainly with a fly rod, and it happens on a regular basis that even a carp will take a fly if it is presented in a natural way. The areas these anglers fish are very often visited by hundreds of carp, and the big carp they've seen are undoubtedly in the 25-30kg category. They are not the only ones to conclude that the IJsselmeer is possibly the best carp water in Europe in terms of numbers and weights of fish. This is something that was first written thirty years ago, and at the time no one believed it!

The IJsselmeer is being fished by a few anglers. Carp up to 30 kilos have been caught by them over the last few years, but have never been made public. They want to keep these captures as their own secret, and who can blame them? I have great respect for these men. This lake is a living and breathing place, full of history and secrets. All you need is the time to find the carp that keep our dreams alive.

Pools and Gravel Pits

Holland has a diversity of waters and amongst them there are pools, gravel pits, small lakes and reservoirs – and they all have different characteristics. These are so many that it is impossible to start to list them.

When you start making plans for fishing the smaller lakes and pools try to get as much information as possible. A few days of research can make your season. The best period of the year for doing this is the wintertime. Try to get old maps from several years back and you will discover some pools that in the early days were connected to a river. In my area I discovered that 32 years ago a pool of 1½ acres was connected to the nearby river. In this type of pool you can catch a strain of old mirror carp. Most of the time we pass these small waters by without knowing that some of them can hold some very big surprises!

Depending on the time of year there are places where the big carp hide themselves in our huge weedbeds and can be very difficult to catch. But on the other hand, during the spring and winter you are likely to be more successful. During the winter? Most anglers think that carp don't move much during the colder weather, especially in these smaller waters, but there

The gravel pit which holds the good old carp.
This is my theatre of dreams.

Bert Gorts with a super common of 16.5 kilos from a small pool.

are always groups of carp which will continue to move and feed, even under the ice. It's my experience that on these pools and reservoirs the productive places during the summer also produce carp during the winter. Hot spots are almost always snaggy areas, or natural feeding spots. Gravel pits have deeper areas than our more natural waters, and during the winter the carp will often settle in these deeper areas.

A beautiful common carp of 21 kilos caught from the canal by Richard Bredenbeek.

A typical hot spot on the Twente Canal.

The weather in Holland is rarely stable for long periods. Changes in temperature occur even during a single day. Rainy days will alternate with sunny days. When you are planning your fishing in Holland you have to be aware of these changes. On the other hand, your fishing on these small waters can be very effective because you can easily change your approach should you need to. Some waters may produce carp during the day, then after a period you can only catch them at night. Why? Because too many anglers walk round the small waters, and it's my experience that the big carp prefer quiet areas to hide and quiet times to feed.

Popular baits on the small waters are dough-balls, boilies and particles. Before boilies and particles were introduced into our fishing most anglers fished with dough-balls and potatoes. Currently most anglers wouldn't even know how to fish with these baits, but I can assure you that when your results on small and high-pressure waters are in decline then you will be successful with these baits. Try it!

Fishing with two rods on a canal in the polder country.

Polders

Holland is a typical polder land: land which in the early days was underwater. Then dikes were built around it to let it dry out. Most anglers find fishing in the polder country involves too much mud, and too much walking. The water isn't very deep so there can't be many big carp. But there are carp there for those who prefer quiet fishing for uncaught fish.

For good results you need to be an all-round angler because of the different situations you find yourself in. Clear, shallow water and lots of weed. The drain sides are of soft mud and there is no bankside cover at all. Walk slowly and gently, make no vibrations, and cast no shadows.

Canals

My friend Roelof Kruithof with a beautiful common carp from the canal.

Well known for its big common carp is the Twente Canal. Many anglers, even from overseas, come over in pursuit of the Twente's monsters. The canal has a variety of fish, and all in a good balance. Bream, roach, enormous pike, and a lot of carp.

Since the early 80s there have been some practical changes concerning the angling. Some sections of the canal have been reconstructed. The wooden walls have been replaced by metal ones, and underneath the water they have deposited big piles of bricks and stones against the walls. For the stalking angler these changes created an unpleasant situation and they had to change their methods.

Carp fishing the Twente in winter is well known, because of the canal's water temperatures. The factory at Akzo uses the canal for cool water, and because of this the water temperature in the winter is slowly reducing. In the canal there is a big population of carp of 10 kilos. Among these smaller fish you will find, and be hoping to catch, the big ones. During the winter the stretch of the canal between Hengelo and Wine has the most constant carp population. During the summer the carp will spread out along the entire canal as far as Almelo.

The number of carp anglers has grown over the years, especially during the weekends, holidays and in the winter. The number one bait is still the boilie, in all its variations. Most of the anglers introduce kilo after kilo into the canal, bucketfuls of all sorts of bait. It's sometimes a miracle that you have a chance of catching a carp. Beneath the surface you can imagine a wall of bait! But because the carp population of the canal is so big you can imagine that they keep feeding on the baits. It's not a typical pressure-water. It's an open water, and maybe that's one of the reasons the carp are still being caught. There are periods when no one catches a single carp, while on other occasions the canal is productive no matter where you are fishing.

Being mobile, for example with a boat, is preferable and will keep you one step ahead of the other anglers on the water. The Twente Canal is a very nice water for carp fishing, but if you go there make sure you are in possession of as much information as possible from other anglers who have fished the venue.

Permits

For fishing in the Netherlands you need a permit called "sportvisakte". You can buy them at the post office for E9.50, which is valid for one year. This is the national permit. Besides this you need a permit from the owner of the water. In any local tackle shop they will give you the information you need. Along with the permit called "Grote Vergunning NVVS" you'll receive a booklet which will name all the waters the permit gives you authority to fish.

Most of the waters in Holland are open for anyone to go fishing, provided you have the national permits of course. There are a lot of waters that are under private control, most of them by a local/regional angling federation, and they have their own permits, some examples of which are illustrated in the text.

Along the river banks there is a lot of land owned by farmers. Enquire at the local tackle shop or the tourist information centre called "VVV". You can find these information centres in almost every place in Holland.

Night fishing is permitted from 1st June to 1st September, but on local waters night fishing is sometimes permitted throughout the year.

The number of rods you are allowed to use in Holland is two unless the owner of a local water has other rules. Check your permit. The penalty for fishing with three rods is about E60.

There are no barbless hook rules.

For further information you can also look on the internet.

www.karperpagina.nl (main page)

www.karperstudiegroep.nl (Dutch Carp Study Group)

www.carpweb.com

Location of Venues

I can mention some waters that have a good head of carp, including some big ones! I have referred to the areas on the map of Holland in which these waters are to be found:

Zwarte Meer, Ketelmeer, Drontermeer, River IJssel, Veluwemeer. On the map sections F6, F7 and F8 (I live in the fishermen's town, Elburg).

Loosdrechtse Plassen – D9 and D10.   Vinkeveense Plassen – D9.

Nieuwkoopse Plassen – D10.   Hollandsch Diep – C13 and D13.

Nijmegen; River Waal – F11 and G11.   River Maas – G15 and G16.

Markermeer – E7 and E8.   IJ-meer – D8.

Amsterdam – Rijnkanaal, near Utrecht/Nieuwegein – E11.

An immaculate common caught from a snaggy, rocky area in the margins of the famous IJsselmeer.

Bait

In my experience the effectiveness of any kind of bait will depend on a number of different influencing factors. The main reason why a carp picks up a bait is because it thinks it is food. When we first introduce a new bait on one of our waters, initially it might not be as successful as we hope. Most anglers will change the bait without giving it a real chance, or trying it at a better time of year. Sometimes it can be frustrating when you blank for several nights, but the more you learn the more you realise how little we understand. This is a recurring theme in carp fishing.

Classification of baits as good or poor is a limitation of our own understanding. For example a bait with a high biological value will have more inherent appeal than one having a lower value. Through the years I have tried all sorts of baits, but my own experience is that my results in our waters in the Netherlands are more consistent with nutritional baits for the bigger fish.

I should emphasise that these are my opinions and that there will no doubt be more extensive bait material elsewhere in the book!

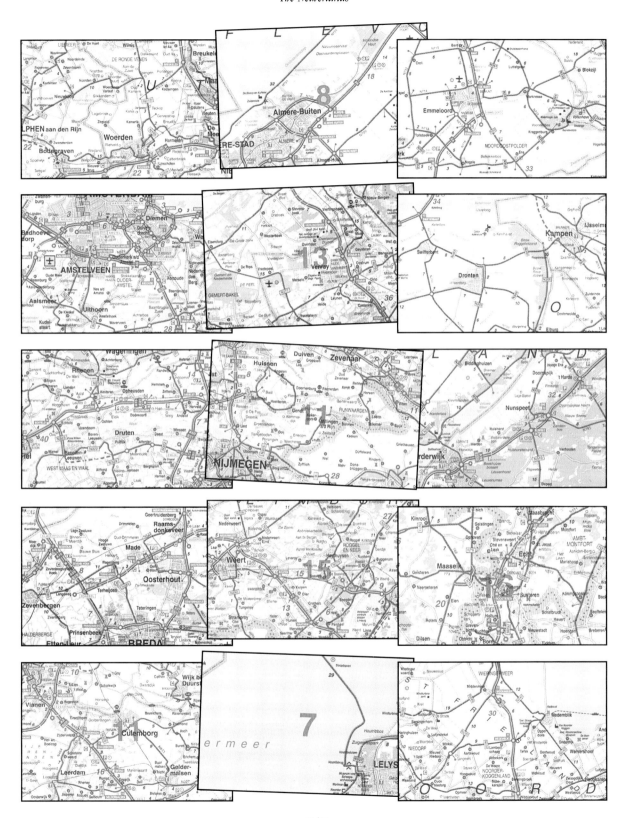

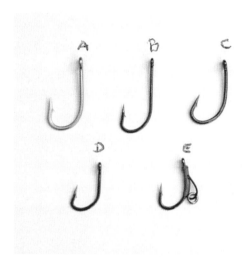

A selection of hooks which are popular with Dutch carp anglers.

My last fish from the 2001 season, a lovely common of 17.5 kilos caught from the canal in November.

Stalking

Because of the variety of its many waters Holland is an excellent place for stalking. There are several methods of stalking carp: pre-baiting, fishing on the drop, and stealthy hunting. In the warmer months most anglers will try stalking when using a floating bait on the surface. A piece of bread, dog or cat biscuit, or floating pellet or boilie.

Every carp angler who wants to set out to hunt for carp using just one rod prefers to find a nice quiet place, fishing no more than two metres from the margin. Carp can be found here because they are always on the search for food, and where will they find that? Not always in the middle of the river or lake, but very often close to the margin. If you become a competent stalker your results will improve more than you ever expected. But because you are fishing close to the bank you need to be really quiet, and move very carefully to avoid any vibrations.

Carp use whatever cover is available. Snags, reedbeds and weedbeds are common holding areas for carp and you will often find them in these spots. The depth isn't of great significance. More important is where you are fishing and the time of the year. In the spring shallow waters and in the winter deeper waters are likely to be the productive areas, for example.

The rod used for stalking must be of special design and powerful enough to hold the explosion from a hooked margin carp in that moment when your float or floater goes under. Everything needs to be in balance; the hook, the reel, line and rod.

When you start stalking a water, walk round and introduce your bait to a number of likely spots, places where you can positively smell the carp. In each of these spots introduce a couple of handfuls of corn, hemp or pellets. Now the time has come for the carp to find our bait and start feeding on it. This is the moment that gives us total freedom of

Swims featuring reedbeds, my favourite areas in the spring.

mind. How can anyone describe the feeling when we see little bubbles around our float and can hear our own heartbeat? This is always very difficult to describe to non-carp anglers!

Choose one of your baited spots and fish it for an hour. If there are no signs of feeding carp then move on to the next place. It can be difficult to say when the carp are present on some waters, but if you take the trouble to come to terms with stalking it can lead to success within a matter of a couple of hours, and will put you one step ahead of many of the anglers who prefer to sit behind their stationary swingers.

Carp are in the margins at different times of day on different venues. On some waters I won't catch any stalked carp at all in the morning, while, on the other hand, another water only produces in the early morning, or at night.

Types of Carp

We have all the types of carp that are commonly encountered: common, mirror, leather, linear, fully scaled and grass carp. In Holland we still find true wild carp, the type of carp that gave me the fever when I first experienced the strength and power of this fish. Comparing strength for weight I have never experienced such an explosion of dynamic power as that you get from wild carp.

From this wild carp came the well-known common carp, the carp we find in most of the waters in this country. There is an organisation called the OVB (formed to promote the improvement of inland fisheries) and in 1957 they began experimenting with the cross-breeding of various carp strains in an attempt to produce different types of fish. The result of this cross-breeding gave us the wild-carp hybrid, which reaches maximum weights of around 35lb. The result of this cross-breeding between wild carp and farm-bred carp means that in the current second and third generation fish there remains only about 25% genetic material from the original wild carp.

This is the common carp which we find in most of our open waters. Many groups studying carp have their preference for fast-growing mirror carp, and during the last couple of years there have been some startling growth rates from Dutch mirrors. Hopefully these latest initiatives will in future promise the potential for catching beautiful, significant carp.

Certain types of carp seem to have a greater preference for certain types of bait, and recognise these baits as food quicker than other strains.

Joop Butselaar with the magnificent Dutch record fish of 31.4 kilos from the Niuewkoopse Plassen.

Dutch Carp Records

If you were to ask any angler if there are record carp swimming in our Dutch waters he would probably look at you and think that you had lost your mind. For big carp you have to go to France, Belgium, Romania etc. But Holland? No way! We're well known for our cheese, drugs and prostitution, but not for record carp.

The first official Dutch carp record was caught on 5th June 1957 by Willem Geestman, a mirror carp weighing 22.5 kilos. The successful bait was potato. It was 34 years before a new record was set when Ron van de Laarschjot caught a mirror carp of 23.7 kilos on 1st June 1991.

On 4th September 1997 Marc Timmermans raised the record to above 25 kilos with a common carp weighing 25.25 kilos. Then, all Dutch carp anglers were surprised when Joop Butselaar caught a carp of 30 kilos on the 29th August 2000 from the Nieuwkoopse Plassen. Joop went on to break his own record on 23rd October 2000 with the same common carp, this time weighing an even more impressive 31.4 kilos.

Who would have thought that carp of these weights would be swimming around in our own little country. And what can we expect from the future?

The following is the full list of official Dutch record holders:

Winners of the World Carp Classic 2000 at Lac Amance, France. Richard Bredenbeek and Thierry Stunnenberg.

Place	Weight	Length	Type	Date	Name
Nieuwkoopse Plassen (?)	22.5kg	93cm	mirror	5 June 1957	Willem Geestman
Maas	23.7kg	92cm	mirror	1 June 1991	Rob van de Laarschot
Maas-Maasbracht	24.1kg		mirror	25 May 1993	Benny de Jong
Maas/Julianakanaal	24.6kg	101cm	common	30 May 1995	Ton Cremers
Nieuwkoopse Plassen	25.25kg	105.5cm	common	4 September 1997	Marc Timmermans
Nieuwkoopse Plassen	27.25kg	105cm	common	9 July 1998	Helmut van Schaik and Joop van Kleef
Nieuwkoopse Plassen	29.5kg		common	1 October 1999	Mark Schuringa
Nieuwkoopse Plassen	30kg	107cm	common	29 August 2000	Joop Butselaar
Nieuwkoopse Plassen	31.4kg	108cm	common	23 October 2000	Joop Butselaar

Through the years Holland has produced several well-known carp anglers and I will mention just a few of them. Jan de Winter; Rini Groothuis, the author of the Dutch carp bible *Karper* and a founder member of the Dutch Carp Study Group; Sjef and Henk van der Hoven, the Kings of Cassien; Leon Hoogendijk, author and successful angler in France; Arnout Terlouw, editor of the magazine *De Karper*; and in 2001 we have the winners of the World Carp Classic at Lac Amance in France. Their names are Richard Bredenbeek and Thierry Stunnenburg.

Conclusion

So now I come to the end of this chapter with a new season of fishing ahead of me, and I'm ready for it. I don't like telling anyone what they should do and how, and indeed I don't have the slightest right to do so. But if I could have one wish fulfilled then it would be that all those people who fish for carp would become more worthy of the name carp angler, and this within all aspects of carp fishing. Learn from the mistakes of others; you can't live long enough to make them all yourself.

If you keep these thoughts in your mind then you are more than welcome to visit our country and I hope that you'll enjoy yourself catching the beautiful Dutch carp.

"Everything has been thought of before – the difficulty is to think of it again." Erwin Vos.

Big-Fish Waters Of France

France is absolutely stuffed full of big-fish waters. Whether they are 10,000-acre water supply reservoirs, 200-acre estate lakes or 2-acre clay pits, this glorious European country is a carp angler's paradise. In this chapter, Tim has asked me to compile a list of venues offering the chance of a big fish weighing in excess of 50lb. There are plenty more than those listed, but I can fully recommend all of the waters described in the pages that follow. (See separate chapters for Lac Forêt D'Orient and Lac de St. Cassien.)

Simon Crow

Abbey Lakes

This famous complex has two waters on-site which are of interest to the carp angler. These are Heron Lake and Fox Lake. Both contain fish of 50lb-plus, with the most famous being a mirror known as The Horse which generally weighs around 57lb. Both are well stocked with twenties and thirties, with the occasional

Crowy with a nice low-thirty from Abbey Lakes – an excellent holiday venue which has carp to over 50lb.

forty. Fishing is only available by prior arrangement, by contacting Rob Hughes on 01948 880884. This is a very easy and very popular venue which isn't far from Paris, about two hours' drive from Calais.

Barrage de Castillon

This is a water not too far from Cassien, and one which has a reputation for fish over 30kg. I heard a rumour that it had done a seventy, but when I asked Gerard Thevenon (a well-known carp angler from Cassien), he could only confirm a 30kg fish (66lb). It is about 1,500 acres in size and is lightly stocked. It is situated at Castellane to the north-west of Cassien, about thirty miles away. The adjacent Lac de Chaudanne also contains some good carp.

The beautiful Etang de Boulet, which has produced carp to 52½lb.

Barrage de St-Etienne-Cantalès

Situated right in the middle of the country to the west of Aurillac, this barrage is close to 2000 acres in size. It was formed by damming the tiny River Cere, and holds some good fish which have made it to over 55lb. It is a deep water with much of the lake being over 30m in depth. Plenty of restrictions so it isn't too carp angler-friendly.

Beaumont de Lomange

This is a famous water which was on the circuit in the 1990s, producing several good fish for the likes of Steve Briggs and Kevin Maddocks, to name just a couple. It is located at Beaumont de Lomange which is just off the A62 motorway north-west of Toulouse. It falls on a campsite with a host of activities, including swimming, volleyball etc. It is a very busy lake, but there are some big fish present. It used to contain a fish of around 30kg, but I believe this fish is no longer there. However, there are still some good 30s, 40s and the occasional fifty to catch. Night fishing is allowed, and fishing is available on day ticket.

Canal de Jonage/Miribel

There are actually two canals here, both of which contain some big carp. They are collectively known as the Canal de Lyon, since they are located in the city of Lyon, bordering the Parc de Loisirs de Miribel-Jonage (see later in the chapter). It is a heavily stocked canal, and not particularly difficult. There are plenty of boats, people and anglers in this area, but the results are there for the taking. No night fishing.

Domaine des Iles

This is a big-fish water within two hours of Calais which regularly produces carp in excess of 50lb. Its lake record is said to be over 60lb, but there are plenty of other good back-up fish also. There are holiday chalets for hire on-site. It can be found just off the A1 motorway at Offoy, to the west of Ham on the edge of the Canal de Somme.

A huge 57½lb mirror from Domaine des Iles.

Domaine de Boux

This famous big-fish water is run by Simon Horton of Excalibur Fishing (tel: 0033 243709839). There are at least two fifties in the water, one of which has made 55lb. The record is over sixty pounds, a milestone which has been reached by two fish, both of which have sadly passed away. Well stocked with 20 and 30s.

Dream Lakes

Dream Lakes is probably the most famous of the holiday tour operators offering carp fishing. This five-lake complex is around four hours' drive from Calais, and details of the venue are regularly advertised in *Carpworld* and *Carp-Talk*. Further information can be gained by calling Graham Greene on 01206 767576. All five lakes contain carp over 40lb, with several of them offering fifties. Lake One houses a mirror known as Two-Tone which has topped 60lb.

Etang au Duc

This lake isn't far from the famous Fishabil centre in Brittany. It can be found at Ploërmel, east of Rennes. It is around 300 acres in size and has produced some good fish over 50lb. It isn't heavily fished, but offers a nice water for anglers visiting this side of the country. You need the national licence for this venue.

Etang d'Aureilhan

Also known as Mimizan, this 700-acre lake is on the west border, to the south of Bordeaux, in the town of Mimizan. It is very well stocked with twenties, with the occasional big fish if you get lucky. The lake record is 53lb. There is legal night fishing in a small section

Belgian carp star 'Magic Sven' Hoebruck with a stunning Domaine de Boux mirror of 50lb+.

of the lake, but the day-only zones are very productive. Tickets are available in the town.

Etang d'Ecluzelles

This lake is a dammed section of the tiny River Eure, and is about 300 acres in size. It isn't heavily fished for its carp, but has produced a couple of good fish over 50lb. It isn't far from Paris, and is found at Dreux which is just to the west of the famous city. The lake lies to the

Kevin Maddocks with an impressive 55lb+ French mirror.

south-east of Dreux and is located in the village of Ecluzelles itself. Tickets are available from the bar in the village.

Etang de Biscarrosse et de Parentis

This is a very shallow water for its size, with some spots being only a couple of feet deep out at 100m range. There are many restrictions on this water due to it bordering a military air force base, but it is still relatively well fished despite this. Located right on the coast near Bordeaux in the south-west of the country, Biscarrosse is quite well

Number One Lake on the Dream Lakes complex, possibly the most famous of the commercial carp fisheries in France.

stocked for its size, with many of the carp being 40lb and 50lb in size. There is at least one fish in the water which has made it over 70lb, but I'm not sure what the lake record is. Night fishing is only allowed in a small section of the lake and for a limited time of the year – April until July or thereabouts. Enquire locally for permits. You can't miss the lake on the map!

Etang de Boulet

Situated in the Brittany region of the country, this dammed river was made famous through the angling of Rod Hutchinson. Rod was one of the early pioneers to Brittany and there are several waters in the area which have swims named after him, as does Boulet. This is a lightly stocked water, with the fishing regarded as moderate to difficult, but the carp do range to over 50lb. There are at least two fish in the water which have made it over this weight, with the lake record currently set at 52½lb. It is heavily weeded in areas with lilies, and fringed by reeds and rushes. It is extremely popular with windsurfers in the summer months, so be warned. Tickets are available from most cafes in the area. It can be accessed in less than an hour from the ferry port of St. Malo, and is situated north of Rennes close to the town of Combourg, where there is also another famous carp water.

Etang de Jonquoy

There are at least two sixty-plus mirrors to go for at Jonquoy, one of which is very close to 70lb and appears regularly in the British press. It is another one of the commercial venues with several operators selling trips, with the most famous being GTS Tours who can be reached on: 01435 873249.

Etang de la Horre

This incredible water, which is around 250 acres in size, is certainly the jewel in the crown for its owner Patrick Bachellier – France's and Europe's biggest producer of carp. La Horre is currently run by British angler David Payne on behalf of Patrick and contains several hundreds of 30s and 40s, topped by a massive 60lb-plus mirror. Formerly known as Boulancourt, fishing is on a pre-booked basis, whereby anglers book a swim by the week. It is located in the Champagne region of the country very close to the famous Chantecoq. To access it, leave the A26 at Arcis-sur-Aube and head towards Lesmont. From here, pick up the D960 and then the D400 to Louze. You will see the signposts from here. For further details contact David Payne of Fishing Adventures on 01536 505791.

The biggest fish in Etang de Jonquoy weighing in at 68lb. The venue holds a number of big fish, and at least two carp in excess of 60lb.

Etang des Landes

Situated right in the middle of the country, about 25 miles south-east of Montlucon near to Gouzon. Landes holds some good fish to over 55lb, with a good head of twenties and thirties. Enquire locally for tickets. It is fairly shallow for its size of 100 acres. Some good fishing is also found locally on Etang Neuf as well as Barrage de Rochebut to the south of Montlucon.

Etang Neuf

There are hundreds of Etangs Neuf around France, with this particular one located north-east of the town of Vitré, around half an hour's drive in an easterly direction from Rennes in Brittany. It is the most picturesque venue you could wish to come across. Heavily covered in lily pads, the lake is around 250 acres and is lightly stocked with carp, one of which has made it over 70lb. This is a lake I first fished in the early 1990s and have returned to now and again as a stopping-off point on the way back to the ferry at St. Malo. Night fishing is not permitted on this water, and you can only fish in selected zones – the section close to the road bridge. Day tickets are available from the house next to the road bridge, but you must also be in possession of a regional licence which you will be able to

The La Horre biggie caught by a Polish angler in 2002.

obtain from selected bars in the region. The average size of the carp is 25lb-30lb.

Grand Etang de Jugon

Jugon has a reputation for being difficult and it isn't surprising when you consider that it is about ten miles long. It can be found south-west of St. Malo, about half an hour's drive away, close to Lamballe. Although the lake itself is ten miles long, it is split into two sections, with the southern section, which is about 300 acres in size, being the most productive for carp. It is very lightly stocked, but they do run to over 55lb. There was a rumour of a sixty from this lake in 2000. Tickets are available locally at Jugon-les-lacs in the bars and cafes.

Lac Amance

This lake is perhaps most famous amongst British anglers for its involvement with the World Carp Classic competition which was held here in 2001 and is the venue which succeeded Lac de Madine. It has been very popular amongst

European carp anglers for several years before this event, with its biggest fish topping the 65lb mark or thereabouts. It is well stocked, with the average size around 20lb. Much of the lake is out of bounds for carp fishing, but there is a legal night fishing section. Fishing tickets at this water also cover the mighty Orient and Temple, and they are available from most bars/cafes in the area. You can purchase both yearly permits as well as holiday ones which last about a month. As a rule fishing is open at Amance between April and November, but dates do vary each

Two super carp from Etang Neuf. Can you recognise the scruffy lad on the left? It's Mr. Crow!

year so check with someone who has knowledge of the lake before travelling. Amance is the most northerly venue of the three famous waters in the Forêt d'Orient, which can be accessed just off the A26-E17 road east of Troyes. It is a man-made lake and is fairly weedy at times. It is also very shallow in places.

Lac d'Aiguebelette

This lake isn't that well fished by the travelling carper so may well offer a good challenge for those in search of one. In 2000 it produced its venue record of 57lb. At almost 1,500 acres in size, Aiguebelette is set in a beautiful valley in the French mountains close to Chambéry. It

Lac Amance – the new home for the World Carp Classic.

isn't well stocked so a good-sized unknown carp may well be on the cards. Night fishing is allowed in specific zones, and much of the lake is privately owned so a bit of research before a trip is recommended. Camping is available close by.

Lac d'Aydat

Another popular water in the summer months due to the campsites nearby. It can be found close to the central city of Clermont-Ferrand, roughly ten miles to the south-west at Aydat. There are plenty of carp of all sizes, with the best making it to just over 60lb. It isn't that well fished by the carp men so could well contain a surprise or two. Very popular with boats. Tickets from the campsites or local bar.

Lac de Bourget

This is another of those unknown quantities which could well hold a big surprise. The water made the headlines in the year 2000 for the capture of a seventy-plus mirror to a pleasure angler (see Monster Carp chapter), but has produced the occasional 50-plus to the few carp anglers who sample it. It can be found in the mountain region north of Chambéry just off the A41. It is very lightly stocked and regarded as being very, very difficult.

Lac de Carcès

Right down south in the territory of Cassien, lies Lac de Carcès. This isn't a

Prolific big-carp catcher Andy Chambers with an Amance forty.

heavily fished water, but it does have a history of big fish. Tickets are available in the village of Carcès itself. It is found to the west of Cassien, just off the A8 motorway, about thirty miles east of the city of Aix-en-Provence. The lake record is rumoured to be around 30kg.

Lac de la Liez

Liez has a history for big fish, but on the negative side, it also has a reputation for being difficult to fish due to the locals and stringent garde de pêche. It has produced at least one definite seventy, with several other good back-up fish, including two mid-sixties. At almost 300 acres it is a dammed river just off the Canal de la Marne. It is found at Langres, 150 miles to the south-west of Paris. It is well fished by many European anglers and is on the circuit for big fish. It's one of three big-fish waters close to Langres, with the others being Réservoir de la Mouche and the Réservoir de Charmes. Tickets are available from the bar on-site by the dam. Night fishing is allowed in the specified sector.

French big-water scene. Morning mist and an angler out in a boat playing a fish.

Lac de Madine

This 2,500 acre venue was the birthplace for the popular World Carp Classic carp match which first hit the carp scene in the late 1990s. It has been on the European circuit for quite some time, having produced several big fish to almost 70lb. It is quite well stocked with several fish around the 40lb mark, but very few over 50lb. Its best fish in recent years is a 67lb mirror which was moved to a local lake in Toul. It is controlled by some strange rules, but fishing is open to all. Much of the lake is out of bounds to anglers but there are several night fishing areas which seem to change on a

Above left: Lac de Madine – only four hours from Calais. Above right: Simon Crow with one of three forties in four days from Madine taken during the filming of Rod Hutchinson's Dream at Madine two-part video set.

yearly basis. Places for these are supposed to be booked in advance by contacting the 'office de pêche' which is located at the number two entrance to the lake. To access Madine, take the A4-E50 to Metz, leaving it around the Verdun region when you pick up the signposts for the lake.

Lac de Pareloup

This huge reservoir is around 2,000 acres in size and is located close to Rodez in the south of the country (you can't miss it on the map if you find Rodez). A couple of years ago this was the talk of the French carp scene, having produced several big fifties on a regular basis, including one catch of three 50s and a sixty in the same session to one angler. It is a fairly untapped water with details of the catches closely guarded by the locals. Tickets are available in the bars close by at Salles-Curan as well as in the tackle shops in Rodez and Millau. I am unsure about the rules regarding night fishing.

Lac de Passion

A well-stocked water which boasts a superb head of 20s and 30s, as well as several bigger fish, topped by a low-sixty mirror. It is less than three hours' drive away from Calais, and can be found to the north of Paris. It is a commercial holiday water which can only be fished by prior arrangement. For more details contact Paul Smith on: 01708 526754.

Lac de Soustans

This coastal lake is found at Soustans, to the north of Bayonne in the south-west of the country. This is a very busy lake with boats and swimmers, especially in the summer, but does produce well. It isn't overstocked for its size (around 1,000 acres) but carp are in there to over 55lb. Tickets are available in the bars/cafes at Soustans.

Lac de Vassivière

Vassivière is around 2,000 acres and is one of those steep-sided waters very typical of France. It has depths ranging to over 100ft, but there are some fantastic fish to be caught. The lake record is a mirror of 58lb, but there are rumours of bigger. It is quite well fished all

Rod Hutchinson has caught big carp from numerous waters in France. This mid-forty common is from the Commons Syndicate water.

Big moment on a big French venue. The anglers and onlookers gather for the weighing of a big fish.

year round by anglers from all over Europe. It can be found to the east of Limoges, close to the town of Peyrat-le-Chateau. It is fed by the River Maulde which is rumoured to contain big carp.

Lac de Vouglans

This incredible water stretches for over twenty miles in length! Located close to the Swiss border to the east of Chalon-sur-Saône it lies in a steep valley with depths ranging to over 100ft in places, some hundreds of feet in others. It is well stocked with commons as well as mirrors, with the average size being around mid-twenty. It offers a good chance of a 40lb common and rumours are that it could contain fish much bigger than its record which is around 57lb. It is a very snaggy water in places, with the margins being very steep. There is no night fishing around much of the lake, with very limited access. A boat is essential.

Max Cottis of Fox International has been consistently successful in France. Max returning a typical big French mirror.

Lac du Causse

Known as Brive on the circuit, this water was in its prime in the early 90s before it was *vidanged*. Then, it was a haunt for many a Continental carper, including the likes of Kevin Maddocks, Alan Taylor and Zenon Bojko. A lot of the fish were sold during the *vidange*, but several escaped the nets and have flourished as a result. It was also stocked with smaller fish, many of which are now reaching 30lb-40lb in weight. It isn't a heavily stocked water, but is certainly capable of producing the odd surprise, including 60-pounders. It is located about 70 miles south of Limoges in the south-west region of the country, at the town of Brive-la-Gaillarde. The lake is actually south-west of Brive at a place called Larch. It is a beautiful water set in the hills of the Dordogne valley. It features in Beekay International's *Euro Carp Quest* video.

Cliff Fox is better known for his carp gear than his carp catching, but he can catch them! Cliff with a mid-France forty-plus.

Lac du Der Chantecoq

This venue has to be the most famous of all French carp waters, apart from Cassien. Chanty, as it is known on the circuit, is situated close to St-Dizier in the Champagne region. At roughly 12,000 acres it is a massive inland supply reservoir which contains a huge head of carp, the numbers of which I wouldn't like to guess at. It first hit the carp scene in the late-1980s when rumours of some impressive hauls of 30s were being passed around the grapevine. Perhaps the most famous British angler associated with the water then was Alan Taylor who made some incredible catches which were covered in the *Angling Times* newspaper at the time. It is heavily fished all year round by anglers from all over Europe, although in the late 90s, stringent rules regarding night fishing were implemented to overcome poaching and the general behaviour of anglers on the water. Today, the lake is controlled by a team of guards, and night fishing is by prior arrangement only. There are around 30 night fishing swims and these must be booked in advance by calling Maison du Lac on 0033 326726343. Much of the lake is available to day fishing, but there are several sections which are closed for angling. It has an incredible density of 30lb and 40lb carp, and it probably

Steve Forster and a 53lb mirror from the legendary Chantecoq.

A classic example of Lake Salagou's commons. The angler is Andy Chambers. This fish made the front covers of both Carpworld *and* Carp-Talk.

offers you the best chance of a 50-pounder in the world. The lake record is currently over 70lb, and there are rumours that there are at least two or three fish around this weight; although I only know of one. Night fishing permits must be paid for in advance, and all visitors must also be in possession of an AAPP (Associations de Pêche et de Pisciculture – the national licence) which is available from several bars/cafes around the lake.

Lac du Salagou

This very famous carp water is well stocked with commons ranging to almost 60lb. The lake record is a mirror of just over 60lb. Tickets are available at the nearby tackle shop in the town of Lodève, which is about ten minutes' drive to the north of the lake, or at the cafes/bars at Clermont-l'Hérault which is slightly closer. Salagou is right on the southern French coast, to the west of Montpellier, and there are several campsites in the region. Much of the lake is closed for night fishing, and anglers visiting the lake should have a rod pod because of the rocky terrain. Very snaggy, but a good chance of a 40lb-plus common.

Lac du Temple

Another famous water in the Forêt d'Orient park, Temple is a man-made reservoir of around 3,000 acres. Fishing is exactly the same

Frank Warwick catches them wherever he goes. Frank with a big French mirror which just missed the magical 50lb mark.

as per the other two lakes in the park with regards to tickets and its closure, but Temple hasn't yet lived up to the reputation of its sisters, although it has produced carp over the 60lb barrier.

Les Quis

Not far behind Dream Lakes as being the number one holiday water in France is Les Quis. This impressive complex of four lakes is situated at Bray-sur-Seine just off the A5 motorway to the east of Montereau-Faut-Yonne. There are several big fish on the complex, including a huge common which is just short of sixty. Trips are by prior-arrangement only and fully inclusive. More details from 0208 8571244.

Maurepaire

Another of David Payne's waters. Maurepaire is Dave's baby, a water which he has developed himself over the years, and one which is quickly developing an impressive status for 40lb-plus

Carp angling legend Rod Hutchinson with a Maurepaire near-forty.

mirrors. There are several fifties in the water also, both commons and mirrors. It is situated in the Champagne region of the country, close to Dave's other waters in the Forêt d'Orient. Contact Dave on 01536 505791 to book a trip.

Miribel Jonage (Le Grand Large)

This is a mightily famous carp water in France, although one not really that well known on the English grapevine. Le Grand Large contains some massive fish, certainly close to, if not over, 70lb (I think the lake record is just short of 70lb). There are many fish over 20kg (44lb) and there is an excellent chance of a fifty. It lies close to the city of Lyon, with the Parc de Miribel clearly signposted. There are several lakes in the Parc, with the best being Le Grand Large. Each year there is a famous Enduro held on the lake, an event which is covered well in the French carp fishing press, the norm being a winning team with a mid-fifty and several forties and thirties.

Rainbow Lake

Rainbow Lake hit the headlines in the mid-90s when it received many of the big fish which were *vidanged* out of Lac du Causse (aka Brive). It is also known as the 'lake of islands' due to the large number of islands which are present. It is a very snaggy water, but boasts some fabulous fish, including a mirror which has topped 60lb. It is close to Bordeaux in the west of the country, and can only be fished by calling Pascal on 0033 556657089.

Réservoir de Bouzey

Bouzey is lightly stocked but offers the chance of a fifty-plus. The lake record is just over 60lb. It is found to the west of Epinal in the east of France, about 50

One of Rainbow Lake's numerous fifty-plus mirrors.

miles from Nancy. It is a pretty reservoir of around 250 acres, and is ideal as a back-up water to try if you are heading off in the direction of the River Moselle.

Réservoir de Charmes

This famous venue is one of three big-fish waters close to Langres which is to the south-west of Paris. It can be accessed just off the A31 motorway. Rumours suggest there may be three fish which have made it over 70lb, but I can confirm that there is at least one well-known mirror which gets caught at least three times a year. Charmes was hit by the 'traffic' of carp in the 1990s when a number of its big fish were taken and stocked into commercial carp fisheries, including one of the biggies which weighed over 60lb. At the time of writing (May 2002), Charmes is closed for repairs to the dam wall, but it is due to open again next year and the carp have not been *vidanged*. The average size of the fish is upper-thirties, but there is an excellent chance of a

Rod Hutchinson on one of his target waters of the 90s, the Orient.

whacker. Very well fished by a lot of Continental anglers and fairly tricky as a result. Tickets are available from the bars/ cafes close by. There is more bank space for night fishing here than at the nearby Liez.

Réservoir de la Mouche

Part of the three-reservoir complex at Langres, Mouche contains a few good fish close to 30kg. This water is regarded as the easiest of the three in the region, with the average size around upper-twenties. There is night fishing allowed in the specified zone, and there are regular garde de pêche checks.

River Doubs

Some of the best spots for this small river are around Besancon in the east of the country, close to the Swiss border. It isn't a very long river,

A line-up of River Lot fish taken from a European River Tours trip in mid-2001. For more details on fishing this river contact 01702 580807.

running for almost 100 miles, but the carp can be found all along its reaches. As with a lot of French rivers, the commons are the most prolific, with these running to low-forties, with the mirrors being the better stamp of fish which reach mid-fifties. Some good areas to try on the Doubs are: Montbéliard, Baume-les-Dames, and anywhere with features near Besancon.

River Garonne

The Garonne is a big-fish river, having produced several carp over 60lb in the past. The average size of the fish, however, is around 10-12kg with a lot of them being commons. The mirrors are generally regarded as being the bigger fish. Some good spots are found at the Barrage de Cazères; Grenade near to Toulouse; Agen; Aiguillon where it meets the River Lot; the big river junction at Moissac where it meets the River Tarn; Bourret to the south-east of Castelsarrasin; and Cordes-Tolosannes to the south-east of Castelsarrasin.

River Loire

This is a river I have fished a lot over the years, especially during the early 90s. It is over 400 miles in length, with the carp well spread out. The average size is around 20lb, with the river record being more than 60lb. There are legal night fishing sections in some areas, with the most popular being at Angers right in the city centre. Some good areas include: close to Deciz, Fourchambault and Gien. There are also several power stations which run alongside this river, which can result in some good winter sport.

River Lot

This particular river runs into the River Garonne close to Bordeaux and runs for about 100 miles in a westerly direction. It has been heavily fished for many years, being one of the first French rivers to receive much attention from the travelling carp angler. It has several dams or barrages along its course, with the best known being Cabanac at St. Geniez d'Olt. It was here where the River Lot record was caught in the late 90s at around 65lb. It is well known for its commons, there being an excellent head of 30lb fish, but there are some big mirrors amongst them too. Most bars in the region will have information on night fishing and where is best for bigger fish. The national licence will cover you for most areas.

French angler Thierry Canal with a lovely forty from the River Moselle.

Set in the most stunning scenery in France, the River Moselle is home to some gigantic carp, including the second biggest carp ever caught from that country.

River Moselle

This is France's best-kept secret, having produced several awesome carp over the last few years. It was this river which produced the country's second biggest fish ever, in the shape of a 78lb mirror to Emanuelle Walt (see Monster Carp chapter). The Moselle can be found at the eastern side of France, with its most famous stretches being in the Metz area. As always with rivers, the big-fish spots are very localised, but carp are well spread along its course, from the higher reaches down to the slower-moving reaches at Nancy. Some of the better catches are made to the north of Metz, near Thionville, close to the industrial areas where warm water outflows and large flood basins can be found. It is a very picturesque river with a variety of features, ranging from wide sections with plenty of boat traffic around Metz, to the slower meandering and heavily wooded areas of Nancy. Enquire locally for permits.

River Saône

The Saône is a particularly long river, running for around 500 miles or so. Carp are caught all along its length, with the majority being commons of around 20lb. Big fish are very localised, with Chalon-sur-Saône being a good starting point since many carp over 50lb have been caught from here. Famous Dutch angler Leon Hoogendijk lives in Chalon and he believes that this river may one day produce a French or even world record carp. Local knowledge is essential for big fish, with most stretches being open for day fishing only. Enquire locally for night fishing zones and permits.

River Seine

I'm not really sure how to write about this famous river since it contains carp

Leon Hoogendijk with a River Saône fifty – one of two taken during the floods of 2000.

A River Saône forty-plus common. There aren't just big catfish in this river!

all along its length. From its most northerly reaches to the south, it has produced good carp for many, many years. Certainly its most famous sections are on the south-eastern side of Paris, around Fontainebleau and Montereau, where it joins the River Yonne. The latter is in fact the section of river which produced Marcel Rouviere's world record carp from 1981, whilst the former is probably one of the most famous areas of river in France with carp anglers, having been the haunt of many a British angler in the late-80s. Most of the River Seine is open to carp fishing, but much of it, like many sections of French river, is closed for night fishing. Anyone wishing to target this river would be wise to do a

lot of research and source legal night stretches, and those which regularly produce big fish. Many of the big fish areas are very localised, with fish of 50lb-plus and 60lb very common. It is a very wide river in places, with some stretches reaching 250m, so expect a variety of fishing conditions. The national French licence must be purchased before fishing.

St Croix

This famous lake is on the route to Cassien and is well known to anglers. No huge fish as far as I'm aware, although the lake is well stocked with a good head of 30s and 40s. The lake record is around the mid-sixty mark, a known fish, and it does receive a fair bit of pressure despite restricted access and night fishing. Dave Plummer used to run trips to this water. Camping is available close by. It lies about 70 miles to the north-west of Cannes.

Villeneuve de la Raho

Right on the Spanish/French border is this little-known venue which has produced carp to over 70lb. It is very lightly fished, but is a popular water with tourists because of a campsite right on the bank. It is found to the south of Perpignan, just off the A9 motorway where you will see signs for the venue. There is a fishing shop nearby which sells permits. Night fishing is allowed in a very small section of the lake. There is a good stock with the average size being mid-twenties.

It's not all boat work in France. Mally Roberts chucking out at a French syndicate water.

The author of this chapter in action at the end of another magic day of carp fishing in France.

One Week in Heaven

We publish two monthly carp magazines and frequently get letters from readers asking for guidance about going away for a week's fishing. As a rule they are going to France for a week on a holiday venue, a water of anything from 5 to 15 acres. How do they go about fishing such a water? What sort of bait will be most suitable? How much gear should they take with them? And so on, and so on. Some of these letters are well over a page long! The following is intended as guidance to anyone going abroad for a holiday session, although some of the comments may be equally applicable to anyone making a one-off visit to a water in this country. For many family anglers this week of fishing is probably their one opportunity each year to leave the real world behind them and lose

Family occasions for us, the Margot sessions. Jemima with a good fish, getting a helping hand from friends Micky Sly and Russell Price.

John Lilley returning a mid-thirty common to Margot. The fish was a good forty at the time this was written. The popular water contains a high number of big fish to 50lb+.

themselves in the world of carp fishing for seven days. Hence the title of the chapter!

What do I call a holiday venue, and where are they?

Holiday venues represent the changing face of carp fishing and a list included here would be out of date by the time the book appears. They are usually up to about 15 acres in size (often much smaller), well-stocked waters with facilities for the anglers on site, and – in the case of some of the French venues – very often transport from a pick-up point in England included in the package. In the pages that follow I mention some we've fished, and others which have been in operation for many years and look set to be around for many years to come. Holiday venues of the type focused on in this chapter are mainly French, but there are other types of holiday fishing packages on offer for fishing in France, Canada, Romania and South Africa. Check out the advertising in *Carpworld* and *Crafty Carper* for details of some of them. Get hold of a copy of the Carp Fishing News book *Holiday Carping* by Simon Crow for more details. Holiday carp venues are a rapidly growing and extremely popular part of the carp scene.

Planning and Preparation

Margot koi. This one was a low double but we've landed them to almost twenty pounds here, and to mid-twenties at Chalet Lake.

The starting point to any trip abroad is the planning. Even before you begin to find out about how to fish the venue you need to plan what you are going to take with you. I can only give you guidelines in a number of categories here. Trips abroad can be split into three main types. By plane. On a package tour. Under your own steam. Overall your main concern will be with the fishing. For the first two types of trip your baggage will be limited and it becomes a question of how much you can cram into your weight allowance, or the number of baggage items you can carry with you.

Aeroplane trips. Start by finding out what the baggage allowance is, and what items are available for hire – or as part of the deal – at the other end. When you are flying you want to save as much of your weight allowance as possible for angling indispensables, extra clothing, and bait. I'm writing this in the light of the experience of three trips to Raduta and one to South Africa. On each occasion the only area I felt under-gunned in was bait. I'll come back to that aspect later.

For plane trips you need to weigh your baggage. Keep checking as you put it together. In Canada, the USA and South Africa you are catered for, or you are able to buy similar foods to those we eat in this country. For Romania I take the angling essentials, then top up with dehydrated foods – paella and pastas – and bait. At Raduta you are supplied with a bedchair,

cooking equipment, gas, pots and pans and can hire a bivvy. I'll deal with the special angling requirements of Raduta in a separate chapter. We are looking at guidelines here.

You are limited to a specified number of items of luggage on some trips where you are picked up in England and taken to the water by bus. Again, are there any major items of luggage available at the venue? What bait is available at the other end? Work backwards. If you can hire a bedchair and a bivvy, do so. You are usually well fed on these packages, and there are regular trips to the local shops, so don't overload yourself with food. The angling essentials – make a list while you are sitting fishing, not while you are daydreaming at home, where you are likely to overlook vital little things like reels, and rods! Take as much

On tour. The facilities at Margot are excellent, but we take the caravan as Mary's sleeping HQ, and the mobile bar and cafe! Micky Sly's bivvy is as near to the bar as possible.

Enjoying a lovely session in the Corner Swim at Domaine de Boux.

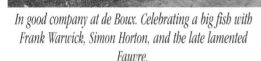

In good company at de Boux. Celebrating a big fish with Frank Warwick, Simon Horton, and the late lamented Fauvre.

specialised bait as you can carry. Spare clothing, particularly for France, where they seem to have more rain than Manchester! Any special food requirements you have.

If you are driving to a venue you can, in theory, take as much gear as you can carry. If four or more of you are going don't underestimate just how much tackle and bait you are likely to take. But given the space you can take all you want, and what you mainly need to know about the amenities at the venue concern the freezer facilities – are there any freezers for bait storage? – and the boat situation. Are boats permitted? Is/are there boat(s) on site? We look at boats elsewhere, but it is my experience of French holiday venues that most of the boats on these waters are inadequate, but usable. If possible take your own boat(s). If there isn't one, and they are permitted, then take one. And a life jacket.

Planning the fishing

OK, all that's necessary, but a bit dry. What about the fishing? Well for starters I'm going to have to do some homework. I need to know as much as possible about the venue before I can start to answer the questions I need to ask myself about the target water. English carpers have been going abroad for nearly twenty years now. Europe isn't the continent of naive carp that armchair carpers in this country think it is. Yeh, there are some prolific waters, just as there are in this country. Many of the best-known, regularly advertised

59lb 2oz mirror from de Boux going back. I caught it again the following day at 58lb 14oz!

waters are popular holiday venues. They are under pressure throughout the spring, summer and early autumn. The carp may have started out naive and catchable, but a few years of constant pressure have educated them. They are probably becoming increasingly bait-dependent, but reluctant to get caught. So that's a starting point for weighing up the angling and tactical approach to the water.

You're after a big French fish? Let's put something into perspective here, and that is the number of times known French big fish get caught. All that pressure and they get caught three or four times each year. Like Bazil, and Mary used to... A maximum of four headline-making anglers **per venue** out of hundreds. So don't go to any overseas water thinking the target fish are a pushover and that any old baits and any old methods will do. In advance I plan in terms of the hardest fish in the water to catch. That's the one I want. As elusive as the Big Black Common in Birch – and I've no idea how to catch her! Any water I go to I treat as the hardest in the world – because it could well be fishing that way the week I am there!

So the starting point to any carp session, home or

Friend Alan Atkins with a de Boux mirror of 51lb+. This is an ideal water for renting as a party and enjoying the seclusion and the private fishing.

abroad, is to get your mental attitude right. And to get your thinking and mental attitude right there are things you need to know. How big is the water? How long has it been open to Brits? How many anglers will there be on it while I am there? Is the use of a boat permitted? Is there a going bait? Are there freezer facilities? Are there crayfish, poissons chat or crabs in the lake?

An aside. "How big is the water and how many anglers are there on it at any one time?" These are two questions you need answering before you even book a trip to an overseas water. Anyone who reads *Carpworld* will know that Domaine de Boux, Etang de Margot and Chalet Lake are three of our favoured overseas holiday waters. Much of our social holiday fishing is at these venues. You can book them as a private party. In acreage they are roughly 12 acres (5), 15 acres (8) and 20 acres (6) respectively. The figure in brackets is the maximum number of anglers allowed on the venue at any one time. Chalet would take up to 8, otherwise the figures are sensible. That's not intended as a recommendation for the venues, just to give you guidelines for the sort of angler per acre maximum which I consider about right for comfortable, relaxed holiday fishing. The economics involved will make it difficult for some venue owners to limit numbers to this level, but on

Paul Musson with one of the big mirrors Domaine de Boux is famous for. This one weighed in at 48lb.

the other hand some are squeezing every last penny they can from their waters by overcrowding them. "How big is the water and how many anglers?" is a big ask before you and your friends commit yourselves to a venue.

We need a reference point. Let's say the water's ten acres and that there will be too many anglers on there while you are fishing it, i.e. more than six. It's been open to the Brits for over six years, which means the carp have learnt a thing or two. There is a going bait, which I'm going to be a bit nervous of because the biggest fish will have already been caught on it and may have learnt to feed on it with extreme caution. You can forget swims because the chances are you won't be in one of the best, and you've got to come up with something meaningful from the one you get. (If you get in one of the best swims your hard work and planning will have given you the chance of the session of a lifetime. Plan in terms of the worst-case scenario and hope you come up with the best!)

You start with the negatives to give yourself a chance of coming up with some positives. Let's look at some of the real nitty-gritty.

Feeding hot-spot. The well appointed dining room in the up-market lodge at the Dream Lakes complex.

The lodge at Chalet Lake, a remote water in eastern France which we enjoyed fishing four years in succession from the late 90s.

Bait

If I'm fishing the same bait as everyone else on a water I feel as though I'm engaging in some kind of communal lottery. I'm waiting for my number to come up – and we all know how long it takes for a lottery number to come up! If ever. Bait has to be your edge. If you are going to Dream Lakes, Les Quis or one of the more popular holiday venues bait can be a tough one to think your way round. I'd take some of the going bait (in case...), two very effective ready-mades, and a proven quality food bait, in ready-made form and as a frozen bait.

Well you did ask!

To me a small water demands small baits. I'd look on 14mm as a maximum size for this type of venue. Go bigger and there is a danger the carp will stop and examine each bait they encounter. You've got a week to get the fish feeding with a view to catching some of them. Small baits are a way of overcoming pressure, and they are available in 10mm from most bait companies. Better still, do what an increasing number of thinking anglers are doing and take a selection of baits in a mix of sizes. Keep the carp guessing as to exactly where the source of danger lies.

When I get in the swim my starting point is 10 kilos of a mix of the baits spread all over the area of swim I've chosen, or have been allocated. Just introduce them everywhere and anywhere in what you can reasonably consider to be your patch of water. The first time you do this you'll scare yourself to death, as I did. I did it to get the fish on the bait. I reasoned that the fish would be spooked from the changeover from one set of anglers to the next (us) so I wasn't likely to catch anything the first night anyway. So I filled in, firstly to give them a taste for my bait(s), and secondly to invite them to come and feed on

Author Tim with a super 42lb 4oz mirror from Tony Miller's lovely, well-stocked Etang Meunier big-fish venue near Limoges.

my patch on a regular basis. When you apply this quantity of bait you realise just how quickly carp go through bait! On the type of waters we are discussing here invariably I catch on the first night using this tactic!

I rarely, if ever, fish pop-ups on overseas waters. I'm a reluctant pop-up user anyway, but even confirmed users agree they are nothing like as effective on many French waters as they can be here. (Although I very rarely use pop-ups in this country, either.) Of the overseas waters I've fished Lac de Madine is the only exception to this generalisation, but at 2,500 acres Madine doesn't really fall into the category we are discussing here!

What happens after the initial baiting? Keep the bait going in. I settle to 5-6lb (give or take) of boilies per day after the initial saturation. Where boats are allowed keep the baits well spread out. Where no boats are in use you can go tighter. Think what the normal baiting approach is likely to be, then opt for the opposite, or an alternative, tactic. Always be guided by the reactions of the carp. Adopt different approaches on a couple of rods to find out what sort of baited situation is the most effective.

Groundbaits and Bait Application

Is there use of boats on the water in question? The answer to this determines my thinking on bait application and the use of back-up baits (groundbaits). Carp anglers tend to be lazy and lacking in initiative. If there is a boat available they will be willing to apply groundbait, and the carp will be accustomed to encountering all sorts of sophisticated baited spots made up of pellets, seeds, chopped baits and all variations thereof known to man and carp.

On waters of this type such situations will be losing their effectiveness, if they have not already done so. No boat? The old throwing stick or catapult comes out, and groundbaits are largely forgotten. Not entirely. You will get the odd angler who works at bait application with a spod – but who wants to work on holiday?

Chalet is famous for its stunning commons, and contains numerous mirrors and big catfish. Micky Sly with a typical mid-thirty common in typical Chalet weather.

So a venue with no boat use is more likely to respond to imaginative groundbaiting and hard work than a venue where the use of a boat is allowed. In this context hard work and initiative are a definite edge, and a spod rod (plus spare spods) and marker float rod (plus spare marker floats) are indispensable aids.

I'll clarify what I'm saying about pressured carp, boats and groundbait situations to avoid misunderstandings. When we first went to Fishabil in 1993 we were told that the carp were shying off beds of bait! "They won't shy off our beds of bait!" John Lilley and I rather cockily told Raphael Faraggi. We had taken frozen Big Fish Mix. We guessed that the fish were becoming nervous of beds of brightly coloured, strong-smelling ready-mades. We were right. But that was last century! We are many years down the line from 1993. Boat-water carp will still be visiting beds of bait, and will be eating from them. With great caution. If ever there was a good-news-bad-news scenario it is beds of bait for pressured, bait-dependent carp! The easier it is for the anglers on a venue to apply beds of bait, the more accustomed carp will be to being confronted by them, and the greater the pressure they are under when feeding. That is the history and syndrome you have to think your way round when you visit a water for a one-off visit.

For instance, if you can use a boat start by forgetting about round boilies.

There is an anomaly with groundbaited situations though. In goes the bait, and the carp steer clear of it, or feed on it with great caution. Then, as the days pass, they accept its presence, start to feed on it more strongly, and by day three or four familiarity, or competitive feeding, has started to make the carp more careless and more catchable on the baited area. So if you are putting down a bed of bait on a strange water be aware that the area may not produce for a few days, but may then get better as the week progresses. Once you've got them visiting seeds, or pellets, slow down on the bait application. The smell of food has infiltrated the lake bed. The carp will keep coming back. Don't spook them by overdoing introductions of new bait. The harder you make them work the greater the chances they will pick up the hookbait. Most of my fishing is done around, or well away from, a focal bed of bait, but I keep a close eye on the area in case the carp start to get carried away in their feeding on it.

My choice of groundbaits* is proven and predictable – because they are effective. Hinders' 3mm Mini-Betaine pellets have worked wherever I've used them. Hinders' Slicker pellets. Hemp is still in its comparative infancy in terms of overseas fishing, and effective wherever it is used. Seed mixes can be electrifying, but may not pull you a big fish. Tigers you always need with you in case underwater pests make fishing boilie hookbaits impossible. (We look

A chunky Chalet 40lb 12oz common for yours truly, one of 31 20lb+ fish in a prolific week's fishing in August 2000.

at meshing hookbaits elsewhere in the book.) Chopped tigers are a brilliant groundbait. Carp go on eating tigers long after they will get caught on them. Oat groats have a big early impact, are easy to prepare, and may not have been done to death on many overseas waters. Groats and hemp was a favourite seed mix before the more comprehensive mixes

Check the rules of a water before you burden yourself with tons of groundbait. Some holiday-type venues have groundbait restrictions and bans.

were introduced in the mid-90s.

I've given some thought to the next tiger: a crayfish- and poissons chat-proof hookbait to follow tigers. Best I can come up with is chopped brazil nuts, fished among seeds and mixed nuts. Brazils have a good carp-catching record, but I don't know how many really big fish they have accounted for. Nor have I experimented with seeing if they will carry a flavour. They catch carp though. It's worth experimenting with alternative hookbaits for overseas waters. Sabotage of hookbaits by crayfish and poissons chat can happen on an alarming scale on some venues, and the feeling of just not knowing if you are fishing effectively or not soon undermines your confidence.

The best product I've encountered for making very hard hookbaits is Richworth's Pop-up Mix, in either the straight or the Fishmeal version. No need to make pop-ups with it, either. I find a mix of one-third Richworth to two-thirds base mix produces buoyant, slow-sinking bottom baits. (The one-third/two-third ratio is for Trigga. Experiment with your own base mix to find the right ratio.)

Ignore the instructions on the Richworth Pop-up Mix bags. Thoroughly combine the two mixes, then treat the powder as a normal base mix. Egg, or eggs (**not** water as Richworth suggest*), liquid additives, gradually add the powder to produce a firm, doughy consistency, then roll out. Boil for up to three minutes. Dry out, freeze, then air-dry. You finish up with billiard ball hard baits which are very attractive to carp. Be warned. Carry a drill with you when you use these baits. You can't get a baiting needle through them.

Former carp record holder Roddy Porter casting out at the prolific Fishabil lake in Brittany. Lovely fishing in a beautiful remote setting.

(*Recent experiments indicate that the more Pop-up Mix you include the more unstable the mix becomes where eggs are used. One-third Pop-up Mix to two-thirds bait mix produces terrific hard baits. Where the ratios are reversed the end product isn't as satisfactory, which is presumably why Richworth recommend the use of water rather than eggs. See Special Hookbaits chapter for more information on this subject.)

When you are groundbaiting start out by using alternative approaches. Pellets are more effective on some waters than others. The same goes for seeds. Try ringing the changes on the hookbaits, too. I tend to fish my favourite bait as the hookbait, but when you are using a number of different baits vary the hookbait approach. I've just come back from South Africa. I fished a water where the bigger fish preferred a local going bait to the faithful Trigga I'd taken with me. I wasn't slow to pick up on this and my two biggest fish came on the local bait, made by a bait company called Edge Baits. Thanks Johan!

It pays to carry some attractor baits with you for use as single hookbaits. Check out Frank Warwick's brilliant chapter for more guidance on this aspect! I've started to use these over the first couple of days of sessions during the period when I'm building up the carp's confidence in my main bait. But my experience is that once the main bait has been established hookbaits as similar as possible to the main bait have repeatedly proved to become increasingly effective as the session wears on, at times to the point that the carp won't pick up anything else.

Be Different

I guess we've already covered the "be different" aspect earlier, but you've got to extend it to your angling tactics, too. When I'm thinking surprise tactics I take Birch Grove as a starting point, and on my travels I try some of the approaches I use there.

Frequent recasting with one rod works surprisingly well on numerous waters. It's a useful tactic when you are getting hookbait interference, too. Not worth trying on pressured waters? Quite the opposite. On small pressured waters the carp will often investigate any splash. You cast out, they go and check out what it's about, and possibly have a go at the hookbait within minutes of the cast. If they don't like the look or feel of the bait it may be put in quarantine and avoided by the carp, however long it sits there. Recasting invites a re-examination. A surprising number of takes at Birch Grove come within minutes of a recast. On small waters I work on the premise that the carp are masters of their environment and fully understand where the food sources and the likely sources of danger are to be found.

PVA bags. Who bothers with PVA bags while they are on their holidays? Who bothers with PVA bags on waters where a boat is allowed? Experiences at Fishabil and elsewhere have suggested that on a 'boat water' bags can make a difference of 8-1 on takes. Carp accustomed to singling out a hookbait from the groundbait seemed to be completely floored by PVA bag presentations. 95 fish in four days at Fishabil in August 2001 startled – and exhausted – me. I knew PVA bags had given me and Briggsy an edge when we won the 2000 World Carp Cup at Fishabil, but I didn't realise how big an edge until I fished them from the dam wall on a pleasure session.

You've got a week. If you're allowed three rods, fish six or seven different spots, and rotate them. Keep the bait going into all of them, watch for movement, don't over-pressure any of the spots. Carp which can have a meal on your bait without the presence of tackle start to relax. If you only bait and fish the same number of spots as you fish rods, all the spots are under tackle pressure all the time. Try to avoid this.

Margins

Not all swims have a suitable margin spot but when possible always keep at least one rod in the margins – and by margin I mean as tight to the bank as possible. It doesn't matter how busy the bank may seem from the point of view of feet coming and going. That isn't pressure to carp, and they become accustomed to it over the years. During the difficult periods at peak times one of the most productive spots at Cuttle Mill used to be straight under the rod tip. You don't bait such spots, other than with a discarded hookbait occasionally. Carp love margins, and overseas fish are no different. The fish are there anyway. Fish them for one fish at a time, and don't kill the margin spots by baiting them.

The well-appointed house overlooking the lake at Etang Meunier, a stunning venue for a week's holiday fishing in France.

Depth

I've always been interested in the depth of the water I'm fishing, but I never realised the real significance of depth until I started fishing overseas and using a feature finder. There are depths, there are feeding depths, and there are big-fish feeding depths. They all vary from venue to venue, and to start with it's as well to cover a variety of depths as well as a variety of spots.

You need to keep a very open mind when you fish a range of overseas venues. For instance Etang de Margot is just as perplexing as Lac de St. Cassien. There's a variety of depths in Margot, but most of the fish consistently prefer to feed in 3½-4 feet, or shallower. A couple of months later you go to Cassien and find the fish are feeding at 50 feet!

If someone shows you a feeding spot on a water check the depth. It may be the key to understanding the fish's feeding habits, and your swim. One of the first questions you ask at Cassien is: "What depth are the fish being caught from?" Briggsy starts out by trying four different depths. At Madine the preferred depth was 6-8ft, with a marked liking for potamogeton beds, particularly in very hot weather. At Domaine de Boux when there was no weed the preferred open-water depth was 8-9ft. Many of the productive margin spots on French waters are very shallow, and easily overlooked. My only Margot forty came from 16" of water. Very shallow margins along the wood side at Chalet are productive. Don't rule out areas on the basis of the depth. Watch, experiment and find out for yourself.

Psychological Warfare

I fish a number of holiday venues of the size and/or type we are discussing. I look on them as the Birch Groves or Cuttle Mills of France in terms of the degree of thinking required to get inside the heads of the carp. Pressure soon starts to have an effect, and the carp soon learn to avoid capture. So the first lesson to learn about any overseas water is that it may not be as easy as you hope it might be.

I've found that all overseas waters respond well to quality bait fished in quality condition. Sealed freezer boxes are an important part of our baggage. No freezer at Chalet means extra precautions. There are freezers at Domaine de Boux and Margot, and at many other holiday-type venues. Failing freezers you need to air-dry your frozen baits well in advance, or check to see if packing them with sugar – as Briggsy advocates – or salt, another known preservative, works with your mixes. Air-drying is a necessity for bait to be taken on a plane trip, firstly because a freezer box would add too much weight to your precious baggage allowance, and secondly because air-dried baits are lighter than frozen baits. My next trip to Raduta is eight weeks away as I write this and I'm already steadily building up a supply of air-dried baits for the session.

You have one chance to make a hit on holiday trips. You can't wear the fish down by feeding them till they are virtually eating out of your hand as you can on a local water at home.

Jemima and Pip starting their carp fishing careers on the small lake at Lac de Madine in 1999. Not really what you would class a typical holiday venue, but Madine is a super place to spend a holiday, and the small lake is full of carp to 20lb+.

Your rigs may have to be more sophisticated than you normally fish – mainly because of the time element involved, but because of the ongoing pressure on the fish, too.

Thinking and analysis play major parts in your planning and strategies for the waters we are considering. It's no good me saying "well, fish it like this" because if you all went and did that, the essential element of surprise would be lost. Think big. Think different. Try to get inside the heads of the carp. What are they nervous of? What are they reacting against? What won't they have seen before? What will take them off their guard?

If you want a big fish from the venue try to find out where they are caught from, and the tactics that have led to their downfall in the past. You can often find common denominators that you can work into your own approach to make the chance of success more likely. For instance nearly all my really big overseas fish have come from spots I have just started covering, be it on day four, five or day ten of the session. On the other hand, there can be a build-up of action from spots baited throughout the week. If you want action and a big fish then split your tactics and keep finding new spots in the swim for one or two rods.

The second point I would make about big fish is that all mine come later in the session, rather than sooner. I've had six fish over 55lb. These have come on days 4, 5, 6, 7, 8 and 10 of the sessions. The Cassien fish of 57lb I caught in November 2001 came on the fourth night, the earliest I have caught a really big fish on my overseas sessions.

When you are hoping for a big carp all your efforts from the moment you start planning, or get in your swim, are a build-up towards the capture, however late in the session it occurs. If you start getting jaded mentally look on your swim occupation as a prolonged pre-baiting exercise. If you started fishing a swim on your local water after four days' pre-baiting you would be brimming with confidence. When you are occupying that swim you have to guard against the opposite effect and a lack of success undermining your confidence.

Don't confuse a one or two-week session far from home with an ongoing campaign on your own waters. Overseas you are starting from scratch in terms of the accumulation of knowledge, building the carp's confidence in what you are offering them, and getting inside the carp's defences. You are trying to cram a season's – or a lifetime's – fishing into a few short days. It takes a very special approach. A combination of belief, and understanding, and a willingness to wait for the kettle to boil. Carp fishing can be about waiting. Learn to become a good thinker, and an imaginative experimenter – and a good waiter.

Timing and Luck

We went to Chalet Lake in 2000 and had an extraordinary week. Alan Atkins had a 42lb+ mirror and a stack of other fish, including 25 over 20lb. I had a 40lb 8oz common, among 31 fish over 20lb. We went for the same calendar week in 2001, and Alan and I couldn't catch a cold! I had two fish and Alan had one! Micky Sly and John Lilley did OK, but not on the scale of the catches of the year before. The fish just weren't feeding as they had done the previous year. On the other hand, the late August Margot trip was unusually kind to us and we had far more fish than usual between us. I had 50 fish to 37lb, including

Further afield... Martin Davidson and Gary Hoden of African Gold landing a fish at the prolific Donaldson Dam just outside Johannesburg.

Martin Davidson of African Gold on the front cover of Carpworld *133 with a 50lb+ common from Snagmere. Carp magazines carry advertising from numerous companies and individuals offering carp fishing holidays.*

45 over 20lb, far better than any previous result I'd had there. But no forty-plus!

So you plan, and think, and work, and give it your best shot, but to some extent you can only play the hand you are dealt. Carp are not machines, and none of us quite understand what provokes a spell of abandoned feeding, or why they can switch off just as quickly. Visitors to Birch Grove are well aware of this phenomenon!

In advance every trip is going to be the session of a lifetime. But I always have a built-in safety valve, a little voice that tells me to be ready to put it down to experience if the session I'm travelling to doesn't live up to expectations. We've all had our share of disappointments. How you live through them and cope with them sorts the men from the boys. Anglers who whinge about the hard times at carp fishing shouldn't be carp anglers!

The planning and the anticipation are among the most enjoyable aspects of carp fishing. If you draw a bum feeding week don't blame the guy who runs the water. He's disappointed for you, too. Just learn from the experience, try to figure out why it didn't work out, and go back the next time with all the answers at your disposal, and hoping that this time the carp join in the party! There is an old adage that luck evens itself out. At the moment that is a very worrying thought for me. Surely I can't have that much bad luck building up for the next couple of years!

A long time ago I learnt a very valuable lesson from Albert Romp, and it has stood me in good stead ever since. We were at Cuttle Mill on a charity event. There were fish showing all over the pool, but no one was catching. I walked down the bank to Albert to ask him what was going on.

"They're not feeding. If they were feeding someone would be catching."

Crowy with an African Gold monster of 55lb+ from Klaserie Dam.

Words of wisdom, and advice that I relate to carp generally, and big carp, wherever I fish. What a water is producing is a barometer of the way the carp are feeding. If others are catching and you aren't then start to rethink what you are doing. But very often when you go to a strange water you are waiting for what you are doing to start working. There is a degree of brinkmanship in making the most of a week's fishing on a distant water. Until they start feeding strongly you aren't going to catch them. Work on getting them feeding and finding the spots to catch them from and catching them will follow. Don't let your mind panic because of a couple of days of inactivity. If you start making changes for the sake of it you can undo all the good planning and hard work that has gone before. Get it right before you go, and fish it right when you get there. Whatever happens don't underestimate the degree of difficulty of some of the overseas waters. Many of them are under far more ongoing pressure than the majority of home waters I fish.

Lac de St. Cassien

Steve Briggs

There can be few carp anglers around today who haven't heard of Lake Cassien. In the relatively short time that it's been known to us it has become probably the best-known carp water in the world. Thousands of anglers venture abroad each year in search of carp, and the figure is rising all the time. Without a doubt France is now the most popular destination – but it wasn't always like that. Until the early 80s anglers were content just to fish waters on home soil, for the most part not even realising that there were carp worth pursuing elsewhere. It was the discovery of Cassien that changed all that, and while it was inevitable that anglers would one day venture further afield it was this great water that got the ball rolling.

Lac de Saint Cassien – to give the lake its correct name – was brought to our attention back in September 1984 when, for the first time, a picture of a Cassien carp was published in this country. The picture appeared on the front cover of *The Carp Catcher*, the then official magazine of the Carp Anglers Association, and showed the captor, Paul Regent, holding a mirror carp of 35lb. The story was that Paul, along with angling friend Kevin Maddocks, had travelled down to the water for an exploratory trip to check the potential of the lake after receiving some information about it. During the limited time they had available Paul managed to catch three carp, the 35-pounder plus two other mirrors around mid-20s, all of which were taken on sweetcorn at close range.

The carp angling potential of the place was clear from the start – but there was another reason for Paul and Kevin's interest in the water. Their plan was to run trips to the venue through Paul's company, Regent Coaches. These trips became known as the Regent trips and they gave many people their first taste of carp fishing outside this country. Not surprisingly there was a lot of interest from the start. At this time in the mid-80s a forty-pound carp was very rare in

Starting place for many trips to Cassien, the famous Chez Pierre's.

All loaded up and ready to go in front of Chez Pierre's.

277

this country, and most of the big-fish waters were well known and well pressured. The potential that Cassien offered was almost unbelievable, with miles of unfished bank space, and hundreds of uncaught carp – with a high percentage of these being between thirty and fifty pounds, and a lake record which already stood at over 72lb!

Obviously it was these figures that first grabbed people's attention, but there was more to it than that. The location alone made it special. Cassien is situated close to the French Riviera in the far south of the country, and being just a short drive from such places as St. Tropez, Nice, Monaco and Cannes it is in one of the most glamorous areas in the world.

Then there's the weather. This part of the world has always enjoyed a better than average climate. Summertime temperatures rarely drop below 80°F, and even the winters are far milder than most other parts of Europe.

The first Regent trip was during the winter, towards the end of January 1985, but although the anglers fished for seven days, no fish were caught, which gave the first indication that the carp in this lake weren't prepared to give themselves up that easily. However, the seed had been sown and many others decided to take on the long journey in search of some uncaught monsters. Among them were such names as Max Cottis, Phil Harper, Roger Smith, Phil Smith, Joe Taylor

Playing a 40lb-plus mirror in the Island Bay – South Arm.

A long-awaited 41lb 6oz common from the bottom of the West Arm.

and, of course, most famous of all, Rod Hutchinson. Rod was the biggest name in carp fishing at the time, and was among the first people to be really successful there. His early writings about Cassien were an inspiration to many people, myself included. He quickly amassed a tally of huge carp in a few short sessions, including seven 40lb + and three in excess of 50lb. Max Cottis had the enviable result of being the first English angler to land a carp over 60lb with a huge Cassien carp of 68½lb. That capture ensured a place in carp fishing history for Max, but the fish he caught was to become even more famous some time later when it fell to another English angler called Kevin Ellis. On that occasion the fish weighed an incredible 76lb. I wonder if he realised, as he struggled to hold the fish, just how famous that capture would make him? From that moment on the carp became known to everyone as the Ellis fish, and the swim he fished is still known as Ellis Point.

That capture got the whole fishing world talking about Cassien, and many of our respected names were confident that the lake could hold fish in excess of 100lb. In reality the Ellis fish was almost certainly the biggest fish in the lake at the time, although that could still change at any time. There was one more capture of this great fish to an English angler when it was caught by Dave Walker at its highest ever weight of 77½lb. Almost unbelievably this fish beat Dave's previous best carp by an incredible 72lb! Which just goes to show that dreams can become reality at Cassien. That capture is still the biggest fish to be caught from the lake, and also the biggest carp ever caught by a British angler. Sadly it was the last time it would grace the banks as just a few days later the great fish was found dead. A sad loss, but it certainly wasn't to be the end of the Cassien big-fish stories.

Not surprisingly the fishing was dominated by the English in those early years, although it didn't take too long before anglers from other countries were making their way down there. There were very few French carp anglers at the time but one of the first to take up the challenge was Didier Cottin, who spent many hours watching the British go about their business, before going on to catch quite a few decent Cassien fish himself, including the famous Moby Dick, which he named after catching it at 57lb. Of the other anglers who were making their mark in those days, the Van den Hoven brothers from Holland were certainly among the most successful, as was

A big part of my Cassien fishing – changing swims. Here I'm travelling down the South Arm in the area of the Pylon Swims, moving from the Banana to the Bridge Swim during the December 2000 session with Tim.

the German Geert Abelo, along with his friends Tilly and Roland. These were the anglers who featured in the TriCast adverts that were around at the time. Together all of these anglers helped to put Cassien on the map and make it one of the most popular carp fishing venues in the world today.

Like many of the big waters across Europe Cassien is a man-made reservoir. The valley where once a stream ran through was dammed at one end and was then filled with water to form the lake. Because of the layout of the land there were great variations in depths and features, all of which goes towards making the lake one of the most interesting there is to fish, and making it one of the most beautiful as well. The lake is made up of three arms of water that are joined in a central area. The arms are known as the North Arm, South Arm and West Arm – for obvious reasons! There is a general tendency to treat the arms as separate pieces of water, although they form part of one lake

At the end of 2001 the water level was the lowest I had ever seen it. The plateau in front of the new Blue Boat swim is normally well underwater.

which covers roughly 1,200 acres. The fish can, and do, move freely around the lake.

The South Arm was the first area to attract attention from anglers. It's certainly the most accessible area for visitors. The A8 Autoroute runs through the main part of the Riviera and passes within a few kilometres of Cassien. By leaving the A8 at Adrets and following the D37 you soon find yourself at the start of the South Arm. The D37 runs the full length of the South Arm before crossing the famous road bridge and going on to the towns of Montaroux and Fayence. The four restaurants for which Cassien is famous are all situated along this stretch of the A8. They are Arboussiers, Pecheur du Lac, and the better known Gerard's and Pierre's. These restaurants are normally the starting point for trips to Cassien. Pierre's was the first of the cafés to be associated with carp fishing, although in more recent times it's fair to say that Gerard's has taken over as the most popular Cassien angling HQ (see map on page 283).

The restaurants supply the permits which everyone needs for fishing, but they are also useful for supplies, equipment and, of course, secure car parking space. For these reasons the South Arm was the first part of the lake to be fished seriously. They weren't the only reasons though. Cassien can be a daunting water for first-time visitors and the depths of the lake can quickly drain the confidence. The South Arm contains plenty of angler-friendly features, with shallow bays, plateaux and – depending on the water levels at the time – some islands, too. The maximum depths are found in the old river bed which runs through the entire course of the lake. In the South Arm this generally means depths of between 40 and 70 feet*.

The beginning of the South Arm is where Rod Hutchinson did a great deal of his early fishing at Cassien. It's still a popular area, but for different reasons now. The prolific catches that used to take place there are far less common now, but this part of the lake has built up a reputation for producing some of the biggest fish in the lake. At any one time there could be a lot of fish in the South Arm but generally speaking it's now more of an area where you may have to sit it out for a while. But the rewards can be there.

Cassien attracts many different types of carp anglers from around the world. Some just want a holiday and a carp – any carp. Others specifically target the biggest fish in the water. Most of the big-fish hunters tend to head for the South Arm in their quest for a 30-kilo fish. Of the big fish that

The Cassien water level can vary by up to 15 feet. The references in this chapter are to depths when the lake is at its normal winter level.

Where many of the fish head for in May – the reedy part of the West Arm spawning bay.

A sunny December morning in the North Arm, looking towards the Picnic Table swim.

A warm summer's day in the Plateau Swim.

are around today a mirror known as Lucy is generally accepted to be the biggest in there at the moment, having been caught at over 70lb. She seems to be resident at the top end of the South Arm, as many big fish such as Half Moon and the Big Leather have been in the past. Just why these fish should be attracted to this area of the lake is a bit of a mystery, but many of them appear to be loners, and they are also the old fish of the lake. It's possible that these fish have lived in the area for many years – possibly going back to before they were pressured by anglers – and old habits die hard.

Further along the Arm is Gerard's café, an area which has produced more big fish over the years than any other area of the lake – many of them to Gerard himself who has spent a great many hours fishing from the beach in front of his café. The café itself is currently run by English angler Martin Russell and his wife Rachel. Martin has made a name for himself in the past running the Cassien Experience trips to the lake. This business has now passed to Lee Picknell, but, just as before, Gerard's is used as the base for the trips. Cassien is not an easy big-fish water but Martin and Lee have landed four good fifties between them – two each – which shows that they are well capable of giving excellent advice about the venue, as is Gerard himself.

Friend, Simon Crow, with a hard-earned mirror of 43½lb from the South Arm. March 2002.

To the right of Gerard's the South Arm widens out into an area generally known as Island Bay. Much of the water is fairly deep in this part, but it can be a productive spot at the right times, and it was this part of the lake that produced Dave Walker's biggest ever Cassien carp in the late 80s. At the end of the Arm is Pierre's café, which is by reputation the most famous of the cafés. It was from here that most anglers used to start their trips, and meet up for a social, too. Some of the get-

Lee Picknell, who runs the Cassien Experience trips, with a Cassien mirror of 56lb from the margins near Gerard's café in the South Arm.

The area of the two South Arm 'No entry' signs. From here down to Gerard's is a slow big-fish area that was popular with the earliest Cassien anglers in the 80s.

281

togethers between anglers such as Johnny Allen, Albert Romp, Roger Smith and Kerry Barringer, and of course Rod Hutchinson himself, are still talked about today, and for the history lovers Pierre still keeps a couple of old photo albums that show many of the old faces and the fish that Cassien was famous for. Few people realise that Pierre's café was the scene of some of the early meetings for carp anglers in France, and one of the first people to host a slide show there was our own Ritchie MacDonald. In more recent times Pierre has retired and passed the café and shop on to his son, Phillippe, who now runs it with his wife Veronique.

The West Arm is by far the smallest of the three arms, ranging from 70 to 150 yards wide. Because it's the smallest part of the lake it tends to be overlooked by many of the visiting anglers, but it can produce plenty of fish at times. Generally speaking the West Arm has a reputation for producing fish of a lower average weight than the rest of the lake. That's not always the case and every year some very big fish do get caught from here. Perhaps the big difference is that none of the big fish are known to spend much time in the West Arm and are likely to be travelling fish.

At the bottom end of the Arm you have the well-known areas of the Blue Boat swim, Ellis Point and the boat club. These have always been popular spots and still top many anglers' lists of favourite swims. What makes these areas so appealing is the fact that

Tim bivvied up opposite Gerard's during the extreme low water levels of late 2001.

One of the islands in the South Arm's Island Bay, with Pierre's in the background.

the lake narrows down at these points, so any fish moving through are funnelled down and are much easier to intercept.

Moving up the arm we come to Roche American, popular because it's one of the few places that are fairly easily accessible by car. During the summer months it's a popular area with many people and can become very busy. As the lake heads up this way the depths increase considerably, but although they would not normally be classed as shallow, they are by Cassien standards. The deepest parts here are between 20 and 30 feet in the old river bed, and 12 to 20 feet in other parts.

Towards the far end of the West Arm is the area for which this arm is most famous – the spawning bay. This bay is closed to anglers for much of the year, and for obvious reasons. It is the one part of the lake which is certain to be visited by the carp at a known time of the year. The time is of course spring, and although the bay itself may be unfishable, many big catches have been made by anglers who have timed it right and fished the areas just outside the bay as the fish have been moving in to spawn.

The North Arm is the most extensive and deepest of the three arms. It seems almost laughable now but in the early days few people even considered fishing this area; it was considered too deep to catch carp from. How different that is

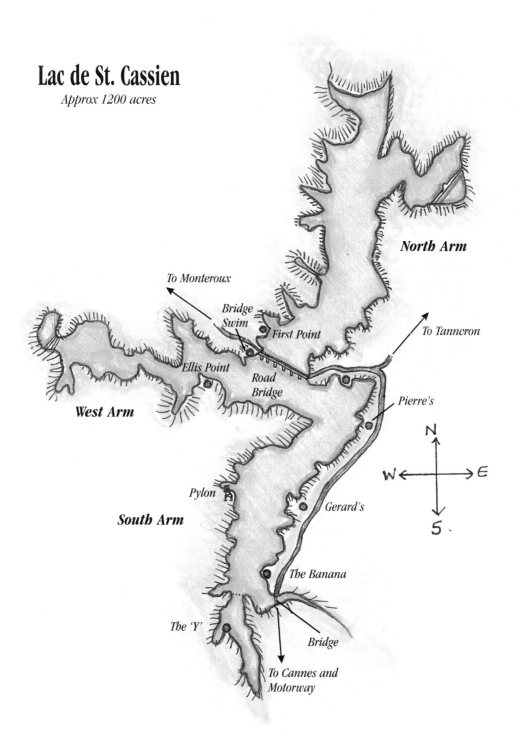

Lac de St. Cassien

Approx 1200 acres

To Monteroux

Bridge
Swim

First Point

North Arm

To Tanneron

Ellis Point

Road
Bridge

Pierre's

West Arm

N

W ← → E

S

Pylon

South Arm

Gerard's

The Banana

The 'Y'

Bridge

To Cannes and
Motorway

today, for the North Arm has become the most heavily fished of all the arms. Apart from a couple of places most of this arm is only accessible by boat, which makes it the quietest and most remote part of the lake. The top end of the arm is at least an hour's row from the nearest café, but with a boatload of tackle you can probably double that time.

At the bridge end of the arm there's a series of points on the West bank, aptly named the first, second and third points. These are the most popular swims in this part of the lake, and normally the most productive. Although the depths start to drop quickly as you go up the arm these first three points all have extensive plateaux out in front of them, but beyond these areas the arm quickly drops off to over 100 feet in places.

The middle part of the arm appears to be the most featureless but there are many swims here that are worth a go. Perhaps the most famous swim in this area is Moby Dick Beach which earned its name after Didier Cottin caught the fish of the same name from here in 1990.

North Arm first point 51½ from the late 2000 session with Tim.

Much of the water here is very deep but there are a couple of very noticeable features. One is a largish plateau half way up the arm. The other is again a raised area, but the difference with this one is that it is almost in the centre of the lake, and although it isn't very wide it does extend for some distance, starting from the third point and going on up the arm for almost its entire length. Much of this feature is over 40ft deep, but year after year fish do get caught from here.

At the top of the arm the lake is at its widest and deepest. Depths of anything up to 150 feet can be found here and much of the fishing is done at fairly close range to the bank. This area is often used by the fish as a holding area when they are put under extreme pressure. It is one of the few areas where they can sit in mid-water knowing they won't be bothered by anglers' lines and baits – until they have the urge to go down and feed again.

Unfortunately for anglers the Dam area of the lake has now been made out of bounds. The stretch of water leading up to the dam is effectively a small arm in itself, leading to a largish bay, where the dam is situated. Although there were only ever a couple of swims in this area, at times they were among the best on the lake, especially when they had been neglected for a while. Now it is a safe haven all year round, and undoubtedly it always holds fish. Is that such a bad thing? Probably not. The fish in Cassien have come under an increasing amount of pressure every year and it's right they should have an area they can retreat to when the need arises.

The last part of the lake is the main central area where all three arms join. The reason why this area can be popular is obvious. The Cassien carp can be very nomadic, and they

A very sparsely scaled mirror of 50lb 6oz from the North Arm's Second Point swim, December 1998.

have to pass through this central area on their travels. The best known of the swims in this area is known as the Bridge Swim. This swim has accounted for many famous catches down the years, including, of course, when Tim Paisley landed Half Moon Scale at 63lb along with several other good fish. It's not hard to see why the swim is so good. In addition to the fact that it covers the bridge pillars there is also a very appealing plateau between the second and third pillars at the western end of the bridge. The downside of this part of the lake is that it is easily accessible for anyone, and the peace and serenity that Cassien is known for is rarely found here. That is enough to put many anglers off the swim, and yes, I do list myself amongst those anglers!

Over the years Cassien has proved itself to be an excellent water for carp growth. Many waters have had peaks and troughs in their history. Most of them have just a short period when they produce something special, or the odd very big fish. Cassien is different. From the time it was first discovered by carp anglers it has held carp in excess of 70lb, and several over 60lb. Several different fish have made it over 70lb, from the Ellis fish, through other well-known carp such as Matilda, and on to Lucy, which tops the list today. The number of growing fifties in the water suggests that this trend of

A fish known as the Little Linear at 49lb 4oz from Roger and Kerry's swim halfway up the North Arm.

An early Christmas present. Christmas eve 1997, 48½lb.

Still my Cassien personal best. 61½lb from the area of the West Arm spawning bay, May 1987.

producing a succession of big fish over the years will continue into the future.

Why should this lake suit the carp so well and produce a succession of big fish? There's no one factor which makes the difference; it's a combination of many things. The climate certainly suits them. The temperature in the South of France is high for much of the year, regularly being around 25°C, and often much higher than that. The high temperatures continue late into the year, which gives the fish a longer growing period than in other areas.

But the high temperatures alone are not enough to ensure that the carp will grow big. The difference comes in the early part of the year when cold water runs into the lake from the surrounding mountains. As a result of this the carp in Cassien have never really spawned successfully. Although they visit the spawning bay each year and go through the motions of spawning nothing ever seems to come of this. This could be because of the influx of cold water.

Unsuccessful spawning seems to be important for producing big fish. That other famous big-fish water, Lake Raduta, has very severe winters (it freezes over) but has a stock of very big fish. When you look around at other countries with hot climates like Spain, Portugal and Cyprus, the carp breed very successfully in these countries, but very large carp are few and far between, and their waters are more likely to be overrun with smaller fish.

Carp need a good supply of food to grow well and reach their full potential. Over the years carp anglers' baits have been accepted as part of the Cassien carp's diet, but baits alone are not

My friend Joss Sunbert from Holland with one of the numerous big Cassien fish he has accounted for over the years.

enough to produce very big fish, and of course the Cassien fish grew to immense sizes before boilies were ever introduced. The food that formed the main diet was, and is, crayfish; there is little by way of other natural food in the lake. The mainly sandy, rocky bottom doesn't lend itself to the type of natural food that we associate with many carp waters. But the rocky terrain and abundance of snags and, importantly, the good quality of the water are a perfect combination for crayfish, and over the years they have thrived in Cassien. Carp are quick to make the most of any food source and the signs of the number of crayfish they can eat can often be seen in the sack after a fish has been retained for a few hours. This could also explain why the smaller species in the lake, such as bream, tench, and roach, have failed to reach any great sizes. But anything that is a potential crayfish eater, such as chub, catfish, and of course carp, have all prospered.

Over the years several stockings have taken place. Most of the fish have been introduced at weights of under 20lb, but it's been proved time and again that these fish have the potential to reach forty pounds in a very short period of time. The fastest growth I've personally noted was in a mirror of 21½lb which I caught in October 1986. Two years later, almost to the day, a friend of mine caught the same fish at a weight of 41¼lb! A gain of twenty pounds in two years. This is by no means a unique growth rate and at the time of writing there are probably more fish over forty pounds in the lake than at any other time in the history of Cassien. Not all the fish in Cassien grow at this sort of rate. Some fish I have a record of have virtually stood still, or just put on a few pounds, although at the other extreme a fish my mate Simon Crow caught at 22lb five years ago now weighs over 50lb!

Age plays some part in growth rates. Of the originals that we know are left in the lake, most have levelled out in terms of weight, and some, including the Big Leather, have even started to go back. They can all fluctuate in weight though. One fish I caught twice in the space of a month a couple of years back actually increased in weight by four pounds during that period. So for targeting the big fish it's important to choose the right time of year as much as any other factor.

What about methods for Cassien? There's little doubt that the Cassien carp have seen virtually all the modern-day rigs and baits available to carp anglers. Many of the best-known and respected anglers from around the world have travelled to this Mecca of carp fishing in search of its prized inhabitants. In the early days the fish were far more naive and quicker to seize the opportunity of a free meal. Consequently with our advanced methods many big fish were caught without the anglers having to work too hard for their results. Perhaps that's a bit unfair on those early pioneers –

Above left: Ritchie MacDonald struggling to lift one of his 1985 big Cassien fish. This one weighed 43lb.
Above right: Max Cottis became the first English angler to catch a carp over 60lb when he landed this Cassien monster of 68½lb in the summer of 1985. This fish later became known as the Ellis fish when Kevin Ellis caught it at 76lb.

although I was one of them! – because Cassien itself doesn't present an easy challenge.

The difference was that in those early days anglers' baits were a novelty and the fish would travel great distances in search of them, and take very little caution in eating them. The real pressure didn't start until 1994, when night fishing was legalised on Cassien for the first time. Prior to that time some anglers took the risk of night fishing, but those who were caught had their tackle confiscated. This was enough to put most anglers off taking the risk, but once night fishing was allowed it was like opening the floodgates. Being able to camp on the bankside meant that anglers could stay for longer periods, and at any time of year as, until recently, Cassien has always been open all year round – an unusual state of affairs on the big-fish waters of France.

Location is vital on the huge, sprawling venue. The biggest problem here is that wherever you are on the lake the area of water you can see at any one time is very limited. Even if you are in the same arm as many of the fish there is no guarantee that you will find them. The fish do jump, which often gives their presence away, but when they are under pressure they are more reluctant to show themselves, or restrict their leaping to areas where they know they are safe from anglers. For this reason many anglers adopt a mobile approach in the hope that if they don't land on fish straightaway they will find them by trial and error.

There are different groups of fish in varying numbers around the lake. It is not uncommon to catch a fish from a swim then have no more action for several days. On other occasions it is possible to have consistent action in one swim over a period of days, or even weeks.

Roger Smith with a stunning Cassien South Arm fish of 55lb, caught during his session with Rod Hutchinson in 1985.

Many of the anglers who specifically target the biggest fish in the lake will often sit it out in an area where they feel those fish are most likely to be. In the past many of the big fish have been loners, as some of the older big fish are now. The younger big fish that have grown on in recent years may well be a different prospect. Having grown up in groups they seem quite happy to stay that way, and now there are some groups of fish that hold several forties and fifties, and maybe even bigger fish. It could well be that the older residents were once part of large groups and as time has passed fish have died, and they have ended up as lone survivors, choosing to say apart from the groups of younger fish that have been introduced.

What it actually takes to catch a Cassien carp isn't easy to explain. There are several different outlooks from a variety of anglers, but at the end of the day Cassien seems to be a law unto itself. Just when you think you've got everything worked out Cassien has a funny way of coming back and kicking you in the teeth, as if it's letting you know you are never going to get the upper hand.

For a long time using big beds of bait was virtually the kiss of death. Apart from the very early days using a large amount of bait would do little more than scare the fish away and ensure that you would struggle to catch a fish. For many years the accepted way to catch the carp was to use bait sparingly, perhaps putting out just ten or twenty boilies each time a hookbait was dropped. However, in recent times there have been some very large catches to anglers using what can only be described as a great deal of bait. Just why the fish should have changed in this regard could be down to various reasons. For one, many of the fish are relatively new, and may well react differently to heavy baiting for that reason alone. Secondly, so much good bait has been introduced in recent years that they are just naturally more drawn

One of the first French anglers to fish Cassien. The famous Didier Cottin with Moby Dick at 57lb, caught in 1990 from the productive swim which now bears that name in the North Arm.

to it. Either way Cassien is one place where it is very difficult to have any fixed theories on where the fish will be, or how they are likely to get caught. For me this is all part of the attraction of the place. You simply have to keep working if you want any sort of consistent success. There is no one method, or area, that can be relied on to produce fish all of the time.

Good quality baits are a good starting point – as they are on most waters. In the past few years the tendency has definitely been towards good food baits, although in the course of a year the Cassien carp see a large number of different baits, and get caught on quite a variety of them. But by and large the bigger and better catches do come to the better quality baits.

Perhaps the biggest stumbling block for many anglers at Cassien has been with the use of flavours. To me it has been very noticeable that the carp will often avoid baits with high flavour levels. I first realised this when I knew I was on fish, but was only getting runs when the baits had been in the water for over 48 hours. If I had been changing the hookbaits every 15 or 20 hours I would have received no action at all. I discussed this with a few friends who had witnessed similar things happening, and our conclusion was that the baits were only acceptable to the carp once much of the flavour had leaked out. We decided that halving the amount of flavour used should do the trick, and it did. The baits with lower flavour levels caught fish far more quickly, in some cases within minutes of the bait being introduced. Of course there are many other factors to take into account but I'm sure that many anglers have gone away from Cassien frustrated and fish-less simply because they were using flavour levels that were too high, and unacceptable to the fish.

Particles have been used with great success through the years. In particular tiger nuts have been very popular at Cassien. Although they had always been used on the water it was during the mid-90s that they really took off in a big way. It wasn't just that the carp liked them either.

Gerard of Gerard's Cafe at Bois de Callian with the famous Lucy at an all-time high of 70lb+.

Tigers proved to be a very effective way of combating the crayfish and poissons chat that can prove such a nuisance when using boilies. After much use the carp have become more wary of tiger nuts, and although the carp still eat them there are a reducing number of captures on them each year.

The most difficult aspect of Cassien to come to terms with are the depths. Understanding the depths of Cassien, and how the fish use them, can lead to a better success rate. This is one area where Cassien really is different from most other carp waters. As with location it is vitally important to fish at the right depth, although just how deep you have to fish depends on conditions and the time of year. The right depth could be anything from 2-3 feet, or down to over 70 feet! The mere mention of placing a bait at anything from 50ft to 70ft is enough to have newcomers to Cassien shaking their heads in disbelief, but the fish are comfortable feeding at these sorts of depths, and get caught there regularly. Anglers have expressed concern about the effect it has on carp, bringing them up from those sorts of depths, but it seems to have little or no effect on them. They are used to moving from the surface to the bottom of their own accord, unlike a deep-sea fish which may live its whole life in the deeper water.

Echo sounders are one of the best possible aids for fishing Cassien and locating its features. Although I did fish there in the past without an echo sounder I must admit that now it is difficult to imagine fishing effectively at Cassien without one. There are no hard and fast rules about depth, but there are guidelines which can give you a starting point. As a general rule it's fair to say that the warmer the weather the deeper the fish will go. That's a hard one to come to terms with. In England the carp in most of our waters will come to the surface and bask in the heat. But that's not the case at Cassien, and in over sixteen years of fishing there I've never seen a fish cruising on the surface.

The water temperature and oxygenation are the factors that influence the carp to be at certain depths. During the hottest period of the year, which is normally July and August, the fish can regularly be found at around 50ft. This state of affairs usually carries on through September and October as well. This is not to say that the carp won't visit the shallower water, because at times they will, in search of food. In particular the fish will often search for food around the many small beds of potamogeton that grow around the margins of the lake. This can happen at any time of year, but there is more of a tendency for them to visit the margins when the water is at its highest level.

Low water levels seem to push the fish into deeper water. It's mainly as the temperature starts to drop that the fish are more likely to be consistently found in the shallower water. I'm sure this is because cold water is naturally drawn downwards, and the warmer water rises, meaning that the most comfortable levels for the fish are nearer to the surface. I've generally found that during December I would expect the fish to be somewhere between 18ft and 30ft, then going on to January and February their favourite depth would be more like 10ft to 20ft. These are only my findings, but there are always captures that go against the grain, and there are some anglers who firmly believe in sticking with the same depths all year round. No one can stand up and say that they have all the answers, but there is little doubt that depths do play a major factor in the fishing at Cassien.

Of the anglers who visit the lake the ones who have become most successful in the long term are the ones who have worked hard, thought about their approach, and have managed to develop a feeling for what makes the lake tick. Unlike many waters, time on the bank alone is not enough to ensure success at Cassien. Many anglers have found to their cost that just sitting it out and waiting for something to happen is not enough to ensure success, and is often a recipe for failure. If you go there with an open mind, positive thoughts, and with the right tools for the job, anything is possible.

Thousands of carp anglers have visited this great water since its discovery, and it has gone from being virtually unknown to one of the most famous and respected waters in the world. People have been frustrated, enthralled, disillusioned, excited and captivated by Cassien, and no matter what their experiences have been the most common reaction is that people can't wait to get back there. Since September 1984 this water has rarely been far from the headlines, such is its reputation and its ability to consistently produce huge carp. And although it's true to say that these fish are far from easy to catch, that is all part of the equation that makes Cassien so special.

Perhaps what the lake has lost over the years is some of its mystery, although that is inevitable with so many anglers from so many different backgrounds and

When dreams come true... Rod Hutchinson with his personal best of 58lb 6oz from Cassien in 1985.

nations sharing their experiences and pooling their knowledge. But we are still a long way from knowing all the great lake's secrets. What the future holds is anyone's guess. More and more anglers visit the lake each year and a Cassien carp – especially one of the big ones – is a much sought-after prize. I've experienced the good times and the hard times there, and I wouldn't change any of it for the world. There is no doubt in my mind that Cassien is a one-off, a special place where dreams are made – and long may it continue.

Cassien material

There is plenty of Cassien coverage in books by foreign authors, but surprisingly little in English carp books – although the venue has received widespread attention in magazines and weeklies. The following books include Cassien material for those who want to read further about the French carp fishing Mecca.

Carp Now and Then – Rod Hutchinson.
Ritchie on Carp – Ritchie MacDonald.
Carp – The Quest for the Queen – John Bailey & Martyn Page. Cassien chapter by Phil Smith.

Half Moon Day

Briggsy sold Cassien to me during the World Carp Cup at Fishabil in June 2000. He'd been in love with the place since the mid-80s. I'd never been. We arranged a trip for a fortnight session in late November.

The middle of the lake from the Bridge Swim with the bridge to the left, and the South Arm round the headland to the right.

First Cassien carp at 10.30 p.m. on the eighth night. 44lb 4oz.

Arriving at Cassien with a trailer full of gear on a wet, windy late November day, worn out from an 18-hour journey, was one of the most daunting carp fishing experiences of my life. A week in without a fish and the water wasn't getting any less daunting...

We started in a South Arm swim I now know as the Banana. Five days in Briggsy had caught two fish. I was still blanking. We moved to the Bridge Swim. One night of traffic and car lights and Steve was on the move again, into his beloved North Arm. The Bridge felt good and I stayed put. Steve's friend Joss gave me the necessary confidence.

"I have eight nights. If I stay put here will they come to me?"

"Oh yes. They will come to you."

I prefer waiting to chasing, so I waited.

On the third night in the Bridge, the eighth of the session, they showed up. Well one of them did. 10.30 p.m. A blistering run to the margin rod to my left. An anxious five minutes with a weeded fish, then relief as my first Cassien fish, a mirror of 44lb 4oz, was in the net. Relief is probably a bit of an understatement, although that was the prevailing emotion.

The next morning brought a mirror of 28½lb. 10.30 p.m. that night another mirror of 43½lb. All three fish from the margins. Steve was travelling long distances to take the pictures, so he moved onto the North Arm's First Point swim 500 yards to my left, one of his favourite spots and a swim he was very familiar with. That night – Sunday – it was his turn for the 10.30 p.m. run, and my turn to take the pictures the morning after. 42½lb. You had to get the feeling there was a shoal of good-sized fish in the area. I kept spreading the Trigga baits over a couple of acres to encourage the fish to hang around.

The weather was wet and windy, blowing down to the bridge from the north. When the cloud occasionally broke at night the clear sky revealed a half moon, on the wane. I'd never been much of a moon phase student, but I reflected that the double capture of the Domaine de Boux fish at 59lb 2oz and 58lb 14oz

Same time, same rod, on the ninth night. 43½lb.

The big-fish action provoked a further move for Briggsy, down to the First Point in the North Arm.

thirteen months earlier had come in exactly the same moon phase. The connection crossed my mind, but I didn't set much store by it at the time.

Monday was quiet. Keep the bait going in. Keep looking for better spots to position the hookbaits. My three fish to that point had fallen to a margin bait in 14ft of water,

The following night it was Briggsy's turn for the 10.30 p.m. fish. 42½lb from the First Point in the North Arm.

The Bridge Swim from the open water.

positioned next to a weedbed of potamogeton and Canadian pondweed. I was thrilled with the three-fish catch – obviously – but commented to Steve that I would love a Cassien fish from the open water. So I was getting greedy already!

That day I repositioned all three open-water baits. One in 12 feet on clean gravel or stone at the top of the plateau: one at 25 feet (Briggsy's favourite Cassien depth) halfway down the plateau; one at 40 feet at the foot of the slope. Up to that point I couldn't find a 25ft spot that excited me, and the 40ft bait had rather been going through the motions, too. That day I spent a long time out on the water looking for more meaningful features. You can't spend enough time looking. It's amazing how easy it is to miss what look to be very obvious spots once you find them. When I return to Chalet or Margot it takes me ages to pinpoint features I know the rough position of from previous trips. It's easy to think you have covered an area exhaustively, when all you have done is carry out a superficial examination.

Eventually, and to my surprise, the screen revealed a stunning spot at 25 feet. A circular fringe of weed about 6ft across, with a clearing in the middle. Four or five slow passes over the feature pinpointed the clearing in relation to an H-block marker, and made precise placement of the snowman hookbait possible. A couple of handfuls of chopped baits, pellets and chopped tigers followed the hookbait down onto the new dinner plate.

40ft was beyond my previous fishing experience. Keep a bait at 40ft for the big

The marker shows the margin spot just beyond the weed that produced four of my fish from the session.

fish, I'd been told, and I did so. Without conviction. That day fate was smiling on me. Again the feature finder came up trumps. A pronounced feature of some sort where the plateau slope levelled off to 40ft. A couple of old tree stumps in a slight hollow, I think. The sort of spot you would use as a landmark on a boring trip across open ground. Or possibly even a food trap. It looked right, other than that it was at the very unlikely feeding depth of 40ft!

Tuesday 5th December. The night and the half moon had almost run their course. I was up at quarter to six, moving as quietly as possible in deference to the margin spot, although I wasn't in a period that had produced up to that point. Coffee. Sit listening. Watch the sky starting to lighten beyond the hills opposite. How many half-lights and

5th December, 6.15 a.m. A hard-fighting margin fish of 39lb.

dawns had I sat through in my carp fishing past? How many more to come in my carp fishing future? The most magical time of all for me. Another couple of hours or so and the night would be over and the next chance would be hours away, the following night. I like to be awake during the possible feeding times, and on most waters there is activity, or a feeding spell, around or just into daylight. Hope was fading with the thinning of the darkness though.

Quarter past six I got up to stretch my legs. As I stood by the rods the margin buzzer gave a single bleep. Fish around? I didn't have long to wait. Within a few seconds that rod was away, and I lifted the hook gently into the running fish. It made for the arches, and I had an anxious twenty-minute scrap with a very powerful carp. I finally netted it under the bridge, then struggled to lift it up the stony slope onto the bank. 39lb. Another bronze beauty, and brother chip to the two forties. I was casting the margin rod, using Lockey's foam on the hook, and pulling back to check it was clear of the weed. Back in position, and back to the coffees and

the waiting. Was that it for the day?

Daylight brought the first really good-looking day of the session. A light breeze from the west, with a thin cloud covering, slowly clearing. I rang Briggsy at quarter past eight to tell him about the fish. He'd had nothing but thought the conditions looked good for more action. He was right. While we were talking the forty-foot rod roared off! My first Cassien open-water run, and from the deep water rod at that!

This one gave as good an account of itself as the earlier fish, and I suppose I was a tad disappointed with the 23lb common that eventually revealed itself. Course I shouldn't have been disappointed with the fish. I knew that at the time. Five days earlier I'd have been euphoric about it. And it wasn't really the fish I was disappointed with; it was simply that it had felt huge in the deep water.

Half eight by the time I'd landed it and sorted out. Three rods still in position. Risk a run-out in

Same day, 8.15 a.m. I was on the mobile to Steve when the open-water 40ft rod roared off. 23lb common.

the boat to reposition this rod? Almost I didn't, but then the thought that the fish wouldn't be on its own crossed my mind, the end tackle was rejigged, and the snowman Trigga hookbait was rowed back out to the forty-foot spot.

I rowed back, secured the boat, put the kettle on, and reached for the phone to acquaint Briggsy with the details – when the same rod was back in action! No heroics this time, and I guessed I was playing a fish of similar proportions to the common. Pleasantly wrong. A stunning Italian-type mirror of 44lb 2oz. A gorgeous, clean-looking carp. Three Cassien fish in 2½ hours. This time I didn't hesitate to put the bait back out there, then rang Briggsy to bring him up to date.

"I'll come and take the pictures shortly," he announced.

I didn't want to drag him out of the swim at feeding time, and told him so.

"No, they'll feed late in these

8.45 a.m. and the 40ft rod was in action again. Super mirror of 44lb 2oz.

conditions. I'll come down now then I can get back on the case. Besides, I want to come and see what on earth's going on down there!"

The high cloud was starting to burn off and the day was warming up. Steve did his usual brilliant job with my cameras, the fish went back, the lovely fella made all the right noises about the result, and at about ten to eleven he set off back on the 500-yard trip to his swim.

I remember feeling a bit emotionally drained about it all. I didn't know the water well enough to relate to Steve's feeling that there might be more to come. I'd enjoyed a morning result beyond all expectations and as far as I was concerned the next feeding time was some hours in the future, that night, or the following morning. I was in neutral, enjoying the moment. Three fish in a Cassien morning? Savouring the occasion would be more accurate!

I'd been wearing waterproof trousers for the photo session to withstand the repeated pans of water over the fish. I sat on the bedchair to pull them off. A single bleep to the 25ft rod didn't register as having any significance, until the indicator tightened to the rod. A take! Up went the rod, and this time you just knew straightaway that what was on the end was not little. 110 yards away the proverbial slow-moving sandbag set off up the plateau towards the bridge. That did not look like good news. I kept the pressure on and made for the boat. Then the fish changed its mind, changed direction, and I was able to play it from the bank.

I was pressuring it, but it was sort of doing what it wanted. The concrete area of the swim has water round two sides, with a bay on the right. The fish set off right, and the heavy pressure had it swinging into the bay. I hustled across to the right-hand side of the swim, halfway along the side of the bay. I was joined by two French anglers who must have seen me playing the fish from the bridge. I glanced round at them and recognised one as Cassien fixture and very well-known French carp angler Christophe. Their presence made me doubly anxious. Please don't drop off.

The fish chugged around the bay, then eventually the pressure started to have its effect and ten minutes or so after the take it neared the net. I'm a patient netter. Don't even try for them until they are on their side and clearly ready to be pulled over the mesh. It doesn't always work out that way, but this one came in at the first time of asking. As it came on its side my immediate impression was that it was as big as it had felt. As it came over the mesh I decided it was bigger than that. Playing it I was hoping it would go forty. Seeing it I thought it might go fifty. I had no aspirations or expectations beyond fifties.

Not until I tried to lift the net up, that is! No, not even then...

Christophe's friend went across to the bivvy area for the unhooking mat. I disconnected the arms from the handle, rolled the mesh around the fish, and heaved it up onto the mat. The Frenchmen looked after the fish while I collected the scales, weigh sling and sack.

Christophe was studying the fish when I got back.

"How big?" I asked him.

"Maybe 27 kilos." I tried to convert but my mind wouldn't cope with it, other than vaguely recalling that the de Boux fish was about that weight. Christophe half turned the fish to check its right shoulder.

"This is Half Moon Scale, the fish all the English would love to catch." He may have called it Moon Scale. I

Half an hour after he took the pictures of my three fish Steve was back in the boat headed in my direction. "How would you like to photograph this 51½lber I've got in the sack?"

now refer to the fish as Half Moon Scale, because of the moon phase and the shape of the distinguishing scale.

I zeroed the scales and left the weighing to Christophe and his friend. The verdict took for ever.

"Exactly 63lb."

What can you say, other than, "Thank you"? I mean you can't act as though it's an everyday occurrence, but on the other hand you don't want to make a complete gibbering ass of yourself. Dammit, we are English... So we settled for carrying the great fish across to the bivvy area, and I secured the sack in the margins. The helpful French guys went on their way, and as they departed I garbled my excited thanks for their help yet again.

63lb! Fact is I'd wondered if I would ever beat the personal best of 59lb 2oz from Domaine de Boux, and this magnificent creature in the sack had done it for me within thirteen months.

I reached for the mobile to ring the long-suffering Steve. No answer. I walked across to the bridge to look up the lake to his swim. His boat was headed in my direction! That confused me. Did he already know? As he approached it became clear that here was an unusually animated Steve, who is a laid-back sort of guy at the most volcanic of times.

"How would you like to come and photograph this 51½lb mirror carp I've got in the sack?" was his opening

The Bridge Swim at Cassien

Depths for water levels on 5th December 2000

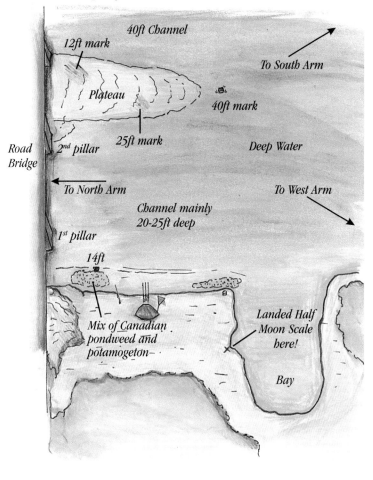

Road Bridge

12ft mark

40ft Channel

To South Arm

Plateau

40ft mark

25ft mark

2nd pillar

Deep Water

To North Arm

To West Arm

Channel mainly 20-25ft deep

1st pillar

14ft

Mix of Canadian pondweed and potamogeton

Landed Half Moon Scale here!

Bay

The bridge from the area of Pierre's. The North Arm extends to the right on the other side of the bridge.

gambit.

What can you say? We'd parted company barely half an hour previously, and in the meantime he'd had a fish of over 51lb, and I'd had one of 63lb. I was chuffed for him, and told him so. It was his moment, and I didn't quite know how to tell him about my fish. I couldn't pretend it hadn't happened though!

"Have you heard of a fish called Half Moon Scale?"

"Of course I have. It's the best-known fish in here." I should have known – but didn't – that it's Steve's heart's ambition to catch this great mirror. I felt guilty for not even having heard of it!

"Well it's in my sack, and weighs 63lb." It says much for Steve's disposition that I knew I could safely give him this news and live to tell the tale... This exchange took place between me on dry land and Steve sitting in the boat. We moored the boat and he joined me in the swim. Excitedly we went through the virtually simultaneous captures that had just been enacted in our two swims.

Steve had got back to his swim after the photography session, moored the boat, and noticed that he'd had an occurrence on one of his long-range rods. Nothing there. As he reeled in, the line to the second rod he'd left out tightened up, with the lovely mirror of 51½lb on the end. A remarkable occurrence, not least because Steve had just known that there was going to be late morning action that day.

The sky cleared and the sun came out. We had marvellous conditions for photographing the two fish. Martin Russell – now of Gerard's, then running trips under the St. Cassien Experience banner – called in to see how we were doing, and promptly set off for a couple of bottles of champagne. Briefly, for that single afternoon, we had the shorts and T-shirt weather that Briggsy had promised me when we were planning the trip. We drank to the memorable day and the run of fish, then we went our separate ways back to our swims to prepare for the night ahead. The session continued on the two-day course it still had to run.

Quarter to midnight that night I had a fish of 37lb 12oz on the rod positioned at the top of the plateau. The fish got stuck early in the fight and I had to go out in the boat in the middle of the night to net it. Around midnight I found myself out over the plateau ready to net it, but with the landing net back on the bank! Silly! I settled for getting the fish under control, laid the rod down in the boat with the clutch set to give line in an emergency, and "rowed" the fish back to the bank. It dutifully followed, like the proverbial dog on a lead. By the time I finally put the net under it the mirror must

Simultaneous capture with Steve's 51½. The magnificent Half Moon Scale at 63lb, with the identifying scale in evidence on the fish's right shoulder. We took the shots of the right flank second, and the strain is starting to show.

Fifth fish of the day. 11.45 p.m. and the rod at the top of the plateau was in action, resulting in this mirror of 37lb 12oz.

have wondered what on earth was going on!

After all the soul-searching about depths all four rods had produced in a single, remarkable day of five Cassien carp in less than 18 hours! At the time of writing I've spent 38 nights on the marvellous venue, for just twelve carp – five of them, including the biggest, coming that day. The more I fish Cassien the more extraordinary the memory of that occasion becomes. As Briggsy put it during the afternoon, sun-blessed champagne break, between us on that one morning we'd caught a twenty, a thirty, a forty, a fifty and a sixty. Heady stuff.

Tuesday, 5th December 2000. In my memory one of the most joyous of carp fishing occasions. Half Moon day.

The Mighty Orient

John van Eck

talking to

Simon Crow

When it comes to hard waters they don't come much harder than the mighty Forêt D'Orient's great lake in France. This huge, lightly stocked reservoir is home to some of the biggest carp in the world. The venue's big fish include the much sought-after Bulldozer, France's biggest common carp, as well as the lake record mirror known as Willy, which topped out at 34.2 kilos (75lb 6oz) when caught in 1996 by French angler Jerome Gigault. In this chapter we take a look at the famous lake through the eyes of Dutch angler John van Eck, one of the most successful catchers of big carp in Europe. Thanks also to Simon Crow for his help with this material.

Big-fish weather and difficult fishing conditions brewing. The beginning of a storm on the Orient.

The calm after the storm. Sunset over Italie.

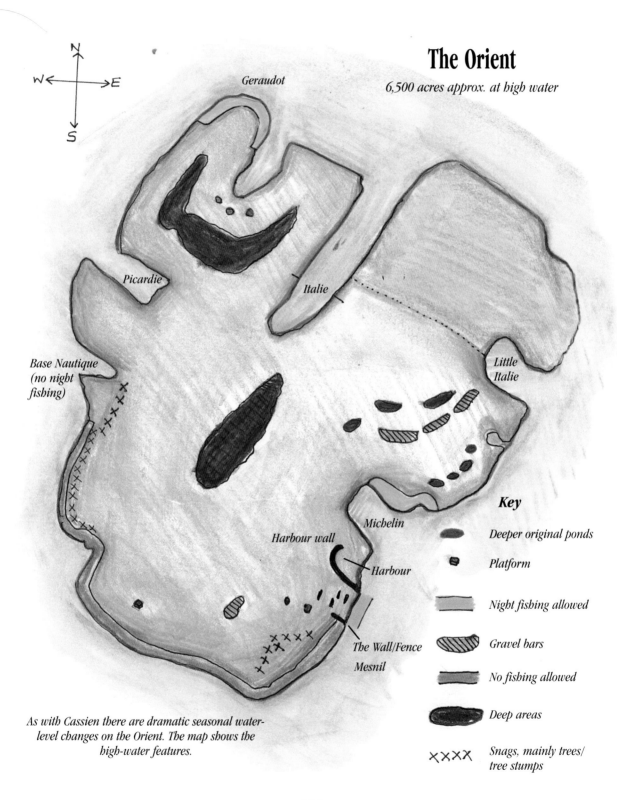

The Orient

6,500 acres approx. at high water

Geraudot

Picardie

Italie

Base Nautique
(no night
fishing)

Little
Italie

Key

Michelin

Harbour wall

Harbour

The Wall/Fence

Mesnil

	Deeper original ponds
	Platform
	Night fishing allowed
	Gravel bars
	No fishing allowed
	Deep areas
XXXX	Snags, mainly trees/ tree stumps

As with Cassien there are dramatic seasonal water-level changes on the Orient. The map shows the high-water features.

In the early 90s most of my carp fishing was done in France. We were looking for new waters with big carp. We wanted to catch big carp, but we also wanted them to be virtually uncaught as well. So we kept our eyes and ears open for every possible bit of information about big carp from France. At the end of 1992 there was an article in the Dutch fishing paper 'De Viskrant'. The fish that were published

The author's friend, Robert Paul Naeff, with two of the very big fish he caught from the Orient during the 90s. We think both these lumps weighed 50lb+.

included at least one big fifty and a few forties. There was no mention of the water's name, and we didn't recognise it, either. But the grapevine started to work overtime and within a month or so we knew the location and the name of the water. It turned out to be the Orient.

It was obvious that the water had potential. A big fifty is proof. The Orient is in the same region as Lac du Der Chantecoq – which we had been fishing that year – but it was quieter. Du Der, with its very fertile clay bottom and crayfish population, was proof enough that this sort of lake had enormous potential to produce big carp. Both were reservoirs. At that time we didn't know much about the population of the Orient, but we were convinced of its potential.

In May 1993 a good mate of mine, Robert Paul Naeff, made a trip to France. He decided to have a look at the Orient and fished it for a few days, catching fish to 43lb. In addition to the information Robert acquired about the lake, on the grapevine we heard more news of very big carp being caught from the venue. Robert and I planned a ten-day trip for the end of June.

When we got there most anglers fishing the lake were concentrating their efforts on

A very special fish. John's biggest fish at the time, and still a personal best at the time of writing this. 68lb from the month session in 1995.

John with a 42lb mirror from the month-long session in 1995.

The last fish from the 1995 session. 41lb going back.

the swims reachable by car. We were convinced that by using boats we could fish some areas where we would be on our own. That turned out to be much harder than we expected. Because of the high water level at that time of year there were very few fishable swims available. To anyone who has never been to the Orient in spring this is very, very hard to believe about such a massive inland sea. But when there is an underwater area of more than 100 yards covered in trees and bushes before you reach the bank proper, with more than two metres of water in front of the trees, there is simply nowhere to fish.

The size of the water didn't faze us. By then we were used to fishing huge waters, having fished Du Der the year before, which is even bigger than the Orient. Also we were used to fishing big waters in Holland. Once you have taken the first step to fishing such big waters and have become accustomed to them it doesn't really matter what size they are.

On that first session we finished up at the top end of the large peninsula called Italie. It was a matter of dropping into a swim where we could fish from dry land and out of the way. There were hardly any swims. The top end gave us plenty of room to play with and a good view of the lake.

The first night was very exciting. We fished in separate swims about 50 yards apart. We always go to France equipped to fish in this way. You are far more efficient like this than fishing together in the same swim, in addition to which the area of the swims was quite restricted. We could only get to each other by wading through the water! About eleven

Hiding away to fish a less pressured area.

302

o'clock that night I heard the first fish jump very close to the bank, and it sounded like a lump. It made me shiver, and it came out a few more times. Quite a few more fish jumped that night as well.

At 3.00 a.m. I got my first run, but unfortunately I lost it against a tree stump of which there were many in the swim. Tree stumps are definitely a big problem in some swims on the Orient. The next morning I learnt that Robert had also lost a big fish, which he reckoned to be very big. It could have been the big 'un that jumped a few times. Very exciting stuff, although it would have been nicer if we had managed to put those fish on the bank.

After the first night the main shoal of fish seemed to have moved

In some areas remains of the tree stumps are an unbelievable hazard.

out of the area, but some were still around. During the week of the first trip I ended up with nine runs, losing five of them. One was definitely a good forty, which I lost because of a hook-pull just short of the net on the last night. I saw the fish clearly, so that was quite disheartening. Of the four fish I landed the biggest was a 37lb mirror. Although I had a

The Orient was Rod Hutchinson's target water for a number of years. Rod with one of his many fish from the venue.

few fish the loss rate was far too high, so attention had to be paid to the style of fishing over the tree stumps.

I didn't return to the water in 1993, which was a stupid mistake. The first year is always the best, but with the restricted swim choice and the lake getting busier by the minute I turned my attention to pioneering other waters. I did fish the water a few times in 1994, including a short visit with Rod Hutchinson. I caught some fish, but the biggest was 39lb. I still hadn't caught one of the big ones, so a change of plan was necessary for 1995. I decided not to fish the venue in the spring and summer, but only in the autumn.

It had become obvious during 1993 and 1994

Hot, calm and sunny. Not a good time to be fishing the Orient.

that the Fence area, or the Wall as they call it, definitely produced the goods during the months of September and October. We formed a plan between eight of us, which included Rod Hutchinson, Mally Roberts, my friend Robert, Piet Vogel and his two friends Bertus and Henk. The plan was to try to keep fishing that one area for the two-month period, swapping the swims over to one another. I don't know if this is the right thing to do but during the first week I fished there that year over 70 anglers arrived to fish that same area, so really it turned out to be the right thing to do at the time!

Everything was planned far in advance, down to the smallest detail. The first team of four started at the end of August. I came in halfway through September and I fished there for a complete

Wet and rainy weather and the fish are feeding. A typical view of the angler pressure in the night fishing areas on the Orient.

Spot the bivvy! Being inconspicuous in a less pressured area of the lake...

month, just to be sure I would be there during the period when the fish would have a feed. The first week the going was tough and I think I only caught three fish. On Friday of that first week, the 22nd September, I caught my personal best carp (still is to this day), a 68lb mirror. All the planning, preparation, worrying if we would get the swim and so on had already been more than worthwhile. Just incredible!

The next week and a half we started catching quite well. I had another 27 fish in this period, including two more forties at 41lb and 42lb. Everyone who was fishing our area was having good fish. The weather was terrible. Lots of wind and rain with a few storms in between, but we didn't mind; the fishing was good. On the Thursday of my third week the sun came out, the wind died, and the fishing died. For the last week and a half no one caught a thing.

Rod again, with a good fish caught in typical Orient feeding conditions.

In 1996 I concentrated on the rivers in France so I only fished the Orient for two weeks in September, more or less having a social with Rod and Mally again, but the fishing had become much harder. I was down to fishing a very small area, as well. I ended up with five fish up to 38lb. My fishing of the water has slowed down since the mid-90s. I fished it very little in 1997, then in 1998 I fished a two-week session in May, catching only two fish, but good fish. Mirrors of 41lb and 50lb. My last session there was a week's blank in May 1999.

Everyone wants to know about the fish in the Orient but I always find this a very difficult question to answer, especially for such a big water. The stocking levels were definitely a lot lower than Du Der. The Orient is a lake of 2,300 hectares (approx. 5,680

Precious moment. Wrestling with a big Orient fish on the muddy banks. You just have to put up with the conditions to be there at the right time.

acres). If I were to guess at say 2,000 carp, that would not result in even one carp per hectare, and I think that at the time I was fishing it the stocking level was no more than that. After the first two years we knew that there were at least two mirrors around 30 kilos, and of course the big common, Bulldozer, which topped 31 kilos at her best weight. Later

on we estimated there to be a further ten fish over 25 kilos, which is of course an unbelievable stock, but still low in total numbers.

I really cannot put a number on the forties that were in the venue at the time, but I'm sure a lot of people overestimated the number. The biggest carp in a water soon become the best-known fish in the lake, not only because they are big (the big fish normally respond very well to anglers' baits) but mainly because the stock of big carp is always smaller than most people think, with a great many repeat captures

Left: Mally Roberts with one of a run of fish when Mally, Rod and their European friends were making a determined assault on the Orient.
Right: Rod again with yet another big Orient fish in stormy, wet conditions.

occurring. I never believe the stories of uncaught eighty pounders being in there. Although you cannot fish all areas of the lake the biggest fish often get caught very early in the fishing life of a venue.

The Orient isn't an easy venue to fish. All swims produce now and again, depending on the weather and the wind direction. All swims can be dead at times, then a week later someone has a big result there. The three night fishing sections of the Wall, Michelin and Geraudot, are good sections from which to catch fish, although at Geraudot I wouldn't really fish into the bay itself. Further on perhaps, but night fishing isn't allowed there. The Peninsula Italie holds a few good swims, but also a lot of snags, and Bay Nautique has also produced good fish in the past.

Weather is a very important factor on the Orient. If it is hot and sunny and there is no wind you really are wasting your time. But the wind blowing into your swim can be very productive, provided, of course, the wind isn't so strong that you can't fish – which happened to us on quite a few occasions!

Because of the low stocking density, location is all-important. We soon learned that because of the size of the Orient you could be miles away from the fish. Moving onto the fish isn't easy, either. First of all you are only allowed to fish small areas of the lake. Secondly, trying to find the fish in a lake as massive as the Orient is very difficult. Lastly, in spring and summer swim choice is very restricted because of the high water level. Come autumn moving swims is hard because of the long distances you have to wade through serious mud!

I tried to apply a semi-mobile approach, trying to make the best swim choice and fishing that swim for a few days. If in that time nothing comes your way, you move swims. Sitting in the same swim is definitely not the best option. I know of two guys who fished one swim for ten weeks, waiting for the carp to turn up. The result? A total blank!

Because of the low carp population you simply have to endure the blanks – which brings me on to two other very important factors, time and perseverance. If you can't handle a few days, or even weeks, of blanking I would say the Orient is not the water for you. It is not only the blanking though. If you fish in the woods you have the animal life, as well. The mosquitoes will attack you all day and night, and when you want some kip the frogs will keep you from sleeping with their noisy concerts! You also have the mud in the autumn – everything gets covered in it – as well as the bad storms.

The right equipment is a very important factor. If you are not equipped for this sort of big water steer clear of them, otherwise your visit will result in disappointment. You need a big reliable boat with an electric engine, plenty of heavy-duty battery power, a fish finder, a life jacket, big reels and a solid bivvy which can handle storms. In addition you have to become accustomed to the big-water style of fishing, including

German star and Hutchinson Dream Team member Christian Finkelde with a recent capture of a big carp from the Geraudot Bay area of the Orient.

John with a hard-won prize. 50lb from the May session in 1998.

playing fish from a boat on your own as well as rowing baits out on your own.

In terms of bait this is down to the angler's personal preference. On such a big water you need to be very confident in your bait so you can concentrate on other things. I have been using Rod Hutchinson's flavours and mixes for many years now. I have also used ready-mades from a Dutch bait company. All the baits I've used have been successful.

It's important to consider the hardness and size of your bait, because of crayfish and other nuisance species. I think that for this sort of water you're either looking for a sweet bait in a neutral mix (for example Hutchy's Scopex with Protaste and Sweet Appetite stimulator in the Carpcraze boilie mix) or a fishmeal bait. If you're in doubt about bait you can't go wrong with Hutchy's MC Mix combined with Monster Crab flavour and Shellfish Sense Appeal.

Bait application is always a difficult one to call. Sometimes heavy baiting works; sometimes not. If you have a successful session by piling it in this does not mean that if you pile it in again next time you are there it will be a mega successful session again. The two main tactics I fished were with spread-out rods with not too much bait around the hookbait – about fifty free offerings if there didn't seem to be many fish in the area. The other method was to use quite a lot of bait – 2-5 kilos depending on how many fish you were expecting – over a fairly large area, fishing the rods spread out over the area. I hardly used particles on the Orient. In my opinion they only draw the attention of unwanted species. In addition, the use of particles is a very popular method, so it is one of the first approaches the fish get wary of.

Very important as well, I think, is that we used to leave the rods out for two days or more, depending on the crayfish activity. Very often we would

The Orient's most famous resident, and arguably the most famous fish in France. The stunning Bulldozer in September 1999, caught by Sebastien Poulatier at 30.2 kilos from Geraudot Bay.

Pole position. John fishing the famous Fence Swim on the Orient.

Flood conditions in the spring with very few suitable fishing spots available.

Pretty, but not really feeding conditions. A peaceful Orient sunset.

catch on the rods which had been left out for a few days. You need very hard hookbaits which will survive in the water for days to be able to fish this tactic. Rod Hutchinson's Clawbuster Mix was designed to make hookbaits to overcome the attentions of crayfish claws over long periods of time!

To finish I should make the point that the Orient has changed in the few years since I was fishing it regularly. There has been a great deal of controversy surrounding the *vidange*** which took place at the venue in the late 90s. To be honest I have no firm information about the *vidange*, other than that it happened, and that the lake was not drained totally dry. My own thoughts are that during the *vidange* some fish from the old stock definitely died, and others were taken out. At the present time there are still fish in there from the original population, including the big mirror known as Willy and the common called Bulldozer, but that's all I can say about it. How many of the original fish remain I simply don't know.

Since the *vidange* they have stocked the lake with new carp. I have heard a number of 3,000-4,000 new fish mentioned, but it is anyone's guess. Today the reality is that a far larger number of anglers fishing the venue are going to catch fish, mostly twenties and the odd thirty. Occasionally one of the remaining bigger fish gets caught, which still makes it tempting.

** A vidange takes place on many of the French reservoirs every few years. The lake is drained down, and the reduced area of water netted. Prior to the French carp fishing boom the carp were sold cheaply, or given away for fertiliser, or as food. Now the value of carp in France is rising and stocks are being looked on as an asset. Many of the original fish remained in the Orient after the vidange, but it is not an unknown phenomenon in France for once well-populated waters to be denuded of fish – as, on occasion, frustrated visiting anglers have discovered after they've fished empty waters for a day or two!

Raduta and Records

Cassien is here to stay as a prime carp water, and I suspect that Lake Raduta in Romania is, too. At the time of writing it is the world's ultimate big-fish water. In its sprawling 2,500 acres live monster carp which have grown on naturally. It has produced at least five different 70lb-plus fish. The current world-record fish – a mirror – lives in Raduta. The current biggest known common in the world lives in Raduta. Of course size isn't everything, but down the years it has been the big fish which have consistently hit the headlines, and Raduta looks set to keep making the headlines for many years to come.

The lake was formerly known as

The sun rising on another Raduta big-fish day. The Shepherd's Cottage stretch in the foreground, with Becker's Point in the background just to the right of the rising sun.

Lake Sarulesti. It was formed in the late 60s in what may seem a controversial manner to us. A river valley running from Bucharest south-east to the Black Sea was selected for flooding when then-president Coucesceau's regime decided to raise the level of the Danube for navigation purposes. Raising the level would result in the low-lying villages and dwellings in the valley being flooded, and the valley dwellers were given just two days' notice to quit. Among the sites to be flooded were carp-rearing farms. There wasn't time to remove all the carp, which became part of the fish population of the flooded valley, the newly created Lake Sarulesti. The combination of huge areas of untenanted water, a very low stock density, the flooding of the land, and the growth potential of the carp, resulted in the fish growing at a remarkable rate.

First British trip to Raduta in 1998. From left Mally Roberts, Rod Hutchinson and Kev Clifford.

In the 70s current owner Robert Raduta purchased the water from the government to build it into a tourist hunting and fishing attraction, and renamed it Lake Raduta. The government which took over from the deposed Coucesceau is keen to erase the autocratic image the country has inherited from the former regime,

Dutchman Henk von Dorn with the world-record mirror at a weight of 77lb 15oz, caught from its home patch in World Record Bay.

and sets great store by promoting tourism. Raduta was a professional sportsman, a successful tennis player, and a successful coach to the very talented tennis players that Romania produced in the 80s and 90s. Ilie Nastase and 'Pancho' Vilas were Raduta tennis protégés in their prime. Raduta put a purchase scheme to the government and was able to buy the lake as a potential tourist attraction.

Robert Raduta is a fisherman as well as being a tennis player and coach. He was interested in the zander that inhabit his lake, and fished for them regularly. One morning he noticed a group of feeding carp on a shallow plateau outside the hotel. He fished a single grain of maize on the spot and within five minutes the biggest of the group picked up his bait. The fish put up a terrific scrap but Robert landed it after quarter of an hour, and was amazed to find that he had caught a giant mirror weighing 78lb! Mounted hunting trophies are a feature of the walls at Hotel Raduta, and Robert wanted the great fish set up. There was no suitable taxidermist in Romania, so the fish was sent off to Austria. The taxidermist was an angler, who happened to know a carp angler... Word got round about this enormous

mirror carp that had appeared from Romania, and the leading Austrian carpers weren't slow to investigate and visit this interesting new lake! They first fished the water in the autumn of 1997. Global carping guru Simon Crow wasn't far behind them, and through the efforts of Simon, Rob Hughes and Kevin Clifford at *Carp-Talk* the British started fishing the water in April 1998, less than a year after the Austrians and Germans.

Since that time the lake has become a Mecca for carpers from all over the world. It has produced innumerable big fish, including the world-record mirror for Austrian Christian Baldemann at 82lb 3oz (see Simon Crow's Monster Carp of the World chapter), and a number of other carp weighing in excess of 70lb. The record fish was first caught from World Record Bay in October 1997 by Jurgen Becker at 74lb. It was subsequently caught at the world-record weight and then by Dutch angler Henk von Dorn at 77lb 15oz in May

A German angler's capture of a stunning Raduta mirror of 64lb.

310

Lake Raduta, Romania

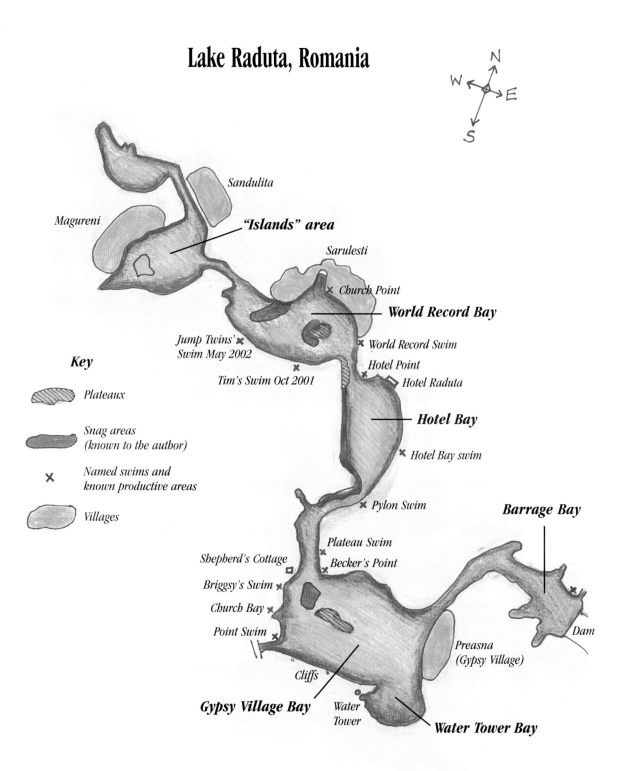

Sandulita

Magureni

"Islands" area

Sarulesti

× Church Point

World Record Bay

Jump Twins' × Swim May 2002

× World Record Swim

Hotel Point

× Hotel Raduta

Tim's Swim Oct 2001

Hotel Bay

Key

Plateaux

Snag areas
(known to the author)

× Named swims and
known productive areas

Villages

× Hotel Bay swim

× Pylon Swim

Barrage Bay

Plateau Swim

Shepherd's Cottage

Becker's Point

Briggsy's Swim ×

Church Bay ×

Point Swim ×

Preasna
(Gypsy Village)

Dam ×

Cliffs

Gypsy Village Bay

Water
Tower

Water Tower Bay

1999. The first British capture of the fish known as the Big Common was by Paul Jones in August 1998 at 61lb (most Raduta Brits feel this could have been a mis-weighing and that the common probably weighed a great deal more than the recorded weight) and it was later landed by Austrian Kurt Grabmayor in October of the same year at 70lb. The fish became the biggest common ever to be caught by a Brit when Alex 'Sandy' Hough landed it at 72lb in May 1999, and the author took over Sandy's 'biggest common' title when he caught the fish at 73lb 13oz in May 2001, the second biggest weight recorded for the fish and the biggest reported carp in the world for that year. Sadly this great fish died in May 2002. See the postscript at the end of The Biggest Carp in the World chapter. Check out Crowy's Monster Carp chapter for details of big carp from the venue.

Fishing the lake is restricted, naturally by the conditions, and artificially by an imposed limit on the numbers fishing the venue at any one time. The limitation on numbers is largely a practical one. You need a boat to fish the venue, and there aren't enough to go round. Robert Raduta regulates the numbers, and gives all the countries who want to fish the venue a fair crack of the whip. At the time of writing, booking

Carp! contributor Simon Horton with his gorgeous Raduta common of 56lb.

Cheshire angler Chris Fowke with a typical Raduta common of 53lb from Becker's Point.

How big! Paul Jones' capture of the Big Common was recorded as 61lb, but the look of the fish and the 70lb+ captures either side of this one suggest that the weighing may have erred on the light side!

by Brits is through Rob Hughes and Simon Crow of Xtreme Carping, and they organise up to three trips to the venue each year, usually in May, June and October.

The fishing is restricted during the summer and winter by nature. The lake freezes up in the winter and the area warms up to unfishable levels in the summer! The first year the Brits fished the water

The South Bank of World Record Bay looking east towards the islands and the Sandulita end of the lake.
Inset: Rob Hughes and Stu Wallis bivvied up on the south east corner of World Record Bay.

trips went out right through the warmer months, but the heat of midsummer made the journeys largely an uncomfortable waste of time, not simply because the climate was too hot, but because the fish didn't feed in such conditions. Trips are now only arranged at times when weather and water conditions make catching possible.

Format of Trips

For Brits all the Raduta trips are by air. The reception at Raduta is friendly, and Romania is a friendly-feeling country, but it is also reputed to be bandit country. If you go there by road you are at risk of being held up. Robert Raduta is clearly of some influence in Romania, and when you are on a trip to the lake you have Raduta immunity from the normal pressures of life in that country! You are picked up at the airport, and dropped off there on the return journey. While you are on the lake you are in his care, and that seems to be clearly understood by all concerned.

A story to illustrate Robert's influence. Simon Crow had been asked to take some bedchairs out for the Raduta tackle armoury, and these were to go with Simon and party on the flight from Heathrow to Bucharest. At Heathrow bureaucracy stood in the way and the bedchairs were to be classed as excess baggage, which would involve a large and unwanted financial transaction. The harassed receptionist was persuaded to get in touch with Romania to clarify the position. She eventually returned, looking crestfallen. "The chairs are to be booked through as the pilot's personal baggage."!

The flight from Heathrow takes three hours, the two-hour time difference meaning you arrive in Romania late afternoon. The journey from Bucharest airport to the lake takes an hour or so. You arrive in the dark, so you can either go out into the night and set up in the dark, or you can have a meal, and a drink, and a social in the hotel. I've tried both alternatives, and both versions have something to be said for them. The drawback to the overnight stay in the hotel is that you finish up with a headache, although the enjoyment in the evening's drinking which causes it almost makes it worthwhile!

Fact is that if you are single-minded and organised enough you can be fishing Lake Raduta within six or seven hours of taking off from Heathrow airport. On my first trip to the lake I had a double-figure fish in darkness on the first night.

Equipment and Supplies

Price of the trip includes a bed, gas, a double-burner stove, cooking equipment and eating utensils. Take a kettle otherwise you have to boil water in a pan. You can hire a bivvy. Do so. Save as much of your 50 kilos baggage allowance as possible for clothing, tackle and bait. Order as much of the bait that is being sent out by the organisers as possible, then take some of your own, too. You can't have enough bait with you at Raduta: you want a mixture of

Steve Briggs bivvied up on the Hotel Point at low water level, with the hotel in the background and Hotel Bay to his left.

The author with one of the fish that was stocked for the 1998 World Cup, here weighing in at 46lb 12oz in October 2001. Caught from World Record Bay.

ready-mades and quality bait, if possible.

Take a special rod case for the plane trip. Baggage handlers look on items of luggage as a challenge! I use a KIS rod case. It's adjustable length-wise, takes six (reel-less) rods, two landing nets, and storm rods. The Bazuka rod case that some of the guys use looks equally sturdy and spacious. Pack it out with bait. The weight of the rod case doesn't seem to get counted in the baggage allowance.

I take a large rucksack and a carryall, plus the camera case and another bag for hand luggage. The

Thomas Angerer with the only recorded capture of this common of 70lb 10oz (see Monster Carp of the World chapter).

camera case and the 'living' bag are hand luggage and not included in the baggage allowance. You need all the tackle requirements in the rucksack and carryall. Keep essentials to a minimum to save weight for bait. Take as much pellet as you can. Changes of clothing. Dehydrated foods for a change of diet. Vesta Paellas are generous, light to carry and easy to prepare. As are dried pastas. You can buy soft drinks, lager, chocolate, and biscuits out there.

The tip of the iceberg. One of the formidable Raduta snags is just showing above the water, giving a hint of what lies beneath the surface.

Amenities

The first thing that strikes you about Raduta is what a civilised place it is. The single-storey hotel is well appointed. The food has improved out of sight from the early trips, when very few people could stomach it. I find it nourishing and plentiful, and I'm a fairly choosy eater. The boat comes to visit you twice a day and takes your order for drinks and food. You sign a chitty for everything you order and receive a bill at the end of the trip, which you are expected to pay in dollars. They haven't yet heard of credit cards in that neck of the woods! These bills vary considerably. Crowy's once amounted to a frightening $7 (he haggled), while heavy drinker Rob Marsh's came to $500! I think his mate Stu Wallis's drink bill may have been included in that!

The hotel is open to you if you want to take time off from the fishing, and have a shower, a drink and a meal, or even a night away from the bivvy.

The Lake

Like the food and service the lake has improved considerably since the earliest trips, judging by comparisons made by the earliest visitors. Prior to the Raduta World Carp Cup in 1998 the lake was partially drained and some of the most pernicious snags removed. Not that you would guess that from studying some of the areas through a fish finder – but I'm assured that the snags are nothing like as bad as they were originally.

"Nothing like as bad" is strictly comparative. The fact that you are fishing a flooded valley with much of its flora and furniture still intact means that by any standards Raduta is a very snaggy lake. Wherever you fish on the lake the area of your swim has to be very carefully plotted to give you a clear idea of where the dangers lie. I look round for likely areas, then work back to the bivvy to see what lies between the rods and the spot I fancy.

Snags are trees, bushes, buildings, a graveyard and so on. The underwater terrain undulates a great deal. As you can see from the map on page 311 the lake is a series of big bays – the biggest, Church Bay, is estimated at around 700 acres – connected by flooded valleys where the original river ran through the countryside. I reread a Simon Crow *Carpworld* article about Raduta as one of the reference points for this chapter. In the article Crowy describes the banks as being "littered with rubbish washed up from the remains of the sunken village and dwellings." Well the banks were natural and clear when I was there – apart from evidence of human remains being washed up in the area of the sunken church – so this is another aspect that has improved considerably since the early days.

Regulars divide the lake into the left-hand side and the right-hand side (looking out from the hotel). The Big Common always comes from the left-hand side. The world-record mirror comes from a small area of World Record Bay, which is to the right. I've included as much detail as possible on the maps, some of which I've accumulated from fishing the water, and some of it from articles by other anglers.

On the two trips I've been on the anglers seemed to gravitate towards the familiar landmark swims. I think an impression has built up from the early days that the fish are very localised. If they were they seem to have changed their habits! While

World Record Bay looking across towards Sarulesti and the swim that has produced the world record mirror on the three occasions it has been caught. The swim in question is in shadow above the tips of the author's rods.

It's not all sunshine at Raduta. The sudden windstorms and torrential showers are a frequent feature of the venue.

I have been there they've either been well spread out, or very mobile. The fact that the action comes and goes, and that at different times you may find shoals of different-sized fish in your swim, suggests the fish are mobile.

Popular swims which didn't produce much by way of big fish while I was there included the Pylon, the Hotel Point, Little Church Bay (as opposed to the vast area of Church Bay), the Water Tower and the Headland. Some of these names may be my own, so I've marked all the

Gypsy Village Bay.

swims with the names I know them by.

The Barrage seems to be a consistent area, although the dam area itself is reported to have been closed to fishing since Rob Marsh's exceptional result there a few years back. At the other end of the lake there have been some outstanding results from the area known as The Islands in both the spring and the autumn in recent years, although I think these may have come as a surprise to the regulars. Crowy and his partner had a stack of fish from this area in October 2001, but only one big 'un.

An acknowledged big fish area, Hotel Bay, with the hotel in the background. The picture was taken from the area of the popular Hotel Point. Inset: The remarkable Robert Raduta.

The Plateau in the cut-through from Hotel Bay to Church Bay seems to be a consistent producer of big fish, suggesting that it is a holding area or on a regular patrol route. There were a lot of fish showing in this stretch of the lake when we were fishing the Shepherd's Cottage stretch in May 2001.

The Gypsy Village area, the Shepherd's Cottage stretch, World Record Bay and Becker's Point all produced consistently while I was there. If you like privacy there are drawbacks to the Gypsy Village swims and the swims on the Sardulesti Sat side of World Record Bay. In these areas you have the relentless company of local youngsters to brighten your life. Pass! I've marked the swim the world-record fish came from. There is a plateau about 150 yards out from this swim, and that is the spot the world-record mirror has been caught from on the three occasions it has been put on the bank. Anyone who can live with the close-range scrutiny of a couple of young teenage boys for a full session deserves to catch that fish!

Becker's Point seems to be a very consistent swim. It's an ideal interception point, and covers some well-featured areas of Church Bay. The talented German angler Jurgen

Returning a scale-perfect Raduta common of 48½lb to World Record Bay during my May 2002 session with Simon Crow.

Becker and partner Norbert Ulshofer won the 1999 World Cup from this swim, and the Point produced two fifties to Brits during the April/May trip of 2001. Chris Fowke's fish pictured earlier was one of a brace of big fish he caught from the Point while I was there. The second-placed team in the 1999 World Cup – from Macedonia – fished a swim on the Shepherd's Cottage stretch, across from Becker's Point.

In October 2001 I fished the far side of World Record Bay across from the village of Sarulesti. I had eight fish over

Looking out onto Hotel Bay from the veranda dining area of the hotel.

40lb to 55lb. In the early part of the year I suspect the fish may be in shallower water than I fished in October. We were catching in depths down to 17ft in October, but the most productive depths earlier in the year had been 8ft-12ft. (Robert Raduta feels that when the fish are feeding 8ft-9ft is the preferred depth.) I had some of the Record Bay fish

Briggsy returning his biggest Raduta common of 53lb, caught from the Gypsy Village area in April 2001.

from my near margin, which borders the course of the old river, but most came at extreme range in the area of a snaggy plateau. There were snags away to my left where the lake narrows down, and a great many smaller fish showing in that area. I fished a rod there for two or three days but it only produced smaller fish and grass carp.

Smaller fish and grass carp are a hazard at Raduta. During my first session on the venue I had 105 carp, including over 70 doubles! Exhausting. In October grass carp were the enemy. Nearly forty of them up to 30lb, with most of them in the 25lb-30lb bracket. Grass carp are mental. They won't go in the net. Then they jump out of it when they do go in. Then they flap all over you, and the bank, very powerfully. Then they cover you with spray as you try to gently return them. They seemed to respond to strong-smelling baits better than the big carp did.

But never mind the doubles and low twenties. Never mind the grass carp. It's the *cyprinus carpio* the amazing water holds that carp anglers go for, and in two sessions in 2001 I had 25 carp over 30lb, including thirteen thirties, ten forties, a 55lb 4oz mirror and a 73lb 13oz common. It takes the prospect of fishing like that to get me digging into the piggy bank and enduring getting on an aeroplane! I'm a very reluctant flyer, but when needs must, you just have to go for it.

Summary

At the time of writing Lake Raduta is deservedly losing its initial reputation for poor food, poor service, unbearable heat, impossible snags, and very few fish. The food has apparently improved out of sight. I found the service to be absolutely excellent, although there can be a language barrier if you draw the wrong boatman to look after you. The heat is said to be unbearable in July and August, and it was getting pretty hot when we left in early May. But most of the trips are planned to take place in weather conditions equivalent to the best we can hope for in this country.

Bucharest airport, a three-hour flight to Heathrow, and home in time for tea – or lunch even, if you live as close to the airport as Briggsy!

Even the roads are better than they were when the Brits first started fishing the venue. Lake Raduta as a tourist attraction is taken very seriously, and Robert Raduta clearly has influence in high places. Most of the road from Bucharest airport to the lake was relaid prior to the 1999 Carp World Cup!

The snags need some thought and planning, but they have been dramatically thinned, another improvement we have the 1999 World Cup to thank for. And a great many new fish were introduced for that competition, with far more fish being caught now than during the early trips. I think this is mainly due to the restocking, and partly due to the fact that some of the older fish have started to turn on to boilies as a food source. When you catch bigger fish from Raduta, Crowy anxiously pores over the pictures to see if they are originals or stockies. Most of the fish over 40lb are originals, but some are stockies, and the growth potential of the environment suggests that more and more of the new fish will make it through to 40lb+ and 50lb+ in the years ahead.

Has Raduta peaked in terms of size of fish? Rod Hutchinson has always maintained that the best growth period for a water is prior to fish coming under angling pressure. The Raduta fish grew huge naturally. Captures slow growth rate. But in the case of Raduta there are genuine grounds for optimism. Such is the size and uncompromising nature of the venue that you've got to think there may be uncaught monsters. And what if you get a fast grower with big potential who loves her boilies? In terms of size Cassien peaked some time after anglers started fishing it. The same could well happen at Raduta.

But the big fish that are such an attraction don't surrender themselves. My capture of the Big Common was the only time it came out in 2001, and it was the only seventy the water produced that year. The world-record mirror hasn't been landed since 1999. These are big, powerful, tackle-wrecking fish. You've got to be there when they feed. You've got to get them in front of you when they feed. And if you can get them to pick up a hookbait you've got to get them into the landing net. Fishing Raduta takes more planning and more specialised tactics than any other water I've fished. If you are going there for the first time, take on board some of the comments in the feature finding and snag fishing chapters. When you go to Raduta you relearn carp fishing as most of us know it!

And you dream! The odds of landing a seventy are far shorter than winning the Lottery. That's what makes Lake Raduta carp fishing's current theatre of dreams. And by the time this book appears the water could well have already written another dramatic chapter or two about its big fish – and made a few more dreams come true.

Rene Hawkins with a significant capture from the Islands area of the lake, a typical Raduta big common of 58lb.

The smiling faces of Simon Crow and Rob Hughes tell the story. Si with the first British capture of a 50lb-plus from Raduta. 53lb.

The Monster Carp of the World

Simon Crow

We all dream about catching the biggest carp that swims, and there certainly are quite a few lads now trying to do just that. The growth of global carp fishing over the last decade has been immense, with many anglers now pursuing the ultimate goal in the sport, a world-record carp. In this chapter, Tim has asked me to compile a list of big fish which I know have been caught or discovered from around the world and which have been backed up by photographic evidence.

I will confess that I am no expert when it comes to keeping records, so if anyone knows of any fish which are missing from this list, which should be on it, I would welcome any details (I can be contacted via *Carp-Talk*). All of those I've listed are over 70lb, and for the benefit of those who get stuck with any of the weights, I've used 2.2064lb to 1kg. Let's have a look at them:

The ninety – The former Yugoslavia

Each year there are literally hundreds of reports on the grapevine about giant carp having been caught, but very rarely do the photos ever turn up despite wild claims of authenticity. As far as I'm aware, this is the only genuine carp which has been recorded at above 90lb, and is the biggest carp (*Cyprinus carpio*) ever photographed.

It hit the headlines in the year 2000 (around October time) when *Carp-Talk*

uncovered a story which came via German angler Emir Caro. Emir is no stranger to big fish on the Continent, and through family or work connections he stumbled across the pictures of this giant mirror which weighed 41.3kg (91lb 2oz). It lived in a lake in the war torn area of the former Yugoslavia. When the photograph of the mirror was taken it was obviously dead, and rumour has it that it was found dead that day, having been killed the previous day by poachers. Apparently most of the poachers in Yugoslavia use dynamite as 'bait', causing an explosion and then netting the fish out. This one missed the nets, but turned up in the margins the following day. The man in the photo is said to be the venue owner, and when you consider that the people involved with the photo had no reason whatsoever to lie about its weight, since they knew nothing about carp fishing, you have to believe it. In my eyes, it looks massive. I would never question that this fish is the biggest carp discovered to date.

The monster carp reported from the former Yugoslavia which is said to have weighed over 90lb!

Since its discovery, Emir Caro has visited the lake several times, but thus far has only caught carp to mid-twenties, despite losing two fish which he believed to be much bigger. He has also discovered that another lake close to this venue has farmed commons of 31.2kg (68lb 14oz) and 32.5kg (71lb 11oz).

American bow-shot mirror – unknown lake in Minnesota, USA

Despite hundreds of rumours, this is the only real evidence of really big carp in the USA that has thus far come forward to the British angling press. A picture of this giant

321

mirror being held by two bow hunters appeared in *The Century of Carp Fishing* book on page 119, and although some disbelieve its reported weight of 84lb, we can't ignore the fact that the USA offers a lot of potential to the global side of the sport. The lake where this fish is said to have been bow-shot is very weedy, and I believe the angler who discovered its whereabouts was fisheries consultant Bruno Broughton. As you can see from the photo, it has obviously visited a taxidermist!

The world-record fish – Lake Raduta, Romania

The history of this fish is covered elsewhere in the book, but there are a few things I'd like to mention about its top weight before passing. I'm very, very sceptical that this fish weighed 37.3kg and should be regarded as the world-record carp. I dealt with the story of this capture when it was caught by Christian Baldemann in May 1998. As the news broke that a big

The American 84lb mirror which was shot with a bow. Some say it doesn't look its reported weight.

carp had been caught from Romania, I spoke to a lot of the witnesses as well as the people who were at Raduta around this time. I myself had just come back from the lake two weeks earlier. For sure the capture by Christian was a remarkable feat. I don't want to take anything away from the lad or his achievement. There is enough back-stabbing in this sport as it is, but unfortunately for Christian, we are dealing with a world-record claim here and not just a personal best carp so surely it must fall under a slightly different headline.

The facts about the capture are that initially the report was that a carp weighing 37kg exactly had been caught from Raduta by an Austrian. This was initially confirmed to me by Philippe Barabinot of France, a very good friend of Robert Raduta, who was at the lake at the time. Phil said that the fish had been caught at a weight of 37kg, not one gram above, not one gram below. It had equalled the then record weight of Marcel Rouvière.

Two days later I then received a call from Phil to say that the weight was wrong and that it weighed 37.3kg and was a world record. *Carp-Talk* then ran the story of the world record and I spoke with Helmutt Zaderer as he stood with Christian and obtained the details about the catch.

Two weeks later, I then spoke with Kevin Maddocks who had been out at Raduta as the Austrians pulled off the lake. Kevin described to me how he spoke with them in the bar as they were celebrating Christian's catch and two weeks of fishing (one other Austrian had caught a seventy as well). Kevin told me he had asked them what they had caught, and they told him a 37kg mirror, a new world record. Apparently he then questioned the world record bit with them, saying that 37kg exactly equalled Marcel Rouvière's fish. It was only when Kevin returned home and saw *Carp-Talk* that he saw the weight was reported as 37.3kg and a new world record, and not 37kg as they had initially told him.

Where this story begins to cloud over is here.

Christian Baldemann with his 'record' mirror which weighed 37kg when initially reported, and then 37.3kg a few days later.

Marcel Rouvière with 'my' world record carp of 37kg exactly from 1981.

Coincidentally, Kevin's meeting with the Austrians happened during the two days that the weight reported by Philippe Barabinot changed from 37kg to 37.3kg. It doesn't take a genius to see faults in the story, but I'll leave it for the Austrians to tell us their version of events. Only they know the real facts.

The Yonne fish – The River Yonne, France

This amazing fish is what I consider to be the world-record carp at 37kg exactly. It measured a staggering 1m 20cm around its girth and 102cm in length. The carp was immediately killed and taken to the local post office where it was weighed in front of several witnesses including the local Brigadier of Police. It is very unlikely that this fish was weighed wrongly with so many people around. It was caught way back in July 1981 by French pleasure angler Marcel Rouvière, who was fishing the small stretch of River Yonne that joins the Seine at Montereau and which is a tributary of the mighty River Seine.

The report, which is featured in French magazine *La Pêche et les Poissons* at the time, covers in details the capture and how it was weighed and certified by high-ranking members of the local village. I can't believe that back in 1981, when the British style of carp fishing wasn't even in its infancy in France, that a man aged 60 and several witnesses would have any reason to inflate the weight of this catch.

The Fish on the Wall – Lake Raduta, Romania

This fish doesn't have a particular name so I've called it 'The Fish on the Wall', because that is where it lives! This is the giant mirror which really started the ball rolling with this now famous lake. It now hangs on the wall in the hotel.

History tells us it was only caught once, with its captor being either Robert Raduta or Roman Costica. When I first heard about Lake Raduta, the stories were accompanied by pictures of Roman Costica holding this carp, which was reported to weigh 78lb. *Media Carpe* in France ran a story about Costica catching this fish, with all of the details about its capture clearly printed. *Carp-Talk* worked off the basis of this information, but when I first visited the lake, Robert Raduta told me that he was in fact the captor and not Costica. His

Left: The fish that started it all. I'm posing with the big mirror that lives on the wall in Robert Raduta's hotel. I can only dream that one day I may hold a carp of this size! (Picture courtesy of Kevin Clifford.)

323

*Emanuel Walt and his big surprise from the mighty
River Moselle in eastern France.*

excuse for not having his picture taken with the fish was because he was wearing a suit at the time! Having seen video footage of a 70lb-plus common being caught from Raduta's small lake, when several locals were pictured holding it, personally I think this fish may indeed have been caught by Robert, who at the time, had no idea what he had just caught!

The Moselle mirror – The River Moselle, France

I think the capture of this giant mirror by Emanuel Walt really did put the Moselle firmly on the global carp fishing scene. Since its capture there have been countless anglers scouring the banks of this eastern France river in search of an unknown whacker. I personally know half a dozen anglers who live close to the Moselle and they all have personal best carp over 25kg to their credit. It is an amazing river with a lot of untapped potential.

I spoke to Emanuel at the French show known as Sapel in 1998 and he told me that he fished hard for this particular fish, putting in considerable time having seen it on several occasions. During that session, which I believe lasted over 40 consecutive nights, he also caught carp over 60lb. There is no doubt that the big mirror was full of spawn at the time of capture, but what a creature. It was witnessed by several anglers and its weight was recorded down to the finest gram. I don't know of any other anglers who have caught this fish. Its history is rather patchy.

De Groten – The Kempisch Canal, Belgium

Towards the end of October in 1994 Marc Pieret broke the Belgian record with a whacker from the Kempisch Canal. It weighed approximately 68lb (31.6kg). Three months later, on Saturday 21st January, well-known angler Ronnie de Groote, then a member of the Belgian Nashbait team, caught that same mirror carp at 33.8kg to smash the record. Another two months later and Ronny's fellow Nashbait team member, Phil Cottenier, became the current Belgian record holder when he caught the same fish, known as De Groten (The Biggun), at a weight of 34.6kg. The date of capture was March 19th 1995. Up until today this giant fish remains the biggest carp ever caught in Belgium. The massive fish was caught again on one other occasion from its home, before it was moved.

*The official Belgian record. Phil Cottenier with his
massive 34.6kg mirror.*

Willy – Forêt D'Orient, France

This mighty mirror carp is the current lake record for the awesome Orient Lake. Known as Willy, the huge mirror achieved its all-time high when it was landed sometime during 1996 by French angler Jerome Gigault. Its weight was a massive 75lb 6oz. The fish takes its name from previous captor Willy van Hulten from Holland, who I believe was the first to capture it in 1993. On that occasion, Willy weighed in at

69½lb. The fish has been caught several times over 30kg, including its second best weight of 74½lb when it was caught by Jean Alexis Delabarre.

It now weighs somewhere in the region of upper-sixty to seventy pounds, but the fact that it doesn't get caught much must mean that it could pack the weight on and possibly surpass even its own top weight so far.

The Bulldozer – Forêt D'Orient, France

The world's biggest common, known as The Bulldozer, first made the headlines when well-known Dutch angler Leon Hoogendijk caught it at a weight of 31.8kg. Leon became famous all over the globe through this capture, because not only did it put the Orient on the map with regard to its potential, but also because the fish was a common. Never before had a common carp ever been caught anywhere close to this weight. It really was a

Big fish angler Leon Hoogendijk with Bulldozer at 31.8kg.

giant at the time, and I remember the centre page pull-out which appeared in *Carpe Magazine* (a French magazine) at the time. It was an incredible photo of Leon in the water with the fish draped over his knees.

I don't recall anyone ever having caught the Bulldozer before Leon, but I can confirm that it was caught by several anglers after him, including French angler Sebastian Poulatier. Michael Brechtmann, a German angler, claims to have caught this mighty fish at 75lb exactly in 1995, which to date is the largest common carp ever reported in the world. It still lives in its incredible home, and occasionally makes an appearance around the mid-sixty/low-seventy mark.

The Kevin Ellis fish – Lac de St. Cassien, France

A fish that became known as such after British angler Kevin Ellis caught it in the summer of 1986 at bang on 76lb. Kevin was the second person to catch this very famous fish after fellow British angler Max Cottis caught it at upper-sixty in 1985; a catch that appeared on the front cover of *Coarse Fisherman*.

Kevin banked the giant mirror from the first point into the West Arm of Cassien, a swim now known as Ellis Point. The mirror was subsequently caught by Dutch angler Leo van de Gugten at 75lb 11oz, I think in the summer of 86, but

Kevin Ellis, with the fish which he made famous. What an incredible carp!

I can't be exact with the date, and then by Sjef Van Hoven at over 74lb. It was then caught by British angler Dave Walker, who landed it at its highest weight of 77lb 9oz. Sadly the fish died shortly after Dave caught it, but its history still remains as the venue's biggest ever carp to date.

Sandy's common – Lake Raduta, Romania

This huge common is named after Cheshire angler Sandy Hough, a regular visitor to Lake Raduta. Sandy was the third angler to catch this giant in the spring of 1999 when it weighed 72lb exactly. Prior to Sandy it was caught by German angler Michael Quak at bang on seventy pounds, its first ever capture, in 1997. It was then caught by

325

I looked round the corner of my bivvy and saw this thing on Sandy's mat! At 72lb my eyes nearly popped out of my head.

British rod Paul Jones at 61lb during a trip organised by *Carp-Talk*, and then Sandy. Following his capture it was banked by Austrian Kurt Grabmayor at 70lb exactly in September 1999, Helmutt Zaderer at 74lb in May 2000, its largest ever weight, and then a Dutch angler I don't know the name of at 68lb (not sure if these are Dutch pounds or British – the picture is on the wall in the Raduta hotel) in September of that same year. Author Tim Paisley was then the last to catch it in May 2001 (see separate chapter).

South African mirror – Unknown lake, an hour from Johannesburg

This is the only genuine photo I have in my possession of a monster from South Africa, although there are plenty of rumours doing the rounds about other biggies. The monster common, reported to have weighed 74lb, is said to have been caught from a venue not far from the city of Johannesburg. Martin Lowe, one-time owner of African Gold (a carp fishing travel company), told me: "This fish isn't the only biggie to have been caught from this venue. It has a good history of big fish, although very few people have fished for the carp. The fish weighed 74lb and is a common, although it looks a bit battered since it has been set-up. It's a big open venue, just over an hour's drive from Johannesburg, and it is untouched by modern-day carp anglers."

Several fish identification experts have seen the pictures of this whacker, and all are of the opinion that it is indeed a biggie. Kev Clifford revealed: "I've taken a few measurements of the fish in Photoshop and estimate its length to be around 4ft. A carp of this length should weigh somewhere between 60lb and 70lb, depending on its condition, possibly more if it is very fat."

The Italian record – Unknown lake in the district of Vicenza, Venzia

This fish put Italy firmly on the map with regards really big carp. Although there have always been rumours of big fish in the country, it is always photos that start

Martin Lowe and the big mirror from the South African lake. Kevin Clifford believes that this fish may well have weighed its reported size.

tongues wagging. Top Italian carper Roberto Ripamonti was the first to report the news to England, when in an e-mail to *Carp-Talk* in the summer of 2001 he wrote: "The new record came from a big gravel pit in the district of Vicenza, Venzia. It was caught by Riccardo Munarin and weighed 71lb 3oz. His angling friend Ermes Perin netted the monster and shortly after I went along to witness it. This is not the only big fish in this lake. Riccardo held the previous record at 60¼lb. I weighed the new record and took the following measurements: length 110cm, height 42cm, not including the

Vicenza, Venzia, Italy. The official Italian record which was caught by Riccardo Munarin and weighed 71lb 3oz.

fins. I hope this fish will put an end to some of the rumours which are floating around about Italian carp. I saw this fish. I weighed this fish. It is a fish which I consider to be the very first Italian record since we don't have any official way of verifying them."

The Bourget mirror – Lac de Bourget, France

I briefly covered the capture of this mirror in a *Carpworld* feature in the winter of 2001. It weighed in at 32.4kg and was landed in the month of June 2000 by Thierry Guabello, who fished 300 metres out in a boat. It took the poor fella 80 minutes to land the beast, and it measured 1m 5cm in length and 1m 7cm around its girth. Sadly, the fish died shortly after capture. I'm not sure whether this was of natural causes or whether it was killed by the captor. The angler who caught it was fishing for zander at the time, with a small roach deadbait on the hook. This was the first real biggie reported from the lake, which can be found in the Jura region of the country.

Unnamed Orient mirror – Forêt D'Orient, France

I don't think this fish has a name. It first broke the seventy-pound barrier in the winter of 2001 when it was caught by French angler Patrick Baillon. Its exact weight was 32kg, with it coming from only 2ft of water. I don't have much history about this fish, other than it was caught by Dutch star John van Eck in May 1998 at 50lb! In just over three years, the fish had packed on just over 20lb. Remarkable!

It is easily recognised by the straight upper-lobe of its tail, which looks as though it has been damaged at some stage of its life.

Matilda – Lac de St. Cassien, France

This is another big Cassien mirror which was caught by a British angler in the mid-90s and which slipped by me whilst compiling the *Century of Carp Fishing* book late last century. Apparently a picture of this fish appeared in the British press around 1995 when it was caught by a British angler known as Julian. It weighed around 70¼lb on that occasion and was caught from the second point in the North Arm. Its top weight was around 72lb in its better years, but nothing has been seen of it for six or seven years. Rumour is that the fish is dead, but... who knows?

Liez mirror – Lac de Liez, France

Another fish which I don't have a name for. This mirror has been landed a few times around upper-sixty, but this year, 2002, it was caught at 32kg exactly in April. If this is the same fish which is the 'known biggie' in Liez, then its picture appeared in *Carpe Magazine* in the later part of the 1990s. According to my sources, this fish is a male and is slowly creeping up in weight despite many people saying that it is past its peak.

Spawny Common – Lake Raduta, Romania

To my knowledge there has only been one recorded capture of this fish. There are several fish in Raduta which have only been caught once or twice in the five years which it has been fished for carp. As an example, the 52lb which I caught in May 1998 hasn't been caught since either.

Thomas Angerer (left) and his spawny common from Raduta in May 1998. To my knowledge this fish hasn't been caught since.

mark, and that was in the summer of 2000 by Les Bois de Callian owner Gerard Thevenon. On that occasion it went 70lb 2oz and fell from the plateau just in front of his café. This fish was immediately recognised as being the same fish which Cassien legend Didier Cottin caught just over twelve months earlier, again from the South Arm, at just over 24kg.

Lucy has a regular haunt in the South Arm and this is where most of her captures seem to come from. It has, however, been caught from the North Arm on the odd occasion. According to my records, the fish has thus far fallen

This particular seventy I think we can say was full of spawn when it was caught. It fell to Austrian angler Thomas Angerer and was caught during the same week that the Raduta big mirror was landed by Christian Baldemann. Thomas caught the fish from the right-hand side of the lake, I think from close to the island area. It weighed 32kg.

Lucy – Lac de St. Cassien, France

This famous mirror is the current best in the great lake. To date, it has only been caught once over the seventy-pound

Cassien maestro Gerard Thevenon with his famous capture of Lucy in the summer of 2000.

twice to British rods; the first time to Greg Strelley at 61lb in 2000 and then in March 2002 to Brett Green when it weighed a few ounces more.

John Buckley's Mirror – Lac de St. Cassien, France

This is another of those mysterious Cassien originals which has just disappeared. John Buckley hit the headlines in the late 80s, around 1988, when he landed this beast at just over 70lb. It was landed from a marginal set of reeds from the third point in the North Arm, and a feature about its capture appeared in *Carp Fisher* shortly after, titled Margin Monster.

Other than John's capture of the fish, all I know about this giant mirror has come from Steve Briggs. He tells me that before John caught it, it was landed at 64lb a year earlier. Its

John Buckley and his margin monster from Cassien.

The Chanty record fish, caught here in 1998 when it weighed 27.3kg to French angler Nicolas Ladriere.

top weight is rumoured to be around 76lb, and that capture is also supposed to have been by a British angler – its picture appeared in Pierre's café at the time.

Reservoir de Charmes biggie – France

I don't know a great deal about the biggie in this water, but there was a report in *Media Carpe* in the late-90s of a 32kg mirror. I don't have the captor's name or the details about his catch, but grapevine opinion is that there is at least one seventy in this water, some say two and some say three! It was drained down and *vidanged* in autumn 2001 as part of the national reservoir repairs, but I don't know the state of the fish or fishing at the time of writing.

Orient mirror (Leon's 29½kg) – Forêt D'Orient, France

This is one of at least four different fish that I know of which have been caught at over 70lb from this magical water. It is reported in Leon Hoogendijk's book from 2001 known as *Carpe Révélations* – pictured on page 223. Leon is holding the very fish at 29½kg in 1994 and has a footnote under its capture saying that it was subsequently caught in 1999 at 32½kg.

Italian common – Ripasotile Lake, Italy

My records show that this fish was first caught by big-fish angler Sandro di Cesare when it was reported at 70lb 8oz in *Carp-Talk* during the winter of 1999. At the time, the venue was a closely guarded secret between Sandro and his angling partner Roberto Ripamonti, mainly, I believe, because there was restricted access to the water since it was in the grounds of a private estate. The venue has been publicised under several different names including Reite Lake. I believe the one in the title was made up by Roberto and his colleagues and is its grapevine name amongst anglers. The only other capture I know of this fish was at sixty-plus a year later, again by Sandro – a report of which appeared in Nutrabaits News in *Carpworld* 124.

Sandro di Cesare with the first 70lb-plus carp to be reported from Italy, in the shape of this stunning common of 70lb 8oz.

De Recordvis – Nieuwkoopse Plassen, Holland

Known as The Record Fish in Dutch, this huge common has been steadily creeping up to its current weight for several years. It has held the record since 1997 when it weighed in at 55lb, a weight which was described as "the milestone of the decade which would take some beating" in a feature about the fish which appeared in *Carpworld* issue 126 in March 2001 by Dutch angler Evert Aalten. In August 2000, the great fish surpassed everyone's expectations when it reached a massive 30kg, and to date its highest recorded weight was in 2001 when it went just over 70lb. It has been landed by several anglers over the years, including Joop Butselaar, Mark Schuringa and Marc Timmermans, as well as British angler Mark Adams who landed it in May 1997 when it weighed a mere 24kg (see p247, 248).

The Record – Lac du Der Chantecoq, France

I'm guessing with this one, which I know I shouldn't. All I know is that Chanty holds at least one definite seventy-plus at the time of going to press and that it is a known mirror which has been out a few times. My records show that the record fish is the same big mirror which has been caught regularly since 1997 when it weighed just over 26kg. In 1998 it weighed 27.3kg when caught by French angler Nicolas Ladriere, and it has since slowly crept up to its top weight, recorded in 2001, at 31.8kg.

Other seventies

This is where it starts to get a bit difficult. There are so many rumours of big fish around the world that it really is hard to separate the good reports from the bad ones. In the last few lines of the chapter, I will attempt to draw it to a close by mentioning some of the seventies which I don't have pictures of but which appear to be more than just mythical rumours. All of the carp I have singled out above have recorded captures that I have photographic records of, either out of magazines or as hard copies sent to me through the post. The following are strong reports of venues which have produced 70lb-plus fish:

- Villeneuve de la Raho, near Perpignan, France – There is said to be a low/scraper seventy in this water, but I have never seen any pictures of it. This water is located right on the French/Spanish border.
- Etang de Margot, Brittany, France – When this lake sprung to the forefront of the commercial venues in France in the late 1990s, it was reported to contain a seventy-plus mirror. It was never caught during its first two years of opening, but may well have graced the banks by the time this feature appears in print. Some reports suggest that the fish was sold by its fish farmer owner before the lake became high profile since it is a known fact that the venue had been on the market for quite some time prior to this.
- The River Seine, France – There have been countless reports of seventy-plus fish from the great river.
- Etang Neuf, Brittany, France – This very picturesque venue close to the town of Laval is said to have produced at least one 70lb-plus carp.
- Lake Raduta Small Lake, Romania – What was once a section of the great Romanian lake is now a small commercial fishery of around 200 acres – it was separated from the main lake by the creation of a road. It holds at least one common of 66lb which was caught by respected Italian carp angler Massimo Montovani, but the venue's owner, Robert Raduta, says that it has produced a different common of 72lb – a fish which I have video footage of, but one which has very hazy information surrounding it. Robert told me in May 2002 that the fish was caught by a float angler who was using light tackle. Robert tells me that this lake holds at least four 30kg commons, one of which is estimated to be around 40kg.
- Abagadsset River, Pretoria, South Africa – A monster of 82lb is reported in the *Century of Carp Fishing* book published by Carp Fishing News in 2000 on page 126. The fish was apparently found or caught in 1954.
- Bon Accord Dam, South Africa – Again from the *Century of Carp Fishing* book published in 2000, on page 126, there is mention of a carp of 83½lb from 1934.
- The St. Lawrence River, North America – Several reports of big fish have come from this incredible river.
- Lac de Madine, France – This high-profile carp venue in the east of France is said to have an unofficial carp record of 32kg.

- Undisclosed lake, Hungary – The Hungarian record is said to be a monster of 33kg which was caught from a lake in the south of the country. My good friend Kurt Grabmayor from Austria has only recently informed me of this fish, and I have every reason to believe that it is genuine.
- Undisclosed lake, Hungary – Kurt has also heard a rumour, which is very strong, of a 32kg mirror having been caught from another Hungarian venue. The whereabouts of this lake are being kept very quiet at the moment because it could well produce a real whacker! Watch this space as it is a very new find and one which may do something special soon!
- Undisclosed lake, southern France – I don't know the exact details about this lake, but I do know that a 70lb-and-ounces fish was reported to *Carpworld* in 2000 by Rod Hutchinson field-tester Nicholas Kerninon. It was then subsequently reported in *Angling Times* in June 2002 when caught by David Sutto weighing 71lb.
- Lac de la Liez, France – Rumour is that there are at least two seventies, but the only one I have ever seen in print is the same fish.

- Lac de Charmes, France – I've heard all sorts of rumours about the big fish. At one time there used to be talk of three or four different 70s, but I think there are at least two definites.
- Miribel Jonage (le Grand Large), France – one very big fish which may have been out at just over seventy, but which I can confirm has been caught for definite at just short of the magical weight.
- Palahatchie Lake, USA – A 74lb carp is listed as being a Mississippi state record in a book titled *Carp in North America* published in 1987. The fish was caught by Curtis Wade on 13th June 1963. It is not known whether this fish is a *Cyprinus carpio* or a Buffalo carp, which are common in North America.

David Sutto with his summer 2002 capture of the mirror of 71lb from the mysterious Trout Lake in southern France.

Conclusion

I have no doubt there are several carp waters around the globe holding monster-sized fish which would easily qualify for this list, but are not included. This is the first ever time, as far as I'm aware, that anyone has ever tried to compile a set of global records of this type so I only have my own contacts and memory to work from. I don't profess to be some sort of historical record keeper either – I have enough difficulty remembering the weights of my own fish captures let alone other people's – so I expect there will be a few additions to this list. If you would like to share these with me, or remind me of them, I would be only too happy to hear from you.

Global Big Carp List

The following is a list of big carp reported caught or discovered dead in other circumstances. We've taken a cut-off point of 70lb as the lower limit for the list. Si's commentary makes it clear that there are doubts surrounding the reported weights of a few of the fish recorded here, including the so-called world record fish! 70lb=31.75kg.

Weight	Captor	Venue/Country	Date
91lb 2oz (m)	n/a	Yugoslavia	Oct 2000
84lb (m)	bowshooter	Minnesota, USA	?????
82lb 3oz (m)	Christian Baldemann	Lake Raduta	May 1998
81lb 3oz (m)	Marcel Rouvière	River Yonne, France	July 1981
78lb (m)	Robert Raduta	Lake Raduta	April 1997
77lb 15oz (m)	Henk von Dorn	Lake Raduta	May 1999
77lb 9oz (m)	Emanuel Walt	River Moselle, France	Sept. 1998
77lb 9oz (m)	Dave Walker	Lake Cassien, France	June 1986
76lb 2oz (m)	Phillip Cottenier	Kempisch Canal, Belgium	March 1995
76lb (m)	Kevin Ellis	Lake Casien, France	1986
75lb 11oz (m)	Leo van de Gugten	Lake Cassien, France	1987
75lb 6oz (m)	Jerome Gigault	Forêt D'Orient, France	1996
75lb (c)	Michael Brechtmann	Forêt D'Orient, France	1995
74lb 8oz (m)	Jean Alexis Delabarre	Forêt D'Orient, France	?????
74lb 6oz (m)	Ronnie de Groote	Kempisch Canal, Belgium	Jan 1995
74lb+ (m)	Sjef Van Hoven	Lake Cassien, France	1988
74lb (m)	Jurgen Becker	Lake Raduta	Oct 1997
74lb (m)	?????	Johannesburg, South Africa	?????
74lb (c)	Helmutt Zaderer	Lake Raduta	May, 2000
73lb 13oz (c)	Tim Paisley	Lake Raduta	May 2001
72lb 4oz (m)	Markus Pelzer	Gravel Pit, Germany	Aug 2002
72lb (c)	Alex 'Sandy' Hough	Lake Raduta	April 1999
71lb 10oz (m)	Captor Unknown	Forêt D'Orient	1999*
71lb 8oz (m)	Thierry Guabello	Lac de Bourget, France	June 2000
71lb 3oz (m)	Riccardo Munarin	Vicenza, Italy	Summer, 2001
70lb 10oz (m)	Patrick Baillon	Forêt D'Orient, France	Nov 2001
70lb 10oz (m)	Angler Unknown	Lac de Liez, France	April 2002
70lb 10oz (c)	Thomas Angerer	Lake Raduta	May 1998
70lb 8oz (c)	Sandro di Cesare	Reite Lake, Italy	Dec 1999
70lb 7oz (c)	Leon Hoogendijk	Forêt D'Orient, France	Aug 1992
70lb 4oz (m)	Julian ?????	Lake Cassien, France	1995
70lb 4oz (m)	John Buckley	Lake Cassien, France	June 1987
70lb 4oz (m)	Angler Unknown	Lac de Der Chantecoq	2001
70lb 2oz (m)	Gerard Thevenon	Lake Cassien, France	Summer, 2000
70lb 2oz (c)	Joop Butselaar	Nieuwkoopse Plassen, Holland	2001
70lb (c)	Michael Quak	Lake Raduta	Oct 1997
70lb (c)	Kurt Grabmayor	Lake Raduta	Sept 1999

Biggest Carp in the World

Day ten of a two-week session at Lake Raduta in Romania. I was fishing the Shepherd's Cottage stretch of the 700-acre Church Bay. Rob Hughes was 150 yards to my right. Sandy Hough was across on Becker's Point, fishing with Chris Fowke. Big-fish man Andy Chambers was quarter of a mile to the right, fishing the area of the sunken church with mate Nobby Caunt. The rest of the British party was spread around the expansive, sprawling 2,500-acre venue.

It was my first trip to Raduta, and I was loving it. Early summer sunshine most days with temperatures in the 70s and 80s. The occasional tidal wave of double-figure fish, with the even more occasional bigger fish thrown in. Up to that morning, 1st May 2001, I'd landed three forties, biggest a new personal best common of 46lb 4oz. Four days to go. A fifty-plus would cap a lovely session. Hughesy is a great bloke to fish with, when he's there, and not asleep. I liked the spot, and I was into the rhythm of the session.

Up at five, with daylight due from six onwards. I drank a couple of coffees and ate one of my surviving Mars bars as the sky lightened in the east opposite me,

Bivvied up on the Shepherd's Cottage stretch of Gypsy Village Bay for a fortnight.

beyond Becker's Point. The previous day had been one of big winds pounding in, and constant action from a shoal of doubles. It had been exhausting, and disappointing. I had two baits in good spots, two in dubious ones. I needed to do

Time for feature finding. Exploring the area where I found the exciting-looking gully.

some exploring and reposition a couple of rods. The area I was fishing had produced too many fish, and was perhaps under too much pressure. I'd been pouring bait into the swim for over a week. The fish knew it was a feeding area. On top of which it was clearly a holding area, although the spasmodic nature of the action and the differing sizes of fish in the shoals suggested that this was a temporary holding area – some sort of transit camp as fish moved from one area of the lake to another. The big winds and constant action of the previous day had precluded feature finding from the boat. The new day was dawning calm and clear. Feature finding

Rob Hughes rig-tying during our shared session on the Shepherd's Cottage stretch.

conditions.

Raduta carp are nomadic. The old river bed ran through the 250-yard-wide valley to my left. It didn't take too much figuring that the old river would be the roadway when the carp were on the move. But the successful Sandy was covering the far bank with one rod, and it wasn't producing action. I'd covered the middle of the river at 24ft for a few days, but that seemed to be too deep for them. I was keen to explore the area to my left. I'd come to the conclusion – rightly or wrongly – that the fish must be moving through on my side of the river, which was why, that particular morning, I was restless to be out with the feature finder to find meaningful spots for two underachieving rods.

I was out on the water soon after it was light. Twenty minutes after first light to about 8.00 a.m. had proved a consistently quiet time. The main body of the snags was straight in front of me and to my right. The lake bed dropped away into a slight gully at about 90 yards, then rose gently to the snag area. I was fishing in front of the snags, locked up solid to avoid losses. I went further left in the boat, following the slightly deeper water, which varied in depth from 8ft to 12ft. I had a couple of H-blocks with me to mark anything significant that came up on the screen.

The water shallowed up appreciably to my left, with an extensive shallows 2-3ft in depth. But as I moved off the shallows about seventy yards out, unexpectedly I suddenly found myself over deeper water. I threw a marker over the side and ran round in a circle. Wow. There was a marked drop-off from 4ft to 8ft. This turned out to be a pronounced gully, down to 12ft to my right, then rapidly shallowing off to 8ft to the left, with the steep drop-off on my side of the gully. It was running at an angle from the snags towards the Shepherd's Cottage. No one had mentioned the feature. It had taken me ten days to find it, and it absolutely screamed patrol route.

Baits included a generous supply of Mainline's Fruit-tella ready-mades, which had accounted for my first two forties on the first two days of the session. I had a few kilos of one of my favourite baits, Mainline's Grange Red, in air-dried form, left. I'd used up a precious 10 kilos of baggage allowance on this bait. I had such belief in the Grange Red as a bait for big commons that by this stage of the session double Reds were the hookbaits on all four rods. My third forty had fallen to the Red.

The only groundbait I had was what was left of the chopped tigers I'd taken. I love chopped tigers on waters where tigers have worked and slowed down. Carp can't resist them, and although they stop

Rob with his friend Chewbacca, who is hanging around waiting for the next free offering.

The common of 46lb from the previous week which confused me when I netted the big fish.

producing, the carp go on eating them. If you use chopped tigers they are always in evidence after you've sacked a fish.

I'd cooked some chopped tigers that morning and used a patch of a few handfuls with half a pound of chopped baits in them as a groundbait focus in the gully. I spread a few Fruit-tella freebies and some of the precious remaining Grange Reds along about 50 yards of the gully, leading in from the left. A double Grange Red hookbait was positioned in the gully, in 8ft of water, just beyond the drop-off, about five yards up-gully from the chopped tigers.

It had taken me two hours to reposition one rod. Feeding time was approaching. I freshened up the other rods, scattered some bait around the area, put the kettle on and was poised for action when the 8.00 a.m. feeding time came round.

Nothing happened.

The sun was climbing the sky and the day started to heat up. There was a mud hole by the left-hand rods and I put my foot in it, splashing mud right up my leg. I washed, then went gathering stones from around the area to fill in the hole. Hughesy was still crashed out down the bank. A picnic party arrived quarter of a mile away on the opposite bank, on the grassy area next to the shepherd's crossing. 1st May. Presumably it was a bank holiday of some sort. The picnickers were between the Austrian anglers fishing the plateau away to my left, and Sandy and Chris on Becker's Point. They'd got a lovely day for their holiday picnic.

It got hotter. I felt irritated by nothing in particular – a combination of a build-up of session fatigue and mild disappointment – and retreated to the bivvy for a power snooze before it got too hot to be indoors. 10.00 a.m. No sooner had I started to drift than the baitrunner to the left-hand rod stuttered and the buzzer sounded. The newly positioned rod! I leant into the fish, but there was nothing there! Uh? I redid the rod, rowed it back out and repositioned it, idly wondering if the "take" had been a line-bite from a big body catching the line between the drop-off and the bait, where the line would be running down at an angle. Yeh, I thought that at the time. I like explanations for the inexplicable.

Hughesy slept on, exhausted from the day of big

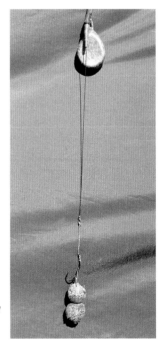

"Photograph everything," Rob suggested when I caught the big common. The successful rig and double Grange Red hookbait hanging against the bivvy shortly after the capture.

A helping hand from Rob Hughes to bring the huge fish ashore.

winds and the double-figure carp onslaught the previous day. Sometimes I envy people the ability to sleep for long periods. I'm a poor sleeper. In any case I feel cheated if I sleep through the unfolding magic of the change from night to day and the first few hours of daylight.

Sorted, I stretched out again. I was catnapping. Drifting. When I'm like that I never know whether I've been asleep for ten seconds or ten minutes. I was edgy. Time was running down and we were going through what I looked on as one of the possible big-fish feeding times with nothing happening.

I'd no sense of anticipation at all...

A buzzer. Derris on for a paddle in the shallow water. The left-hand rod again, dragging line off the screwed-down Baitrunner. Rod up. Sandbagged. It was a feeling you hope for there. Anywhere. Dig in your heels and hang on. When there's nowhere for them to go you can't let them go anywhere. I'd been playing all the fish like that, and it was a frightening experience. You're waiting for the rod to spring back, but that had only happened a couple of times – from cut-offs early on before I'd got the feel of the area, and just once from a hook-pull. My confidence in the Longshank Nailer size 4s was growing with each successfully landed fish.

You shudder looking back. I hit this thing, and hung on, then gradually started to win line. Come here darling. It was a big, heavy scrapper. You're waiting for the line to start grating, or for everything to go solid, but it didn't. I wanted the fish to go left, really, because I knew there was a snag halfway in to my right that had unexpectedly cost me a fish a couple of days previously. But the fish swung right, across the front of me, and the line cut steadily through the water as the unseen carp moved down towards the area of the snag. I laid the rod over and heavy pressure had it moving back. I'm out to the top of the Derris with the landing net propped against my shoulder. The fish settled for a steady, aimless chug

Rob and Andy Chambers taking the strain as they weigh the big common.

round in front of me.

She gradually came closer and ten minutes or so into the fight I thought it might be ready for the net. I gave it a go, and in she came at the first time of asking.

Up to that point you are just playing and landing a carp. Then you see it and reality is at hand. Please be big. It was. A common. A big common, but, unbelievably, looking back my first reaction was not that I'd just landed a monster. Physically its shape was similar to that of a 46lb common I'd landed five nights previously, which confused me. But when I replay the netting in my mind I know that when the nose hit the spreader block the tail was still hanging over the drawstring, and I had to juggle it in. And the back and the gut were touching each of the landing net arms. So why my initial reaction was that this might be the fish of 46lb I'd caught previously I don't know – apart from the vague similarity in shape.

Smile... No problem!

I checked the time straightaway. Always do. It was half eleven. I tried to lift the net by the arms, but failed totally. I was going to say miserably, but my disenchantment of an hour or two earlier had vanished! I called Rob, but he was still asleep.

I detached the landing net arms and wrapped the fish in the net, then moved the unhooking mat to the water's edge. Wet the sling. Zero the Reuben Heatons. I'd decided it was almost certainly bigger than 46lb by this time, and was hoping for 50+. On the Reuben Heatons 50lb is at ten to the hour. I struggled the great fish off the mat, willing the needle to go past 50lb. It went way past, and startled me by settling in the area of quarter past the hour.

Up to that point I had no idea at all what I'd just landed. The unexpected performance of the needle had me lowering the bundle back onto the mat, and taking my glasses off for a closer look at the figures on the scales! I'd never even looked to see what sort of weight was at quarter past the hour,

"How do you hold a fish that big?" Very determinedly! You only get one chance to get shots like that right. I'm actually holding the huge fish against my chest. It was huge!

337

second time around! I struggled the great beast into the air again, with some difficulty, it has to be said. 73lb something. Nearly 74lb. How big!?

Well how would you feel? Thoughts flashed through my head. "Oh you haven't, Tim. You can't have!" I'd caught a mirror of 63lb from Cassien less than five months previously. I'd come to Raduta hoping for a 50. Dreaming of a 60. Now I'd caught this.

I put the sack/sling and fish back in the edge and shouted for Rob again. I was just getting ready to go and rouse him, when he appeared, blinking in the sunlight. He walked up the bank towards me.

"You caught something?"

"Something like that."

I hoisted the fish back onto the mat and uncovered it as he approached. He figured the size of it a lot quicker than I had!

"Oh my God, that is effing enormous!" Which was a somewhat crude but undoubtedly accurate appraisal of the great common's size!

Rob was coming round, and took over, bless him. We sacked the fish as deep as we could.

Captor returns.

After he'd studied the great fish Rob decided it was the same common Sandy had caught at 72lb two years previously. He hollered the news across to Sandy and Chris, who came over with their video camera. Sandy's a lovely laid-back fella. I knew his capture of the fish had been the biggest common ever caught by a Brit. As mine now was. I felt a bit guilty (for ten seconds) about claiming his crown. He seemed genuinely thrilled for me.

Rob commandeered my camera to shoot everything in sight. He rang Robert Raduta, who later turned up with Martin Davidson and a set of scales for the official weighing. While we were waiting for the weighing party Rob went off to give Andy Chambers and his mate Nobby the news. He couldn't resist engaging in a bit of mischief.

"Tim's had a 33."

"That's nice." 33lb fish don't excite much comment at Raduta.

Give it the Terry Hearn salute someone suggested, so I gave it my best shot. I think we all wanted to drag the shared excitement of the capture out for as long as possible.

338

"You're not listening properly are you? He's had a 33."

Realisation dawned and Andy grinned incredulously.

"You mean 33 kilos don't you?"

It was the third time in four years that the great fish had been caught from the swim next to Andy's!

We gathered for the weighing and the photo shoot. I was asked to put a weight on the fish, and after deciding there were 14oz in a pound(!) settled for a weight of 73lb 12oz. Later someone pointed out the mistake and after we'd all studied the video we agreed a

Hotel Raduta is a welcome sight when you are coming in from two weeks on the bank.

weight of 73lb 13oz. The third biggest common ever caught after the Orient's Bulldozer at 75lb, and this same great fish at 74lb.

We had a few bottles of champagne on the bank that night. For the rest of the session Rob and I walked around repeating the weight and shaking our heads in disbelief. The session drifted to a close in lovely weather, and with no more very big fish to report. Even without the big common it had been memorable. One of the most enjoyable sessions I've ever fished.

Departure was Saturday morning. We packed up Friday afternoon and gathered at the hotel for a celebratory meal

Back to civilisation and a celebration dinner with (from left) Rob Hughes, Steve Briggs, South African Henni du Preez, Rob Marsh, Nobby Caunt, Andy Chambers and Stu Wallis.

and a few drinks. The guys were already well into the beers when Rob and I came in, and they gathered on the hotel front to give me a round of applause as we disembarked. I thought they were taking the mick, but it was a jingoistic thing as much as a congratulation for the capture. There were Austrians, Germans, Czechs and French on the water at the time, and a Brit had caught the big one! Yeh! Heads up guys, it's our turn.

The aftermath of the capture has been almost as remarkable as the fish itself. At the Carp Society's Fish With the Stars at the end of the month there was a round of applause for the fish. When I've shown the common at a couple of slide shows there has been a spontaneous round of applause. And when that happens you know it's not the capture they are applauding. It is the fish. We dream about big fish, but does a fish of that size ever figure in our dreams? Not even before or during the Raduta session had I dreamt that particular weight! And at no point in my carp fishing life had I dreamed of catching the biggest reported carp caught in the world in 2001. Things like that only ever happen to other people.

I think Crowy dreams of this fish! And after the capture it was his reaction I liked best of all. Briggsy had put the idea of Raduta into my head, but Crowy and Rob Hughes had made it possible, and when I got there it was Crowy who suggested I try the swim I fished, and had taken me out into the night with boatman Yanous.

"It's only a small-fish swim. It never produces a big fish. Spend a couple of days in here then make a move." Yeh, OK Si. But two forties in the first two days held me there, and the swim went and spoilt its reputation for not producing big fish. So when Rob rang him on the mobile shortly after the capture to tell him what I'd caught Si's very human reaction was: "Well he effing would wouldn't he?"

And do you know, the capture of that fish is still unbelievable every time I think about it? Which is quite often, as it happens. How does it feel? Imagine you've caught it... It's not real is it? That's how it feels!

Proud moment. Awarded the yellow T-shirt for the capture by Robert Raduta.

Postscript

On the 1st of May 2002 Simon Crow and I were fishing together in Raduta's World Record Bay. We received word that Leon Hoogendijk – who was fishing the plateau area of the cut-through from Hotel Bay to Gypsy Village Bay with Phillipe Lagabbe – had discovered a huge common carp dead in the margins. Well over 30 kilos was Leon's assessment: and of course Leon knows a thing or two about big fish! In my heart I knew straightaway that this was the Big Common. The cut-through was a known haunt of the big fish; she was a big old girl, almost certainly one of the originals from the flooded fish farms; and it was a year to the day since I'd briefly enjoyed her company. Leon photographed the fish and later confirmed that it was in fact the Big Common. Crowy refers to this fish as Sandy's Common. I've heard it referred to as Tim's fish. Other countries may have their own names for her. I like to think of her as the Big Common, for that she certainly was. I felt saddened by her passing, and strangely privileged to have been the last one to catch her. Somehow her passing makes the memories relived here all the more precious.

Back Along the Way

The first afternoon of the first Carp School at Horseshoe in 1998. The fish weren't in a cooperative mood but Chris Ball managed to winkle one out off the top to show the youngsters how it is done!

The Carp Society's annual Fish with the Stars event at Horseshoe has become a special angling/social occasion. This is the scene outside the main marquee just before the Friday morning draw. 'Amateurs' pay to fish with high-profile anglers over this weekend.

The final afternoon of the World Carp Cup 2000 at Fishabil. Steve and I have just won the event and are starting the celebrations with the British 'support team' of Mary and Joan.

There are a couple of shortcomings with a volume of this nature. The first is that you are reluctant to put it to bed because you want it to be as current as possible when it is published. The fact that the printers have extended the deadline to within a month of publication date means that the book shouldn't have missed too much by way of last-minute monsters or revolutionary advances!

The second drawback is that because this is essentially a technical/practical book it comes out as a distortion of reality. A life of carp fishing isn't just about trying to catch carp. The friendships, the meetings, the matches, the trips, and the social get-togethers are almost as big a part of the carp scene as the waters and the fish. When 'B.B.' said, "The two are indivisible, the background and the fish," I'm sure he didn't have in mind sharing a bottle of Courvoisier with friends, or popping a few bottles of champagne to celebrate the start of a season, or the capture of a fish. But in sorting through the transparencies and prints for the selection to illustrate *Carp!* some of the shots of the social gatherings I had to reject as irrelevant caught and held my attention, and had me reminiscing about special moments – other than the captures of carp – during the last six years.

Oddly it is the much-maligned carp matches – particularly the international ones – that throw up the most memorable of the social gatherings. In the Winds of Change chapter I referred to the impact Lac de Madine had on my carp fishing outlook. Madine in 98 and 99 was special for all sorts of reasons, certainly not least the party the night before the draw! The World Carp Cup 2000 at Fishabil was equally memorable – win or lose – and made all the more special because of the two-day build-up, and the afternoon and evening of celebrations that followed the win Steve and I were fortunate enough to enjoy.

A marvellous, special memory. The British contingent setting off along the dam wall at Fishabil for the presentation ceremony.

Special friends... *Our annual Christmas celebration in Shropshire with the Gwilts, owners of the Mangrove and Birch Grove. From left: Angela, Harrison, Giles, Oliver, Rob, Mr and Mrs Gwilt (Bill and Elsa) and Mary.*

The usual suspects at the Angling Publications/Carp Fishing News Christmas party. Kev Clifford and Julian Cundiff have already gone home or the line-up would have been even more frightening!

Yateley is the venue for the annual Stoney & Friends Fish-in to raise funds for the Macmillan Nurses. This is the scene at the 2001 event, which raised over £11,000 for the appeal.

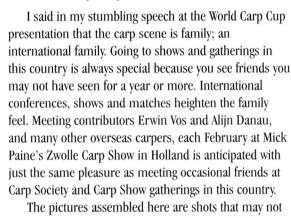

The party about to leave for Bucharest airport and home after my first trip to Raduta in 2001.

I said in my stumbling speech at the World Carp Cup presentation that the carp scene is family; an international family. Going to shows and gatherings in this country is always special because you see friends you may not have seen for a year or more. International conferences, shows and matches heighten the family feel. Meeting contributors Erwin Vos and Alijn Danau, and many other overseas carpers, each February at Mick Paine's Zwolle Carp Show in Holland is anticipated with just the same pleasure as meeting occasional friends at Carp Society and Carp Show gatherings in this country.

The pictures assembled here are shots that may not mean a great deal to all the readers, but... Well I hope I'll be forgiven the self-indulgence of devoting these two pages to friends we've shared some special moments with during the last few years, and special occasions that stick in the memory as vividly as many of the fish I've caught. The final picture says it all. Here's to all of you from some members of the family, and some special friends, who have helped make all my carp fishing years, and especially the last five or six, so memorable and enjoyable.

Thanks for the memories, back along the way.

Here's to the next time. *The* **Carpworld** *team and friends partying at Madine on the eve of the 1999 World Carp Classic event. From left: Alan Atkins, yours truly, Mary, Pip, Micky Sly, Jemima, Dominic Martin and John Lilley.*

Contact Points

Phone numbers and/or addresses for some of the companies referred to in the book. This information is correct at the date of publication, 30th September 2002, but may change with the passage of time.

Abbey Lakes. Contact Rob Hughes.

African Gold, Martin Davidson, PO Box 722, Walkerville, 1876, South Africa. 0027 11949-1958.

Alan Young, 0797 0801493.

Angler's Paradise Holidays, The Gables, Winsford, Halwith Junction, Beaworthy, Devon. 01409 221559.

Angling Books Ltd. As Angling Publications.

Angling Publications, 272, London Road, Sheffield S2 4NA.

Bait Company, The, The Paddock, Nasty, Nr. Great Munden, Herts. SG11 1HP. 01920 438338.

Big Fish Adventure, Mayford Centre, Woking, Surrey GU22 0PP. 01483 740061.

Birmingham Angling Centre, 2, Beech Road, Erdington, Birmingham B23 5QN. 0121 3736627.

Black Cat Baits, 12, Beaumont Court, Church Stretton, Shropshire SY6 6DT. 01694 724126.

Bluebell Lakes, 01832 226042.

Boyers, Wm., Boyer Leisure Ltd., Tackle Shop, Farlows Lake, Ford Lane, Iver, Bucks SL0 9LL.

British Carp Angling Championships. Contact Rob Hughes.

British Carp Study Group, The, c/o John Abbotts, 22, Essex Road, Church Stretton, Shropshire SY6 6AY.

Carp Cabin, The, 300-302, Meadowhead, Sheffield S8 7RQ. 0114 2746458.

Carp Company, The, 3, Stroudes Close, Worcester Park, Surrey KT4 7RB. 020 8715 8342.

Carp 'R' Us, PO Box 4200, Sudbury, Suffolk, CO10 7LE. 01787 282380.

Carp Fishing News Ltd., Newport, East Yorkshire, HU15 2QG. 01430 440624.

Carp Show, The, Carp Conferences Ltd., 272, London Road, Sheffield S2 4NA. 0114 2580812.

Carp Society, The, Horseshoe Lake, Burford Road, Lechlade, Gloucestershire, GL7 3QQ. 01367 253959.

Carp-Talk. Contact Carp Fishing News Ltd.

Carpworld. Contact Angling Publications.

Cassien Experience, The. Lee Picknell, 306, Battle Road, St. Leonards-on-Sea, East Sussex TN37 7BB. 0033 681975275.

Catch 22, Easthough Road, Ling, Norwich, Norfolk, NR9 5LN.

Century Composites Ltd., 58, Hutton Close, Crowther, Washington, Tyne & Wear, NE38 0AH. 0191 4168200.

Chalet Lake, David Rance, Carp Fishers Abroad, High Farm, Kemberton, Shifnal, Shropshire TF11 9LL. 01952 585002.

Chapmans Specialist Tackle, 17-29, Beechway, Ashby, Scunthorpe, North Lincs. DN16 2HF. 01742 858982.

Chilton, Dave. Contact Kryston.

Club Nutrabaits. Contact Nutrabaits.

Crafty Carper. Contact Angling Publications.

Crowood Press, Crowood Lane, Ramsbury, Marlborough, Wilts SN8 2HR. 01672 520320.

Domaine de Boux. Contact Excalibur Fishing.

Domaine des Iles, Bernard Caron, 9, Rue du Moulin, 80400, Offoy, France. 0033 3238110 55.

Dream Lakes, Graham Greene, Gone Fishing, 81, Villa Road, Colchester, Essex. CO3 0RN. 01206 767576.

Dutch Tourist Board. 0906 871 777.

Dynamite Baits, Wolds Farm, The Fosseway, Cotgrave, Notts. NG12 3HG. 01159 899060.

Edge Bait Company, The, 28, Melk Weg, Atlasville, Boksburg, Gauteng, PO Box 6738, Dunswart 1508, South Africa.

ESP Tackle, Adam Penning, 01865 748989

Essential Products, 66, Durleigh Road, Bridgwater, Somerset TA6 7JE. 01278 427634.

Etang de Jonquoy, Contact GTS Tours, 01435 873249.

Etang de Margot. Contact Excalibur Fishing.

Etang Meunier. Tony Miller, 0033 254383996.

European Carp Angling. See Cassien Experience.

Excalibur Fishing, La Volerie, 53200, Gennes sur Glaize, France. 0033 243709839.

Fishabil, European Specimen Angling Centre, Le Lac, 22230 Loscouet-sur-Meu, France. 0033 296 252 766.

Fish in France. Bernie Stamp or Terry O'Brien, 90, Grove Park Road, Mottingham, London SE9 4QB. 020 8857 1244.

Fishing Adventures. See David Payne.

Fosters Specialist Angling Centre, 214/216, Kingstanding Road, Birmingham B44 8JP. 0121 344 3333.

Fox International, Fowler Road, Hainault Industrial Estate, Hainault, Essex IG6 3UT. 0208 559 6500.

Gardner Tackle Ltd., Unit 3B, Merrow Business Centre, Merrow Lane, Guildford, Surrey GU4 7WA. 01483 303262.

Gerard's, Les Bois de Callian, Lac de St. Cassien, 83440 Tanneron, France. 0033 (0) 49360 6763

Giant, Leeda Tackle, 16-17, Padgets Lane, South Moons Moat, Redditch, Worcs B98 0RA. 01527 529030.

Gold Label Tackle, 378, Boldmere Road, Sutton Coldfield, Birmingham B73 5EZ. Tel: 0121 373 4523.

Haiths, J.E. Haith Ltd., 63, Park Street, Cleethorpes, NE Lincs. DN35 7NF. 01472 357515.

Heathrow Bait Services, Ian Russell, Merwood Farm, Stonehill Road, Ottershaw, Surrey KT16 0EW. 01932 877577.

Hinders of Swindon, Bryan Jarrett, Manor Garden Centre, Cheney Manor, Swindon SN2 2QJ. 01793 333900.

Holiday Carp Waters. A Carp-Talk Essential Guide by Simon Crow. Terrific insight into fishing abroad, full of advice and information. Available from Carp Fishing News Ltd. Ring 01430 440624 to check availability.

Horseshoe Lake. Contact The Carp Society.

Horton Management Ltd. As Excalibur Fishing Ltd.

Hughes, Rob, Birchwood Farm, Moss Lane, Whixall, Shropshire SY13 2RU. 01948 880884.

Hull & District AA. 01430 440624.

Korda Developments, PO Box 253, Romford, Essex RM1 4GT. 01708 733668.

Kryston Advanced Angling, Bolton Enterprise Centre, Washington Street, Bolton BL3 5EY. 01204 366556.

Lac de Passion, Paul Smith 01708 526754.

Lac du Der Chantecoq. Maison du Lac on 0033 32676343.

Lake Raduta. Contact Rob Hughes.

Les Quis. See Fish in France.

Leslies of Luton. 89/93, Park St., Luton, Beds LU1 3HG. 01582 453542.

Linear Fisheries, Shimano-Linear Fisheries, 10a, Rackstraw Grove, Old Farm Park, Milton Keynes MK7 8PZ. 01908 645135.

Locke, Martin. See Solar Tackle.

Mainline Baits, 48, Humber Ave., South Ockendon, Essex RM15 5JN. 01708 854129.

Maurepaire. Contact David Payne.

MCF Products, 01233 208555.

Mistral Baits, Alan Parbery, 2, Kings Street, Wellingborough NN8 4RF. 01933 442404.

Motorway Pond. See Hull & District AA.

Nash Tackle, 01702 233232.

Nashbait. See Nash Tackle.

Nutrabaits, Units C1 & C2, Canklow Meadows Industrial Estate, West Bawtry Road, Rotherham S60 2XL. 01709 370990.

Orchid Lakes, Marsh Pratley, Abingdon Road, Dorchester, Oxford OX1 7LP. 01865 341810. 07885 618190.

Payne, David, 01536 505791.

Premier Baits, Units 7 & 8, 3, Wilton Road, Haine Industrial Estate, Ramsgate, Kent CT12 5HG. 01483 583595.

Rainbow Lakes, Pascal 0033 556657089.

Richworth Baits, Streamselect Ltd., Island Farm Avenue, West Molesey, Surrey KT8 2UZ.

RMC Angling, The Square, Lightwater, Surrey GU18 5SS. 01276 453300.

Rod Hutchinson Developments, Main Road, Legbourne, Louth, Lincs. 01507 609069.

Sandholme Publishing. Contact Kev Clifford, Carp Fishing News Ltd. 01430 440624.

Selby Three Lakes, Gordon Fowler, 0781 8092420.

Shimano (UK) Ltd., Unit 1A, Vale Park Business Centre, Vale Park, Evesham, WR11 1GD. 01386 425825/6.

Simon Horton, See Excalibur Fishing.

Solar Tackle, PO Box 22, Orpington, Kent BR6 7XF. 01689 826632.

Sparsholt College, Winchester, Hants SO21 2NF.

Sparsholt Guide to the Management of Carp Fisheries. See Sparsholt College.

Tackle Box, The, 251, Watling St., Dartford, Kent DA2 6EG. 01322 292400.

Tails Up, 13, Kingswood Ave., Hampton, Middlesex TW12 3AU. 020 8893 8000.

Trakker Products, Fulwood House, Cliffefield Road, Sheffield S8 9DH. 0114 2589755.

VBK Magazine, Editor Alijn Danau, C. Cautermanstraat 8, 9040, Gent, Belgium.

Walkers of Trowell, Nottingham Road, Trowell, Nottingham NG9 3PA. 0115 930 1816.

World Carp Classic. International HQ, Suite 111, Victory House, Somers Road North, Portsmouth PO1 1PJ. 02392 827000.

Wraysbury. Contact RMC Angling.

Xtreme Carping. See Rob Hughes.

Yateley Complex. Contact RMC Angling.

Carp! Index